Thresholds

Thresholds

Studies in
the Romantic Experience

Albert Cook

The University of Wisconsin Press

Published 1985

The University of Wisconsin Press
114 North Murray Street
Madison, Wisconsin 53715

The University of Wisconsin Press, Ltd.
1 Gower Street
London WC1E 6HA, England

First printing

Printed in the United States of America

Library of Congress Cataloging-in-Publication Data
Cook, Albert Spaulding.
   Thresholds: studies in the Romantic experience.
   Includes index.
   1. Romanticism—Addresses, essays, lectures.
2. Literature, Modern—19th century—History and
criticism—Addresses, essays, lectures. I. Title.
PN751.C66   1985   809'.9145   85-40365
ISBN 0-299-10300-5

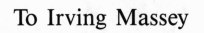
To Irving Massey

Contents

Preface   ix

Acknowledgments   xi

1 Introduction   3

2 Blake: The Exaltation of Fluidity   29

3 Sin, *Verstand*, and the Love of All Things:
   The Vacillation of Coleridge   63

4 Hölderlin's Brink   83

5 Leopardi: The Mastery of Diffusing Sorrow   97

6 Stendhal: The Discovery of Ironic Interplay   110

7 Pushkin: The Balance of Irony   125

8 Baudelaire: The Assessment of Incapacity   139

9 Mallarmé: The Deepening Occasion   162

10 Emily Dickinson's White Exploits   179

11 Dostoevsky: The Apocalypse of Anguish   203

12 The Moment of Nietzsche   220

Notes   245

Index   301

Preface

The Romantic writer, as though perpetually facing a more hopeful version of Poe's Maelstrom, must retain his balance while plumbing profound and mysterious intricacies of emotion and at the same time trying to account for the most powerful and fleeting of thoughts. He must do so while employing the expansive, inherited means of a language, with all the rhetorical associations and expectations this implies, when this sole means of expression comes to seem untrustworthy enough to undermine him through the very instrument that would give him utterance. Such a writer, we have come to learn, must have recourse to the most adaptable of self-tested systems. At the same time he must neither lose his hold on a normativeness and referentiality of utterance nor fall back on the set positions which would remove him from subjection to the indeterminacy that can alone give him being and expression. He must maintain himself on a perpetual threshold, one whose conditions of indeterminacy are too simply described if they are "deconstructed" into their underlying slippages and contradictions, even though we owe to deconstructionist critics a large share of the most delicately calibrated accounts of the elements in such indeterminacies. And indeed, just as this book has gained, I believe, by being written in the climate of deconstructive criticism, so the deconstructive critics themselves, in their insistence on radical indeterminacies and in their attention to fine-tuned fluxes of motivated verbalization, are honorably continuing the dialectical questioning of Hegel, Schlegel, Kierkegaard, and Nietzsche (to say nothing of Sartre and Merleau-Ponty). The implicit nihilism of their possible conclusions, which the vulgar deconstructionists among them raise to an axiom, is belied by the sense of threshold existence radiated in the writing (and also the person) of Derrida, an élan and energy that carries the tone of implicit hopefulness. And tone itself is extensible into something like a propositional structure, as Derrida has effectually said.[1]

While of course there are deep differences from writer to writer, and from philosopher to poet to novelist (and for that matter from painter to musician), the trace of the strenuous impulse towards a future while maintaining a balance of expressive stance can be found in many of the most imposing writers in the Western tradition since the Industrial Revolution. In their language, too, the sense of a "threshold" shows its traces in the impulse to mix levels of expression in ways that pre-Romantic categories like "Menippean satire" cannot really account for. Whole areas of discourse, indeed, will interpenetrate, and philosophy and poetry tend to borrow from each other, a development that in different ways Hegel and Schlegel both deeply discussed. Before them Herder had already generalized the scope of the poetic spirit. Characteristically the poet, and the novelist as well, begins to feel the need to produce a theoretical justification for his work, a justification that gets imbedded into the poetry itself for writers as different from each other as Blake, Emily Dickinson, and Mallarmé.

The play among possible structures, the confluence of strains of discourse, remains tensile in such writers. Their enterprise itself is deeply felt as a sort of threshold. It is never oriented towards the endless regress, the "mise en abîme," of radical self-doubt, though echoes of such doubt enter pronouncedly into literary and philosophical expression at this time. Rather, even in Nietzsche — one may say especially in Nietzsche — the enterprise is oriented in tone and focus, and in feeling, towards the possibility of ultimate resolution, however it may recede: towards the deep convergence of expressed intellect and emotion.

I am here continuing concerns broached in some of my earlier books, chiefly in *The Meaning of Fiction, Prisms,* and *Myth and Language.* This book began as a study of modes of expressing feeling in Romantic and post-Romantic writers, but I was soon caught up in the implications of the condition that the pre-Freudian accounts of depth psychology to be resurrected from such writers as Blake are intricately involved in the pre-Heideggerian modes of thought and manipulations of language. Similarly, I found that the earliest key figures, Rousseau and Goethe, are pervasive enough in their views that they did not need separate chapters to themselves, especially as their works can be more easily summarized than those of Blake or Nietzsche, at least insofar as my particular interests here have treated them. Indeed, instead of adding still further chapters, I have confined many discussions to the notes, with what I feel is some gain in the proportionateness of my presentation, though at the risk of irritating the reader impatient with what may seem digressive argument. It should be noted that translations not otherwise attributed are my own.

Acknowledgments

I have had much help from various quarters, which it is a pleasure to acknowledge, in the long process of writing this book. Many colleagues of considerable learning and wisdom have given me the benefit of their advice by reading all or part of the manuscript and commenting on it, including Thomas McFarland, Irving Massey, Aaron Rosen, Clint Goodson, Edward Ahearn, Arnold Weinstein, and John Grant. My research assistant, Blossom S. Kirschenbaum, has done everything from putting the manuscript effectively on the computer and making an index to providing useful stylistic suggestions. Her predecessor, Angelika Webb, was also of considerable help in this process.

The book was begun in the stimulating atmosphere of the English Department at the State University of New York at Buffalo, and it was finished at Brown University, where I have also benefited from continuing discussion with students and colleagues. Parts of it were written at various times on fellowships from the International Research and Exchanges Board (the Soviet exchange), the Camargo Foundation, and Clare Hall, Cambridge, and I am grateful to all these institutions.

I am also grateful to journals where some of the book has been published in earlier versions: *Novel* (Stendhal), *Costerus* (a small segment of the Blake chapter), *Works and Days* (part of Emily Dickinson), *The Canadian Journal of Italian Studies* (Leopardi), and *Carleton Germanic Papers* (Nietzsche).

Stylistic suggestions are the smallest part of the abundant support and crucial companionship provided by my wife Carol.

Thresholds

1

Introduction

1

For the Romantic Poet every moment is a threshold:[1] the words of the poem express and evoke a state akin to that of a tribal initiate about to enter a liminal experience. Language, as we have come to emphasize, seems difficult to such a poet, a slippery medium. But language also contains at once the power to bring about a state of awareness and the means to define what that state is. Blake and Wordsworth differ from Milton or Thomson in their essential practice of querying the language they use while building out of it a system of definition for the ways in which a person has access to, and creates, privileged states of being.

These states are emotional states, of course, though to rest with calling them that may have the effect of curtailing the intricacy and consistency of how such writers organize experience. The elaborate epistemology of Kant, the constantly self-revising and expanding consciousness of Hegel, are enacted, if never exactly illustrated, in such work, and the long and intricate convergence of poetry with philosophy takes a rich variety of forms. Stendhal offers a sort of dialectic of the emotions in his protagonists as they live through trying to make sense of derivatives from two inherently contradictory systems of ideation. Dostoevsky puts his characters through a constant testing by extremes, where the spiritual, the psychological, the emotional, and the ideological work out inextricable versions of each other. Settling restively for a version of philosophical prose, Nietzsche tries for much the same result. Even so seemingly prim a figure as Emily Dickinson puts her flashlike tiny integers of verse to the task of trying to catch the intricacies of interaction among the spiritual, the psychological, the emotional, and the ideological.

Baudelaire worked out a doctrine at the extremes of experience by poising his statements slowly, in verse of conventional rhythms or in prose-poems. These Baudelaire has curtailed to a verselike precision from the rhapsodies of his model, Aloysius Bertrand. Mallarmé domesticates and genializes his own versions by questioning the language and the rhythms of his phrasing word by word and, finally, "concretely," the very physical dimensions and location of the word on the page. In doing so he produces a rarefaction of language that has the effect of increasing, rather than diminishing, the robustness of his utterances. At the same time he provides a deep assertion of ideal normativeness: it is the words of the tribe that are purified. Hölderlin, too, amplifies a sort of vertigo in the ambivalence between past and future, of realization and failure. A trembling poise shines in his ideas, in his occasional deflections of linguistic usage, and still more in his rhythms; but those rhythms, and also the statements they carry, profoundly assert a transcendence of such ambivalences. "What abides, though, the poets found," he says: "Was bleibet aber stiften die Dichter."

2

"Gefühl ist alles." "Feeling is all," Goethe has Faust say. Like so much else that Goethe imagined, this statement is a bridge between an age that is fading and one that is on the rise. After the Industrial Revolution had taken hold — or in what we persist in calling "Romantic" times — feeling not only drew personal attention from imaginative writers. Several of them shaped a personal universe of perception around a central principle of feeling. Yet the eighteenth century already valued sentiment, and McKenzie's "Man of Feeling" is an exemplary person, while Tristram Shandy and the protagonist of *The Sentimental Journey* give themselves over delightedly to a drift of response.

Such a response, however, has the slightness and randomness of whim. On the side of the person it does not get internalized or analyzed. And on the side of the outer world there are no massive changes or deep actualizations occasioned by feeling. The world stays in place, and the person is left with his feeling, be it the vast pique of the *Neveu de Rameau* (interestingly discovered by Goethe),[2] or the constant flotation of affect in *The Man of Feeling*. In the light of the age that is fading, even Werther is left with his agonies in a world that neither yields to him nor offers true solace. That is why he kills himself. What partially consoles him is the reading of an eighteenth-century sublime-effusion masking as a survival from a northern past — *Ossian*. But *Ossian* will no more give voice to the agonies of Werther than it could, we may presume, to the aspirations and visions of another of its devoted readers, Napoleon. Werther's *Leiden* looks ahead also, but Goethe cannot tell us to what.

Rousseau, as often, provides the key emphasis: "Encore un coup, le vrai bonheur ne se décrit pas, il se sent, et se sent d'autant mieux qu'il peut le moins se décrire, parce qu'il ne résulte pas d'un recueil de faits, mais qu'il est un état." ("One more stroke: true happiness is not described, it is felt, and it is felt the more the less it can be described, because it comes not from a group of facts but is a permanent state.")[3] Alas, this wordless state did not become a permanent one for him; but the large effort to make it so, and to base the desired state on what is recognized by feeling, was one to which the expressive forces of many gifted successors would implicitly subscribe. Nor did Rousseau abandon expression of a sort that admits characterization as "transparent" in Starobinski's terms[4] and as dialectical in de Man's.[5]

On the side of the person, to begin with Blake, the primacy of feeling is analyzed elaborately. It is so deeply internalized that it comes to seem coextensive with the outer world itself, whose massive changes can all be attributed to the variegations of feeling that occasion its deep actualizations. Tharmas, who comprises the tongue in his functions, is elevated to a provisional dominance and a steady equality with other grand, primal figures. Person and world reflect each other, and interact, on the ground of feeling. For Rousseau "the passions are, as it were, the motive (*mobile*) of all action."[6] In the *Confessions* the free man is one who can account for his feelings and submit even to the public act of bringing feelings and failings out into the open so that they can be seen as common.[7] Thus they are rendered harmless: public confession, as in many later therapies, redefines original sin as an imposition of society on an original Pelagian innocence. The purged speaker easily reaches the threshold of a better life.

The figures I will be discussing here have all, in their various ways, faced and deeply articulated ambivalences in feeling, as feeling has come into a powerful and central role. "Praise to the end," Wordsworth says, in the widespread impulse to accommodate even painful experiences. Under a somewhat distorted version of this impulse, as delineated by Mario Praz,[8] pain is sought out for its own sake, in the self or in the other: sadism or masochism predominates in Baudelaire, if he is read somewhat narrowly, and without attention to his powerful and intricate symbolizing; in the nightmare side of Shelley; or in the morbid side of Flaubert; as well as in such as Swinburne, Huysmans, and Wilde. These writers and others, in Praz's view, produce a Medusa figure in place of an Aphrodite.

But this reading will not allow for the force or ambivalence — with hints of an energy that is prospective — even in such praise for the psychic function of "sorrow" as Keats's "Ode to Melancholy":[9]

> Make not your rosary of yew-berries,
> Nor let the beetle nor the death-moth be
> Your mournful psyche, nor the downy owl
> A partner in your sorrow's mysteries;
> For shade to shade will come too drowsily,
> And drown the wakeful anguish of the soul.

Homeopathy, Keats says, will destroy the wakefulness of the state of sorrow, its energy and perceptiveness and alertness to transformation. One must combine the process with its allopathic opposite to force-feed a transformation:

> But when the melancholy fit shall fall
> Sudden from heaven like a weeping cloud, . . .
> Then glut thy sorrow on a morning rose,
> Or on the rainbow of the salt sand-wave,
> Or on the wealth of globèd peonies:
> Of if thy mistress some rich anger shows,
> Emprison her soft hand, and let her rave
> And feed deep, deep upon her peerless eyes.

The speaker insists on maintaining himself on the threshold of a possibility more energized than mere stagnant sorrow. In this situation the control of the verse, its orbicularity, performs a steadying charm to get him beyond what he describes.

The transition from the bright flowers to the eyes of the mistress brings anger, as well as joy and sorrow, into the whole fusion. The experience becomes liminal in its fullness, and transience is the very principle that permits the process. "She dwells with Beauty—Beauty that must die." Consequently, "Ay, in the very temple of delight / Veil'd Melancholy has her sovran shrine, / Though seen of none save him whose strenuous tongue / Can burst Joy's grape against his palate fine." The condition for perceiving either aspect of an ambivalent dynamics between joy and sorrow is a capacity for bringing both into this interdependence. On this path a person may become a hero of feeling, one who will be a sort of constellation of Melancholy, "among her cloudy trophies hung." The "Ay" of the transition affords the emphasis-hyperbole of archaism to its deep turn away from the "no, no, go not to Lethe" of the opening. The poise of the poem is felt to be gained as a triumph of symbolic clearness under the pressure of fluid states.

The charm and equipoise of the ode form steadily reassure the auditor that pain and sorrow will not ravage him in disorder but be recuperated for perception and transformation. In all this movement of identification between the self and outer nature through a contrast between them, and with either state of joy or sorrow through the very transience from one to the other, we are at a more complex point than any sado-masochistic algolagnia or simple Medusean archetype. And certainly further than a formal burnishing of the commonplace. Keats wants to be the master of the feeling, not its slave. His Ode offers an incantation-formula to govern these deep changes.

This process that Keats bodies forth is the more remarkable for his own emphasis elsewhere on the creative side of the somnolent states, in "Sleep and Poetry." "Drowsily" here would seem to go too far, beyond the border of the "Hesperian" fullness that Geoffrey Hartman[10] finds to be a metaphysical condition in the "Ode to Autumn," beyond the "breathlessness" of the superseded psychic demonic kingdom of *Hyperion*, a poem that begins "Deep in the shady sadness of a vale." Joy never enlivens that sadness, but its borderland is one Keats there declares necessary for the poet to visit. He explores it as a liminal experience. And his figure in *The Fall of Hyperion* moves across an expansive threshold toward the monitory voice of a divine figure who is also female, Moneta — a figure whose classical origins are obscure enough to have the ring of Blake's invented deities. In this situation the poet himself effectuates the odd, powerful fusion of joy and sadness that no more submits the joy to be "drowned" in sadness than the valued wakefulness is drowned in sleep. Testing such limits of feeling serves as a vehicle to test other limits, as between permanence and transience (the Nightingale), fullness and emptiness ("Ode to Autumn"), imagination and reality (the Grecian Urn), love and kinds of solipsism ("The Eve of St. Agnes," "Isabella"), mortal and Olympian (*Endymion*).[11] A qualification, a dynamism, a larger horizon, a pretext, some intimation of a threshold, are to be looked for in the widespread Romantic world-sorrow, in the *Weltschmerz* of Leopardi, Clare, Lamartine, Hugo, Bécquer, Shelley, Tiutchev, Nekrasov, Brentano, and many others.

3

We may provisionally allow some force to the extremity of Praz's views, as a measure of the emotional stresses resulting from an *anomie* pervasive after the beginning of the Industrial Revolution. Seen historically, this *anomie* is a sort of negative condition, a psychological counterpart to the increasing anonymity of urban life and the general mobility of populations at many levels, from workers to intellectuals.[12] Seen psychologically, it extends an indeterminacy about recurrences and identities to the very roots of self and language.

Pressure on family circumstances is notable in the origins of most of the English Romantics, whatever class they may have come from. Keats and Wordsworth were orphans, Shelley a lord estranged from his family who broke up his own beginning family under an attraction started in the bosom of Godwin's complicated, reconstituted family. Byron was the quarrelsome child of the widow of a near rake, Lamb the custodian of an insane sister who had killed their mother, while Coleridge was one of a very large brood disturbed in his own family relations. Blake, in whom alone no such disturbances are traceable, nevertheless centers the action of his major Prophetic Books on instabilities of connubiality and filiation.

Wordsworth's experience of trying and failing to set up a family on foreign soil is not unlike the love story recounted in *Villette*. Charlotte Brontë herself experiences *anomie* at school in Belgium. The mythic force of the Brontës, indeed, derives from their being a family whose childhood intimacy was so great that it precludes their going out to found families of their own. Jane Eyre replaces an insane wife killed in a conflagration.

Back home Wordsworth came to poetic maturity during the time when he was setting up an artificial family, through which he supported himself at Racedown by tutoring the "son," Basil Montagu, in a household of which he was the "father" and his sister Dorothy the "mother." The loneliness of Racedown, which they notably remarked on, turned out to be the enabling condition for the expression of a solitary union with nature, of which the obverse is social *anomie*.[13] The "Lucy" poems are about a mysterious dead beloved thought by Coleridge and others to be Dorothy. And indeed in his poems Wordsworth often identified himself with anomic persons on the move in his landscape: the boy of Winander, the mother of "The Thorn Tree," the leech-gatherer of "Resolution and Independence." As though to preserve this focus, he largely excluded from his shorter poems those persons moving into the Lake Country who were rentier exurbanites like himself; there is no one described in the poems who might be a reader of poems by Wordsworth, whereas some of his neighbors were appreciative. And certainly his powers declined as his sociability and position increased. This result is usually attributed to the debilitations of being put on a pedestal, but adulation did not notably change Goethe, in the circumstances of a world still carrying eighteenth-century traces of feudal organization.

Coleridge asserted that "Itard's Savage Boy of Aveyron" was "to be included in William's Great Poem," locating in Wordsworth's imaginative universe the famous extreme example of family-deprived *anomie*, the homeless boy found in the woods and painstakingly brought to language and social life.[14]

Wordsworth wandered and walked over a lonely terrain, but one always the same after his hieratic voyages to Europe. In his wanderings he shows the restless displacement of Shelley and Byron, of Gogol and Hölderlin and Nietzsche, a state of spirit given supremely reductive expression in the poem placed last in Baudelaire's *Les Fleurs du mal,* "Le Voyage." For Shelley a movement ever further eastward resolves problems and fulfills aspirations in *Prometheus Unbound* and "Epipsychidion." Restlessness is the spatial counterpart of *anomie*; to exalt restlessness is at once to exorcise it and to make it the theoretical basis for self-integrating perception. On such a principle may the "spots of time" in *The Prelude* be conceived as cohering. They are encountered in transit.

In sexual intimacy the deepest boundary to cross is the incest taboo, and the anomic shadow of incest passes across the consciousness of many Romantic writers. The household at Racedown was that of a sublimated incestuous couple, and Wordsworth's intimacy with Dorothy has an incestuous tinge. Incest is the anomic form of the family, and it exercises a powerful attraction as a Herculean means for overcoming social impotence. While horror before father-daughter incest freezes the style of *The Cenci* into unparalleled directness, the fantasy of Shelley's *The Revolt of Islam* shows a whole society idealized and revolutionized through the alliance of an incestuous brother and sister. Siegfried in Wagner's *Ring* is born of an incestuous union that leads at once to his triumph and to general disaster. And as Nietzsche points out,[15] it is Wagner who invents this crucial part of the story; the myth does not place just this emphasis on it. Wotan himself is stalled by Fricka's insistence that Siegmund and Sieglinde are transgressors who cannot be permitted the aid of Brünnhilde. Her disobedience and their transgression ultimately bring about the downfall of the gods themselves. But Wagner has Freia object to the adultery (Sieglinde is married), partially displacing the transgression away from the incest. Here he again shows his submission to the sentimental and ideological cross-currents about which Adorno is eloquent and definitive.[16] Wagner has placed himself, and his personages, at an exposed point where waves of extreme feeling can wash over them, and the weaving of myths into leitmotifs is designed to structure those feelings. Instead of defining or analyzing the incest through his plot, Wagner wallows in it poetically: "Schwester! Geliebte!" is Siegmund's admiring effusion. Flaubert in the early *Madame d'Écouy* and elsewhere touches on incest.[17] Byron is likely to have practiced it. For Melville's Pierre the incestuous union with and rescue of his illegitimate sister become the gateway at once to truly penetrating perception and final downfall.

In the light of such powerful cross-currents, the Romantic emphasis on the sublimity of love takes on complexity and strength. Love, too, may draw strength from *anomie*, like the love of Clélia for Fabrice in the

Chartreuse de Parme, intensified by his imprisonment, and then by her adultery with the priest he has become: seeing him only in darkness because she had vowed never to look upon him, sight is subverted by touch. The vow is broken in spirit while unbroken in letter, her love honored and dishonored in one intensifying act. The profession of the Romantic, as wandering tutor or professor, Lenz or Hölderlin, may anomalize or put a theoretical halo on the lover. The beloved herself, for de Quincy and Dostoevsky and Nekrasov, is cast as a blameless prostitute, anomic degradation the first step to unqualified exaltation, without the Freudian qualifications of limited "object choice." Ogarev set up the purified prostitute as a solution to his own erotic dilemmas.[18]

Psychoanalyzing these clusters of relations would only partly explain their persistence in literary representation and their hold on the imagination. The embattlement and the very compensatory defense of the family dynamize and render urgent the intimacy between self and other. Of its very nature this intimacy may be a secret, or have a secret side, or violate one or more taboos: it is the more valued for its power to persist in silence and to overturn opposition. In an earlier period, on the other hand, Petrarch seems almost comfortable with his longing. The lovers in Dostoevsky and in Shelley have no such consolation; they link perilously in a universe of *anomie*, while Eugene Onegin finds *anomie* the residuum of mishandling a proffered love.

Marriage would have sapped Kierkegaard's power, he felt, and *Either/Or* tries to explain why. The ideal of celibacy here becomes antinomized, eroticized, and universalized. Renunciation loses its explicitly Christian base as it gains dialectical power by keeping the lover on a perpetual threshold. In the light of such theory, Don Juan himself get a dialectical foundation. The seducer is an ideal seducer, on a par with the music of Mozart that harmonizes his actions, though his orientation to a future differentiates him deeply from Mozart's protagonist. The Orpheus myth that haunts opera supersedes familial relations: its tragedies are sexual when not explicitly Orphic in the substitution of the boundary between life and death for the shared future of the lovers.[19] *Ernani* borrows from Hugo and *Otello* from Shakespeare to put the aging lover in the position of causing his own and others' downfall. Dynasty and mystery in the *Ring* supervene over the code of family, which Fricka has still managed to enforce. In opera generally the memory of an aristocratic social organization serves to heighten the conditions to be subverted; *Hernani* expresses Hugo's socialist impulses.

Wuthering Heights imposes itself supremely in the imagination as expressing a sublimely fierce renunciation of sublime love in a lonely and wild nature on the part of two distinct, isolated, spiritually unified beings, caught in storms of passion on the threshold of adult life. Such is the mythic core to which Emily Brontë found her way. The novel itself, looked at not in memory but in its actual progression, bases its central plot line on the all-but-total destruction of a family through this unrealized love. Rather as old-fashioned semipornography punished the indulgent by plotting them towards some social penalty, *Wuthering Heights* opens with a prolonged display of sadism on the part of Heathcliff towards all the descendants of the man who kindly took him in off the streets of Liverpool as a gipsy waif and raised him in his own family.

The mythically dominant plot is narrated by the family retainer as an explanation for Heathcliff's conduct. Cathy's rejection of Heathcliff is made to hinge, proleptically and evasively, on the brother's rejection of Heathcliff, in a petulant and impenetrable series of evocations where the theology of the Fall grazes psychological self-justification. She succumbs to the silent force of convention and waveringly rejects the wavering power of the aspiration she and Heathcliff had shared, though the writer sentimentally allows the denial to coexist with the persistence of aspiration. All notions here are at the service of class lines, at once infrangible and insignificant, and of the family, at once dominant and doomed:

> "If I were in heaven, Nelly, I should be extremely miserable."
> "Because you are not fit to go there," I answered. "All sinners would be miserable in heaven."
> "But it is not for that. I dreamt once that I was there. . . . heaven did not seem to be my home; and I broke my heart with weeping to come back to earth; and the angels were so angry that they flung me out into the middle of the heath on the top of Wuthering Heights; where I woke sobbing for joy. That will do to explain my secret, as well as the other. I've no more business to marry Edgar Linton than I have to be in heaven; and if the wicked man in there had not brought Heathcliff so low, I shouldn't have thought of it. It would degrade me to marry Heathcliff now; so he shall never know how I love him; and that, not because he's handsome, Nelly, but because he's more myself than I am." (Chapter 9)

Of course, Heathcliff does know, if they had not been telling each other as much for years, he would only have to overhear this conversation. And he does hear it, for he is eavesdropping at this very moment. Heathcliff's "low" social status must automatically, the language tells us, yield to what the feeling of the novel has been telling us is paramount, the identity-in-love of Cathy and himself ("more myself than I am"). Cathy's will and her feeling are hopelessly at odds; there is no way she, or we, can examine even the discrepancy. She fades into doomed subserviency to class lines that are nowhere examined, though everywhere supremely tested, in the novel. To marry Edgar Linton is "heaven" that she does not deserve, here opposed to a sublime place in nature, the Wuthering Heights where she dreams she wakes "sobbing for joy." Wuthering Heights is a threshold of the wild, a place where childhood familiarity, adolescent amorous awakening, and Wordsworthian nature all sublimely fuse. At the same time, all these floating states are effectually canceled by the assumed rigors of social matchmaking, by a blindness for which Jane Austen would surely have had contempt. Jane Austen herself manages to assimilate personal inclinations to social selection through a long, tensile process of plotted adjustments. In Emily Brontë's novel both society and the person are absolutized, and the "secret" that finds expression in the plot cannot encounter the public fact of class, a given so absolute it can only be half-jokingly made light of. But the values of Love and Nature do find evocative expression, preventing the novel from being used just as Marxian or Freudian parable, the way Freud uses *Gradiva*. There is a disproportion between the contradictory elements, the stated deference to class versus the expressed assimilation to ultimates, Cathy's "secret" referred to immediately beforehand. This very disproportion constitutes a discontinuous explanation of what ails her in the face of her expressed "love" for Edgar Linton. Both "secret" and "dream" themselves, too, are discontinuous from each other, and from Heathcliff's social condition. The language, at this crucial point of the text, jumps with halts and silences, while the feeling both fuses and fails.

The unnecessary elaboration and strange symmetry of kinship patterns in the novel function as an evasion of this central contradiction, as though a branching family tree could lock into the fact that the tree is dead to offer an icon of meaninglessness. The meaning is to be found elsewhere, in the unconnected, and profoundly dominant, love.[20] Heathcliff's behavior somewhat echoes that of Byron immediately after his marriage, but the counterweight to his massively sadistic petulance is more than just psychic damage in the family.[21] And it is also less: the orphan Heathcliff, though he clings desperately to the fact of the loss of his love, has no family: he begins in *anomie*; he emerges from urban slums onto the wild heath.

Love is an antidote to the social process of a reification that is complexly invasive in technological society, as Lukacs and Adorno have variously indicated. *Wuthering Heights* takes place in a backwater, and the backwater itself is an antidote to the domestic *anomie* and reification of the progressively urbanized culture. Instead of lamenting that the village is deserted, as in the eighteenth-century Goldsmith, later writers tend to fantasize the village. In *Wuthering Heights* it is reduced to a couple of households spread out through the country life that for England has some of the character of actualized fantasy. This first urbanized and industrialized country also first and most persistently adapted the pastoral ideal — an ideal that includes a tamer version of love — to the stresses of urban developments in a whole society.[22] In such writings as *Wuthering Heights* and *Jane Eyre*, the Brontës, among other things, are fiercely exorcising their painful acculturation to alien, metropolitan Brussels. The biographer of Charlotte Brontë, as it happens, is the wife of an early urban reformer, Mrs. Gaskell; she deplores what amounts to the destructive effect of London life on Branwell Brontë. And in her own *Cranford* she at once idealizes a past village life and makes it very clear, in the opening, that the village has become a mere exurb to the industrial city, vacated of its menfolk by day. Her characters wander on no heaths, and the novel has a persistent, faint air of missed amorous possibility for its pining characters.

Adrift in the vastness of the city, the characters of Balzac and Dostoevsky find urban existence at once an isolation from love and an opportunity for it. In its role as a consumption center, the city, as Sombart describes it, solidifies an alliance among love, luxury, and capitalism.[23] Yet this alliance is unstable. It is neither available to everyone nor certain for anyone.

4

On the positive side, as a sort of counterbalance to the persistence of *anomie*, the German Romantics soon theorized about the centrality of feeling more precisely than had Goethe. "Thinking is only a dream of feeling, a feeling that has died," said Novalis,[24] and with regard to its processes, he also characterized feeling in a phrase that summarizes the burden of Blake: "Feeling is imaged (organized) movement."[25] Schlegel addresses the principle again and again: "Feeling is the apparently indifferent but really fruitful and complete means of consciousness," a statement that intermodifies another maxim, "The entire play of living movement rests on concord and opposition."[26]

At this dawn of historicism, feeling set some of the tone even for the vision of history, not just in Blake, who calibrated history upon stages of poeticized feeling, and not just in Hegel, for whom the high moment of a historical culture found fulfillment in an aesthetic reading of its dominant trait. For Vico the prime moving force in history was a sort of poetic perception. Rousseau, who drew constantly on actual or fancied historical illustrations to offer substantiation for his views, derived language itself from a sort of primary cry of feeling, distinguishing the spoken language from that of gesture, dictated by need. "We should therefore be confident that needs dictated the first gestures and the passions elicited the first vocalizations."[27]

The fixities of an earlier age did not yield easily of course — or for that matter disappear entirely: Blake's allegorical entities share some kinship with eighteenth-century abstractions, and even with the figures in Renaissance masques. They have strong roots in the apocalyptic imagery of "Old Dissent," as E. P. Thompson has shown.[28]

Music reveled in and systematized this access to feeling. Grand opera came into its own.

> it is a grand opera. . . .
> A tenor large and fresh as the creation fills me, . . .
> I hear the train'd soprano (what work with hers is this?)
> The orchestra whirls me wider than Uranus flies,
> It wrenches such ardors from me
> I did not know I possess'd them![29]

So Whitman says, a devotee of the operatic style and an imitator of operatic arias.[30] In the other direction, from literature to music, Beethoven was led to compose by the rhythms of Goethe's poems, according to Bettina von Arnim.[31] "In music's mirror," she says more generally, "does man's heart learn to know itself."[32]

Nietzsche and Rousseau were both actually composers, combining music and creative thought. As Mendelssohn, who lived in a milieu of philosophers, somewhere says, "The thoughts expressed by music are not too vague for words but too precise."[33] Beethoven associates the Pastoral Symphony with sentiments rather than with specific country sounds, and music in general with a moral sense.[34] Bettina von Arnim[35] declares that few understand what a throne of passion every musical movement is and that passion itself is the throne of music. So readily accessible is music to this use that it is turned into social and pseudo-erotic falsehood by a deceptive woman in Turgenev's *Nest of Gentlefolk.*

Such women are insincere. They commit something like sacrilege in turning a wellspring of pure feeling to false use. Like Proust's Madame Verdurin, who advertises an unfelt cultural piety towards music, they pay the penalty of missing the deep flow and adaptability of personal life that all these novels depict. Feeling is the ground upon which the sincerity and authenticity of this time must base itself, in ramifications that Trilling works out.[36] As he quotes Matthew Arnold:

> Below the surface-stream, shallow and light,
> Of what we *say* we feel — below the stream,
> As light, of what we *think* we feel — there flows
> With noiseless current strong, obscure and deep,
> The central stream of what we feel indeed.

There is a complexity of shame, a *honte,* for Rousseau in the episode where he let a maid get fired rather than confess stealing a ribbon, with all the dizzying dialectic that de Man attributes to it.[37] This complexity becomes possible when it struggles against Rousseau's self-chosen injunction towards candor, and then only through sustaining the feeling that will go through the whole process and survive to find words for incorporating the passage into the *Confessions.* Before the fluidity and depth of the feeling that such writers have found a way to express, terms like "face" or "mask," "sincerity" or "insincerity," fail. They are somehow too coarse, too *grob,* as Staiger says.[38] The writer has launched his enterprise in a finer, more profound language, one that embraces its qualifications while it works them out.

For all this activity it is not necessary that the expressive self become self-conscious: poetry can base itself on interiorization without saying so, though it may choose to say so as the mode of its interiorization. Wordsworth in *The Prelude* does; Leopardi and Hölderlin do not. All three are *sentimental* in Schiller's sense, a term that implies both the centrality of feeling and the self-reflection of the person stressing it. The incantatory pitch of all three poets does not remain on an even level as in the sublime odes of the eighteenth century: it must constantly be recreated, along the line, and the speaking self must thereby be reconstituted. This pitch floats free at its felt center, not in a classless society, though revolutionary programs tend to envision a classless society of the future. It is not that society has become classless, but that the intimate wellsprings of expression do not concern themselves with functions that are derivations of class. The very emphasis on the qualities of landscape has a democratic — a classless and impersonal — side, as Werner Hoffman points out: "Landscape is that segment of the world that belongs to everyone."[39]

To center so pronouncedly on feeling that one's moorings in a particular place and class are somewhat loosened is, in effect, to open up vistas on the past and on the future. Thus a connection may be asserted between historicism and detachment from class. Vico felt obscured enough to write an autobiography as well as a panoramic philosophy of history. Rousseau, a rolling stone with connections easily formed at various social levels, based the arguments in *Émile* and *Du contrat social* on elaborate reconstructions of past social fact, conjectural and actual.

A comparable inclination towards retrospection and prospection, the term of a Proustian impulse, governs Rousseau's sense of how to balance his personal feelings:

> Occupied with my tender nostalgias (*regrets*) all along my route, I
> felt and I have often felt since then as I think about it again, that
> if the sacrifices one makes to duty and virtue are costly, one is well

compensated by the sweet memories they leave in the depth of the heart.[40]

This statement splits into a before and after the *ratio* of St. Thomas, the sound inclination towards the good of a theology that persisted through Renaissance modifications. Memories in the heart serve as the instrument for temporalizing the moral sense; duty and virtue melt, once they have been actualized, into a retrospective feeling.[41]

5

In prose fiction the mingling of styles, what Bakhtin associates with the "carnival" stylistic potpourri of Rabelais, works to serve an evocation of dreamlike mythic material. Bakhtin finds notably in Dostoevsky a "polyphony."[42] And yet Flaubert's work is a monody, and the mythic material in *Un Coeur simple*, as in *Hérodias* and *La Légende de Saint Julien l'Hospitalier*, has become ironized and fixed. Both extremes, the new polyphony and the new monody, attest to deep pressures on the formation of style, pressures beyond those experienced by Rabelais or Diderot, Greene or Richardson.

The problem of "sentimental" stylistic admixtures pervades the evocative use of quasi-mythic material in *Frankenstein*, in the novels of Dickens, in those of Hawthorne. A different register, in Irving Massey's reading, is attained in the myth-haunted orotund raptures of E. T. A. Hoffman.[43]

Even in the Rabelaisian flights of *Moby Dick*, irony and sentiment interfuse in an indissoluble tension, more hyperbolically than in Flaubert, but no less mysteriously.[44] They do so more markedly still in *Pierre*, where Melville urges that we "let the ambiguous procession of events reveal their own ambiguousness" (Book X, III). The protagonist is at the mercy of the deep events that are bearing him along because he has not been able to probe as the author hints one might: "Not yet had he dropped his angle into the well of his childhood, to find what fish might be there; . . . ten million things were as yet uncovered to Pierre." A persistent imbalance between exaggeration and trivialization keeps the sublimation firmly in place and at the same time broadly ironized:

> He stared about him with an idiot eye; staggered to the floor below, to dumbly quit the house; but as he crossed its threshold, his foot tripped upon its raised ledge; he pitched forward upon the stone portico, and fell. He seemed as jeeringly hurled from beneath his own ancestral roof.   (Book XI, III)

The gigantism of Pierre's steps here is as portentous as Melville mocks it for being. The persistent ambivalence of stylistic attitude undergirds and overrides the central ambiguity of a man who faces the truth but takes himself too seriously, to the point where he is finally both ridiculous and transfigured in death. The notions of "catnip" and "Titan" are somehow equally appropriate, and what seems the self-indulgence of the style neither quite settles into self-parody nor quite rises to the high pitch that it sets to fall from:

> Stark desolation; ruin, merciless and ceaseless; chills and gloom,— all here lived a hidden life, curtained by that cunning purpleness, which, from the piazza of the manor-house, so beautifully invested the mountain once called Delectable, but now styled Titanic.
>
> Beaten off by such undreamed-of glooms and steeps, you now sadly retraced your steps, and, mayhap, went skirting the inferior sideway terraces of pastures; where the multiple and most sterile inodorous immortalness of the small, white flower furnished no aliment for the mild cow's meditative cud. But here and there you still might smell from far the sweet aromaticness of clumps of catnip, that dear farmhouse herb. . . . The catnip and the amaranth!—man's earthly household peace, and the ever encroaching appetite for God.
>
> No more now you sideways followed the sad pasture's skirt, but took your way adown the long declivity, fronting the mystic height. In mid field again you paused among the recumbent sphinx-like shapes thrown off from the rocky steep. You paused; fixed by a form defiant, a form of awfulness. You saw Enceladus the Titan, the most potent of all the giants, writhing from out the imprisoning earth; . . . turbaned with upborne moss he writhed; still turning his unconquerable front toward that majestic mount eternally in vain assailed by him, and which, when it had stormed him off, had heaved his undoffable incubus upon him, and deridingly left him there to bay out his ineffectual howl.   (Book XXV, IV)

Pierre is at once a callow youth and something akin to the Titan, who in the attributions here is caught also in a ridicule not distinct from that bestowed consistently upon the protagonist. But in Melville's ambivalence, as it enters the style, the ridicule shades over into admiration, as hyperbole shades over into inarticulateness. The dream-progressions of a mythic romance plot stir up the narrator's language into a silliness not to be distinguished from terror; the unknown is acknowledged, if neither faced nor defined. The threshold is approached in the act of avoiding it.

Such ambivalences as these suggest the presence of some unconscious pressure that has been got into the language of the work.

The conscious and the unconscious move together in human expression at any time, though their proportions and their mode of interrelation may differ. In the language of mathematics human expression approaches as closely as it can a language of purely conscious constituents. And in dreams there takes place as free an expression of the unconscious as possible. Lewis Carroll, Melville's near contemporary, may serve as a paradigm for one mode of calling conscious and unconscious into play, a professional mathematician who wrote about a little girl dreaming, and who injected a free play of fantasy into his mathematical games.

If poetry has come to seem preeminently the mode of language that permits the fullest play to unconscious elements, the proportions will vary within poetry between conscious and unconscious. The surrealist tradition is surely right in seeing Rimbaud as allowing more to the unconscious than do Boileau or Malherbe, even though in the poems of those seventeenth-century writers we may attribute the formal control and the evenness of tone to mechanisms that are analogous to, that may even involve, repression, sublimation, repetition-compulsion, and displacement. The rhythmic afflatus of poetry itself can be taken to signal the presence of the unconscious; the heightening of voice and self-absorption of the poet betray a narcissistic detachment into dreamlike fantasy.[45] The metered forms not only control the unconscious but set up an ordered terrain upon which it can operate without interruption.

Rimbaud derives from Baudelaire, and before Baudelaire, as Béguin[46] reminds us, there is a long tradition of German discussion according special powers to the dreaming imagination. What we have come to call the unconscious was discussed elaborately at the very same time that philosophy was trying to account for imaginative expression and poets were drawing closer in various ways to philosophers. By overemphasizing a reliance on systematic structures, Michel Foucault well characterizes related developments on the conscious side since the Industrial Revolution:

> The critical superrevelation of language, which compensated for its layering into the object, implied that it would be brought near at one and the same time to an act of knowing pure of all speech to that which does not know itself in each of our discourses. It was necessary either to render it transparent to the forms of knowing or to bury it in the content of the unconscious. This explains well the double march of the nineteenth century towards formalism of speech and towards the discovery of the unconscious — towards Russell and towards Freud. And it also explains the temptation to bend one towards the other and to interlace (*entrecroiser*) these two directions: an attempt, for example, to bring into the light of day the pure forms which before any content impose themselves on our unconscious.[47]

Foucault here speaks of two kinds of abstract discourse, symbolic logic and depth psychology. Much more resistant to characterization is the mingling of conscious and unconscious elements in an imaginative discourse that at once submits to and assesses the primacy of feeling, perhaps at the same time coming to terms with an *anomie*.

In imaginative discourse, in poetry, the conscious element does persist. Rimbaud offers not only a vision but an organized, recapturable conception of the city,[48] just as does Baudelaire. For Baudelaire himself, a "classical" control of both meter and rational rhetoric contains the "correspondences." But in Mallarmé, the meter and the rhetoric themselves exhibit disturbances; they allow the unconscious, they exhibit on their surface the fine variations of constant reattunement. Departing from Mallarmé, Valéry is, as it were, forced to purify the classical control to an almost totalized point. Yet the repressed returns in force, and Valéry's most famous long poem presents the ruminations of a giant female Fate spread out upon the stars of the night sky.

The balance between conscious and unconscious is something new in Blake. Coleridge struggles for a different balance between the two. Leopardi and Hölderlin, I will try to show, seem to be contraverting in their rhythms and in their organization the stark message that the bare language of their poems seems to be conveying. Emily Dickinson, free and adaptive in her adoption of images, constructs a process of something like free association in which to conduct her startlingly robust theological discussions.

The literary act, having a certain kinship with dreams, may arise in romantic circumstances that reveal such kinship. Indeed, "The Rime of the Ancient Mariner" was "founded on a dream" of one of Coleridge's friends.[49] The night setting of the round of invented ghost stories, in which *Frankenstein* was conceived, socializes a free association not far removed from dream. Many Romantic writers composed in circumstances not so different from those of a patient reclining on an analyst's couch and opening himself to dreamlike free association. Shelley reclined or rocked while composing, under a tree in England, in a boat in Italy. Pushkin composed on a bed, as later did Edith Wharton, Amy Lowell, and Puccini. Wordsworth took free-associative long walks, on which he conceived of poems. He often refers to dreamlike states in his poems. Tiutchev wrote in a half-sleep. Hemingway's method of writing while standing erect at a sort of lectern may be seen in this context as a kind of Stoic anti-sleep, a physical aid to holding the associations in tow through short sentences, weighting every word.

A supremely balanced hovering between plain statement and deep, nearly unexpressed intimation accounts for the power of the "Lucy" poems. Here, where Wordsworth comes closest to embodying his ideal of writing poetry in the language of "man speaking to men," he also attains a degree of ineffability that floats the language of the poems towards something like a somnambulistic state. I have already referred to the air of repressed incest that seems to linger over these poems. They are almost revenants of language, revenants in language, rather than the acts of communication they pretend to be and so successfully mime. This trait makes them more than just fusions of other forms, "brief elegies that purify both gothic ballad and mannered epigram."[50] The "Erlkönig," about which Hartman also writes,[51] is indeed a gothic ballad; it recounts what might be a dream, and it evokes a nightmarish foreboding. But its language is fairly direct, in addition to seeming so. The language of "A Slumber did my spirit seal" also seems fairly direct, but it is far from actually being so, as many recent commentators have noticed:

> A Slumber did my spirit seal;
> I had no human fears;
> She seemed a thing that could not feel
> The touch of earthly years.
>
> No motion has she now, no force;
> She neither hears nor sees;
> Rolled round in earth's diurnal course
> With rocks, and stones, and trees.

"Thing" in the third line may be taken neutrally for a quasi-pronoun, as in "A pen is a thing you write with" for "You write with a pen." Or it may be taken as an incipient pejorative: "She was once alive; she is now a mere thing, indistinguishable from rocks and stones." Taken the latter way, the second stanza amplifies the attribution. But that stanza itself offers comparable lexical problems. Why in so economical a poem the near reduplication of rocks and stones? Why insist on the distinction by a comma after "rocks"? If rocks and stones reinforce the pejorative, "trees" somewhat cancels it, or seems to. Or is anything pejorative here?

It is not only in such elusive elements of diction that a hovering sense of something imprecise, some dreamy cloud in perception, dominates the poem. The tone itself is elusive, like the ambivalence hanging over charged figures in the unconscious on which the dream, as Freud interprets it, will draw.

Is the speaker celebrating or deploring what has happened to the girl?[52] In any case, does his first sentence carry through the last stanza or not: is all that he says here a part of "Slumber"? "I had no human fears" could mean either "I had no fears at all of the sort that I as a human being could have" or else "The fears I felt were so supernatural I do not even dare to name them except to refer to them by a negative." The "metrical contract" of gothic ballad, and even of ballad generally, would reinforce the second reading, but the metrical contract of funeral epigram would reinforce the first. The colon does so too: the whole stanza in this light becomes an amplified way of saying, "I was oblivious enough not to think she could die." But this oblivion would itself be ambivalent, especially in the light of the death that hangs over the girl in all these poems, and particularly by contrast with "Strange fits of passion have I known," in which "the strange fit" whose story the poem recounts is the thought that the girl has already died before the rider reaches her cottage. The girl laughs at that thought in the poem's final stanza, and the writer comes to tears in remembrance of her laughter. That final stanza, however, is struck from the poem by Wordsworth:

> I told her this: her laughter light
> Is ringing in my ears:
> And when I think upon that night
> My eyes are dim with tears.

The poem itself is comparably simple on the surface. We learn only in its last line what the lover has been thinking, "'O mercy' to myself I cried, / If Lucy should be dead!'" Through the poem he has been approaching her and somehow never reaching her. Since the reunion of the lovers would be the natural terminus of the narrative, the "strange" thought about death substitutes for the unachieved union. Yet there is no dialectic of interaction between love and death. The thinking is suspended, as in a dream, and the motion of the rider, an approach never consummated in the finished poem, resembles traveling in a dream. The poem is offered as a communication "in the lover's ear alone," an anecdote trivial on the face of it, puzzling, and classified by Wordsworth in the poem as an example of "strange fits of passion."

His excision of the final stanza quoted above has the effect of preserving the suspension, of keeping the whole flow of the poem in harmony with a sort of vagueness that sorts well with the logical shifts and tonal uncertainties of "A Slumber did my spirit seal."[53]

The two poems, however, get different labels from Wordsworth. "Strange fits of passion" is classified under "Poems Founded on the Affections," along with "She dwelt among the untrodden ways" and "I travelled among unknown men." The remaining two "Lucy" poems are assigned to the honorific group "Poems of the Imagination": "A Slumber did my spirit seal" and "Three years she grew in sun and shower." In this last poem, too, death is broached as a gradual possibility now become actualized: the identification with Nature of the dead girl in "A Slumber did my spirit seal" is attributed here to the living girl. The language is so evasive that it is not at once clear whether Nature's assertion of claim —"This Child I to my self will take"— amounts to causing the child's death;

actually it merely amounts to establishing a harmony between Nature and the growing girl. Again in the last stanza, the claim-speech of Nature is at once followed by an account of the death. The phrase "the work was done" looks backward in the poem to a budding girlhood but assimilates forward to the death just mentioned:

> Thus Nature spoke—The work was done—
> How soon my Lucy's race was run!
> She died, and left to me
> This heath, this calm, and quiet scene;
> The memory of what has been,
> And never more will be.

"She dwelt among the untrodden ways," too, has been singled out for its nascent contradictions. Concentrating on these, as though Wordsworth were like Donne, has the effect of obscuring the vague intimations he does manage to convey, bringing language within hailing distance of a dreamlike realm:

> She dwelt among the untrodden ways
> Beside the springs of Dove,
> A Maid whom there were none to praise
> And very few to love:
>
> A violet by a mossy stone
> Half hidden from the eye!
> —Fair as a star, when only one
> Is shining in the sky.
>
> She lived unknown, and few could know
> When Lucy ceased to be;
> But she is in her grave, and, oh,
> The difference to me!

Too much is evoked by Lucy for her to be the "Echo" Hartman calls her,[54] though that term gets at some of her elusiveness as a figure. It is her death that is lamented, and this poem, too, has an elegaic ring, yet we cannot say of that writer's assertions whether he responds more powerfully to her life or to her death. Even so rich an elegy for a young girl as Leopardi's "A Silvia" is quite clear on this point. Here we are not sure whether the speaker is someone who simply has remarked on her as he passed repeatedly through the village, or a brokenhearted lover. Without certainty in this matter, we cannot begin to assess how large "the difference to me" is. It might be a capital loss; it might simply be a marked alteration in the human landscape. Again, as in interpreting a dream, we cannot quite be sure that a given episode is not summary rather than episodic, a piece in the puzzle or the whole puzzle itself.

The simple style suggests a likeness of violet to star — and the use of the term "star" in the nomenclature of some flowers reinforces the likeness, itself a topos. However, stars are also different from violets: they are steadier, more permanent, more visible, more elevated, and more unattainable. One could say that in moving from life to death, the girl moves from violet to star. (There is the topos of comparing girls to flowers, and another topos of declaring a dead woman to be a constellation). It is not simply that Wordsworth enlists the likeness between star and violet, or the difference. Rather, he floats the likeness upon the difference, and the ineffable result suspends precision.

So, too, for the contrast between "praise" and "love." The "none to praise," taken against the "few to love" may imply that praise is the harder attainment. The two occupy different universes, and it is not clear whether a tinge of snobbery may color the poem: there are none to praise because nobody she meets is noble enough to accord praise. But, of course, the praise might also have an erotic tinge, and in that light "praise" and "love," too, exhibit both likeness and difference. The moral and social fades into the aesthetic and amorous.

In "I travelled among unknown men," the large abstractions are the familiar Wordsworthian nature perception, England, and Lucy. Nature, country, and girl fade into and reinforce each other in the writer's absence from all three together, an absence become permanent in the death characteristically delayed for mention till the last line:

> Thy mornings showed, thy nights concealed,
> The bowers where Lucy played;
> And thine too is the last green field
> That Lucy's eyes surveyed.

The effect in this last stanza is not exactly one of patriotic affirmation. England and mourning and nature perception have all got absorbed into one state of consciousness, dreamily but without blurring. John Jones contrasts Wordsworth's distinctness with the blur of Ossian.[55] He comments, too, on the frequency of his use of the word "thing,"[56] a frequency that may be taken for a sort of talisman to guarantee a vividness and sharpness to what Wordsworth depicts, in the insisting presence of a contrary vagueness.

In *The Prelude* the subject is evasive at the beginning — and indeed throughout the poem, in spite of the subtitle "The Growth of a Poet's Mind." The states that the poem praises lie beyond definition in the unconscious. The speaker moves into these states and out of them, left with the theorizing that tries to comprise them and yet fades before them. In the face of "joy," these abstract phrasings keep formulating the pleasure principle that Wordsworth asserts to be the basis of his poetry: "The poet's art is an homage paid to the grand elementary principle of pleasure, by which he knows, and feels and lives, and moves."[57]

The actual words in *The Prelude*'s disquisitions elude the formal base they seem to be resting on and instead function more as "fiduciary symbols" than as signs.[58] So there persists at once a mutuality and a tension between the mode of discourse and the states on which the discourse centers. The language will not really revert to the distinct disclaimer of "the inexpressibility trope," even though the long opening of the poem, for two hundred and seventy lines, concerns itself with the problem of having to cast about in vain for a subject. Casting about comes back to the self, which moves out to what it has been feeling. The disparity between the evanescence of what is being discussed and the abstract language used to discuss it keeps a dreamy semi-consciousness afloat.

The encounter with the old leech-gatherer in "Resolution and Independence" occurs in a dreamlike suspension, and the act of coupling poet and leech-gatherer performs an identification arbitrary enough to be referred to interpretations of an unconscious process, since a logical analogy is asserted that does not account for the haunting presence of the figure.

At another extreme, Wordsworth has recourse to haunting, indecipherable sounds, or to the mere babbling of the idiot boy before the moon. The boy of Winander "blew mimic hootings to the silent owls." Wordsworth in "Peter Bell" puts the turning point of the man's whole life at the moment when he hears and moves towards a haunting, indistinguishable sound. The Danish boy sings songs to animals who could not understand him, and "Like a dead Boy he is serene." All these boys repeat, in a sort of reversal, the dreamlike merging-in-isolation of the dead Lucy.[59]

Or, in fuller formulation:

> Dumb yearnings, hidden appetites, are ours,
> And they must have their food. Our childhood sits,
> Our simple childhood, sits upon a throne
> That hath more power than all the elements.
> I guess not what this tells of Being past,
> Nor what it augurs of the life to come;
> But so it is, and, in that dubious hour,
> That twilight when we first begin to see
> This dawning earth, to recognize, expect,
> And in the long probation that ensues,
> The time of trial, ere we learn to live
> In reconcilement with our stinted powers,
> To endure this state of meagre vassalage
> Unwilling to forego, confess, submit,

Uneasy and unsettled, yoke-fellows
To custom mettlesome, and not yet tamed
And humbled down; oh! then we feel, we feel,
We know when we have friends. Ye dreamers, then,
Foragers of lawless tales, we bless you then,
Imposters, drivellers, dotards, as the ape
Philosophy we call you: then we feel
With what, and how great might ye are in league,
Who make our wish, our power, our thought a deed,
An empire, a possession — ye whom time
And seasons serve; all Faculties; to whom
Earth crouches, the elements are potter's clay,
Space like a heaven filled up with northern lights,
Here, nowhere, there, and everywhere at once.
                              (1805 *Prelude*, V, 533–57)

Consciousness and *anomie* before a persistent unconsciousness are both present here.[60] The air of definition is at once approached and undermined by the persistent attempt to offer alternate terms that can be taken, rhetorically more than logically, either as assays at greater precision or fumblings towards unrealized expression. They may also be taken for emphases by repetition, as with "our childhood . . . our simple childhood." The childhood is really not so simple. This excursus follows on an account of the speaker's fascination in his boyhood with *The Arabian Nights*; the general heading is "Books." The very space described in the last line as indeterminate to perception resembles space apprehended in a dream, and the culminating adverbs both exhaust and cancel the possibilities they name.

Here the familiar doctrine of the Immortality Ode is couched in the language of the very philosophy it calls "the ape."[61] The voice, as the rhythms are varied through the passage, catches itself up, rises but is not allowed fully to rise, expands but then qualifies, never fully expressing and never losing touch with the powerful emotional undercurrent on which it is basing a faint embodiment of the principles it reaches towards discussing. The powerful "northern lights" image is not allowed its full climactic force; instead it is dissipated in the alternate spatial adverbs, like a vanishing dream.

The Prelude (a title bestowed after Wordsworth's death) delineates "the growth of a poet's mind," and it uses the language of the more lucid part of the mind as a means for approaching the darker. Its subject is not poetry, and not the person of the poet, but the power prior to poetry that allows the poet to become what he is. The state has privileged moments, the "spots of time." It also has blanks of consciousness, and it offers difficulties:

> Yet is a path
> More difficult before me; and I fear
> That in its broken windings we shall need
> The chamois' sinews and the eagle's wing;
> For now a trouble came into my mind
> From unknown causes. I was left alone
> Seeking the visible world, nor knowing why.
> The props of my affections were removed,
> And yet the building stood, as if sustained
> By its own spirit!   (II, 287-92)

At the same time the achievement of the poem, and the persistence of this passage, too, in identity from 1805 to the 1850 version, testifies to the poet's continuing connection with the undercurrent of half-consciousness. As he says of his college days, "I was a Dreamer, they the Dream" (III, 28).

Wordsworth attributes the possibility of being in touch with such states to the "half-consciousness" expressed in meter, "the tendency of metre to divest language, in a certain degree of its reality, and thus to throw a sort of half-consciousness of unsubstantial existence over the whole composition."[62] Or, in other words, meter transfers language into something akin to a dream state.[63]

In *The Prelude*, the less-than-great poem ("awful burden," I, 235), the "incomplete" poem, and the liminal poem merge in a doubling of tentatives whose accidental image is the facing texts of the 1805 and the 1850 versions, together with the palimpsests of the inspired broken passages and the 1800 "two-book *Prelude.*"

Though the poem proceeds chronologically from infancy to a post-Snowden enabled present, it works as a kind of fantasia of rumination about access to the very power it is celebrating.[64] The experience of the poem and its act of celebration subsume the various doctrines that it offers. They constitute its psychological originality: the three stages of consciousness (Hartman), the third "primal" landscape in addition to the first of past experience and the second of present recapitulation (Jones), the gradual movement from optimism to pessimism (Bostetter).[65] The poem's fine and distinct visual perceptions[66] are at the service of an overriding impulse to express and to master the "half-consciousness" behind the poem's "oscillating up-down pattern of attention."[67] In a deep sense it provides access to a world where "feeling" is undifferentiatedly active, one we have come to call "the unconscious":

> From nature largely he receives; nor so
> Is satisfied, but largely gives again,
> For feeling has to him imparted strength,

And powerful in all sentiments of grief,
Of exultation, fear — and joy, him in mind,
Even as an agent of the one great Mind,
Creates, creator and receiver both.

(1805, II, 267–73)

The effect, as Lindenberger says,[68] is of a "steady probing inward." Wordsworth mimes as well as discusses his experience, but the discussion and the mimetic act are curiously displaced from each other: the procedures of vivifying access are veiled in quasi-abstractions as much as they are veiled in meter. The dream is honored but not allowed to take over.

6

The language of such poems shows persistent instability in the relation between the representational function of language (that which attempts to delineate or represent) and its discursive function (that which engages in the reflective play of signifiers). Coleridge, somewhat against his own poetic practice, was willing to isolate the reflective as the highest function of language. The strength and the evasiveness of such poems as "Kubla Khan," on Clint Goodson's showing, derive from shifts between the mimetic and the discursive functions,[69] as Coleridge exemplifies and evolves his own special sensitive theorizing about language.

His anti-nominalism and his willingness to insist on the philosophical (the conscious) side of poetry put the unconscious side under a fruitful tension. The poem must avail itself of what is anyway a general attribute of poetic language, its tendency, in the very mimetic act of firmly referring to objects, to begin with a sort of interreference. Put simply, "in poetry the words themselves interact, both musically and logically. 'I wandered lonely as a cloud' is not a single flash of observation. The word 'lonely' is identified first with the word 'cloud' before their constellation is referred to a referent in reality. (There may be no real cloud overhead in the poem.) And, further, the referent, a real 'lonely-as-a-cloud' emotional state, goes on to make 'wandered' almost analogical."[70]

The analogy itself takes on dialectical and summary functions, in the form of a persistent discussion of allegory and symbol, and an increased reliance on culminating symbols like the rose of Blake or the blue flower of Novalis. The desire embodied in poetic language is questioned and brought to a point where it will both express a longing and find an image for it. Such depths do the simple "Lucy" poems cover, unlike the neat, contented lyrics of the Renaissance in a superficially comparable style, the shorter poems of Jonson, or even the songs of Shakespeare. Inspected by the modern critic, the ode of Keats becomes a thicket of qualifications, a labyrinth of analogies. And yet each of the great odes expresses and propels a longing while embodying it in a single image: psyche, the nightingale, the urn, Melancholy, Autumn. These images, or figures, borrow the poise and the richly displaced emphasis of allegories. They are not quite allegorical, however, lacking first of all the interaction with other allegorical figures that brings into balance the allegories of Jonson's masques or Blake's Prophetic Books. The urn and the nightingale stand alone. And they also stand aside, elusively evading the function of standing squarely for the idea of the poem. Oddly, the poem measuredly opens floodgates of contemplating what the urn and the nightingale are *not*. Autumn can stand for loss, or for plenitude; the Hesperian image of the harvest figure forestalls by stalling on both, and by containing in preterition an earlier phase of itself whose absence becomes a kind of opposite: "Where are the songs of spring? Ay, where are they?"

Such figures draw, too, on the energy that earlier societies coded into myths. But unlike the figures of myth, which simply mediate, they are both mediating and mediated at the same time. They enter unstably into a combination that then "jells" just for the poised moment of the ode. The interrelations in Blake's pantheon rely predominantly on such instability, rather than charming it away in Keats's fine tuning and sensitive qualifications.[71] The figures in Keats's most ambitious, and persistently unfinished poems, *Hyperion* and *The Fall of Hyperion*, are also only provisionally hypostasized, like the figures in the odes. The language of description in *Hyperion*, accordingly, neither rises to explicit metaphor nor fixes in mimetic constatation. A displacement from such procedures gives force, and a sort of sublated mythic air, to the elaborate sunset passage in that poem (I, 172–229), an almost surrealistic evocation of the sunset through individual, sub-allegorical, quasi-metaphorical properties.

Put differently, an equivalent for myth is brought to approximate the emotive sense of myth through abstraction, and through a machinery of dialectical removes from credence in the myth.[72] This remove from credence attains a stance that has a counterpart in irony, and an elaborate form of irony is the means by which Blake early has access to these dialectical possibilities. As de Man so strikingly shows for their negative side, allegory and irony share affinities in tropological procedure. Blake manages to get beyond irony, while retaining its particular modality of statement. Irony itself gets beyond irony.[73]

The challenge of centralizing his feelings through language enables the modern writer to eat his cake and have it too. At his best he will make the negative and qualified devices of language bend back expressively on themselves, to permit him to bring the flux he feels into an energized harmony while he stands triumphantly just across the threshold of utterance.

2

Blake
The Exaltation of Fluidity

1

Wordsworth aims in *The Prelude* through a language characterized as semi-adequate to feel his way towards the conditions of adequacy. In describing these he stands on the threshold: he celebrates adequacy and strikes an elegiac note over its elusiveness. He strives towards an ideal simultaneity of poetry and language. Now, poetry in general acts to envisage a sort of simultaneity, and all its means converge to that end. Aimed at a version of simultaneity are the devices of echo, incremental repetition, restriction to a particular diction, coherence (or showy diffusion) of figural language, "projection of the axis of selection upon the axis of combination,"[1] and heightened coordination of the various aspects of the speech act.[2] These devices would be useless if they did not have the implied semantic function of declaring at every point of the statement that the statement hangs together in some more than ordinary way.[3]

Prose, by contrast, in its ordinary manifestations, is firmly anchored to an analytic function of moving from A to B. A manipulable prose, indeed, came about, in Western culture at least, only at the point where it found the means to disentangle itself from poetry by inventing philosophy — an approach to centering analysis and producing a theory of the analytic.[4] In an earlier phase a numinous simultaneity in myth was matched and expressed by a poetry of charged terms and fixed, virtually sacral function.

Now, poetry, which must be cast in language, is also inescapably sequential, like prose. And the aspiration to simultaneity must somehow come to terms with this fact. It must enlist, rather than get caught in, the tension between the sequential and the simultaneous. Shelley, in Ir-

29

ving Massey's reading,[5] found a fairly automatic means of doing this. By the time we get to a further point in the poem, or even in the line, we leave behind what we had before. The effect is not the nonsense for which Shelley has been criticized, but rather a dreamlike access to a rapturous state. Simultaneity is, as it were, assumed, and the assumption is pointed up by freedom in sequence from the normal constraints of sequence.

Take the lines from "Ode to the West Wind":

> Thou on whose stream, 'mid the steep sky's commotion,
> Loose clouds like earth's decaying leaves are shed,
> Shook from the tangled boughs of Heaven and Ocean.

There is, it has been argued, no tree discernible here, and yet a tree is referred to. Treating this expression as a slippage of metaphor (Heaven and Ocean do not have boughs they shed on the sky), or even as a loose evocation of nature, will not adequately face its consistency and tonal unity. Nor are the terms just evocative that produce a firm referentiality to things we can see with our very eyes: sky, clouds, earth, leaves, boughs, ocean. The surrealists carried such procedures a step further, and with an added self-conscious flouting of logical sequentiality. In Shelley the sequentiality is neither flouted nor observed. He simply moves ahead serenely in a musical and referential improvisation, one whose notes of freedom are at the same time rigorously given an external structure, that of terza rima. The base of the predication has been subverted. It returns not only in the coherence of metrical and other devices but also as the dissolving features of nature are subordinated to a "windy" feeling of freedom. Outer nature and inner feeling are brought into relation not by Wordsworth's sequential ruminations over the simultaneous, but rather by a kind of automatic assumption that lines written in a half-sleep[6] could attain the simultaneous by subverting the sequential.

Blake had an elaborate theory, we have come to learn, about how outer nature and inner feeling interact. He found as a means for at once expressing and expounding this developing theory a series of poetic procedures that make him, very possibly, the only philosopher-in-poetry who has ever lived. Poets tend to have ideas—borrowed ones, like Pope, or original ones, like Shakespeare or Dante. Dante notably coordinates his own ideas and those of others into an analytic framework. But though the figures in his poetry are richly significant, in accord with his own theory about them, the actual language, like the structure, remains analytic. Parmenides, Empedocles, and their successor, Lucretius, couched entire philosophical systems in verse. The systems, however, remain preponderantly analytic, and the verse is largely palliative or ornamental, honey on the cup so the bitter medicine will be swallowed, as Lucretius said. Lucretius, to be sure, has a powerful "poetic" component above and beyond his philosophical message. We may disagree with him about the honey on the cup, respond to the tense overdrive of his poetic power, and still be convinced that his vehicle is headed at all times firmly in the direction of physical theory. Blake's procedures are of a different order.

In the Prophetic Books Blake turns the simultaneous back on the sequential, first by inventing a kaleidoscopically changing story that is at once endlessly linear and obsessively cyclic. Irony permutes with the absence of irony to undermine a merely predicative sequentiality.[7]

As for doctrine, having deeply identified outer nature and inner feeling, into encompassing simultaneity, Blake renders their relations dialectical by breaking them down into mythlike entities, the Zoas, with all their shadows and emanations. These quasi-allegorical figures are as rigorously sequential as a key term in a philosophical discourse would be. They cannot be melted down into each other, while at the same time the narrative brings about partial fusions that are shown as either a goal to be aspired towards or a peril to be avoided. The sequence of time is referred to the simultaneous moment, and Blake goes Rousseau one better by at once identifying origins with beginnings and dramatizing the identity. This is a distinction Hölderlin may be seen to adumbrate.[8] Blake sublates it by creating a poetic language that moves immediately beyond a prior point of ideation. And finally the doctrine encoded into all Blake's reordered simultaneities of poetic form is a doctrine of oceanic fluidity, one where the psychological elements have a sequential distinctness and at the same time a perilously balancing simultaneity, his kind of perpetual threshold.

If poetry is accorded a philosophical role, questions about signification are opened. These occasioned deep theoretical questioning in Germany — metaphor, symbol, allegory, and irony for Schlegel; myth for Herder and Schelling. Blake, their contemporary, went them one better by building into his verse a theoretically realized function for metaphor, symbol, allegory, irony, and myth. Even the fairly early *Songs of Innocence and Experience* subvert ordinary notions about the use of metaphor to launch symbols and provide an armature for allegory. The bifocal similarity of innocence to experience matches lamb to tiger, one tree to another, rose to sunflower. The similarity flows into antitheses and back again, without any forward sublation, but without any of the closed order that the form of these small poems suggests.

Metaphor posits at once likeness and difference between two objects. It is a "tuning fork"[9] that evokes contradiction because difference is foregrounded, and bypasses it — a "progression" through "contraries" in Blake's terms — because likeness is asserted. It quickly refers to context, both for the differentiation of vehicle from tenor and for the pragmatic[10] verification of its signification with respect to actuality.

Blake universalizes his context and his threshold: his reference is cosmic, historical, spiritual, personal, eschatological, sexual, aspirational, all at once. Consequently the relation among sets of quasi-allegorical entities has an arbitrariness in which the random and the necessary cannot be distinguished from one another because tenor and vehicle cannot be disentangled.

The cyclic or seasonal congruences of a tribal, neolithic culture are thus subjected to a criticism that replaces them not with what came after, some form of rationalism, but rather with a charged and virtualized equivalent of what came before: not an old mythic system, but the essence of a prior mythic system. Myth has been philosophized by being assimilated to an ongoing inquiry of which it is at once a source and a goal unrealizable except by the most wakeful poetry (which it defines).

By virtualizing and dynamizing a microscopic, processive series of events around his interreferring mythical entities, Blake has produced something like an equivalent for such an earliest state, seeing it as an assertion of the reality of mythic beings:

> the Daughters of Albion
>
> Names anciently remembered, but now condemn'd as fictions
> Although in every bosom they controll our Vegetative powers.
> (*Jerusalem* 5.37–39; p. 146)[11]

Romantic attitudes go Renaissance attitudes one better. They exponentialize them. This statement of Blake's transposes the myth-doctrine of Petrarch or Pico della Mirandola (or Boehme or Swedenborg, taking it from the theological side) into a transformational principle whereby what is unknown within the human psyche is all that has been dynamized in the outer world. We are given a dominance of myth without naming myth, one that endlessly factors existences into congeries of archetypes, turning metaphor and myth into versions of one another. In this system every metaphor is a myth, without symbolization. And every myth is a symbol, multiply designating at every point and virtual at its moment in time because perpetually subject to the fluidity of its own self-definition (the metamorphoses of Vala or Orc). The relation of one figure to other beings in the context is always being adumbrated. This relation is never less than total nor more than arbitrary. A modern assertion, "the body is the unconscious," would itself fix, according to principle, this permuting series. Language fails before the task of presenting such a process. Blake says as much in terms that accord well with Heidegger's definition of Hölderlin's *Sagen* towards a grand *Stimmung*. So he phrases his version of the "inexpressibility trope":

> (I call them by their English names: English, the rough basement.
> Los built the stubborn structure of the Language, acting against
> Albions melancholy, who must else have been a Dumb despair.)
> *(Jerusalem* 36.58–60; p. 181)

It is, finally, trivial to say that Blake anticipates Hegel, or that transcendent logical series could be derived from him. Rather he transcends the Hegelian dialectic of making contradictions subsume earlier points in a reasoning process by simultaneously creating and using a theory of philosophic poetry that is itself a giant *Aufhebung* of any of its referents taken singly or together.

Thinking through invented myths to which he assigns a virtual credence allows Blake to fuse philosophy and poetry. What he says in his work constitutes at once a chain of predications whose consistency is defensible and a series of arbitrary inventions whose aesthetic fancifulness the very names of his beings advertise. Heraclitus, by contrast, was trying to take from poetry only that which would be useful for defensible predication.

On the ground of myth he combines abstractions in ways that have a theological force as well as a psychological application:

> Therefore I write Albion's last words. Hope is banish'd from me.
>
> These were his last words, and the merciful Saviour in his arms
> Receiv'd him, in the arms of tender mercy and repos'd
> The pale limbs of his Eternal Individuality
> Upon the Rock of Ages. Then, surrounded with a Cloud:
> In silence the Divine Lord builded with immortal labour,
> Of gold & jewels a sublime Ornament, a Couch of repose,
> With Sixteen pillars: canopied with emblems & written verse.
> Spiritual Verse, order'd & measur'd, from whence, time shall
>   reveal
> The Five books of the Decalogue, the books of Joshua & Judges.
> Samuel, a double book & Kings, a double book, the Psalms &
>   Prophets
> The Four-fold Gospel, and the Revelations everlasting
> Eternity groan'd & was troubled, at the image of Eternal Death!
>
> Beneath the bottoms of the Graves, which is Earths central joint,
> There is a place where Contrarieties are equally true:
> (To protect from the Giant blows in the sports of intellect,
> Thunder in the midst of kindness, & love that kills its beloved:
> Because Death is for a period, and they renew tenfold.)

> From this sweet Place Maternal love awoke Jerusalem
> With pangs she forsook Beulahs pleasant lovely shadowy Universe
> Where no dispute can come; created for those who Sleep.
>
> > *(Jerusalem, 47.18–48.20; p. 194)*

Here the statement of despair on Albion's part leads to a rescue by "the merciful Saviour," whose attitude suggests the raising of Lazarus in a form that transposes the iconography of a Pietà (Jesus holding a dead Man instead of the Virgin holding the Son of Man). The rescue entails Blake's recreation of a sickroom-temple, after the Son has become an image of the Father in terms reminiscent of cliff-bound England ("Rock of Ages"). The temple is supported by pillars that carry upon them unspecified emblems and each a specified book of Holy Scripture. The presence of the Bible in the Temple adapts the location of the Ark of the Covenant, the enshrined Bible, on the central altar of Solomon's temple. Blake here turns iconographic details of scriptural interpretation into the elements of an invented story that becomes a new theology. That theology, in the expansions of the next lines, contains within itself a spiritual definition not only of an anti-philosophy of ambivalent contradiction ("Beulah . . . a place where Contrarieties are equally true") but of the philosophical enterprise itself ("Giant blows in the sports of intellect"). The activity of philosophy is defined, anticipating Nietzsche, by its unconscious emotional component, and perhaps also its parody of theology: it offers "thunder in the midst of kindness" (parodying God the Father?), and a fixing-in-death of its very object ("love that kills its beloved"). The principle to be derived from revealed theology makes death itself something other than this, a fixed but temporary event ("for a period") that contains within itself its own opposite, a principle of revivification ("they renew tenfold"). In effect Blake has used the text "O death where is thy sting, O grave where is thy victory" (I Corinthians 15:55, quoting Hosea 13:14) much as St. Thomas might have done, as the basis for a chain of theological reasoning.

That chain of reasoning, however, is not only brought to bear upon a series of mythological happenings; it exists modally only in the context of such happenings, and it cannot be divorced from that context. So the Holy Scripture cannot be separated off and glossed, as Blake reads it, for the guidance of an institutionalized church: the first whole plate of *Jerusalem* shows Los-Blake carrying a lantern shaped like a sun into a door under an arch that could only be an entrance to the crypt of a church. The Scripture must be vividly reimagined and made continuous with a creative psychic life, at the culmination of which, in the last plate of *Jerusalem* but one (Plate 99), a Jerusalem vaguely androgynous (or perhaps a Jerusalem somehow conflated with Albion or bearing his attributes) undergoes the awakening of a forceful trans-sexual embrace in the arms of a haloed Jehovah figure. The Christian elements converge and dominate as *Jerusalem* progresses, and there emerges something like a demonstration of Schelling's *Philosophie der Mythologie*.[12] Since Blake does, finally, assign credence to Holy Scripture and to the Christian Revelation, his own inventions never quite rise to the status of the mythical elements in Christianity. Nor are those Christian typological components ever redefined into a comparable arbitrariness: the invented myths, carrying with them their borrowings from the Druidic, the Platonic, the Classical, and the Near Eastern, strain towards the Christian types, which come free, clear, and alive in the process. Without their energetic straining the two systems would not move towards harmony but would collapse under overdefinition. As it is, they stand poised as he imagined them, clear and yet mobile in their possibility of definition.

2

The supernatural is not allowed to rest on its theological or anthropological formulas. Instead, Blake makes it coterminous with the natural. The poeticizing of philosophical language, and the theologizing of poetic language, entails the interaction of natural and supernatural, an overriding simultaneity encompassing history and depth psychology as versions of each other — a thesis Hegel was propounding at just about the same time in *Die Phänomenologie des Geistes*.

As Blake gradually found his way into this titanic project, he strangely, and as it were randomly, inverted key terms in his language, doing so "ironically" in such a way as to avoid any tone of irony, except in the satire that was his very first try, *An Island on the Moon*.

In *The Marriage of Heaven and Hell*, Blake uses "devil" to mean "angel," and vice versa. Yet he only reverses these terms intermittently, and sometimes "angel" is a positive term. Thus he bewilderingly subverts the law of contraries, conveying his doctrine — or an aphoristic substitute for one — through shock and irony, while analytic language is subjected to ironic reversals that are transcended by being randomized.

This incipient use of Hegelian contradiction (as Bronowski has in effect called it)[13] did not satisfy Blake, because as he grew into the composition of his major works he left such ironic procedures behind, substituting for them a new approach whereby the Prophetic Books were to be assigned the modality of Scripture by assigning to Scripture the modality of poetry. The cosmic history in *The Marriage* is subjected to irony, whereas in the Prophetic Books, again and again, we are given a transformation, or a series of transformations, instead of an ironic series. In *The Four Zoas* Blake added further scriptural references in revision, as though to insist on the Biblical congruence. At a point where humankind is converging to become the company of the blest, he introduces in the margin the simple reference to another passage from Ephesians, one with a different emphasis: "To the intent that now unto the principalities and powers in heavenly places might be known . . . the manifold wisdom of God" (Ephesians 3:10). Here the viewpoint offers a merger with heavenly beings, and not the wrestling against fallen angels of the introductory epigraph. But the spiritual similarity of the "principalities and powers" is indicated by the repetition of the Greek words *archas* and *exousias*.

Milton presents three categories of persons, defined by theological terms: the "reprobate," the "redeemed," and the "elect." While singly the ironic touch operates on this nomenclature, so that the two "good" ones are really "bad" (at least to the extent of being limited), there is also a Biblical justification for terming the "reprobate," the energetic striver, as "good"— "The stone that the builders rejected has become the head of the corner" (Mark 12:10, quoting Psalms 118:22). The terms "redeemed," "immortals," and "eternals," introduced as early as *The Book of Urizen* (15, 16), reinforce the scriptural self-declaration of the Prophetic Books.

Analytic language wishes to establish credence. Ritual language works on the assumption of a prior credence. The tale of a myth explains what it was that could have engendered credence. Irony radically questions credence by inverting predication.

The language of Blake fuses all these procedures. At once ironic in deviation and mythic in narrative-allegorical set, that language complicates credence more intricately than could analysis (deconstructive or other), ritual, myth, or irony.

If, for example, Blake neither believes nor disbelieves in "Urizen," what is the status of this entity, and of those like him, of Los and Urthona, Luvah and Vala and Enitharmon and all the other beings in his mythic universe? Urizen is not Satan, and neither is he God, though he functions very much like the Satan of the New Testament and the God of organized religion as Blake sees them.

In the formulation of Blake's doctrines, the four Zoas would coexist in a sort of harmony. But then "Urizen" would be unrecognizable, since he could not exercise the dominance of categorization that characterizes him in the Prophetic Books. To call him the "fallen reason" puts him in a perspective at once processive and cosmic-historical, and indeed that is a dimension of Blake's presentation; *The Four Zoas*, read carefully, is all process; the Prophetic Books are a cosmic history.

These epic events are not subjected to irony. Rather, they are qualified by being assimilated into a more direct commentary on existing, authoritative Scriptures. Thus they are modalized:

> Reader! *lover* of books! *lover* of heaven,
> And of that God from whom *all books are given.*
> Who in mysterious Sinais awful cave
> To Man the wond'rous art of writing gave,
> Again he speaks in thunder and in fire!
> Thunder of Thought, & flames of fierce desire:
> Even from the depth of Hell his voice I hear,
> Within the unfathomd caverns of my Ear.
> Therefore I print; nor vain my types shall be:
> Heaven, Earth & Hell, henceforth shall live in harmony
>
> > (*Jerusalem* 3; p. 144)

Here and elsewhere Blake identifies the writing "dictated" to him as the speech of God to him, as though he were Moses or Isaiah. Now, however scripture may be defined as a communicational mode, it has the attributes of commanding assent and credence from its group of auditors, who are defined by assent to and credence in it: Christians are those for whom the New Testament has authority before they read it, Mohammedans those who firmly believe in the Koran. The self-selected group of Blakeans have a different makeup, and also a different relation to the book, since they could not possibly assent before reading. Blake, in a sense, takes care of this question by positing a virtual rather than an actual audience, a romantic audience possessed of prophetic powers. He conveys this in an epigraph from Scripture to that book of his which recounts the transmission of prophetic powers to himself, *Milton:* "Would to God that all the Lords people were Prophets" (Numbers 11:29; *Milton* 1; p. 94).

Instead of just declaring that poetry is at the origin of all thought including history and law, as Vico did, and then constructing an evolutionary theory upon those origins, Blake built "poetry" (which for him, as for Vico, mostly meant what we mean by "myth") into an inspection of a history that he declares in the preface to *Jerusalem* to be "true." Or, as he early says, "The Jewish and Christian Testaments are an original derivation from the Poetic Genius. This is necessary from the confined nature of bodily sensation" (*All Religions Are One*, Principle 6). In the resulting scheme, then, Voltaire and Rousseau became not predecessors or slightly similar antagonists, but scorners — a curious attribution for Rousseau in particular:

> Mock on Mock on Voltaire Rousseau:
> Mock on Mock on tis all in vain
> You throw the sand against the wind
> And the wind blows it back again . . .

> The Atoms of Democritus
> And Newton's Particles of light
> Are sands upon the Red sea shore,
> Where Israels tents do shine so bright.
> > (Poems from the Notebook, 4; p. 468)

Here Voltaire is not different from Rousseau, and the social doctrines of either do not differ in their microscopic particularity from ancient or modern science. Any merely analytic language has the defect of any other. Elsewhere Voltaire and Rousseau are identified with cruel, dominant female archetypes:

> Seeing the Churches at their Period in terror & despair,
> Rahab created Voltaire; Tirzah created Rousseau;
> Asserting the Self-righteousness against the Universal Saviour.
> > (*Milton* 22.40–42; p. 116)

In *Jerusalem* various kinds of intense spiritual blockage become paramount. There the two are identified with a high but veiling angelic entity:

> Here Vala stood turning the iron Spindle of destruction
> From Heaven to earth: howling! invisible! but not invisible
> Her Two Covering Cherubs afterwards named Voltaire & Rousseau.
> > (*Jerusalem* 66.10–12; p. 216)

Tirzah and Rahab are figures in Blake's Pantheon borrowed from the Old Testament, as is the Covering Cherub; Voltaire and Rousseau are historical personages with doctrines that influenced an immediate history of deep preoccupation to Blake and his contemporaries. Beyond the question, not simply resolved, of how by identifying real persons with these Biblical figures Blake is adapting metaphor, there is the equally deep question, within his system itself, of the relation among sets of postulations.

In the *Marriage* "good" and "evil" are inverted, devils being good and angels evil. And then the inversion is made problematic. In *The Songs of Innocence and Experience*, Blake offers another twofold set, which it would not do to make less than complete by assigning these areas to only two of the four Zoas. Still, "Innocence" and "Experience" do overlap with the "Urthona," "Tharmas," "Luvah," and "Urizen" of the Prophetic Books. Both the twofold set and the fourfold set take up the same preoccupations of sexuality and creativity and macrohistory and apocalypse, engaging them in simultaneity. Both sets envisage the cosmic alternations of deep spiritual choice under the management of exalted fluidities. But one set cannot be mapped onto the other; nor can "good" and "evil" be made coterminous with "innocence" and "experience," or with other twofold sets in Blake's terminology: natural and spiritual, or general and particular. Each twofold set is complete in itself, as is the major fourfold set of Zoas; nor will either reclassify the "elect," the "reprobate," and the "redeemed," a threefold set almost wholly resolvable into another twofold set. Every individual who is classifiable into one type in this threefold set would presumably carry within himself, and experience outwardly in the long range of history, the interactions among the four "Zoas" or living creatures that in Blake's developed view inhabit the psyche of every man.

The possibility of positing congruences between twofold and fourfold (or threefold) in Blake would be complicated by his many inclusions — immediate history (the French Revolution), the fact and typological bearing of Biblical history, the physical map of England, an idealized or personified England or "Albion," the functions of such activities as science and architecture and philosophy and poetry itself, such charged elements in nature as sun, moon, stars, and seas, the compass directions with which his Zoas are associated, pre-history (the Druids, the "Wicker Man of Scandinavia," a giant composite sacrifice figure), and Blake's own personal biography. The massive research of the past fifty years into the detail of Blake's pantheon has not got very far, beyond asserting identities here and there, at investigating the kinds of interrelations of those significant areas as they bear on coordinating the twofold with the fourfold set. Nor could it do so without allowing for the transformational principle in Blake's language, whereby simultaneity is made to subvert the sequence that enriches it.

If we take "natural" and "spiritual" (or "supernatural"), for example, as a central binary category in Blake's thought, then that category may serve to distinguish the visible England, or even the national ideal of England, from "Albion." But it also distinguishes either one of these as "natural" (England is a real place with a history) and "spiritual" (Albion is the honorific and typological name for a nation *sub specie aeternitatis*).

Within the Zoas themselves, there are further sets of relations, all of which bear on all the previous ones mentioned. Urthona is the Eternal name for Los, whose name in time signifies the same and yet a separate entity. Urthona has a Spectre, a rational redefinition of his essence; he also has a Shadow, or "the residue of one's suppressed desires."[14] He has an "Emanation," a wife whose signifying term recapitulates the creation of Eve from Adam's rib by way of a word suggesting the flow of water or air (Latin, *emano* = "flow from"). This wife, Los's Enitharmon, may take on independent existence; she may also produce offspring (Orc), who are at once allegories for emotional sequences and Blakean nonce words for actual processes or for congeries of attitudes. The relations of the Zoas with one another are dependent on, and also prior to, the relations for each Zoa among himself, his Spectre, his Shadow, his Emanation, and his offspring. And in one sense all this happens in an individual psyche, which exists at a simultaneous moment and also in the grand sequence of macrohistorical connection to a people for whom equivalent, and at the same time problematically congruent, processes are going through their cycles.

The very existence of multiple sets, twofold and fourfold, allows Blake a fluid and uncontradictory transposition that the fixed entities of a public pantheon would not permit: Homer, and even Ovid, must work within the mythemes given by the culture. Scholars have traced Blake's mythemes, for the most part, to cultural sources, but his eclectic handling of them, and the open modality of his combinations, keeps them adaptable to his purpose at hand. In a twofold set Rousseau and Voltaire are mockers; this does not contradict their more complex function as "Covering Cherubs," or final blockage by misinterpretation of the *spiritual* life (though in the "Mock on" sequence, the emphasis is on their assimilation to natural scientists, Democritus and Newton). Nor does this contradict their masking as those figures, spiritual because drawn from Israel but preponderantly pejorative, Tirzah and Rahab. "Rahab created Voltaire," or natural religion masking as a stifling mystery produces what seems to argue against it but is really its opposite number, Voltaire. Rahab is the mother of Tirzah (*Four Zoas*, VIII, 294), or natural religion exacerbates sex into a sort of prurient prudery, recognizable from Rousseau's own account of his emotional life. So "Tirzah created Rousseau" follows, in a sequence that conflicts superficially with other attributions for both figures but accords with the historical and psychological dimensions that Blake sets out. "Created" suggests birth on the analogy of God's bringing about the world. The verb emphasizes both the spirituality of these processes and their assimilation to, and parody of, God's or the poet's liberating role. Voltaire and Rousseau receive this description in a speech of Palamabron ("pity") and Rintrah ("wrath") to Los ("creative energy"): this and other moments of the speech modulate through the dialectical relation of these entities too, with comparable contradictions on the surface.

Voltaire and Rousseau are "Covering Cherubs" under the destructive spindle of Vala, another female figure of spiritual but limiting function, the "Emanation" of the second Zoa, Luvah. At this particular moment of *Jerusalem*, Vala, rather than Luvah, is functioning as the wife of Albion, and Luvah is being tormented; Albion has not been united to his true wife, "*Jerusalem*, Emanation of the Giant Albion," as the poem's title page puts it. The "Covering Cherub" function is an aspect of blockage or veiling, and the Veil (perhaps with reference to the similar Hindu Maya) is one of Vala's functions. The reason for Voltaire and Rousseau we shortly learn: "For Luvah is France: the Victim of the Spectres of

Albion" (*Jerusalem* 66.15). There is no noun of the five in this line that does not radiate its own identifications and implicit contradictions.

In the fourfold schematism Vala is paired off with Luvah as Enitharmon with Los, Enion with Tharmas, and Ahania with Urizen. But this scheme, too, is adaptable: in *The Four Zoas* Los and Enitharmon are the offspring of Enion by the Spectre of Tharmas (6–7). And Vala has overriding as well as parallel functions; the entire poem originally had the title *Vala*, linking this one Emanation of one of the Zoas with the large, enervating female figure, transpositions and fragmentations of the Great Mother about whose existence Blake could have had only rudimentary anthropological information. Vala and Eno and Rahab have this role in the fourfold set. In the twofold set it is the submissive-dominant young-old woman whose fullest expression comes in "The Mental Traveller."

It cannot be said that Vala is only a false Emanation for Albion in *Jerusalem:* the association is a real one, and productive. There Vala almost merges with Jerusalem, a female figure with whom she had an intimate relationship figured in one of the most striking plates in the poem, Plate 28, the frontispiece to Chapter 2, which shows Jerusalem cupped in a flower embracing Vala, "the lilly of Havilah" (19.40–42). The name, as Damon explains it, implies freedom and love, being drawn from the land east of Eden around which the first of the four rivers flows (Genesis, 2.11–12). As Nature, Vala can either encourage or torment Luvah, Love or The Body, especially under the domination of Urizen; and the torment under dominance causes her own transformation:

Hear ye the voice of Luvah from the furnaces of Urizen

If I indeed am Valas King & ye o sons of Men
The workmanship of Luvahs hands; in times of Everlasting
When I calld forth the Earth-worm from the cold & dark obscure
I nurturd her I fed her with my rains & dews, she grew
A scaled Serpent, yet I fed her tho' she hated me
Day after day she fed upon the mountains in Luvahs sight
I brought her thro' the Wilderness, a dry and thirsty land
And I commanded springs to rise for her in the black desert
Till she became a Dragon winged bright & poisonous
I opend all the floodgates of the heavens to quench her thirst.

And I commanded the Great deep to hide her in his hand
Till she became a little weeping Infant a span long
I carried her in my bosom as a man carries a lamb
I loved her I gave her all my soul & my delight
I hid her in soft gardens & in secret bowers of Summer
Weaving mazes of delight along the sunny Paradise
Inextricable labyrinths, She bore me son & daughters.

(*The Four Zoas* 26.4–27.7; p. 311)

Here the tormented Luvah recapitulates not only his natural role as Love but also those of God the Father, Adam, and Jesus (the lamb in the bosom). As this happens Vala changes from serpent into dragon into infant into mother — with complex anthropological sources and correlations, and also psychological ones, not least the foregrounded existence of this whole account as the fond memory of a tortured and separated spouse.

Later in this poem, regenerated in the heart of Enitharmon, Vala unites with Orc in the form of the Shadowy Female, daughter of Urthona, who transmutes into the shadowy vortex. In *Jerusalem* Vala's function is more ancillary than in the poem that originally bore her name. (And indeed the three major Prophetic Books each has a central female figure with comparable functions: Vala in *The Four Zoas*, Ololon or the sixfold Emanation in *Milton*, and Jerusalem in *Jerusalem*.) As Damon explains, "Jesus took Jerusalem, Albion's Emanation, as his bride, and gave Vala to Albion for his wife (20.40; 63.7; 64.19; 65.71). . . . Vala is still Luvah's Emanation; she is also his daughter." Persisting in opposition, she becomes the Whore of Babylon, fused with Rahab (80.52) in the tabernacle of the Covering Cherub (89.52).[15]

A discrepancy obtains, then, between one phase of the fourfold system and another: the moments of Vala do not stand stably for some given set of attributes. Blake opens poetic windows on a prime Mother Goddess, not by an archaizing throwback and not by a fixed scheme only, but by letting energies of ambivalence play over such figures, as sequence feeds back into a simultaneity deeply abstracted and energized beyond any "Beulah"-like versions of the Neolithic agricultural cycles. Everything becomes liminal. Vala is never allowed to be something simply less than Beulah, the same as or the opposite of Jerusalem, the equivalent of Rahab, the source of a Covering Cherub, or the Emanation of Luvah. In the mainly binary epilogue, "To the Accuser who is The God of This World," a quatrain that concludes *The Gates of Paradise* repeats his inversion of "Satan" and the Christian God:

> Tho thou art Worshipd by the Names Divine
> Of Jesus & Jehovah: thou art still
> The Son of Morn in weary Nights decline
> The lost Travellers Dream under the Hill.   (P. 266)

Yet the last lines here suggest a Urizenic chaos or fixity. The "mild moony lustre" in which Lucifer dreams here most resembles the mood of Beulah, one aspect of the third realm in the fourfold set, "Threefold in soft Beulahs night" (Letter to Thomas Butts, November 22, 1802; p. 693). Blake would seem always to be resting on his principle "Without Contraries is no Progression," but his practice qualifies even that maxim, as his definition does: as he says at the beginning of *Milton*, Book the Second, "There is a place where Contrarieties are equally True / This place is called Beulah." Hence it is not an ultimate state, though the mirror writing on the plate immediately preceding this statement asserts, "Contraries are Positives / A Negation is not a Contrary." This in turn stands under the mirror-engraved motto "How wide the Gulf Unpassable between Simplicity and Insipidity." Day and night reverse sides in the later plates of *Jerusalem*. Blake sometimes reverses his directions; West can exercise the symbolic function normally assigned to East. And the directions themselves are not stable in their functions or even in their spatial definitions:

> And the Four Points are thus beheld in Great Eternity
> West, the Circumference: South, the Zenith: North
> The Nadir: East, the Center, unapproachable for ever.
> > (*Jerusalem*, 12.54–56; p. 154)

But very soon we have:

> And the Eyes are the South, and the Nostrils are the East.
> And the Tongue is the West, and the Ear is the North.　　(59–60)

And a little later:

> And the North is Breadth, the South is Height & Depth:
> The East is Inwards: & the West is Outwards every way.
> > (14.29–30; p. 157)

These assertions may be taken (or not) to supplement those assigning the directions of the Zoas:

> But in Eternal times the Seat of Urizen is in the South
> Urthona in the North Luvah in East Tharmas in West
> > (*The Four Zoas*, 74.28–29; p. 344)

A frequent principle, allowing for conflations as well as transpositions, posits the identity of any one man with others or all:

> We live as one Man; for contracting our infinite senses
> We behold multitude; or expanding: we behold as one,
> As One Man all the Universal Family.
> > (*Jerusalem*, 34.17–19; p. 178)

3

Blake, of course, was by profession an artist or engraver. The two-sidedness of his activity between engraving and poetry, and the very instability between the two attest to the comprehensiveness of his aspiration and to the fluidity he allowed himself in articulating it. The self-questioning theoretical flexibility of his poetic language becomes a sharply significant repertoire of the modes of relation between verbal and visual expression. This repertoire is significant by virtue of its instability from instance to instance. Drawn from a rich cultural context, Blake's illuminations or illustrations are always changing in their relation to a text. Blake almost from the beginning adapted the form in which the engraver gives a pictorial representation of what is described in the text. In the illustrations for Young's *Night Thoughts*, his own graphic imagination exceeded Young's statements so much that Young may have provided some of the impetus for *Vala*, begun on unused sheets from the *Night Thoughts* engravings.

Conventionally an illustration repeats the text, whereas illumination, the medieval practice of amplifying and embroidering letters, just decorates a text sacred enough to be accorded this ornamental attention. And much of Blake's graphic work has the character of illumination, or illumination amplified by illustration. A third convention, the folk tradition of the picture Bible, may also be seen to be adapted in Blake's illuminated works: these texts, written for the barely literate like the modern comic books for which McLuhan and Parker[16] see Blake as a predecessor, differ from illustration by providing the picture not as a pleasing parallel to the text, but as a necessary gloss on it. If the gloss attains a certain abstractness, as in the spiderlike head on a web above a rock under a tree at the bottom of "The Human Abstract" from the "Songs of Experience," then a fourth convention is approached, that of the allegorical emblem book.

All Blake's practice has some of this emblematic abstractness because he aimed at something like an allegorical representation for his graphic work, or at a correspondence to allegory in which the verbal poetry did much of the positive work, and the visual was left to sketch, to underline, or to offset slightly. Even his closest approach to Renaissance canons of representation, his depiction of "the human form divine," while it may be derived through Michelangelo and Winckelmann as well as from Fuseli,[17] abandoned the careful, perspectival practice of his best contemporaries for the "line" or outline of an emblematic being. His trees and clouds are abstractions, drawn on a different base of visual signification from the practice of his near contemporaries Constable and Turner, with their careful attention to exact visual delineation of properties in nature. Nor does Blake pay special attention to the production of the tactile values that on the whole he underrated in Renaissance painting (while paying homage to Raphael); density, hue, and saturation receive scant modulation in his practice. His color symbolism is drained of the richness that

Turner shares with, say, Giotto, Bosch, and Titian. Blake tends to use a simple green for vegetation, yellow for sun, white for innocence, and so on. Only the property of contrast gives his color special vividness, as the yellows, greens, and pinks balanced in "the lark" from "L'Allegro," an illustration for a poem by someone else; or the yellow, red, green, and dark brown of "The Ancient of Days," a separate and independent representation; or the faint pinkish, yellowish, green, bluish, and brown of *Jerusalem* Plate 32,[18] where separately the hues represent merely grass or sky or bodies whose healthy faint flush carries over to the buildings in the background. This plate does not so much amplify the text, where Vala has already "her dark threads cast" (45.67), "clothed in black mourning" (45.47); it supplements the text with what may be regarded as the earlier, more benign relationship between Jerusalem and Vala. Or else it contradicts the text, as the old man on crutches led by a boy may be said to do in "London," since that Song of Experience offers no such hopeful resolution. "The Songs of Innocence" and the "Songs of Experience," however, taken together, do offer hope; and so what looks like contradiction must be here accounted a kind of anticipation, the plate from *Jerusalem* a kind of retrospective.

The tendrils along the sides of many plates do not "illustrate" in any way; they merely "illuminate"; they decorate the text with something vaguely classifiable as instances of creative power in nature. And the abstract or universalized etchings, the "emblematic" ones, do not necessarily illustrate the text at a particular narrative moment; rather they transpose it into another, but equivalent, visual-allegorical statement. Sometimes the illustration glosses just a word or two on the page. Sometimes the pictures constitute a separate and equivalent narrative in relation to one another, as the first six plates of *Milton* do. For some visual figures there may be said to exist an independent pattern of signification, not especially related to any point or even to the whole poem in question; so may one interpret the frequent man, stone, bird, vine, star, leaf, and even serpent. Or again, a single picture may multiply functions: it may contain embryonically what is spelled out in the text; it may also show the twofold pattern of male and female while at the same time touching on some other pattern (as the reprobate, the redeemed, and the elect). And it may also illustrate the story line.

All these many functions of signification for Blake's pictures amount to an instability in the relationship between picture and text, a freedom that reiterates the freedom exalted in the words of the poems. This instability keeps alive the instability, or arbitrariness, attendant upon representing in a visual or verbal image the force of a mythic figure, especially when the figures, like Blake's, are themselves both invented and subject to transformations. There is further instability in the very occurrence, and the relative fullness, of the pictures: some plates do not have them; others have only the simplest illuminations. It may be said in general that the richest pictures come at moments of stress or emphasis, and that the proportion of pictures to text increases markedly at moments of stress or culmination. The stir of the visionary world at its most wrought requires more than one medium for its expression.

All these instabilities underlie a kind of text that is initially presented with a declared fixity. Blake's Prophetic Books constitute, before they are experienced, a paradoxical entity: the hand-crafted "Bible." In the experiencing of words plus pictures, a simultaneity is celebrated whose energy remains liminal and draws its force from the very instability that is the mark of its liminality.

4

The imaginative demands to create so expansive a form appear early in Blake as the pressure to change or vary the form he has in hand. The imaginative gesture of setting himself into a satiric posture towards his society in *An Island in the Moon* brought a transmutation of his poetic impulse from the dexterous sublimity of *Poetical Sketches* to the dual vision finally poised into the *Songs of Innocence and Experience*. These songs began, so far as we can tell, as individual lyric effusions breaking the prose of *An Island in the Moon*. Similarly, ten years later, the allegorical vein of his major "fourfold" vision pressed on him as he surrounded the circumscribed poetic utterances of Young and of Gray with lengthy series of illustrations. Typically, in the illustrations to Young and to Gray, a small central text is overwhelmed by vast semi-allegorical beings. The illustrations here become more dominant than the figures in all but a few of the illuminations in Blake's major Prophetic Books. These beings expand the primal states that Blake was beginning to invent, while roughly at the same time focusing on political revolution in *America* and *Europe*. Finally, perhaps under the pressure of those illustrations, another transmutation of his poetical vision came about.[19] The psychic life and the panorama of human history, inner and outer, now became one large drama of an exalted, perpetual fluidity. The Four Zoas had come to the preponderant position they would have, and the poem *The Four Zoas* came into being.

In the relations among the Zoas there operates a fluidity that it is the main gesture of the three major Prophetic Books to body forth. Even the expansion from one level to four implies not a simple moving up but a dynamic alteration of relations at each level:

Now I a fourfold vision see,
And a fourfold vision is given to me
Tis fourfold in my supreme delight
And threefold in soft Beulah's night
And twofold Always. May God us keep
From Single vision & Newton's sleep.
(Letter to Thomas Butts, November 22, 1802; p. 693)

Even in this schematic account there is a different phrasing accorded each of the four temporary states. And the same dynamic instability is implied in Frye's summary:

As Ulro is a single and Generation a double world, so Beulah is triple, the world of lover, beloved and mutual creation; the father, the mother and the child. In Eden these three are contained in the unified imagination symbolized in the Bible by the four "Zoas" or living creatures around the throne or chariot of God, described by Ezekiel and John. This world therefore is fourfold, expanding to infinity like the four points of the compass which in this world point to the indefinite.[20]

The logical definition of relations among these four entities is itself so complex that it has — justifiably — arrested the attention of commentators, with the unfortunate byproduct of making it seem as though they were not only allegorical but somewhat static. But in his major Prophetic Books Blake has found the means for giving three different slants to series of qualitative psychic and cosmic moments. He has found, we may say, a means to embody the abstract formulation of Novalis:

Now, if he sinks wholly into the contemplation of this primal appearance, the creation-history of nature unfolds before him in newly arising times and spaces like an immeasurable spectacle, and each firm point that fixes itself in the endless fluidity becomes for him a new manifestation of the spirit of love, a new bond between the Thou and the I. The careful description of this inner world-history is the true theory of nature; through the interdependence of its world of thoughts in itself and its harmony with the universe a thought-system produces itself spontaneously as a true image and form of the universe.[21]

To take the *Four Zoas* first, there Blake concentrates on his "Urerscheinungen" directly, and he "unfolds" them so as to include, but not to limit himself to, the "new bond between the Thou and the I."

The poem, through the length of its nine "nights," proceeds through a welter of interactions that produce seemingly total states. These interactions are between the allegorized persons, first between Tharmas, who embraces touch and taste and the senses and the tongue of speaking, and his Emanation-wife, Enion. Then other pairs come into view. But there is also rivalry and interaction between the Zoas, who are males, and chiefly between Urizen and Los.

Characteristically, someone will utter a long speech amplifying loss, or gain, or intent, and the world will correspondingly change. At the beginning Tharmas, through something like infidelity, has lost many Emanations, and he has hidden Jerusalem (here, too, "Emanation of the giant Albion"). He will build a labyrinth, but then he and Enion, in their interaction, mutually refuse a search for other beings. Tharmas consequently sinks into the sea, where he is floating throughout most of *The Four Zoas*, and an aspect of all the action of the poem can be read allegorically as "the floating of Tharmas" (or "the indiscriminateness of linguistic utterances," "the disorder of the senses," or "the potential chaos of sensual immediacy"). From his feet (5.10) issues his Spectre, which the daughters of Beulah name "Eternal Death." However, under the aegis of Enion, Los and Enitharmon are born, and then Enion is left, propelled into Non-Entity. Los and Enitharmon in turn initiate a vast set of interactions that result in Urizen's domination of the cosmos. But he, too, involves himself in interaction, with Los, with the Creative Energy of Enitharmon's offspring Orc, and with Ahania, *his* Emanation, who is awakened by the lament of Enion over the Vortex brought into being by Urizen. Luvah ("the passions") and his Emanation, Vala, enter the body of man at the injunction of Albion (41). In another of its aspects, the whole of *The Four Zoas* is a dream of "the sleeper" Albion. Vala, whose name gave the title to the whole poem in its first version, stands for Nature and Earth—but also for her mate, since she was born first as a double entity, which split and produced the scissiparous birth of Luvah and Vala (83.13–16).

These interactions result in shrinking, groaning, wandering, building, weaving, dancing, celebrating, and other characteristic liminal activities of the figures in Blake. Such activities, themselves indeterminately significant, always result from the interactions that are the constant motive forces along the narrative line of the poem. At various points it is asserted that a number of ages pass. "A first age passed and a state of dismal woe" (351). Though states are often mentioned, and though the figures themselves stably signify their own areas of feeling and perception, the processive welter cannot pause until, in the last line of this poem, "The dark Religions are departed and sweet Science reigns."

The effect of Blake's Prophetic Books is to subject all possible cosmic and psychological action to the principles of his more didactic utterances:

> He who binds to himself a joy
> Does the winged life destroy
> But he who kisses the joy as it flies
> Lives in eternity's sun rise.

The title of this quatrain here (461) is "Eternity"— not a constant state, but an aspect of a principled openness. Not "eternity" but "eternity's sun rise" comes to him "who kisses the joy as it flies." The alternative title for the same quatrain (465) is "Several Questions Answered"— not one, but several, an attribution that would admit of all the multiple applications of such evanescent feelings as are represented in the narrative course of *The Four Zoas*. "Energy is Eternal Delight" ("The Voice of the Devil," Plate 4, *The Marriage of Heaven and Hell*, p. 34), and the energy of perceiving the poem's events may be distinguished from the deprivation of delight in what one of its figures perceives at a particular moment. Both joy and sorrow, in tune with the notions of Wordsworth and Keats, may be productive. "Joys impregnate. Sorrows bring forth" (Plate 8, p. 36). And they may reverse, through going too far: "Excess of sorrow laughs. Excess of joy weeps" (ibid.). Or, in another sequence, from "Auguries of Innocence":

> Joy and Woe are woven fine
> A clothing for the soul divine
> Under every grief and pine
> Runs a joy with silken twine.   (P. 482)

The four earlier Prophetic Books dealing with these figures also center on physical changes in the world that betoken spiritual changes in the figure, and then in the figure of man. In "The Book of Los," the interaction of Los with Urizen keeps producing such changes:

> 2: And the unformed part crav'd repose
> Sleep began: the Lungs heave on the wave
> Weary overweigh'd, sinking beneath
> In a stifling black fluid he woke
>
> 3: He arose on the waters, but soon
> Heavy falling his organs like roots
> Shooting out from the seed, shot beneath,
> And a vast world of waters around him
> In furious torrents began.   (59–66; p. 92)

This book offers a simple conflict between two entities, as do "The Book of Urizen," "The Book of Ahania," and "The Song of Los." Correspondingly, all are in a measure shorter than the blank verse line. When Blake expanded his meter to the septenary— to a line that preserved the variability of the blank verse line while stretching it— he also expanded his representation of interactions to include other beings, and for all three of the major Prophetic Books he moved away from the conflict between the two figures who most preoccupied him, the positive Los-Urthona of

Imagination and the negative Urizen of Reason and control. Tharmas and Luvah are on a par with Los and Urizen in the action of *The Four Zoas*, though Urthona does dominate at the very end. *Milton* centers on a poet who is a dead master, himself exemplary of processive conflict in his soul. *Jerusalem* displaces the Zoas to arrange them around the archetypal-prototypal Man, Albion, and his Emanation, whose name is that of the heavenly city with which she is to be identified.

The effect of these narrative procedures is not only to complicate the action, but to keep it open to the fluidity of the massive feelings that govern it at every point. Nuances of feeling, congeries of feelings, are here hypostatized into active beings. Paradoxically, in the actions themselves, the nuances are structured away: they seemingly lose their fluidity and become Tharmas or Enion, Luvah or Vala, Los or Orc. And yet here to structure nuances away is to structure nuances only: in this achieved figural perspective a wakeful attention to sequence moves to a fluidity that imagines its opposite, a moiré-like simultaneity.[22]

Dante, whom Blake saw as a figure of control but also as a figure of divine inspiration, provides a rational structure. Blake's chief difference from Dante is not that he "invents" his mythology, but rather that the events in his mythic progressions, his "mythemes," are all so fleetingly representative of nuance that they resist formulation or any assessment other than a difficult attention to them as they move past. The strain of keeping some definition of these fleeting figures creates a certain strain on Blake's style and a fixity in the language seemingly contradictory to the fluidity he represents by contrast with the style of the *Songs of Innocence and Experience*. Dante's style, on the other hand, funds its flexibilities and depths increasingly and directly as his theme grows more complex.

Genesis itself, the act of birth, is redefinable in *The Four Zoas* as a byproduct of a condition that at once blocks birth and strives towards it. So Enitharmon is born from the side of Los, Orc from Enitharmon, Luvah from Vala (83.13–16; p. 351). In "The Book of Urizen" (Plate 6), Urizen is rent from the side of Los. Urizen at one point is even the child of Vala: "Vala was pregnant and brought forth Urizen Prince of Light" (83.12; p. 351).

The figures themselves are nuanced in their actions. Altizer, for example, is willing to bring Luvah into congruence with the Savior who is always in view for Blake: "Luvah is a figure symbolizing the universal process of Crucifixion." But, at the same time, "Luvah is not a consistent figure, nor does Luvah ever appear in full clarity; rather Luvah is the figure through whom Blake primarily expressed his own imaginative breakthrough; and he embodies all the ambivalence of an initial stroke of vision."[23] Indeed, the same may be said for many of Blake's figures, preeminently of the "Covering Cherub" who is an aspect of Luvah, blocking-by-releasing in an energetic moment that is obscure and perhaps so because meant to be obscuring.

Blake praises the sexual energies, and he relates them without hierarchization to other energies. Like Shelley, who remarked on the connection between sex and poetry, Blake relates the senses and the passions to the imagination: he relates Luvah and Tharmas to Los-Urthona. But this is done so processively that one can never relegate any one aspect merely to the twofold or threefold of his more didactic formulation.

It is by a kind of prophetic stroke, making the future he envisions take on the fixity of entities bounded in space, that as a painter and illuminator Blake foreshortens all the perspective-depths and freezes all the momentary states that are caught by painters from Constable to Cézanne. The whole tradition of British landscape painting, to say nothing of Turner's proto-Impressionism, passes him by. He theorizes a justification for abandoning the painterly by exalting the line. Yet he has none of the haunting fixity that Kaspar-David Friedrich, in both doctrine and practice, was able to get into landscape as representing states of the soul. Blake represents such momentary states by their seeming contrary, just as he uses fixed diction to depict his fluidities in his simple "outline"-style figures, where such shadings as are represented are subordinated to the obviously allegorical nature of the figure or the scene.

Correspondingly, his diction hardens and his syntax itself is musclebound by comparison with that of his "sublime" predecessors and his "Romantic" successors — or even by comparison with the early Blake of the *Poetical Sketches*. The hard diction, the simple rhetoric of his syntax, like the simple outlines of his pictures, are fixed points in a fluidity so elusive that it can only be represented by the stable elements standing in a tension towards them. In *The Four Zoas* the sea into which Tharmas falls is at the same time the woof of Enion. This has happened because she "died" (not a final act but an aspect of her being), doing so after *trembling* in *terror* because Tharmas *fears* his own *pity* of her (1), and the four italicized emotional reactions are not only processive moments but also aspects. The woof is at the same time a tabernacle for the encompassing female figure Jerusalem. And the woof is also designated as being "nine deep nights," as well as the tongue of Tharmas, either of which could be taken aspectually as some equivalent for the utterance of the poem or its own whole verbal progress, divided as it is into "nine nights."

In one speech Los says, "Then I am dead till thou revivest me with thy sweet song / Now taking on Ahanias form and now the form of Enion" (34.37–38; p. 316). But before long, "Thus lived Los driving Enion far into deathful infinite / That he may also draw Ahania's spirit into her Vortex" (34.97–98; p. 318). Each of these is at once a processive moment and a complexity of aspects at the moment. "Urizen comforted saw / The wondrous work flow forth like visible out of the invisible" (33.9–10; p. 315). The attribution of simile in "like" forbids our drawing a line between visible and invisible, or even making one simply a representation of the other.

When Urizen in his wanderings passes through deserts and then clouds, then rocks and mountains and cities, coming to "forms of tygers and of lions, dishumanized men," then to columns of fire or of water (70.25–37; p. 340), all of these may be taken alternatively as moments of his journey or aspects of his being. They are not successive in the same way that Los's actions are successive; one of Urizen's attributes is not to admit of the most intimate fluidities of feeling, and, therefore, not to embody them. Urizen cannot handle aspects even of the other Zoas, as when Christ becomes man who has become Luvah identified with Orc:

> When Urizen saw the Lamb of God clothed in Luvahs robes
> Perplexed & terrified he Stood tho well he knew that Orc
> Was Luvah But he now beheld a new Luvah. Or One
> Who assumd Luvahs form & stood before him opposite
> (101.1–4; p. 358)

The feelings of Blake, then, by virtue of their complexity provide the occasion for constant transformation, rather than a detachable principle for transformation. At any point one may take the contour of a few psychological-cosmic movements and imply them as a reading of a series of feeling-phases. But any one such set is itself only a phase in the large movement from psychic imbalance and servitude to the freedom of balance. The large movement in *The Four Zoas* is not cyclic, once it has run its course. "Sweet Science reigns" for good, so far as the events of the poem are concerned. But that a cyclic reversion is a perpetual threat and even a preponderant tendency, we may infer from the preliminary cyclic movements that occur over and over again in the poem. Indeed, there are at least a hundred and seven actions of transformation narrated in the frequent long speeches of the participants.[24] The only order one could impose on all this fluctuation would be either a cylic or a progressive one, and either would be provisional or aspectual. Since the entities are themselves free as they combine within the putative psyche of idealized man, they can change themselves, and the world, by the simple process of reacting:

> terrified at the Shapes
> Enslavd humanity put on he became what he beheld
> (53.23–24; p. 329)

As Vala says, speaking of a "dead" Luvah provisionally identified with Christ:

> For he was source of every joy that this mysterious tree
> Unfolds in Allegoric fruit.   (103.18–19; p. 361)

The significations hover, and the Allegory does not enlist the stable referents that seem to belong to the form as a device of signification. Allegory is, so to speak, made to produce its opposite. Such indeterminacy between "visible" and "invisible" is characteristic here, as, for example, in the scales and cubes and stations and looms and atmospheres and eagles that are part of a process in which Luvah involves a Man who is not the redeemed man or the regenerate man referred to elsewhere in the poem, but "Fallen Man" (29.1).

5

Blake's impulse was "To cast aside from Poetry, all that is not Inspiration." As he came to formulate his program, he called on himself and on "Painters! . . . Sculptors! Architects!" to "believe Christ and his Apostles." For the poet this meant turning away from the "artifice" of classical work to "the Sublime of the Bible" (*Milton* 41.7; p. 141).

In *Jerusalem*, where a religious frame is given to the sections of the poem, this set of injunctions is explicitly given a metrical correlative that was implicit in his use of the septenary to begin with:

> When this Verse was first dictated to me I consider'd a Montonous cadence like that used by Milton & Shakespeare & all writers of English Blank Verse, derived from the modern bondage of Rhyming; to be a necessary and indispensible part of Verse. But I soon found that in the mouth of a true Orator such monotony was not only awkward, but as much a bondage as rhyme itself. I therefore have produced a variety in every line, both of cadences & number of syllables. Every word and every letter is studied and put into its fit place: the terrific numbers are reserved for the terrific parts — the mild & gentle, for the mild & gentle parts, and the prosaic, for inferior parts: all are necessary to each other. (P. 144)

Persistently in his earliest work, the *Poetical Sketches*, Blake has tried to stretch the caesurae and the enjambments across a periodic and "sublime" blank verse to achieve such an end:

> Thou fair-hair'd angel of the evening,
> Now, while the sun rests on the mountains, light
> Thy bright torch of love; thy radiant crown
> Put on, and smile upon our evening bed!

> Smile on our loves; and, while thou drawest the
> Blue curtains of the sky, scatter thy silver dew
> On every flower that shuts its sweet eyes
> In timely sleep. Let thy west wind sleep on
> The lake; speak silence with thy glimmering eyes,
> And wash the dusk with silver.
>
> ("To the Evening Star," p. 402)

This is almost too energetic to be Hesperian in Hartman's sense, though it is the very Hesperian topos itself that is Blake's subject.

The first impulse to the *Songs of Innocence and Experience* came up randomly while he was writing prose. In them he generally offers a near-ballad mix to purge "all that is not Inspiration" from the particular poem. In "The Blossom" the unrhymed second line, and a triple rhyme (Sparrow / arrow / narrow) modify the rhythms away from nursery rhyme, while retaining that tonic sound:

> Merry Merry Sparrow
> Under leaves so green
> A happy Blossom
> Sees you swift as arrow
> Seek your cradle narrow
> Near my Bosom.   (10)

A jingle of the popular sort more aimed at adults serves as the base for "Holy Thursday" in "The Songs of Innocence":

> Twas on a Holy Thursday their innocent faces clean
> The children walking two & two in red & blue & green
> Grey headed beadles walkd before with wands as white as snow
> Till into the high dome of Pauls they like Thames waters flow.   (13)

The iambic trimeter of the corresponding poem in "The Songs of Experience," emphasized by end-stopped lines and by strong trochees, becomes a satiric measure, presented without rhythmical admixture:

> Is this a holy thing to see,
> In a rich and fruitful land,
> Babes reduced to misery,
> Fed with cold and usurous hand?   (19)

The tetrameters of "The Tyger" are mainly trochaic, but they are so emphatic that they are made to hover towards iamb. Long syllables notably modify the meter of "Ah! Sunflower," and long syllables prolong away from the measure of song the longer lines of the "Introduction" to "The Songs of Experience":

> Turn away no more:
> Why wilt thou turn away
> The Starry floor
> The watry shore
> Is giv'n thee till the break of day.   (18)

The effect here shades a light plaintiveness into the earnestness of the injunction. A threshold voice is made to accompany the description of a threshold. Not irony but something more delicate, a conflation of opposites, is at work here in the very sound. This also balances by opposition its simplifying counterpart: the regular trochees of the "Introduction" to "The Songs of Innocence" lilt to a simplicity that matches its diction:

> Piping down the valleys wild
> Piping songs of pleasant glee
> On a cloud I saw a child
> And he laughing said to me.
>
> Pipe a song about a Lamb;
> So I piped with merry chear,
> Piper pipe that song again—
> So I piped, he wept to hear.   (7)

Like "The Little Girl Lost" and "The Little Girl Found," this is so simple, indeed, as to hit below the register of the art song, a model for Blake throughout and one that he employs again for the introductions to Chapters 2 and 3 of *Jerusalem*, the final chapter getting an introduction in blank verse. A slowed and solemnized version of art song serves as one of the many and varied epigraphs to *Milton:*

> And did those feet in ancient time
> Walk upon Englands mountains green:
> And was the holy Lamb of God,
> On Englands pleasant pastures seen!   (pp. 94–95)

This is art song modified by hymnody, or vice versa, with all the effect Blake wants of supplanting the "artifice" of the classics, which he has just mentioned.

The septenary itself is freer from "Bondage" than blank verse because the extra two feet confuse the issue. His septenary is more solemn, more modulated than the "fourteener" with which it has sometimes mistakenly been compared. In fact it is a great deal more modulated because the "fourteener" corresponds rather rigidly to its metric pattern, having a fixed caesura and usually a mid-line rhyme besides; it sounds close to doggerel. In Blake's hands, however, the septenary modulates so much as to present difficulties of scansion. It creates at each step a seemingly loose proximity between design and instance. Thus it serves as a splendid vehicle for the "pulsation" of the poet's inspiration as it sweeps across what Blake calls millennia:

> Every Time less than a pulsation of the artery
> Is equal in its period & value to Six Thousand Years.
>
> For in this Period the Poets Work is Done: and all the Great
> Events of Time start forth & are concievd in such a Period
> Within a Moment: a Pulsation of the Artery.
>
> (Milton, 28.63–29.3; p. 126)

Microscopic time and macroscopic are here made to interpenetrate and converge as the defining condition of a perception far more liminal than Kant's a priori time could allow. An idea that anticipates Nietzsche's conception of time is here bodied forth in a verse measure that manages a new ratio of sequence (it rushes forward) and simultaneity (it seems to hold up and pause).

Just when other poets were struggling to adapt Milton by using Milton's own measure, Blake found a way to intensify Milton's Renaissance measure as he intensified Milton's view of archetypal man struggling out of sin. This man for Blake is a realized man: the poet. In *Milton* it is first the Bard who speaks (Plates 2 through 13), who then takes refuge in Milton's bosom (14.8). This poetic impulse brings self-realization both spiritual and sexual:

> Say first! what mov'd Milton, who walkd about in Eternity
> One hundred years, pondring the intricate mazes of Providence
> Unhappy tho in heav'n, he obey'd, he murmur'd not. He was silent
> Viewing his Sixfold Emanation scatter'd thro' the deep
> In torment! To go into the deep her to redeem & himself perish?
> What cause at length mov'd Milton to this unexampled deed?
> A Bards prophetic Song!   (2.16–22; p. 95)

"Milton's track" as he proceeds is to the very center of the Zoas. The diagram of that track in Plate 22 is the most explicit Blake left of the relationship among his allegorical beings. Milton even places red clay (Adamah, "Adam" = earth) over Satan in order to make him look human (19; p. 111). "As an eighth Image Divine tho darkened," Milton proceeds through the cosmos, a shadow and a dreamer, at the same time "Himself; / His real and immortal Self: was as appeard to those / Who dwell in immortality" (15.5–15; p. 108). Very soon this fictional Milton effectuates another enabling poetic transfer by entering the left tarsus of Blake himself (15.47; p. 109), who then manages here his expanded version of Milton's measure, shedding the "monotony" Blake attributes to it.

Since before Blake's youth, the example of Milton's expatiating blank verse had served to liberate poets of Thomson's disposition and Young's from the hegemony of couplet and "sublime" ode alike. And as Blake turned to his new poem, Milton's high-pitched cadence and Latinate inversions had recently filled Wordsworth's ear with a model that was lending *The Prelude* an elevation and a suppleness the ordinary spoken language he aimed at could not have afforded him. In a decade or so Keats would take the reading of Milton as a condiment for diction, then reject him as a constraining influence on his most ambitious long poems, *Hyperion* and *The Fall of Hyperion*.

Blake's *Milton*, in its fairly restricted diction, its ranging septenary line, and its series of rather simple declarative statements, seems farther in technique from *Paradise Lost* than do any of these. Yet Blake's subject, the fall and regeneration of Universal Man, was closer to Milton's than any, and his very high-handedness with it shows how he was able, more than any of these, to adapt Milton for his own poetic purposes.

In Blake's eyes, the poet, if he rises to awareness, can present man's dynamic existence in the intermediate state between the realized Eden of imaginative virtue and the simplifying defection to the hegemony of one of the three lesser "Zoa" domains. Milton, on Blake's showing, fails from Eden, and yet he does try to realize this dynamic, intermediate existence. He has failed to reach a threshold. Some of the obscurity of *Comus* lies in the poet's not quite voicing the middle ground — the full ground of Grace adumbrated in the poem and coming to poetic expression unequivocally only in the last two lines:

> Or if Virtue feeble were,
> Heaven itself would stoop to her.

A similar failure, too, may be seen in *Lycidas*, which merely adumbrates a fusion of the natural level, in which universal nature laments an Orpheus whose head is nevertheless borne down the swift Hebrus; and the supernatural level, in which the dead poet succeeds in becoming a kind of tutelary presence: "weep no more, woeful shepherds, weep no more / For Lycidas, your sorrow, is not dead." Milton himself, twitching his mantle blue in the last lines of the poem, has not worked out his own intermediate state between the dying Orpheus and the Genius of the Shore.

This intermediate state Milton at last portrayed — dimly, Blake asserts — in *Paradise Lost*. Adam is sinful but redeemed. Paradise is lost, but what has been lost is a Paradise the poem evokes in elaborating the loss. The glory of God, the corruption of Mankind, are fused in Milton's poetic vision of the aboriginal parent. Adam, seen by the poet of the poem's invocations, falls to the state of the poet who imagines his fall from the unfallen Eden.

Only in his rhythms does Blake seem to diverge from Milton, and yet it is precisely in his rhythms that Blake reproduces Milton's achievement on his own, original grounds, transforming the Renaissance "justification," in his very sound, into a Romantic aspiration. The septenary of Blake, while superficially different from Milton's blank verse, was adopted by Blake for reasons like Milton's. Blake, in fact, invented his measure. Just as Milton saw, in his avoidance of rhyme, "ancient liberty recovered to the heroic poem from the troublesome and modern bondage of riming," so Blake evolved his measure after finding in blank verse a "monotony . . . as much a bondage as rhyme itself." In his new measure, "every word and every letter is studied and put into its fit place."

Now, Milton's blank verse exhibits one unique feature, which T. S. Eliot describes as "the sensation of a breathless leap . . . communicated by his verse and by his alone." I have elsewhere analyzed this effect, and it would be out of place here to reproduce my argument in full.[25] Briefly, in *Paradise Lost* every accent is felt as successively prominent. Thus in a given line there is not one major accent, as in most verse, including that of Thomson and Wordsworth, but at least four:

Brëaking the hörrid sïlence thus begän

The voice, rising continually to this succession of extreme stresses, produces a tension that, I have argued, is a rhythmic counterpart for the tension developing in the poet's mind as he looks back, fallen himself, to the unfallen world of Genesis.

Blake thought of his septenary as likewise carrying a meaningful force, and also as communicating tone: "the terrific numbers are reserved for the terrific parts—the mild & gentle, for the mild & gentle parts, and the prosaic, for inferior parts: all are necessary to each other."[26] In his "variety" of "cadences" within the "liberty" of the septenary, I believe Blake has given us, on a completely different rhythmical basis, a much closer tonal equivalent for Milton's "breathless leap" than is to be found in the long paragraphs of *The Seasons*, *The Prelude*, or *Hyperion*. (By this I mean not that Blake's rhythm surpasses these poets', but only that his ear is, in effect, closer to Milton's.) The septenary, unlike the monotonous "fourteener," does offer a variety of rhythms, which Blake constantly produces with it (one slash equals a minor caesura, two a major caesura):

(1) There is in Eden / a sweet River / of milk / & liquid pearl,

(2) Nam'd Ololon; // on whose mild banks / dwelt those / who Milton drove.

(3) Down unto Ulro: // and they wept / in long resounding song

(4) For seven days of eternity, // and the river's living banks,

(5) The mountains // wail'd! // & every plant that grew, // in solemn sighs lamented.

(6) When Luvah's bulls / each morning / drag the sulphur Sun / out of the Deep

(7) Harness'd / with starry harness // black & shining // kept by black slaves

(8) That work all night at the starry harness, // Strong and vigorous

(9) They drag / the unwilling Orb: // at this time / all the Family

(10) Of Eden / heard the lamentation / and Providence began.

(11) But when the clarions of day sounded // they drown'd the lamentations,

(12) And when night came // all was silent in Ololon: & / all refused to lament

(13) In the still night // fearing / lest they should others molest.

(Milton, 21.15–27; pp. 114–115).

The septenary allows a wider range of caesurae than blank verse, as many as four or five to a line — just about as many as the major accents in Milton's line, in fact. The tension within Blake's septenary, flowing in varied cadences, resembles Milton's tension, if more slackly. A sense of rising and falling is produced. Because the line is so long, it can absorb an occasional enjambment almost as if it were another caesura. This sense of rising and falling corresponds, I would assert, to the perpetual tensing and slackening of purposes in the fourfold struggles of these Blakean epics, just as Milton's pitch keeps a perilous height of control against the Satanic dissolution.

In the first of the lines quoted, the cadences, separated by minor caesurae, are fairly even, just as the temper of the sweet river is composed of Beulah-like milk and liquid pearl:

> There is in Eden / a sweet River / of milk / & liquid pearl.

Here the voice verges on urgency — and produces its longest cadence — in naming the location, "There is in Eden," a place beyond Beulah and therefore, when named, more energetic even in rhythm than the "sweet River" with its milk and pearl. This "mildness," mimed in even caesurae, carries on into the next line, which rises most on "Ololon," a character who later in the poem as the "Sixfold Emanation" rouses Milton to Edenic action. In the third line, though, introduced by this group of lines' most pronounced enjambment, the phrase "Down into Ulro" is followed by a major caesura, the strongest so far. The phrase and the attribution alike lengthen at the end: "in long resounding song." This quickly breaks up, after the even longer "for seven days of eternity, and the river's living banks," into short distressed cadences playing out in the "solemn sighs," lamented in the rhythm as in the words of this passage.

The next line contrasts a strength of one of the Zoas to this lamentation. It seems to give Luvah, the second of the Zoas, a hegemony undeserved but seemingly impregnable — because steadied by the cadences — even as in the first line. Here, though, the rhythm is far more packed, dominated by accented syllables that are so strong as to seem syncopated more often than not after the first caesura:

> When Lúvah's búlls / eách mórning / drág the súlphur Sún oút of the Déep.

Of course any poet utilizes his rhythms; Blake does so in a very special way, by working his caesuras hard, and by creating his major effects either within the great variety of a single line or in the flow over a long paragraph. The line-to-line variation, midway between one line and the long paragraph, is the area in which most poets do their most effective rhythmic work. But Blake, like Milton, does not pay his closest attention to line-to-line variation; he creates a tension within the short haul of the individual line, and at a high pitch over a long paragraph, by increasing the number of variations within a given line. His rhythm establishes Blake, in a metaphorical sense (which was the only way he meant it), as the "incarnation" of Milton he claims in his poem to be. And beyond this, the long line, long enough to dominate other units of the verse, floats in an ever fluid simultaneity.

6

All the fluidity of psyche that Blake found the terms for in his major Prophetic Books allows for a transcendence of the alternatives of equivalence posed by Lacan between the Kant and the Sade who were Blake's earlier contemporaries.[27] Blake's vision transcends as it unites the categorical imperative and the universality of the pleasure principle by allowing a cosmic latitude to the perceptions of the individual. "Allegories are things that Relate to Moral Virtues Moral Virtues do not Exist they are Allegories and dissimulations But Time and Space are Real Beings a Male and a Female Time is a Man Space is a Woman." So Blake, in "A Vision of the Last Judgment" (p. 553). His formulation invites to a dialectic between the sense of sexuality and the very basis of perceptual representation. Such a dialectic is parallelled in the instability between the words

and the illuminations of his texts, and this statement itself is in a cata-
logue for an exhibition. For Blake, self-consciousness, Nature, Experience,
Others, and the Order of Society are all themselves "visionary forms dramatic" (*Jerusalem* 98.28; p. 255). The connections among these entities,
as less comprehensively for Rousseau, Chateaubriand, and Wordsworth,
guarantee a wholeness of feeling as a possibility that a properly managed
fluidity may find an access to: "Attempting to be more than Man We Become less." These words of Luvah stand as a warning against any less
poetic attempts to formulate that fluidity (*The Four Zoas*, 135.2; p. 388).

Even in the relationship between man and God, Blake posits a sort
of instability, varying the terms fluidly[28] and permuting his own utterances against the Bible. On such a scale, and with such possibilities of
transformation, Blake's prophecy about the function of the imagination
could be made to include Poe's *Eureka* or Shelley's "Epipsychidion."

The theology of imputed identity between Christ and his followers is
itself subjected to a sort of dialectic. The epigraph to *Jerusalem*, "Jesus
is one" (*Monos ho Yesous*), invites us to bring any being there into congruence with an encompassing Savior. The point is made many times at
moments of the poem, notably by Los in his assertion of identity with
Albion:

> We live as One Man; for contracting our infinite senses
> We behold multitude; or expanding: we behold as one,
> As One Man all the Universal Family; and that One Man
> We call Jesus the Christ: and he in us and we in him,
> Live in perfect harmony in Eden the land of life
>
> (34.15–21; p. 178)

The next-to-last line here echoes a phrase from John; *Jerusalem* invokes
the Savior rather than the Muse (5.20); and yet its dynamic principle of
fluidity makes it distinct from both Scripture and commentary on Scripture. What is true of such persons as the Daughters of Los in this universe:

> Every one a transluent Wonder: a Universe within
> Increasing inwards, into length and breadth, and heighth:
>
> (14.17–18; p. 157)

is comparably true of the "minute particulars" (also a phrase Blake uses)
of the physical universe, "A grain of Sand . . . translucent and has many
angles . . . every angle is a lovely heaven" (37.15–18; p. 181).

Once he had found the terms for these fluidities, Blake could abandon
the dialectical ironies of *The Marriage of Heaven and Hell* and his an-
notations to Swedenborg. "There is no Limit of Expansion! there is no
Limit of Translucence" (42.35; p. 187). The principle that "Time is the

Mercy of Eternity" (24.71; p. 120) permits an act of poetry in time to open up what he might have called the Western Gate, the gate of "Tharmas" and so of Language, into a theological perception—the only kind of theology possible except for the silent feelings in the inspiration of their illumined fluidity:

> For a Tear is an Intellectual thing;
> And a Sigh is the Sword of an Angel King
> And the bitter groan of a Martyrs woe
> Is an Arrow from the Almighties Bow!
>
> (52.25–28; p. 200)

In the light of all this, the transformations of a man and a woman alternatively from youth to age through their reactions to each in "The Mental Traveller" schematize the fluidity only provisionally. For Blake the provisional is enough. In one of its aspects the fluidity attains an excess which is a road that leads to the palace of wisdom. The thresholds keep resolidifying as they dissolve.

3

Sin, *Verstand,* and the Love of All Things
The Vacillation of Coleridge

1

What Blake gradually achieved, the fusion of poetry and philosophy, Coleridge aimed to achieve; he spent his life in the effort to integrate thinking, expression, feeling, and the posture that would turn this legendary talker into some version of a systematic philosopher. This philosopher would remain a poet if possible, but aimed at least to retain the essence of poetry in the heart of his system.

Coleridge began with the intention of building philosophy and theology together with his poetry. As McFarland says, "Coleridge was ideally committed to an equilibrium — an interchangeability really — in the poetic and the philosophical functions."[1] The ratio between poetry and philosophy, the relations between them, remained both powerful and unstable throughout his life — an albatross, so to speak.

In "The Rime of the Ancient Mariner," Coleridge parallels the Blake of "The Mental Traveller" in choosing a ballad framework for a tale that connects the natural and the supernatural. The diction of the ballad reduces language to the essentials that the artfulness of art song implies are its proper subjects, while the ballad meter associates the tale to a fundament of common human concerns. Credence is conveyed in the assurances of a tale ringing as though it had become legend. But credence is a problem for the Ancient Mariner, who is doomed to recreate it each time from the beginning, by arresting the Wedding-Guest — a narrative frame superadded to the simpler ballad outline. It is of just this poem that Coleridge adduces his doctrine of the willing suspension of disbelief.

In 1817, twenty years after conceiving his ballad, Coleridge appended as an epigraph a passage in Latin from the seventeenth-century geological apologist Thomas Burnet about the relationship of the natural to the supernatural world. The epigraph at once offers and avoids an explanation of the spiritual transactions presented in the poem, while at the same time echoing some of Coleridge's deepest theological and philosophical concerns. It draws on a line of thinking that deeply preoccupied him, since it was the component of love, and of the spiritual activities in the human psyche generally, that for him supplied part of the philosophical basis for a rejection of Spinoza's account of continuity between the natural world and God as a kind of substance. At the same time, this seventeenth-century figure, Burnet, derives from a line of thinking already superannuated by the great thinkers like Kant and hermeneuts like Eichhorn who informed Coleridge's constant meditation. Nor did Burnet, even so much as the Bacon who was another favorite of Coleridge's, have for him the sense of maximal authority with which, in the area of theology, the Scriptures or even the Church Fathers would have been invested. Here is his quotation from Burnet (I have indicated by ellipses the passages that Coleridge excised):

> I can easily believe, that there are more Invisible than Visible beings in the Universe; and that there are more Orders of Angels in the Heavens, than variety of Fishes in the Sea; but who will declare to us the Family of all these, and acquaint us with the Agreements, Differences, and peculiar Talents which are to be found among them? It is true, human Wit has always desired a Knowledge of these things, though it has never yet attained it. . . . [Seventeen lines of text omitted, discussions of "souls, genii, manes, demons, heroes, minds, deities, and gods" with interpretive references to the Neo-Platonists, the Gnostics, and St. Paul.]
> . . . I will own that it is very profitable, sometimes to contemplate in the Mind, as in a Draught, the Image of the greater and better World; lest the Soul being accustomed to the Trifles of this present Life should contract itself too much, and altogether rest in mean Cogitations; but, in the mean Time, we must take Care to keep to the Truth and observe Moderation, that we may distinguish certain Things, and Day from Night.[2]

Coleridge's omission of the two passages about angels and devils — an omission longer than the passage that he has quoted — tends to conflate those beings with the *Naturae invisibiles* ("Invisible beings") apprehensible in the world itself, while displacing them into it. He does so in a manner comprehensively similar to the doctrines of the Spinoza with whom he carried on a lifelong battle in his mind. Left without the specificity of "orders of angels . . . genii, manes, demons," and so on, the *Naturae invisibiles* would come to seem indistinguishable from the *res extensae* of Spinoza,[3] just as, taken by itself "He prayeth best who loveth best / All things both great and small" (614–15) could serve as a slogan for watchful accord with the Spinozistic *substantia* and its ultimate indistinguishability from God. Spinozism, however, as Coleridge said,[4] was an atheism, and within the poem itself, as it goes beyond Spinozism, there are two beings whom Burnet would surely have classified among those mentioned in the passages Coleridge suppresses. These are the "Nightmare Life-in-Death" and her consort Death, whose dice game for the soul of the Mariner some take for the central event of the poem.

In these allegorical figures, however, we may see at once a conflation and a displacement. The half-won dice game is equivalent in agency to the prayer that allows the Albatross to drop from the Mariner's neck. Thus Chance (the dice game) and Contrition (the prayer) double as the resolving mechanism, coexisting in such an unresolvable doubleness that they simultaneously displace one another and repeat one another.

The Nightmare Life-in-Death, in her visible presence, is a momentary avatar, since the epigraph must identify her as one of the *Naturae invisibiles* of the poem. She incorporates the attributes of the Great Mother powerfully enough to have served Robert Graves as a summary of her functions:[5]

> *Her* lips were red, *her* looks were free,
> Her locks were yellow as gold:
> Her skin was as white as leprosy,
> The Night-mare Life-In-Death was she,
> Who thicks man's blood with cold.   (190–94)

Allegory here at once displaces myth and draws on the awe that myth is created to handle. Coleridge's most elaborate revisions of "The Rime of the Ancient Mariner" have to do with the descriptions of "Life-in-Death" and her actions. Once she throws the dice, however, she does not go through with Robert Graves's plot of either seducing or destroying, let alone inspiring, her object, unless the tale he is doomed to tell is taken as an anguished equivalent for such inspiration. Indeed, the Mariner has, so to speak, been displaced from his role as Consort to the Goddess in Graves's plot.[6] Psychological figures like those of Blake are here supernaturalized, externalized, and put into a tale that harrows when told but does not really evoke full credence.

The Mariner is displaced in favor of Death, who otherwise is only a passive partner, and loser, in the dice game. His tale is obsessive rather than inspired, somewhat along the lines of Coleridge's definition of madness.[7] It is Coleridge himself who, on the evidence of the poem, is inspired, an inspiration he could look back to in the years of "dejection" during which he first copied down this passage from Burnet (1801–1802) and then added it as an epigraph to his retrospective triumph, after presumably having abandoned most of the numerous projects of 1795–96.[8] These projects precede the poem, and the poem itself is a sort of substitute for them.

But the substitution or displacement by a partially similar work operated even more generally in Coleridge's oeuvre than is usual in the persistent indirection of creative focusing. It is considerable evidence for what McFarland calls the "diasparactive" element in the Romantic, the human consciousness — a tendency to fragment and distract as a counterforce to the tendency to construct.[9] On Eleanor Shaffer's showing, "Kubla Khan" is a kind of substitute for or precipitate of purposes left over from a projected epic on the events recounted by Josephus, "The Fall of Jerusalem."[10] *Biographia Literaria* holds ideas in place, as Coleridge reminds us, until he can get to the never really broached *Magnum Opus*. "Christabel" stayed on his desk more than twenty years waiting to be "completed," and it is a sort of substitute for another poem in the vein of "The Rime of the Ancient Mariner," itself a version of another project, a poem or prose narrative about the wanderings of Cain on which he was supposed to collaborate with Wordsworth and of which a few prose fragments did get written.

The suggestion that Coleridge write a ballad came up spontaneously on a walk with the Wordsworths. He fashioned the first version into a poem that could be given pride of place in *The Lyrical Ballads*, a supernatural lead-off for the "supernatural" half of the task, the "natural" half being assigned to Wordsworth. The quotation from Burnet that was added in 1817 is presumably designed to reinforce and make more explicit that initial allocation of imaginative focus. The supernatural beings are themselves made explicit more in the marginal glosses, which speak of the angels and demons that were elided in the quotation, than in the body of the poem. There the link between natural and supernatural is always blurred at crucial points, as it is in the quotation from Burnet that Coleridge offers us. The poem, like the *ingenium humanum* ("Human Wit") of the quotation, always desires a "knowledge" or conception of these things (*notitiam*) but never attains it or touches at it (*attigit*). Burnet's word for "desire," *ambivit*, means more ordinarily "circle round" or "compass"— a motion of the intellect around the supernatural beings much like that of the Ancient Mariner, who *ambivit* around the globe.

Instability governs the appearance of the Albatross, an early and dominant motif of the many touched on in the poem.[11] The Albatross, "as if it had been a Christian soul" (65), occasions, or else coincidentally co-occurs with, the breaking up of the ice that was "all between" and "all around." Or else its eating does:

> It ate the food it ne'er had eat,
> And round and round it flew.
> The ice did split with a thunder-fit;
> The helmsman steered us through! (66–70)

Is the sequence here *post hoc* or also *propter hoc?* And is it the appearance of the bird or its act of eating that is significant? Because our choice is blurred here, we can only "circle" (*ambivit*) the connection between natural and supernatural. We never "touch" it; but it does not go away either. The same portent and perplexity, carried in the simplicity of the declarative, formal suggestion of certainty in the ballad stanza, obtains of the next event:

> I shot the Albatross. (82)

This is the last line of Part I, immediately followed by the first line of Part II:

> The Sun now rose upon the right. (83)

There is a recurrent natural explanation for the sun's position: the ship has crossed the line. The unique supernatural explanation, heavily implied by the direct sequence, and by the portentousness of sequence in this poem as in ballads generally, is qualified by the succession of still graver events upon the death of the Albatross. The mariners "all averred I had killed the bird / That made the breeze to blow" (93–94), though in fact the breeze, the "good south wind" (71) which "the Albatross did follow" (72) — rather than the other way around! — "still blew behind" (37) after the death of the bird. And shortly the appearance of "the glorious Sun" leads the mariners to cancel their attribution: "'Twas right, said they, such birds to slay / That bring the fog and mist" (100–102). Their contradiction nullifies their superstition, except that they were right the first time, and soon: "We stuck, nor breath nor motion; / As idle as a painted ship / Upon a painted ocean" (118–19).

Or were they right the first time? The natural Universe here is mysteriously responsive to the internal spiritual motions; the bird drops off when the Mariner can love the water serpents. So we cannot rule out the possibility that the dead calm has come upon them as a result of their superstitious vacillation, the immediately preceding event, rather than because one of them has shot the bird (the motif of the cursed ship's passenger, as found in the stories of Arion, Dionysus, Jonah, and St. Paul).

While entertaining this doubt, we cannot disengage their hanging of the Albatross "instead of the cross" (141) around his neck from the over-whelming mysteriousness of a situation that involves both natural and supernatural. And in some sense the Mariner is the greatest sinner among them; he is also — unlike Cain — in some sense the most deserving, since the dice game between Death and Life-in-Death leaves him as the sole survivor. The others — the "four times fifty living men"—"dropped down one by one" (216, 219) immediately thereafter.

Many events directly involve his person — the shooting of the Albatross, the dice game, loving the serpents, the dialogue between the Polar Spirit and his fellow daemons, the charge of the Hermit that brings about the need to tell his tale. None of these events is free of the fusion of natural and supernatural, but none fuses them in the same way, and none can be firmly paralleled to any other. At one point the Mariner, trying to pray as he looks between the dead men on deck and the "thousand thousand slimy things" in the sea (230–43), is subjected to an influence identified by no marginal note, which could be a small wind or an evil spirit or an internal prompting, any one of the three or any combination:

> A wicked whisper came, and made
> My heart as dry as dust.   (246–47)

Death and Death-in-Life are alike as spirits, as mates, and as messengers of something like death. They differ in their gender, in the "life" component for the woman, and in their attitude towards the Mariner: the one dices for his absolute annihilation; the other, who "wins," returns him to a kind of life. This duality is repeated on a more advanced spiritual stage when the "fellow daemons" of the Polar Spirit hold a dialogue about him:

> 'Is it he?' quoth one, 'Is this the man?
> By him who died on cross,
> With his cruel bow he laid full low
> The harmless Albatross.
>
> The spirit who bideth by himself
> In the land of mist and snow,
> He loved the bird that loved the man
> Who shot him with his bow.'
>
> The other was a softer voice,
> As soft as honey-dew:
> Quoth he, 'The man hath penance done
> And penance more will do.'   (398–409)

The "softer voice" is oddly only concessive, and the Hermit who "shrieves" him hears a confession that turns out to be just the narrative we have run through. The duality between confessor and penitent is, as it were, preserved, since the words of absolution are not spoken and the "penance more" would be lifelong. The recital of the story we have heard to the Wedding-Guest is in fact just one instance of it. The world remains his threshold, a perilous one where the natural cannot rest from being haunted by the supernatural.

The stylistic simplicity of the ballad form in "The Rime of the Ancient Mariner" serves to keep blurred the points where a convergence takes place among Coleridge's 'major preoccupations: his definition of perception in the natural world, extended at just this time in his life by the study of Kantian transcendental logic; his questioning of the relationship between the natural and the supernatural realms, over which Spinoza hovers as a presence whose breadth McFarland has taught us; his development of a theology in the light of the new criticism of Eichhorn and others; and his preoccupation, in that theology, with questions of conscience, guilt, penance, and redemption.

In the first case, the faculty, Imagination or *Einbildungskraft*, that makes poems derives, in the Kantian perspective (as again McFarland shows us), from the interacting faculties of the mind in its epistemological grounding. These, in turn, both exemplify and provide for the sorts of contradiction, of instability or vacillation, that I have been reading into "The Rime of the Ancient Mariner." "Fancy and Imagination are Oscillations," Coleridge says, "*This* connecting Reason and Understanding; *that* connecting Sense and Understanding."[12]

It is in the realms of guilt, consciousness, and free will that Coleridge finds the most convincing refutations of the Spinozistic God. In Barth's reading,[13] Coleridge's theological concerns through his study of the higher criticism were philosophized to the point that they produced a version of the *sensus plenior,* the broader sense, in Scripture. But in the poetic practice of "The Rime of the Ancient Mariner," the broader sense operates without the sort of divisibility into discrete allegorical levels[14] that Dante projected for his poem about a spiritual journey. Dante likewise bases himself more explicitly on Scriptural interpretation; so Coleridge quotes an earlier Scriptural interpreter, Thomas Burnet, for his afterthought of apologetic justification.

The Mariner's final message to the Wedding-Guest, disjoined from his tale in a word of farewell, and his final words, repeat his response to the water snakes when he "blessed them unaware" (285; itself repeated 287):

> He prayeth best, who loveth best
> All Things both great and small;
> For the dear God who loveth us,
> He made and loveth all.   (614–17)

Asserting the benignity his tale nowhere allows, the Mariner has here transposed the Spinozist *sub specie aeternitatis* into a conventional, somewhat sentimental Christian-homiletic view of the Creator. In context these words have not lost wholly the phatic air of the simple Farewell, begun a few lines before (610). The benignity is a sort of increment, and a paradoxical one, in the light of the Mariner's repetitive penance. Nor do the last words depict the Wedding-Guest as receiving exactly the spirit of one "who prayeth best":

> He went like one that hath been stunned,
> And is of sense forlorn:
> A sadder and a wiser man,
> He rose the morrow morn.   (622–25)

We are left, then, not with the lesson of God's benignity, but with an accrual of wisdom from the energetic transposition of harrowing events into benignity.[15]

2

For "The Rime of the Ancient Mariner," the function of the poem itself is to make a large cast towards problems of theology, and even philosophy. Philosophy and theology are also the terms for Coleridge's definition of the "secondary imagination." That middle term in his three-part formulation[16] is given only once in all his work. Its instability and its very dependency on the "infinite *I am*"—which itself operates at some midpoint between a post-Cartesian *Cogito* and God's "I am that I am" to Moses from the burning bush—make it flow into those "other" areas of Coleridge's persistent meditation. It is not only that he invents a new form, the "lyrical ballad," just as "Christabel" also offers a new form recognized and imitated by Sir Walter Scott.[17] "Kubla Khan" comparably fuses the literary and the theological so that Eleanor Shaffer can define it as a fusion of traditional ballad and sublime ode legitimated by its high-critical focus on the Apocalypse.[18] And it is not only that Coleridge displaces the usual form and content of ballads. They tend to offer a single event, told in simple language, often involving a voyage, a marriage, supernatural occurrences, weather portents, and even revived dead men,[19] just as does "The Rime of the Ancient Mariner." The form and the content have been displaced into a theological questioning about the interactions of the supernatural with the natural.

Moreover, there is more at work in the poem's ultimate signification as a quasi-solution to theological problems than just the new Romantic fusion of tenor and vehicle in its use of images. Other poets perform this fusion with Coleridge's — or Blake's or Wordsworth's — dialectic of working out abstract problems through the poem.

To put it somewhat differently, one may separate the *De Doctrina Christiana* of Milton from *Paradise Lost* as clearly as one separates the *De Monarchia* from the *Divina Commedia*. The prose work may be used as a gloss on the poem, but each stands firmly separate. With Coleridge, on the other hand, looking at his total intellectual enterprise, one can see such masterly poems as "Kubla Khan," "Christabel," and "The Rime of the Ancient Mariner" as substitutions for unwritten poems, instances of somehow failed statement in the moral or theological realm. Others have stressed the hide-and-seek of sexual problems in "Christabel." These appear in sharp relief if contrasted with their analogues, the comparable father-stepmother-daughter triangles in *Titus Andronicus* and *Cymbeline*, where the father is comparably deaf to the fears of the devoted daughter. The only mystery about the "incompleteness" of "Christabel," indeed, is this characteristically Coleridgean hanging fire. It completes the particular tale when the father's hospitality to the daughter of an old friend is made to cover for a decisive furthering of erotic commitment away from the distinct, though hinted at, apprehensions of Christabel herself, the banishment of the retainer-poet sealing the implied engagement:

> 'Why, Bracy! dost thou loiter here?
>
> I bade thee hence!' The bard obeyed;
> And turning from his own sweet maid,
> The aged knight, Sir Leoline,
> Led forth the lady Geraldine.

Coleridge, of course, called the poem incomplete: he felt he had more to write. But then he nearly always felt this way about his writing. Anguish over the hastiness or incapacity or inconclusiveness of the writing act at a given moment furnished him, in deep prescience, with the modality for carrying it "through." Even "Kubla Khan" can be regarded as a completed act in the mode of the fragmentary epic, as again Eleanor Shaffer points out, in spite of Coleridge's convincing account of the circumstances that made it incomplete. Who, without Coleridge's accompanying tale of apology about the person from Porlock, would ever guess the poem to be unfinished? Who, without his own statement of intention to write further, would take "Christabel" to be unfinished either? Coleridge's utterances often have a momentary look; they are occasional, but they also fail their occasions on the one hand and transcend them as ribs for a dimly discerned structure on the other. His vacillating stance, the work declared to be virtual rather than actual, and the fluidity of the theological and philosophical problems it voices all reflect each other in the particular complex of his hesitant articulation. His genius was to operate powerfully under a lawlessness of his own origination, to adapt to him a remark from the *Biographia Literaria.*

Something of originality and consistency obtains for the *Biographia Literaria* itself, though on the negative side it is a hasty, semi-plagiarized draft for one of several large works never written, a shapeless "haystack of a book" in Herbert Read's phrase.[20] Coleridge first called it "Autobiographia,"[21] and it offers the mode of not just autobiography but autobiography-merging-into-treatise, autobiography-justifying-group-literary-practice, autobiography-evincing-ad-hoc-literary-principles. Since it constitutes the first modern work of philosophical literary criticism, it must be seen as a sort of lucky hit in its form as well as a quasi-deferral and a quasi-failure. Coleridge's form often has the guise of a lucky hit — like the ballad of the "Rime" and the apocalyptic epic fragment of "Kubla Khan."

The fragment, in Pascal beforehand and Nietzsche after, permits a sketchlike attempt at definition to suggest the contingency of shadowy matters that are not permitted to press the utterance into categorical shape. Such fragments by implication elevate a momentariness of thought, its liminal status, into a principle. A step towards more complete utterance, and they become what they already partly pretend to be, units in a demonstrated consistency. A step in the other direction towards more rounded and poised succinctness and they become aphorisms, maxims that imply a fixed order in the Renaissance usage of Erasmus, Vauvenargues, Chamfort, and La Rochefoucauld. Such aphorisms take on a fully philosophical cast in the hands of Coleridge's near contemporaries Joubert and Friedrich Schlegel, of Novalis, Nietzsche, and even the Shaw of the *Maxims of a Revolutionist.*[22] Become philosophical, the fragment manages to shy its utterance in the direction of a definition that can suggest a lucky hit only if the target is kept at a certain distance, if the launching of the shot retains its contingency. The fragment as such advertises its liminality.

An *essai* is a shot at a lucky hit, too, a "try," a literary form that advertises not the fragmentariness, but the arbitrariness, of its collocations.[23] The arbitrariness perforce induces philosophical tentativeness. It induces as well some revelation (and at the same time concealment) of the self-conscious narrator, whose self-consciousness is also revealed and concealed as it spills over in various directions, an *esprit ondoyant et divers* indicating the liminality of his utterance.

But only at Montaigne's Renaissance stage of merely posing such questions can the essay form serve a large-scale verbal integration of experience. When the question of self-consciousness fully emerges with Rousseau, not just as a Cartesian starting point for demonstration but as a deep convergence between personal and societal definition, then something like autobiography emerges, and the essay becomes "occasional" in the hands of Coleridge's friend Lamb. Coleridge, whose attention-span would seem to lend itself to the essay form, was not notably successful when the pressure of his living circumstances brought him to issuing essays in regular succession: "The Watchman," "The Friend," and "The Statesman's Manual." We read these works not as wholes, but to re-render them as fragments, to mine them for gems of definition, the same way we handle his pieces on Shakespeare. These lectures or oral essays are notable for no conventional presentational strategy, and for no brilliant mosaic juxtapositions, but rather for marvelous fragmentary insights that imply unstated and undeveloped hierarchies of deduction and principle. Even Emerson, the essayist *par excellence*, is most notable when most Montaigne-like: when the tang of his personality is freed and some arbitrary bit of self is touched on. What is the philosophical status of Emerson's assertions? We cannot grant him the grounding of Coleridge or Nietzsche; he cannot really be made to hold up without being translated all but totally into the argument of some prior thinker. Nor do his contingencies point a direction as Nietzsche's do. Kierkegaard, by contrast, qualifies his philosophical speculations by ironically intricate autobiographical masks and contexts; but he is never an essayist. The lucky hit of the *Biographia Literaria* gets its directional bearings from the fragments (sometimes translated paragraphs from Schelling, much like the quotations in the *Notebooks*), from the essay form, but most predominantly from the mode of autobiography, which provides the narrative line, submerging the fragment and evening out the tentativeness of the essay.

Rousseau's concerns were not alien to a Coleridge who somewhat valued him,[24] and who blocked out an "Essay on the Passions"[25] — passions at whose mercy he felt for much of his life. But except for a faint undercurrent of apologetic aside, this element, a dominant one for Coleridge, is edited out of *Biographia Literaria*. There he opts for the liberating condition of the subject announced by its defining adjective and terminal word; it is to be *literary*, asking about the growth of awareness about the dimensions of *poetic* practice. Not only is it literary, but it avoids self-consciousness even about its own literary form. The self enters only to apologize for not being more rigorous or to explain how it has come to hold the view that will then be expounded. The backtracking itself is never reflexive, though the writer backtracks to explain reflection.

In this higher achieved prose work, as in his poetry, Coleridge's strategy is to evade the extremes of what would seem to be desirable, a conceivable plenitude of linguistic expression. Partly by accident, to be sure, he reproduces in another form the unfixable violations of "The Rime of the Ancient Mariner." He avoids the plenitude of full philosophical expression on the one hand — Kant or Schelling or Hegel — and on the other hand the plenitude of an autobiographical reminiscence that retrospectively plumbs what is most urgently and intimately of personal concern to the writer in his feelings. We might have approached the program of Rousseau's *Confessions,* the short span of exposed anguish in Hazlitt's *Liber Amoris* and the *Confessions of an English Opium-Eater,* or the expatiating and comprehensive narrative completeness whose full circle and self-hallowing tone is implied in its title, its very orotundity, Chateaubriand's *Mémoires d'outre-tombe.* We might have been given the easy transpositions of *Dichtung und Wahrheit.*

Even with Coleridge's formalized focus on the growth of a literary mind — which parallels the concern of Wordsworth's "growth of a poet's mind" in *The Prelude* — the autobiographical mode is inescapably stagey: the writer announces to the reader that he is leading him into the formative anteroom of his defensible opinions. Coleridge, as it were, pulls himself up short before just the communicational implications of this staginess, borrowing from it the license to digress and the appeal of revelation (much as the Mariner fixes the Wedding-Guest), but not permitting it to dictate the nature of his content. *Biographia Literaria* is about as unrevealing as such a document can get while still remaining recognizably within the register of autobiography.

3

The tentativeness by which, finally, we recognize the profundity of Coleridge appears in the aspirations his poems may be taken to embody. In that light they become something other than the realized and clearly poised imaginative wholes of the sort suggested by the definitions of *Biographia Literaria,* the kind of poem about to be realized in just a year or so by the odes of Keats.

Each of these odes takes a clear emblem that it writes up to, writes around, and keeps stable. And still the perceptions are made in these odes to quiver round the feelings. All resemble each other in imaginative structure. Coleridge's poems, on the other hand, aspire in one direction towards theology ("The Rime of the Ancient Mariner," "Hymn before Sunrise in the Vale of Chamoni"). In the other direction they aspire towards confession (the Conversation Poems, "Dejection: An Ode"). It is only in the theological projections of Coleridge, themselves unrealized, that theological definitions of the relation between natural and supernatural are brought into a congruence touched on but qualified in the "shriving" of "The Rime of the Ancient Mariner."

So, in the central matter of the employment and significative direction of the images in his poems, only the very early Coleridge, from whom Wimsatt draws his illustrations, comfortably fits his definition of "the structure of Romantic nature imagery."[26] "Both tenor and vehicle . . . are wrought in a parallel process out of the same material. The river landscape is both the occasion of reminiscence and the source of the metaphors by which reminiscence is described. . . . The interest derives not from our being aware of disparity where likeness is firmly insisted on, but in an opposite activity of discerning the design which is latent in the multiform sensuous picture." The last sentence splendidly describes what we feel to be going on in the poems of Wordsworth, Coleridge's chief example in his criticism and his constant, interactive measure for his own efforts. But it will not account for what happens in Coleridge's later poems, where the design is often not "latent" so much as it is manifest — at the end of the "Aeolian Harp" and "Hymn before Sun-rise in the Vale of Chamoni"— or else it is so urgently approached as not to be accounted for by latency, as in "The Rime of the Ancient Mariner" and "Kubla Khan." As Clint Goodson tellingly demonstrates, "Kubla Khan" vacillates between representation and evocation in its poetic language.[27]

Coleridge's own well-known definitions of the poetic image extend Wimsatt's account of its latent design. For all the complexity and philosophical testing that Coleridge derives from the German idealist tradition, it is "likeness," and a continuity of function from the self-assertion of God down to the most casual image, that he stresses. Likeness organizes, and in a sense overrides, the threefold distinction of *Biographia Literaria*.

> The Imagination then I consider either as primary, or secondary. The primary Imagination I hold to be the living power and prime agent of all human perception, and as a repetition in the finite mind of the eternal act of creation in the infinite I AM. The secondary Imagination I consider as an echo of the former co-existing with the conscious will, yet still as identical with the primary in the *kind* of its agency, and differing only in *degree*, and in the *mode* of its operation. It dissolves, diffuses, dissipates, in order to re-create; or where this process is rendered impossible, yet still at all events it struggles to idealize and to unify. It is essentially *vital*, even as all objects (*as* objects) are essentially fixed and dead.
>
> Fancy, on the contrary, has no other counters to play with, but fixities and definites. The fancy is indeed no other than a mode of Memory emancipated from the order of time and space; while it is

blended with, and modified by, that empirical phenomenon of the will, which we express by the word Choice. But equally with the ordinary memory the Fancy must receive all its materials ready made from the law of association.

Here, while Coleridge's concern is mainly to buttress a separation of Imagination from Fancy by the highest authority possible, the very necessity to do so implies that in a given instance there would be enough resemblance between the products of the Imagination and the products of Fancy that we would have to pause very carefully before separating them. And indeed, if the terms are applied that he uses above to distinguish primary from secondary Imagination— *kind, degree,* and *mode* (italics Coleridge's) — then they could suffice also to distinguish Imagination from Fancy.

The persistent attempt from Goethe on to distinguish allegory from symbol is found somewhat oddly in the hands of writers like Coleridge, Melville, and Kafka, who are themselves drawn to allegory. This interest is only to be explained if the similarities between the two, and especially what are perceived as the difficulties of allegory, are sufficient to permit for a positive interaction between the terms:

> Now an Allegory is but a translation of abstract notions into a picture-language which is itself nothing but an abstraction from objects of the senses; the principal being more worthless even than its phantom proxy, both alike unsubstantial, and the former shapeless to boot. On the other hand a Symbol is characterized by a translucence of the Individual or of the General in the special or the Universal in the General. Above all by the translucence of the Eternal through and in the Temporal. It always partakes of the Reality which it renders intelligible; and while it enunciates the whole, abides itself as a living part in that Unity, of which it is the representative. The other are but empty echoes which the fancy arbitrarily associates with apparitions of matter.[28]

This account of language, which follows the tradition from Locke and Condillac through Hartley, makes allegory a sort of equivalent for fancy, as defined above, in handling "objects," "counters," and "fixities," by finding its ultimate source in "objects of the senses." The last sentence here names fancy explicitly. Symbol, too, is defined here most clearly in the "translucence" adduced "of the Eternal through the Temporal." It functions much as the secondary imagination does in its echo of the "infinite I AM." However, this definition does not really rule out the possibility that the superficial similarity between allegory and symbol would permit an allegory to be used as a symbol, just as fancy may subserve imagination.

Something like this process would seem to be Coleridge's intention in "The Rime of the Ancient Mariner," and something like this positive and cumulative force of allegory is what Coleridge attributes to *The Faerie Queene*: "The true sense [of allegory] is this,— the employment of one set of agents and images to convey in disguise a moral meaning, with a likeness to the imagination, but with a difference to the understanding, —those agents and images being so combined as to form a homogeneous whole."[29] The terms "imagination" and "homogeneous whole" make it clear that "allegory" is now pressed into service to do the work of what Coleridge calls "symbol" above. I am not suggesting that he exactly contradicts himself, but rather that a hierarchy of similar entities — imagination and fancy, symbol and allegory — may be seen either as a hierarchy, and so distinguished, or as similar, and so either associated or even identified. Here fluidity of terms and fixity of terms approach each other unstably. "Metaphor" is the current term for what Coleridge calls symbol, or else "myth," but he goes on here to subcategorize "metaphor" under "allegory," and then to parallel "mythology" in a proportion with "symbol": "This distinguishes it [allegory] from metaphor, which is part of an allegory. . . . Narrative allegory is distinguished from mythology as reality from symbol." But again, the circle is closed in Coleridge's application of Origen for a typological reading of Adam and Eve:

> the transgression of Adam and Eve was a Muthos, *en grammasi ebraikois* — an idea shadowed out in an individual instance, imaginary or historical— . . . 'In Adam all die'— or Adam and Eve were Individuals, in whom it *first* took place: in this alone different from all other Men and Women. In the former the Individuality is rightfully assumed— in the second it is recorded— the Truth is the same in both, and both alike are Mythic, and belong to Mythology.[30]

The reference to the transcendence of the Individual and of Time (which he has also discussed here) makes Mythology do very much the work that the Imagination-Symbol does by seeing the General in the Individual and Eternal in the Temporal.[31]

The very associative ease with which Coleridge moves around among these terms suggests not only that they had many aspects for him but that their employment would not be stable in his own practice.[32] And this is the case in such a poem as "The Aeolian Harp." To adopt a simple and relatively neutral typology (while bypassing or "bracketing" all the intricate problems of sign relations among the signifier, the signified, and the referent), we may say that any act of naming first constates or at least *refers* to an object. Second, in a poem it may take that reference to offer *analogies* to something else: "My love is a red, red rose," a girl is a flower in certain respects. This second process, usually involving images (metaphors, symbols, tenors, vehicles, hypotyposes, even metonymies, etc.), may itself be incorporated in a third, comprehensive inclusion of the image into some sort of universal system. This third, *systemic* use may employ a sort of prior given, as Blake's "rose" partakes of the preimagined Blakean universe. Or the systemic may be developed in the course of an experience that the poetry recounts, as in Wordsworth's *Prelude*, where we refer the waterfall not to some prior system but to the moment it is recounting, a moment that gathers up paradoxes and difficulties of the momentary designation, "the stationary blast of waterfalls," into a systemic sense that has been developed through the events narrated in the poem, but that the contradiction between "stationary" and "blasts" somewhat subverts.

We often think of poetry, and define it, as centering on *analogy*. Keats's odes, for all their subtlety, satisfy this expectation, poised neatly on a single object out of which they evolve analogies. A poetry of simple *reference* is possible, but felt to be minimalist; the short poems of Landor confine themselves largely to this function. Poetry that reaches towards *system* offers difficulties both to the poet and to the reader; it has taken us more than a century to begin to read Blake's Prophetic Books and *The Prelude* properly. And Shelley, for a while, was too easily dismissed because in his hyperbolic and almost free-associative practice he swept *reference, analogy*, and *system* all up into one hazy "mythmaking" fusion: "The Ode to the West Wind" and *Prometheus Unbound* are fantasies glorying in the possibility of system rather than productions of a system.

Coleridge is elusive not only because he carried the possibility of systematizing with him as a constant aspiration, and as a leaven for producing aphorisms. He is elusive in his poems, and for the same reason. Whereas it is easy to weave a consistency, and also to establish a hierarchy, among fancy, imagination, symbol, metaphor, and myth as he uses these terms for prose definition, in his actual poetry Coleridge may shift abruptly from a concentration on *reference* to an assertion of *system*, bypassing the *analogy* that, it would seem, he himself feels should bear a central role in poetry, whether as "allegory," "metaphor," "symbol," or instance of the "imagination." "The specific symptoms of poetic power" crucially involve image making. "The Aeolian Harp," however, begins in referential depiction:

> My pensive Sara! thy soft cheek reclined
> Thus on mine arm, most soothing sweet it is
> To sit beside our Cot, our Cot o'ergrown
> With white-flower'd Jasmin, and the broad-leav'd Myrtle,
> (Meet emblems they of Innocence and Love!)

> And watch the clouds, that late were rich with light,
> Slow saddening round, and mark the star of eve
> Serenely brilliant (such should Wisdom be)
> Shine opposite!

Every item here is a *reference* to an actual scene — the nestling wife, the cottage, the overgrowing flowers, the clouds, the evening star. Almost as though to undercut the symbolic fluidity of universal feeling in which the poem will culminate, Coleridge translates the Jasmin and the Myrtle into the fixities of staple equivalence, allegories preserved in the *langue* for the Myrtle and for the color of the Jasmin. He even suggests the propriety of another allegory, giving it a capital, for the serenely brilliant evening star: "Such should Wisdom be."

There is an interplay here: "With white-flower'd Jasmin, and the broad-leav'd Myrtle" constates exhaustively, so to speak, because in poetic botany since Chaucer's time "the flower and the leaf" composes all the growths on a plant. "White-flower'd" is even redundant: it distinguishes the species from "purple jasmin" (and so initially the white serves a purpose of *reference* rather than of *analogy* to innocence). But "broad-leav'd" has no such classifying function, making its constated opposition to "white-flower'd" not only comprehensive but also disjoined into the very disparities the end of the poem will celebrate. A color identifies, a shape describes, "white" and "broad." Both are gathered up fixedly as "meet emblems," and this interplay stays at the tone of conversation as it performs the function of reference. It seems to be eschewing the very sort of poetic power that Coleridge valued. Yet his avoidance of rich analogy has the positive effect of supporting a new, conversational mode of poetry. The speaker of such poems reaches towards a dimly present auditor — or towards his soliloquized self — to name persons in the distance powerful and absent.

The poem goes on referentially and lumps together the humble "bean-field" with the potentially symbolic sea just before it constates and names the presence of an actual lute set up in the actual window. The adjective "simplest" describes a minimal instrument (as opposed to a more complicated lute) rather than its linguistic use in the poem — the look of the lute and not its meaning:

> How exquisite the scents
> Snatch'd from yon bean-field! and the world so hush'd!
> The stilly murmur of the distant Sea
> Tells us of silence.
>   And that simplest Lute,
> Placed length-ways in the clasping casement, hark!

Once he gets under way with analogies for the sound of the lute, however, Coleridge produces a tumbling series of associations, as though analogy will not stay still for its "esemplastic" unifying:

> Such a soft floating witchery of sound
> As twilight Elfins make when they at eve
> Voyage on gentle gales from Fairy-Land,
> Where Melodies round honey-dropping flowers,
> Footless and wild, like birds of Paradise
> Nor pause, nor perch, hovering on untam'd wind!

This very process immediately brings him up to the assertion of a universalizing "life" principle which Owen Barfield has discriminated as a fundament of his system,[33] and which therefore may be taken to invoke, as well as to suggest, the *systemic* in the poem — but not to bring it about interconnectedly, as Wordsworth and Blake both do:

> O! the one Life within us and abroad,
> Which meets all motion and becomes its soul,
> A light in sound, a sound-like power in light,
> Rhythm in all thought, and joyance every where.

Here Coleridge the Philosopher (adding this passage later to his poem) speaks in meter, as he continues to do, suggesting the universal doctrine only as a possibility: "What if all of animated nature, / Be but organic Harps diversely fram'd / That tremble into thought, as o'er them sweeps / Plastic and vast, one intellectual breeze, / At once the soul of each and God of all?" This tentative notion, Spinozistic as it were, is rejected by the mere look, the "more serious eye," of the woman who is constated as lying in his arm. Her Christian caution that bids him "walk humbly with his God" lays a burden of inescapable guilt on such speculations in the face of the *Deus absconditus*: "For never guiltless may I speak of him, / The Incomprehensible! save when with awe / I praise him, and with Faith that inly *feels*." The movement from *reference* to *system* draws dizzy inference from its *analogies*. This movement is self-canceling. Confession voids as well as closes the cycle of theologizing, resigning from the richness of possibility by assigning fullness to an emptiness of feeling. The poem's last line joins "Peace, and this Cot, and thee, heart-honour'd Maid" as constated possessions of the speaker. So the moon in "The Nightingale: A Conversation Poem" is constated as a sort of psychological aid. It hushes the crying baby Hartley Coleridge. The anecdote of its doing so displaces Coleridge's ruminations about refusing to read the usual metaphorical meanings into the actual nightingale that he has been hearing. So in "This Lime-Tree Bower My Prison," the scenes he at once misses and evokes, as a result of his refusal to go out on a walk with his friends, are equaled by what he has "marked" in the bower itself.

I do not wish to rule out a kind of dialectical play between absence and presence in these situations, and it could be said that qualifying the nightingale is a rhetorical mode of access to its metaphorical attributes, eating one's poetic cake and having it too in the face of resistance between word and image. What Coleridge refers to himself as seeing in the lime-tree bower is cast into a double negative, which could be worked through its own dialectic: "Nor in this bower, / This little lime-tree bower, have I not marked / Much that has sooth'd me." But mainly this poetry works through a curious avoidance of the very qualities in poetry that Coleridge values so intensely as to have provided the most commanding definition of them in English.

In "The Rime of the Ancient Mariner," the relation between the natural — in language, *reference* or constation — and the supernatural, or the *system* of orthodox theology, is subjected to questioning by what would seem to be the contrary device of the trappings of a fixed *analogic* structure, an allegory. Consequently the contrariness nags at us in the sense of the events, as between the chance of the dice game and the dreaming contrition of the Mariner. And it also nags at us in the details. Is the "ice, mast-high, . . . As green as emerald" mainly a constative *reference* drawn exactly from a voyager's narrative? Or is it especially *analogous* to the supernatural? Is it part of the allegorical system? Its portent derives from our being unable to settle these questions. We stand on their threshold as on that of the supernatural (guilt and contrition and spiritual beings) and the natural (the wedding). And, on the other side, the "silly buckets," clearly *analogous* to the redemptive cleansing they accompany and therefore drawn into the *system* of supernatural purgation, are doubtful as to *reference*: we cannot be sure they were not merely dreamed, or that the cleansing water fills them:

> The silly buckets on the deck,
> That had so long remained,
> I dreamt that they were filled with dew;
> And when I awoke it rained.
>
> My lips were wet, my throat was cold,
> My garments all were dank;
> Sure I had drunken in my dreams,
> And still my body drank.   (297–304)

There is a congruity here between natural rain and the dreams that are a penitential access to the supernatural. But the role of the buckets is uncertain as to its signification of the constative. "Sure I had drunken in my dreams" could mean either that the Mariner dreamt he drank or else that he actually drank while he was also dreaming. "Still my body drank" insists on the continuity between dreaming and waking in any case, but the uncertainty of the constative reference preserves the air of portent that holds the Wedding-Guest and is felt to move the Mariner on through his course.

Thus in the figurative patterns of his poems, as in the significative function of the poems taken by themselves, and in their relationship to the activities of philosophy and theology, Coleridge has found a series of strategies for suggesting a possible consistency while producing actual disjunctions.

4

Hölderlin's Brink

1

Confronted by a world that he perceived to be permeated by intimations of gods who had (paradoxically) disappeared, Hölderlin, after finishing his philosophical studies, gradually centered on poetry as the means to express and define those intimations. His terms were theological — fate, time, gods, demigods, the holy. The frequent nubs of predications in the poems that enlist such terms have been decoded by Heidegger for a sort of archetypal, and balanced, representation of the human situation.[1] And yet, in the onward surge of the poems themselves, the speaker conveys a kind of "oscillation" between despair and wonder.[2] He stands on a brink; he deplores the possibility of getting beyond it while uttering the strophes that announce his capacity for seeing beyond. He makes balanced lyrics out of what could be described as the predicament of Coleridge. Heidegger characterizes this language as an "oscillation-structure" (*Schwingungsgefüge*) of Saying, and states that "through this pulling-apart of interdependent words the hint at a speech about the gods obtains a great and distinctive breadth."[3]

Hölderlin broaches an activity as a thinker ever on the threshold of realization by stirring his verses into an elevated tone that most resembles the sublime of the eighteenth century. However, the deep philosophical component of these poems and their aspiration towards an explanatory fullness transform them into probes beyond merely formal poise, as though Collins and Blake had merged in a single figure.

As for his ideas themselves, they tend to try to define the breadth of the speaker's situation in a late historical time. Germany is a reverberant present home, a sort of domesticated threshold, while Greece serves as an ideal past, an impossible future towards which the speaker nevertheless aspires. Where Schiller had addressed the matter of the past as a professional historian, splitting it from his poetry and moralizing it in his plays, Hölderlin personalizes the past in the quick of his poetry. The past becomes expressed as a hovering presence whose accidentally accessible energies may or may not carry him to a sense of the future.[4] The future, as envisioned, still is continuous with the past in its power to transform longing into joy; it is not the separate, and too quickly collectivized, Utopian future of Schiller's "Ode to Joy." Nor does Hölderlin, like Winckelmann, pause to contemplate the glories of Greece as they have been realized in stone. Rather he invokes, and thereby evokes, the emotions attendant upon a loss of the flow between men and gods, between men and nature, of which Greece is the exemplar. Hölderlin explicitly defines the opposition between his situation and that of the Greeks in terms of "drive" (*Trieb*) and "goal" (*Ziel*). "The hardest thing in it appears to be that antiquity seems to be wholly against our original drive, which is spent in imagining the unimagined (*das Ungebildete zu bilden*), and in perfecting what is original and natural"[5] (4.221). And this hardest of difficulties (*schwerste*) is just what he set himself to take the measure of.

Thus the problematic continuity is broached in the act of creation, via the extensions of language (Heidegger) and the limits of language (de Man),[6] between the life of the psyche and the history of man, and also between these and the easy effusions and cataclysmic comings-into-being of visible nature.

This continuity, which partially parallels the dynamics between past and present, nature and psyche in Blake, is not schematized, as it is in Blake, but rather is funded into the rhythmic possibilities of natural language. Visible nature serves as a source of such visions, as in Wordsworth, yet "the gods" and the past loom equally over the psyche, and visible nature is not a sole privileged source. The balanced alertness in Hölderlin's poems is thus brought to share a powerful mediation between absence and presence. So in *Diotima*:

> Denn ach, vergebens bei Barbaren
> Suchst Du die Deinen im Sonnenlichte,
> Die zärtlichgrossen Seelen, die nimmer sind!
> Doch eilt die Zeit. Doch siehet mein sterblich Lied
> Den Tag, der, Diotima! nächst den
> Göttern mit Helden dich nennt, und dir gleicht.   (1.242)

> For Ah! in vain among barbarians
> Do you seek your own in the sun's light;
> The tender-great souls who are no more!
> Yes, time speeds. Still my mortal song sees
> The day, Diotima! the one that names
> You next to the gods, with heroes, and resembles you.

The song in a posited future will see the day that names Diotima, in conjunction with gods and heroes, and the song also brings her into comparison with them. Yet the person on whom these near identities-to-be are said to pivot is herself an inquirer, seeking her own in the sunlight, the "tender-great" souls. Such terms as *ach* and the "no more" of *nimmer* serve to body forth a suspension of hope and regret. Natural light and supernatural beings induce powerful poetic gestures in the speaker and silent longings in the Diotima who is twice in the first two lines told "du schweigst." Well might she be silent, since among barbarians her seeking is to be in vain, except that this poem defines the perception of what is said at the same time to be unsearchable.

The stretching of human capability here, a Romantic topos, takes on a special temper in Hölderlin by virtue of the striving for a measured balance among the charged elements—the gods, the psyche, the past, the act of the poem, the future, and a homeland both real (Germany) and ideal (Greece).

At another vantage the continuity is asserted between depth of thought and vitality:

> Wer das Tiefste gedacht, liebt das Lebendigste.

> Who thought the deepest, loves what is most living.
>   ("Sokrates und Alcibiades," 1.260)

The strategy of naming here is not either classical or neo-classical. But the combination of notions strikes a balance that might be called classical. Hölderlin finds in Sophocles what Keats, less temperately, found in "Melancholy" ("Burst joy's grape upon his palate fine") and Wordsworth in nature ("Praise to the end") — the doctrine that will fuse joy and sorrow:

> Viele versuchten umsonst das Freudigste freudig zu sagen.
> Hier spricht endlich es mir, hier in der Trauer sich aus.

> Many have tried in vain to say the most joyful with joy;
> Here at last it speaks out to me, here in sorrow.
>   (*Sophokles*, F, I, 179)

Here the contradiction resides not in the feeling so much as in the means for expressing it, where a kind of allopathy is called for in the language.[7] The poet lends Diotima a voice for that whereof she is silent. And the emblematic progress of natural and supernatural events is said to proceed in silence also:

> Und Moos wächst und es kehren die Schwalben,
> In Tagen des Frühlings, nahmlos aber ist
> In ihnen der Gott.

> And moss grows and the swallows turn
> To the days of spring, but inaccessible
> Is the god in them.
>
> (*Der Mutter Erde*, 2.125)

The elusiveness of a speech meant to comprehend what a silence embodies is derived from the intersection of natural and supernatural in the life for which Hölderlin represents himself as seeking terms:

> Was ist der Menschen Leben ein Bild der Gottheit,
> Wie unter dem Himmel wandeln die Irdischen alle,
> Sehen sie diesen. Lesend aber gleichsam, wie
> In einer Schrift, die Unendlichkeit nachahmen und den Reichtum
> Menschen. Ist der einfältige Himmel
> Denn reich? Wie Blüthen sind ja
> Silberne Wolken.   (2.209)

> What is the life of man an image of godhood,
> As the earthly all wander under heaven, and they
> See these. Reading, though, likewise, as
> In a script, men imitate endlessness
> And the kingdom. Is the onefold heaven
> Then rich? Like blooms indeed
> Are silver clouds.

Another medieval trope, the "book of nature," turns to a sort of mystification.[8] The tentativeness of the process forbids our congealing these assertions into a doctrine of a relation between imitation (*nachahmen*) and infinity (*Unendlichkeit*). The first term has a long history from Plato on, while the second, not usually coupled with it, names one Romantic ultimate. To the relation between imitation and infinity, Hölderlin applies, as it were, the light touch of qualification. Paired also here with infinity is *Reichtum*, a term that does not sort with either of the other two. *Reichtum* is repeated at the very end of the poem, when the paleness left as the blue goes out of the sky is not "riches" but a sign or indicator of riches, "Anzeige des Reichtums." A simile is appended to it, "wie Erz," like ore. Here, on its first occurrence, *der Reichtum* immediately raises a question — precisely a question of what may be attributed to that natural sky (where the blue is later mentioned) for which the language of Hölderlin has the same term as for the supernatural heaven, "Ist der einfältige Himmel / Denn reich?". The earthly *wandeln* under heaven. To *wandeln* — "wander" or "change" or "traffic" — is not to be "onefold," *einfältig*, itself a stronger and more physical term than "simple" (*einfach*). A contradiction between *einfältig* and *reich* is not stated, but only wondered about. Indeed, the question implies that the possibility of a resolution has in fact already been broached by the context in which *Reichtum* is paired with *Unendlichkeit*. The answer to the question is another flower simile: "Wie Blüthen sind ja / Silberne Wolken." If the clouds in the heaven are silver, they are indeed rich. And either they contain the possibility of being manifold rather than *einfältig* when such a simile can be posited of them, or else, when they are filtered through human language, they are stammered into a pseudo-manifoldness, since it takes the irreducible doubleness of a simile to describe them.

The onus of assertiveness is vested not only in the syntactic sequence, where the simile answers the question about the heaven's being *einfältig* and *reich* at the same time. The assertiveness is also vested in the parenthetical *ja*, displaced from being a direct answer to the question and made to underscore the simile. "Worte, wie Blumen entstehen"—words or the clouds partake of the transience of the beautiful, a deep dramatization of Goethe's later bare assertion, "Alles Vergängliche ist nur ein Gleichnis." Yet words, for all their displacement, do possess, and in poetry do exemplify, an evocative power:

> O nenne Tochter du der heiligen Erd!
> Einmal die Mutter. Es rauschen die Wasser am Fels
> Und Wetter im Wald und bei dem Namen derselben
> Tönt auf aus alter Zeit Vergangengöttliches wieder
> Wie anders ists! und rechthin glänzt und spricht
> Zukünftiges auch erfreulich aus den Fernen.

> O thou daughter of holy earth, name
> One time the mother. The waters roar at the cliff
> And storms in the wood and at its name the same
> Vanished godliness from old time rings again.
> How different it is! And justly it shines and speaks
> The future also joyously from the distances.
> (*Germanien*, 2.152)

Naming serves to evoke both past and future, and the very "unreadability" (to use a current locution) of the juncture between "glänzt und spricht" contributes to the mystery of arousal declared to reside in the proper use of words—the high poetic use. This use, as Heidegger emphasizes, begin though it may in evanescences, comes to term in a triumphant permanence: "Was bleibet aber, stiften die Dichter."[9] ("What abides, though, do poets found," 2.189).

The movement from past to future here may be called well-nigh Hegelian even in its lineages of deep spiritual processes derived from the existence of *Germanien*, as in the Germany of *Die Phänomenologie des Geistes*. Yet it never solidifies to become a Wordsworthian, let alone a

Hegelian, doctrine. It retains its tentativeness, the mark of its origin in evanescences of responsive feeling, as essential to the bloom of what it is perceiving.

In the process of his poems, as in his view towards experience and towards the history of Greece or Germany, Hölderlin locates the possibility (the word is his) of expression and realization in the proper wakefulness towards transience and passing away. So he formulates the notion abstractly in his essay "Das Werden im Vergehen" ("Becoming in Passing Away," 4.282–87).

> Ein Bestehendes selber wirklicher scheint und reales oder das sich Auflösende im Zustande zwischen Seyn und Nichtseyn im Nothwendigen begriffen ist.
>
> Das neue Leben ist jezt wirklich, das sich auflösen sollte, und aufgelöst hat, möglich (ideal alt). Die Auflösung nothwendig ist und trägt ihren eigentümlichen Karakter zwischen Seyn und Nichtseyn. (283)

> Something that subsists of itself appears more actual and real, or what resolves itself in a condition between being and non-being is conceived in necessity. . . .
>
> The new life is now actual, which shall resolve itself and has resolved itself possibly (ideally old), the resolution necessary, and bears its particular character between being and non-being.

"On coming-to-be and passing away" again is a classical philosophical conception. It is the name of a treatise by Aristotle. Hölderlin, however, here transforms the classical. He reads the experiential force of something that precedes poetry into a quasi-Hegelian area between Being and Non-Being. The other terms are among those he uses in the elaborate stenographic equations of his notes for an essay on poetry, "Wechsel der Töne" (4.238–240). There *Wirklichkeit* ("actuality") is associated with the naive and with lyric, *Notwendigkeit* ("necessity") with heroism and epic, and *Möglichkeit* ("possibility") with idealism and the tragic. All three terms appear in the second of the quotations above. However, these terms do interpenetrate, in keeping with Hölderlin's predilection for nascent fusions. As Lawrence J. Ryan points out in his elaborate application of these formulae to the body of Hölderlin's poetry, all three "tones" are possible for lyric (p. 69).[10] Ryan goes on to attribute combinations of them to specific poems, pointing out even in the public spirit of Hölderlin an unsteadiness and a dynamism (p. 352). One may find a comparable wavering, a permanent threshold-consciousness, in the political poems of Leopardi, Blake, and Coleridge. But even in Blake this wavering is not so persistently quickened by the recovery and future-orientation of a stubbornly elusive purposiveness.[11]

Incapacity stands as a constant menace in this poetic expression, incapacity not through human falling away, but rather through the necessary human embroilment in the transience of existence. Rivers are a common figure for this transience, and Hölderlin has frequent recourse to them: the Rhein, the Ister or Donau, the Neckar. In *Andenken* it is the Dordogne, and the Garonne, against whose flow in the last stanza he erects his emblematically assertive final line, "Was bleibet aber, stiften die Dichter" (2.189).

Even the direct expressions of the transience fated for humankind contain a counter-energy, as in the last stanza of *Hyperions Schiksaalslied*:

> Doch uns ist gegeben,
>   Auf keiner Stätte zu ruhn,
>   Es schwinden, es fallen
>   Die leidenden Menschen
>   Blindlings von einer
>   Stunde zur anderen,
>   Wie Wasser von Klippe
>   Zu Klippe geworfen,
>   Jahrlang ins Ungewisse hinab.

> So it is given us
>   To rest in no state,
>   There vanish, there fall
>   Suffering men
>   Blindly from one
>   Hour to another
>   Like water from cliff-ledge
>   To cliff-ledge thrown
>   Yearlong down into the unknown.   (1.265)

There is a marked prolongation of the last line; it is a foot or two longer than any in the stanza. It is even longer than the concluding lines of the first two stanzas ("Heilige Saiten"; "Ewiger Klarheit"), to which, as a counter-expression, it begins to assimilate. The open, slow syllables rhythmically belie the very rapidity of the preceding simile: they move much more slowly than water thrown from cliff-ledge to cliff-ledge.

This change of rhythmic prolongation may be taken to hint that man is not in fact entirely divorced from those beings it is he, after all, who perceives, in the opening of the poem: "Ihr wandelt droben im Licht / Auf weichem Boden, seelige Genien! "[12] ("You traffic up there in the light / On soft ground, blissful spirits!") "Und die stillen Augen / Bliken in stille / Ewiger Klarheit." ("And the still eyes / Look in still / Eternal clearness.") In another, later emphasis, "Viel hat erfahren der Mensch. Der Himmlischen viele genannt, / Seit ein Gespräch wir sind / Und hören können voneinander." ("Much has man experienced. / Named much of the heavenly / Since we are a conversation / And can hear one another," 2.137).

The climax of *Hyperions Schiksaalslied* emphasizes the acute sense of loss, and the attendant feeling of uncertainty, out of which Hölderlin projects his very feeling of futurity, "ins Ungewisse hinab." This sense of loss has two faces. Taken by itself it opens only into a sorrow of deprivation. But taken together with the act of poetic saying and the opening of a future, it quickens the spirit into an access of perceiving intently what is declared to be missed. The threshold faces both ways as one plunges on "Blindlings von einer / Stunde zur anderen, / Wie Wasser von Klippe / Zu Klippe geworfen."

The distance from Greece is a special version of the keenness-in-loss, and *Der Archipelagus* imagines Greeks themselves suffering the poignance of such loss under Persian attack. Contemplating such a situation brings Hölderlin back to his own condition of wakeful belatedness:

> Aber Freund! wir kommen zu spät. Zwar leben die Götter,
> Aber über dem Haupt droben in anderer Welt.

> But friend! We come too late. To be sure, the gods do live,
> But overhead up there in another world.
> ("Brod und Wein," 109–10; F, I, 251)

Empedocles hovers on the brink of total loss in total fulfillment as he protractedly prepares his disappearance into the crater of Aetna, seen in the distance while he lays injunctions on his disciple:

> Die Schwere fällt, und fällt, und helle Blüht
> Das Leben das ätherische, darüber.

> The heaviness falls and falls, and light blooms
> Life the ethereal over there.
> (*Empedokles*, dritte Fassung, 307–9; 4.132)

The limbo of secret purpose permits the resolution of the two states, not by any logical or dialectical series, but rather by their interpenetration in the mood of the imagined speaker. There is no "drama" in *Empedokles*, and none is needed. The problematic state of the protagonist provides sufficient occasion for the canvassing meditations on nature and the soul.

Rivers are compared to men too. And the perversity of the human condition is made more explicit, though not separated from perception either; the end of *Stimme des Volks* celebrates the savage self-sacrifice of the people of Xanthus, who drove their children into the flames of a mass suicide, making themselves heroes as their ancestors had been against the

Persians. Still, Hölderlin's last statement declares the necessity of interpreting such sagas, thus foregrounding, as neither Pindar nor Corneille would have done, the crucial role of linguistic and poetic manipulation:

> und wohl
> Sind gut die Sagen, denn ein Gedächtnis sind
> Dem Höchsten sie, doch auch bedarf es
> Eines, die heiligen auszulegen.   (1.53)

> and indeed
> Legends are good, for they are a memorial
> To the highest, yet there is need, too,
> For someone to interpret the holy.

Hölderlin takes an issue connected with the origin of speech, a live philosophical puzzle for Herder and Rousseau,[13] and runs it along in *Stimme des Volks* (2.49) as part and parcel of his nostalgia for prehistoric origins, the "time of the Gods," when what we know as a past would have been a future.

2

As Michael Hamburger points out, over the seminary gate at Tübingen stood the motto "Aedes Deo et Musis Sacrae."[14] This seminary is almost next door to the tower on a river bank where, as it turned out, Hölderlin spent the last thirty-six years of his life. The firm coupling of God and Muses calls for no theoretical justification on Hölderlin's part, in the mode of Poe's *Eureka* or Coleridge's projected *Magnum Opus*. Rather, it calls for a constant balancing act whereby the role of God and the role of poetry are given their proportionate share without a fixed positioning. The poet is awake on the threshold that is at the same time a brink. The perception of the divine brings about a deep process in men.

> So ist der Mensch; wenn da ist das Gut, und es sorget mit Gaaben
> Selber ein Gott für ihn, kennet und sieht er es nicht.
> Tragen muss er, zuvor; nun aber nennt er sein Liebstes,
> Nun, nun müssen dafür Worte, wie Blumen, entstehen.

> So is man; when the good is there and a god himself
> Cares for him with gifts, he knows and sees it not.
> He must bear it beforehand; and now he names what is dear to him.
> Now, now must words for it, like blossoms, arise.
>   ("Brod und Wein," 5.92–93)

At the end of this whole cycle, which begins with the divine presence and proceeds through human suffering, words are compelled (*müssen*) to be produced—as automatically and creatively as natural ornaments, as flowers. This is finally a positive and triumphant, if deeply qualified, act. Enacted is the broad ground on which "God and the Muses" coexist in creative interdependence, a response, as it were, to the injunction early in the same poem:

> So komm! dass wir das Offene schauen
> Dass ein Eigenes wir suchen, so weit es auch ist.   (2.91)
>
> So come, that we may see what is open
> That we seek our own, far off though it be.

The assertion holds, even in the face of the deep doubt and isolation that the poet expresses, again in the same poem, when "die Himmlischen" come thundering in an ominous form resembling "die Noth und die Nacht" (2.94).

And there is no irony in Empedocles' apotheosis by self-destruction. Revising his play over and over, Hölderlin persistently shies away from that climax. Hölderlin himself, in the short poem celebrating his poet's leap into the volcano, says he is held back by love from such a leap (1.240).

Keats's "negative capability"—"being in uncertainties, mysteries, doubts, without any irritable reaching after fact and reason"—has here been dramatized and, as it were, rendered negligible through its complete fulfillment, in a measured series of statements where equipoise and wakefulness feed each other. Keats's own poetry, on the other hand, at its sculpturesque best strives towards, and attains, a golden sleep of incessant virtuosities. "Sleep and Poetry" names the set of Keats's vision. "Deep in the shady sadness of a vale"—this beginning of *Hyperion* could not be paralleled in Hölderlin; yet Keats has, compensatorily as it were, a power for the mimetic resurrection of lushness that also in Hölderlin could find no parallel. The glory of Hölderlin is the stripping of a Romantic feeling to its measure in the absolutely gnomic, to an abundant series of deep saws that cheer the very state whose trembling contradictions they rise to the act of naming.

Even the saying about intermittences is intermittent:

> Nenn' ich den Hohen dabei? Unschikliches liebet ein Gott nicht,
> Ihn zu fassen, ist fast unsere Freude zu klein.
> Schweigen müssen wir oft; es fehlen heilige Namen.
> Herzen schlagen und doch bleibet die Rede zurück?
>
> Do I thus name the high ones? A god loves not the unbecoming.
> To seize him is our joy almost too small.

Often we must be silent. Holy names fail.
Hearts are beating and still does speech hold back?
(*Heimkunft*, 99–102; 2.99)

In this passage, which could almost have been written by Rilke, there is a kind of readiness of heart-prompted speech that compensates for, without resolving, our obligation to be silent because our joy is too small to grasp God.

3

The rhythmic anchorage for this vision is sometimes an adaptation of classical meters. Hölderlin's hexameters and elegiacs are more hyperbolic, longer in their sentence-runs, and less modulated than those of any Greek and Roman poets — except the philosophers. His hexameters resemble not Homer or Callimachus, Vergil or Ovid, but rather Empedocles and Lucretius. Yet he has no system in view, for all the projection of one in *Wechsel der Töne*, and no narrative either: the hexameter is turned to the use of meditative fantasia, as though he were trying to find a poetic equivalent for the union of subjects in his early thesis on the parallels between Proverbs and Hesiod's *Works and Days* (4.176–88).

Where the hexameters are impetuous, the Odes are adapted from the Alcaics (and Asclepedians) of Horace, for all Hölderlin's emphasis on the Greeks. They are measured — but not according to the Horatian inter-reverberations of multiple adjustments, word-to-word, within a line. The markings of Hölderlin's measures come in larger units than Horace's, and his balance is simpler, permitting him, as it were, to turn his attention to intensities of meaning. The platitudinous Horace, on the other hand, vests all his intensity in the rhythms and sequenced associations of syntactic interplay, in ordonnances of sound and conventional sense.

Where Horace has many pauses, Hölderlin, by contrast, sets up one caesura, which creates a simple interplay between an initial phrase longer in the first long line, shorter in the second long line. Such a pair is followed by a feminine ending in the third, short line, and a final fourth line, sometimes without strong caesura:

Du schweigest und duldest, / und sie versteh'n dich nicht,
Du Heilig Leben! / siehest zur Erd' und schweigst
Am schönen Tag, / denn ach! umsonst nur
Suchst du die Deinen im Sonnenlichte,

Die Königlichen, / welche, wie Brüder doch,
Wie eines Hains gesellige Gipfel sonst
Der Lieb' und Heimath / sich und ihres
Immerumfangenden Himmels freuten,

Des Ursprungs noch / in tönender Brust gedenkt;
Die Dankbarn, / sie, / sie mein' ich, / die einzigtreu
Bis in den Tartarus hinab die Freude
Brachten, / die Freien, / die Göttermenschen.   (2.28)

You are silent and patient, and they do not understand you
You holy creature! You see the earth and are silent
At the beautiful day, for ah! just in vain
do you seek your own in the sun's light,

The kingly ones who, indeed like brothers,
Like the blest top of a grove otherwise
Enjoyed love and the homeland
And their ever-embracing heaven,

Mindful of the origin still in the ringing breast,
The thankful ones, they I mean, who solely faithful
Brought joy all the way down to Tartarus,
The free ones, men of the gods.

This contrast between masculine and feminine endings is a main device in Hölderlin, used adroitly also in the much different, invented stanza of *Hyperions Schiksaalslied*. Normally one expects a masculine ending to end a complex syntactic run. The trail-off of the feminine ending, a standard device in Hölderlin, holds the voice back in something nearer silence than a stressed syllable would. This holding back while pressing forward suggests that there is something more to say and that so much is unsayable that a near lapse into silence is musically enjoined on the singer.

In another, later development, Hölderlin releases a wide pendulum swing for the lengths of his free lines:

O Insel des Lichts!
Denn wenn erloschen is der Ruhm die Augenlust und gehalten
    nicht mehr
Von Menschen, schattenlos, die Pfade zweifeln und die Bäume,
Und Reiche, das Jugendland der Augen sind vergangen
Athletischer
Im Ruin und Unschuld angeboren
Zerrissen ist . . .

O islands of light!
For where there is extinguished fame, delight of eyes, and no
    longer maintained
By men, shadowless, the paths doubt and the trees,
And kingdoms, youth-land of eyes, are gone,
More athletic
In ruin and inborn innocence
Is torn . . .   (*Patmos*, spätere Fassung, 61–67; 2.180)

The strange emphasis of "Athletischer" stands like a fragment of sculpture, in metrical isolation, and the fits and starts of utterance provide a sort of sound equivalence for "islands of light."

4

The leaps of rhythm run to the "islands of light" in the words. Expression is finally disjoined and rapturously made paratactic in such a late hymn as this fragment:

Und mitzufühlen das Leben
Der Halbgötter oder Patriarchen, sitzend
Zu Gericht. Nicht aber Überall ists
Ihnen gleich um diese, sondern Leben, summendheisses auch
                    von Schatten Echo
Als in einen Brennpunkt
Versammelt. Goldne Wüste. Oder wohlunterhalten dem
                    Feuerstahl des lebenswarmen
Heerds gleich schlägt dann die Nacht Funken, aus geschliffnem
    Gerstein
Des Tages, und um die Dämmerung noch
Ein Saitenspiel tönt. Gegen das Meer zischt
Der Knall der Jagd. Die Aegypterin aber, offnen Busens sitzt
Immer singend wegen Mühe gichtisch das Gelenk
Im Wald, am Feuer. Recht Gewissen bedeutend
Der Wolken und der Seen des Gestirns
Rauscht in Schottland wie an dem See
Lombardas dann ein Bach vorüber. Knaben spielen
Perlfrischen Lebens gewohnt so um Gestalten
Der Meister, oder der Leichen, oder es rauscht so um der
                    Thürme Kronen
Sanfter Schwalben Geschrei.
Nein wahrhaftig der Tag
Bildet keine
Menschenformen. Aber erstlich
Ein alter Gedanke, Wissenschaft
Elysium.
                    und verlorne Liebe
Der Turniere.
Rosse, scheu und feucht.   (2.249)

And to sympathize the life
Of demigods or patriarchs, sitting
In judgment. Not everywhere, though, is it
Like them for this, but life, humming hot also echo of shadows
As in a focus

Gathered. Golden desert, or well-maintained
                    with the flint and steel of the life-warm
Herd at once night strikes sparks from the polished stone
Of day, and around twilight still
Is a sound of strings playing. By the sea whispers
The crack of the hunt. The Egyptian woman, though, sits
                    with open breast,
Always singing from care, arthritic the joint,
In the forest, at the fire. Signifying good conscience
Of the clouds of the seas of the constellation
There rustles on by in Scotland as on the lake
Of Lombardy a brook. Boys play
Accustomed to pearl-fresh life thus around forms
Of the masters or corpses, or there rustle thus round the towers crowns
Cry of soft swallows.
No truly the day
Pictures no
Men's forms. But first
An old thought, science
Elysium.
                    and lost love
Of the tourneys.
Steed, shy and damp.

Without any theory especially behind it, this poem is already using the devices of the Acmeist or the Projectivist, Mandelshtam or Olson.[15] The jets of expression, to continue with anticipatory comparison, are definite enough to keep it unlike Apollinaire, and they are finally logical enough to be unassimilable to surrealism. The doctrine has now become a series of "shadow echoes" or "burning points." More mysterious than the comparable figure in Giorgione's *Tempesta*, "Die Aegypterinnen," in Hölderlin's usual half-inexplicable contrast (*aber*), offers a bundle of oppositions between singing and pain, youthful maternity (the open breast) and age (the arthritic joint). A vaguely late medieval glimpse of horses straining before a tournament competes with a sweep in space from Lombardy to Scotland, the play-aspirations of boys, towers, swallows, paradise, and (of all things) the emphatic and rhythmically suspended word that does not quite confine itself to what the nineteenth century will make of it: *Wissenschaft*, a golden waste indeed. *Wissenschaft* here lingers in its etymology. Surrounded by such company it will not join Hölderlin's schoolmate Hegel. Its desert is golden.

These images are not echoes. They are simplex — so much so that, again, they engender a sort of fear in their timeless isolation. The desired measure seems not to exist on earth. The freedom of the poet is precariously to body forth a balanced equivalent for freedom.

5

Leopardi
The Mastery of Diffusing Sorrow

1

Leopardi early overdefined his identity as that of the classical scholar. This negative identity called forth, as it were, a positive one, in which, as for Blake, Coleridge, and Hölderlin, philosophy and poetry played crucial roles. So did the definition of emotional states, which he expressed in ways that made them indistinguishable from philosophical positions, the goal Nietzsche was later to strive for.

Leopardi began at a neutral point, in solitude, turned wholly and austerely to the study of the past, till gradually he perfected a vernacular voice for that which the past, in its conditions, could not have expressed. In his work poetry and philosophy reach still another equilibrium — the philosophy providing a theory that will purify the poetry and liberate the poetry from itself. The philosophical *Zibaldone* lends weight, as background, prelude, and accompaniment, to the poems.

In the isolation of his father's library, Leopardi first, prodigiously, set himself to the mastery of that exactitude towards classical antiquity which drew other equally cloistered but less inspired minds after the Industrial Revolution, a maximizing retrieval of data backed by a faith in the set significance of one hallowed past. He became a prodigy of classical philology. Behind and around this faith, so to speak, something that would negate this exactitude by engulfing it was gathering head, a process of speculation and an accompanying expression of it in the splendid control of a diffusing sorrow. Meanwhile it was to Wolf and Cardinal Mai — the addressee of almost his first long poem (1.7–9)[1] — rather than Winckelmann, that Leopardi gave his intellectual attention. And soon he would, so to speak, leap right beyond Winckelmann, from painfully close con-

97

centration on the detail of minor classical writers[2] to the incorporation of classical examples in a vast meditative effort — subphilosophical but somewhat extraliterary. The *Zibaldone* ("miscellany") is not to be paralleled in any Renaissance poet's commonplace book; it would not be matched and surpassed till the extensive *Cahiers* of Valéry. In its four thousand five hundred and twenty-six pages, Leopardi over a fifteen-year period kept exalting by implication and example the very process of the mind at work in thinking. He returned again and again to just the sort of topic that the more formal Valéry would still more protractedly address — the nature of perception, the philosophical implications of the literary use of language, the ontological status (as we would say) of art.

Underplaying the sort of classificatory intelligence needed for exact philology, and also the intelligence of the philosopher, Leopardi located the poems he suddenly began to write between these two activities. These poems are rhymed meditations at first anchored in a reverence not for the idea of antiquity but for antiquity as seen through the eyes of the philologist. He slacked off sharply at philology as soon as he began his poetic work. And the prose meditations of the *Zibaldone* took place as a kind of defining accompaniment, a private stock-taking, rather than the public justification that the Renaissance poet-critics and their followers advanced in the England of Wordsworth and Coleridge or the France of Victor Hugo.

Leopardi makes the distinction fairly early (2.110–11), for linguistic use, between "parole" with "immagini accessorie" and "le voci scientifiche," providing a framework where philology and philosophy might be lumped together under the latter category.[3] However, just as the modern philologist tries (vainly!) to banish impressionism from his discriminations, and the philosopher of the Humean tradition (though Leopardi leaned towards Plato) emphasizes a radical skepticism, so Leopardi tried for a poetics that would increase emotional overtness through a deliberate scaling down in his style,[4] "antiretorica" by comparison with his predecessors if not with the twentieth-century poet. He would seem to have pushed the *voci scientifiche* (in his sense) to produce an effect on the reader. While he elsewhere[5] stresses the continuity between ancient and modern, it is along these lines that he distinguishes between them, between Ovid and Dante: "And in the same way Ovid, whose mode of depiction is enumeration (like modern descriptive sentimentalists, etc.), leaves the reader almost nothing to do, whereas Dante, who awakens an image with two words, leaves much for the imagination to do" (*Zibaldone* 57, 2.39).

In Leopardi's own practice the simplicity or "poverty" of his style was achieved through successive manuscript drafts, where characteristically he replaced forceful words with less emphatic ones.[6]

2

This concentration of verbal effect left him free to connect and centralize high points of feeling, the current of "pessimism." This attitude, by refusing to entertain illusion — or its counterpart in hyperbolic diction — was able to bring together the two great Romantic themes, nature and love. Wordsworth deepened the first only, so to speak, by nearly sacrificing the second (and Coleridge remarked interestingly that Wordsworth was incapable of love.) "Lucy" for Wordsworth is a distant object not too different in what she evokes from the Highland lass or the old leech-gatherer. Shelley, who did write about love and also about nature, presents nature only as a sort of backdrop for love, where Leopardi manages to bring both into the feeling of his diffusing sorrow. And where Shelley yearned for Italy and sketched on vast canvasses countries that lay ever further east, this Italian made what was close to home yield a full crop of sentiment — the hillside near his home in "L'Infinito," the field outside his door in "La Ginestra."

Leopardi undercuts the typical Romantic version of the distant *locus amoenus* by putting an Icelander at the Cape of Good Hope ("Dialogo della Natura e di un islandese," 1.114–17), who expresses radical dissatisfaction with all the environments on earth. He imagines a sort of global threshold.

The beloved is conceived powerfully enough to draw charged area after charged area into her orbit:

> Torna dinanzi al mio pensier talora
> Il tuo sembiante, Aspasia. O fuggitivo
> Per abitati lochi a me lampeggia
> In altri volti; o per deserti campi,
> Al dí sereno, alle tacenti stelle,
> Da soave armonia quasi ridesta,
> Nell'alma a sgomentarsi ancor vicina
> Quella superba vision risorge
> . . . .
>
> Raggio divino al mio pensiero apparve,
> Donna, la tua beltà! Simile effetto
> Fan la bellezza e i musicali accordi,
> Ch'alto mistero d'ignorati Elisi
> Paion sovente rivelar.

> There returns before my thought sometimes
> Your likeness, Aspasia. Sometimes fleetingly
> Through places inhabited it shines to me
> In other faces; through deserted fields,
> In the clear day, or under silent stars

As if awakened by sweet harmony,
In my soul already close to being stunned
Does that superb vision rearise
. . . .
A divine ray appears before my thought,
Your loveliness, Lady! A similar effect
Does beauty have, and musical accords
That seem to reveal deep mystery
Of Elysiums unknown.   (*Aspasia*, 1.35)

3

In "Il Risorgimento" (1.25), Leopardi makes explicit the doctrine that corresponds to and partially defines his energy of nostalgic recall. It is one akin to that which Wordsworth made a main source of his own creation. Leopardi reproduces the central notion of the "Ode: Intimations of Immortality from Recollections of Early Childhood."[7] But he scales it down, so to speak; he proverbializes it, investing it with doubt and shading it towards melancholy:

Credei ch'al tutto fossero
In me, sul fior degli anni,
Mancati i dolci affanni
Della mia prima età.

I believed there would wholly be
In me, at the flower of my years,
Lacking the sweet troubles
Of that first age of mine.

The notion is stated baldly, but the feeling behind it is no less powerful. It comes up again in the *Discorsi*, and in his sketch for an autobiography. Like everything else in Leopardi's poetry — like love and like the infinite-yearning response to nature — it partakes of a grave sense that man fulfills himself by being unfulfilled, and that consequently, as the short lines make rhythmically emphatic here, there is no doctrine that can be singled out as the whole basis for other perceptions. Remembrance is a force in "A Silvia" and also in "Le Ricordanze"; the force has the effect of stepping up the yearning of the imagined speaker rather than of providing a comforting explanation for it. Again:

O come grato occorre
nel tempo giovanil, quando ancor lungo
La speme e breve ha la memoria il corso,
Il remembrar delle passate cose,
Ancor che triste, e che l'affanno duri!

How welcome there occurs
in the time of youth, when hope is still
Long and the course of memory is short,
The remembrance of things that are past,
Even sad ones, and those whose distress endures.
                                              ("Alla Luna," 1.18)

Here the exaltation comes as a high moment in the process of thinking. In "A Silvia" the nostalgia is stepped up not only by the long lines
that break the restraint of short ones, but also by the rhetorical delay
of essential information — we are not told that Silvia is dead till the next-
to-last stanza. The act of memory then is brought to focus suddenly after
being lingered over protractedly. What seems to be the appeal of an old
lover — "Silvia, rimembri ancora" — turns out to be the rumination of a
mourner.[8] There is and can be, therefore, no vibrancy of response in the
person so tenderly addressed; Silvia is deaf, being dead, and the rhetoric
places the pall of death over a vividness like that of love, investing the
afterlife with a yearning towards possibility. It becomes a threshold in
spite of itself. Elsewhere, in the "Dialogo di Tristano e di un amico" (1.180–
85), Leopardi places many of his most characteristic ideas in the mouth
of Tristan, who says little or nothing of the love for which his name stands.
"A Silvia" offers no *Liebestod*-fusions, but rather the vigorous evocation
of a feeling so broad as to include love or death, depending on the immediate focus:

Porgea gli orecchi al suon della tua voce
. . . .
Lingua mortal non dice
Quel ch'io sentiva in seno.

I gave my ears to the sound of your voice
. . . .
Mortal tongue cannot tell
What I felt in my breast.   ("A Silvia," 1.26)

Once expressed, the sentiments have the air of commonplace. On the
evidence, they are not so; no one is just like Leopardi in the way that
others are like Musset or Schiller. In the "Dialogo d'Ercole e di Atlante,"
Hercules has let the earth fall and nobody on it has noticed that he did so.

And the sentiments may also seem casual. But that they are not so appears in the restraint of the poems, and also in Leopardi's fairly low es-
timate of Byron, who seems to him arbitrary and unsuccessful precisely
in his delineation of feeling (*Zibaldone* 226; 2.100–101) when he calls attention to feeling in a self-defeating way: "The poor lord sweats and ex-
erts himself so that every least phrase, every least juncture, may be origi-

nal and new." Leopardi contrasts this procedure unfavorably with Goethe's in *Werther* (*Zibaldone* 261; 2.111). But as he himself says in the significantly titled "Il Pensiero Dominante":

> E tu per certo, o mio pensier, tu solo
> Vitale ai giorni miei,
> Cagion diletta d'infiniti affanni,
> Meco sarai per morte a un tempo spento.   (1.33)

> And you for sure, my thought, you alone
> Vital to my days,
> Delightful cause of infinite distress,
> Will be extinguished with me some day by death.

Thought alone is vital to his days, the cause, itself single, of infinite desires, and therefore unsensationally present in the death this very process may be taken to imply. The attention, the traces of aspiration, the orientation of this speaker can already, without exaggeration, be called pre-Heideggerian.

4

In the "Storia del Genere Umano" (1.79–85), men are created alike and bored with this condition; "Jupiter" then differentiates them, and they are delighted, but gradually they come to feel *tedio*. The poems of Leopardi follow this fable, coming to terms with tedium by recreating conditions in which it is at once realized and wakefully resisted. The agency for the realization is a lyric poetry, which Leopardi declares to be the superlative kind of superlative human speech, in a statement that anticipates Heidegger's deductions from Hölderlin: "Lyric can call itself the peak, the height, the summit of poetry, which is the summit of human discourse" (Zibaldone 245; 2.106).

His poems, as he reached his mature expression, lean more emphatically on the alternation of long and short lines than do the *Rime* of Petrarch, which he edited. In his hands this alternation becomes an instrument that breaks and rises to fullness, breaks and again rises, the terminal line being always a full one. Even in poems of constant hendecasyllables, like "L'Infinito," a version of this effect is gained by the resolution of caesurae before the final line, turning that classic terminal resource to an affirmative where *dolce* predominates over *naufragar*:

> Sempre caro mi fu quest'ermo colle,
> E questa siepe, che da tanta parte
> Dell'ultimo orizzonte il guardo esclude.
> Ma sedendo e mirando, interminati

Spazi di là da quella, e sovrumani
Silenzi, e profondissima quiete
Io nel pensier mi fingo; ove per poco
Il cor non si spaura. E come il vento
Odo stormir tra queste piante, io quello
Infinito silenzio a questa voce
Vo comparando: e mi sovvien l'eterno,
E le morte stagioni, e la presente
E viva, e il suon di lei. Cosí tra questa
Immensità s'annega il pensier mio:
E il naufragar m'è dolce in questo mare.   (1.17)

Ever dear to me was this lone hill,
And this shrubbery that on every side
Shuts out the ultimate horizon's view.
As I sit and gaze I fashion interminable
Spaces across the distance and superhuman
Silences and a quiet most profound
In my thought, until my heart is very close
To taking fright. And just as the wind
I hear rage among these plants, I start
Comparing that infinite silence to this voice
And the eternal comes to aid my memory,
And the dead seasons, and the present one,
Which lives, and the sound of it. And so in this
Immensity my thought drowns itself:
And shipwreck to me is sweet in this sea.

This poem begins by speaking of a view that is shut out by shrubbery and then imagined, much as does Coleridge's "This Lime-Tree Bower My Prison." On such a threshold absence and presence both define the actual situation, while the rhythms keep the aspiration of the voice aimed forward.

From the fourth line on, for nine lines, not only does every line enjamb until the colon at the end of the fourteenth; every line except the ninth contains a caesura that is a more marked pause than the (enjambed) line-ending. The process follows the recapitulations of the *pensier* that is the only important noun repeated in the poem, except for *silenzio*. There are near synonyms and related words for each, *mirando, odo, comparando* comprising moments in *pensier* while *quiete*, repeating *silenzio*, is given the longest word in the poem as a qualifier, *profondissima*. This word, in turn, as a superlative, belongs to the large cluster of "absolutes" in the poem: *sempre, tanta, ultimo, interminati, sovrumani, infinito, l'eterno, immensità*. Cumulatively they mime the inundation that the unbroken last line rhythmically expands to name. *Dolce* seems more important than *naufragar,* not only because of its central position in the line but also because the reader is finally accorded the satisfaction of resolution after so many short, breathless, suspensions. He is like a tired swimmer finally with relief going under. Some strange process is at work in which a word normally used of ships, *naufragar,* may be applied to a human being — only partially applied by a sort of metonymy, since the imagination would have to supply a vessel in which to be shipwrecked. However, the verb is present — *è,* "is," and not "would be"— as though in some way the act of uttering the poem has already amounted to ship-wrecking, a suggestion heightened by the immediacy of the last modi-fier, *questo —* "*this* sea"— when he has begun by saying that the scene is not visible.

The poem follows Leopardi's general practice of gradual climax. So in "Le Ricordanze" the series of apostrophes comprising general words presented in broken rhythms crests in the naming, and thereby the sug-gestion of "arcana / Felicità":

> E che pensieri immensi,
> Che dolci sogni mi spirò la vista
> Di quel lontano mar, quei monti azzurri,
> Che di qua scoprò, e che varcare un giorno
> Io mi pensava, arcani mondi, arcana
> Felicità fingendo al viver mio!

> And what immense thoughts,
> What sweet dreams, did the sight inspire in me
> Of that distant sea, those azure mountains,
> That I discern from here, and thought one day
> That I would cross, arcane worlds, arcane
> Felicity fashioning for my life!

Immensi, dolci, spirò, lontano mar, azzurri, scopro, giorno, pensava, mondo, arcana, felicità, fingendo, viver, mio — we are back in the word-florilegium of "L'Infinito." The thought crests, and crests again, and crests again, unwearied in facing its own weariness. The landscape is conceived as a threshold the speaker longs to cross.

There is negative concession or preterition in the very opening of this longish poem:[9] "Vaghe stelle dell'orsa, io non credea / Tornare ancor per uso a contemplarvi" ("Vague stars of the Bear, I did not believe / I would ever return to the habit of contemplating you") — but this is just what he is doing. He is there returning to contemplate these stars as they twinkle over his father's garden. He moves between vagueness and pre-cision, just as the first word of this poem does, since it can mean either "vague" or "wandering," as well as "beautiful." The second sense, the precise one, is itself applied somewhat imprecisely, since the constellation does not exactly wander but rather moves through fixed positions in the heavens. The word that literally translated from the Greek means "wandering star"— as the professional classicist Leopardi certainly knew — is *planet*, the opposite of the fixed stars in the constellation of the Great Bear.

Vaghe, then, the first word of "Le Ricordanze," opens it on a strong and yet evasive tonic note. Having said that the stars are vague and beautiful as well as wandering, the poet can wander through an exploration of what may be evoked through a scene of remembrance and the topic of memory generally. For Leopardi is willing to invest almost the whole poetic effect into a kind of vagueness and indefiniteness of diction: "Not only elegance, but nobility, grandeur, all the qualities of poetic language, even poetic language itself, consists, if I observe it well, in a mode of speaking that is indefinite and not well defined, or always less defined than prosaic or vulgar speech" (*Zibaldone* 1900–1901; 1.517).

Between the fixed and the wandering, the mind of the speaker takes account of a sentiment at once vague and precise, thinking back to his life as a boy and the end of his joys: "ove abitai fanciullo, / E delle gioie mie vidi la fine" ("Where I lived as a boy / And of my joys I saw the end"). In its rhythm and its diction, as in the doctrine it espouses, the poem succeeds in diffusing its sorrow by staying triumphantly sub-Wordsworthian. "Le Ricordanze" are only what may be evoked in a comprehensive look at the evening landscape under the stars. And yet there is a concentration. In the drafts (*abbozzi*) of "L'Infinito," there is a Petrarchan green laurel tree covering a large part of the horizon, which disappears in the final poem, along with the leaves of some plants (1.73).

5

For Leopardi even *naufragar* is *dolce*. We are beyond the Romantic agony. The sorrow is so diffuse in its confrontation of the infinite that it shades into joy, without simply delectating in sorrow. Joy, *allegrezza*, Leopardi declares to be a necessary component of poetry (*Zibaldone* 205; 2.93). And of the hovering between sentiments in "La Ginestra" he says, "I do not know if laughter or pity prevails" (1.44). It is the infinite in love that brings pleasure to men (*Zibaldone* 1017–18; 2.295–96). And melancholy is powerless without an aura: "the imagination and even the sensibility that is the melancholic does not have force without an aura of prosperity, and without a vigor of spirit that cannot stand without a twilight ray, a gleam of happiness" (*Zibaldone* 136; 2.69).

Poetry, through its strategy of sending the indefinite in pursuit of feelings aimed at the infinite, avoids the trap of thought-definitions already characterized in the early ode *Ad Angelo Mai*:

> Ecco tutto è simile, e discoprendo.
> Solo il nulla s'accresce.   (1.8)
>
> Behold all is alike, and as it appears.
> Only nothing increases.

The process of being disappointed by an image also manages to transcend the confusion of disappointment:

> Che la illibata, la candida imago
> Turbare egli [l'occhio] temea pinta nel seno
> come all'aure si turba onda di lago.
>
> That it [the eye] feared to stir up the innocent
> And shining image depicted in my breast
> As the wave of a lake is stirred up in the breezes.
> (*Il Primo Amore*, 1.16)

Dante's *lago del cor* (*Inferno*, 1.20), as well as Dante's meter, has been taken over and made the locus of a never-ending dynamic process of perception. Poetry, and art generally, Leopardi says, aims at truth, not beauty ("Non il Bello ma il Vero o sia l'imitazione della Natura qualunque, si è l'oggetto delle Belle arti"; *Zibaldone* 2; 2.3). It takes, in effect, its subject at the point where the true philosopher feels discontent at the incompleteness of his reasonings: "Nessun maggior segno d'essere poco filosofo è poco savio che volere savia e filosofica tutta la vita" (*Pensieri* XXVII; 1.224). But all life is what the poet might try to express, just because the sentiment he feels in a natural setting (*una campagna*) inspires vague and indefinite ideas of the highest delight, as though one were chasing a butterfly without catching it.[10]

And yet, on the other hand, as he says in "Amore e Morte":

> Quando novellamente
> Nasce nel cor profondo
> Un amoroso affetto,
> Languido e stanco insiem con esso in petto
> Un desiderio di morir si sente.   (1.33)
>
> When newly
> There is born deep in the heart
> An amorous affection,
> At once languid and tired in the breast,
> A desire to die is felt.

The desire for a fullness of sentiment is powerful enough to shade over almost instantly from love to death, and without any morbidity. The terms themselves are comprehensive in their psychology, and they delineate a sequence: a precise, if comprehensive, effect.

There is a kind of hidden paradox here between goal and procedure and in the use of understatement and indefiniteness in a poetry that aims at unvarnished truth-telling. Images and terms in the language here are not adornments but instruments towards bodying forth something like a complete description.

The act of moving towards silent apprehension itself enjoins silence, as in the *silenzi* and *quiete* of "L'Infinito." Or, as he says in "La Sera del Dì di Festa":

> tutto è pace e silenzio e tutto posa
> Il mondo, e più di lor non si ragiona.   (1.17)
>
> all is peace and silence, and the whole
> World rests, and there is no more talk of them.

These poems achieve an air of having totalized experience by going through the thought process of coming up, in repeated attempts, to name such a totality.

Such a process stands behind "La Ginestra," the proleptically or synecdochally significant broom plant toughly and heedlessly growing outside the poet's door in a beautiful landscape right beside a volcano:

> Qui su l'arida schiena
> Del formidabil monte
> Sterminator Vesevo,
> La qual null'altro allegra arbor né fiore,
> Tuoi cespi solitari intorno spargi,
> Odorata ginestra,
> Contenta dei deserti. Anco ti vidi
> De' tuoi steli abbellir l'erme contrade
> Che cingon la cittade.   (1.42)
>
> Here on the arid spine
> Of the fearful mountain,
> The exterminator Vesuvius,
> To which no other tree or flower gives joy,
> You scatter your solitary tufts about,
> Odorous broom plant,
> Patient in deserts. So I saw you
> With stalks embellish the lone countryside
> That girds the city.

The poem must be taken with the epigraph from John 3.19 that immediately precedes this opening: "Men loved darkness rather than light." So seen, the broom plant is first addressed as a contrast to human activity, an implicit counter-example rather than an analogy to the human condition. Plants seek the light rather than shun it, as this Biblical passage says men do. And plants beautify the desert. However, the analogy is also present: it can be said that man, too, is like a tough plant growing on the side of a volcano, since the line that follows emphasizes the brief life and the unexpected end of the city: "la qual fu donna de' mortali un tempo" ("who was mistress of mortals for a time"); and the word *donna*, here denotes "rule" (whereas the humble broom plant rules nothing, like the "uom di povero stato e membra inferme" later on). *Donna* also raises all the associations around the word *donna*, a desirable woman from Dante on. The verb *abbellir*, applied to the broom plant, is not to be divorced from the *contrade* and the *cittade*: it is that which the broom plant beautifies. So that the analogy, subtly, begins to work against the contrast, creating, again, the vagueness and indefiniteness that Leopardi has insisted is the proper means for poetry.

As the poem gathers force the analogy emerges into an emphasized predominance:

> Depinte in queste rive
> Son dell'umana gente
> *Le magnifiche sorti e progressive.*

> Depicted on these slopes
> Are the human race's
> *Magnificent and progressive destinies.*

Here Leopardi employs the italics he scorns Byron for using so frequently. Irony establishes the analogy; man claims the italicized definition that could differentiate him from the broom plant, but is thrown back by catastrophe into that humble state. The immediate reference of the lines here, however, is not to the broom plant on these slopes, but to the ruined cities, Herculaneum and Pompeii. The landscape here contains traces of history as well as analogies to men: the process has become more involved: it is irreducible either to a nature mystique or to a rhetorical meditation on transience, allowing in its vagueness for both, and for an emotion that comprises both:

> Or tutto intorno
> Una ruina involve,
> Dove tu siedi, o fior gentile, e quasi
> I danni altrui commiserando, al cielo
> Di dolcissimo odor mandi un profumo,
> Che il deserto consola.

> Now one ruin
> Comprises everything

Where you are sitting, gentle flower, and as though
Feeling sorry for the hurts of others, to the sky
You send of sweetest odor a perfume
That would console the desert.

The pathetic fallacy is broached but only grazed: the broom plant is "*quasi* . . . commiserando," and it is for the observer that the plant sends a most sweet odor to the sky; it consoles the desert *for him*. Again the ideal landscape of classical tradition and such Romantics as Shelley has been subverted by stubborn natural fact: no *locus amoenus*, but a tough plant growing in a *deserto*. In one sense, then, Leopardi illustrates his own epigraph: he loves the darkness of his example more than an ideal light, and men do build on the side of Vesuvius where he is living. But then he transcends it: he finds light even there. And he manages to fuse all these possibilities into a single expressive sequence "La Ginestra." The act of diffusing sorrow accommodates sorrow to an indomitably energetic perception.

6

Stendhal
The Discovery of Ironic Interplay

1

Irony, by inverting the normal constative thrust of language, throws into question the normally neutral link between auditor and speaker. Thereby it intensifies that link through a constant testing, implicitly orienting it towards a future. In this way the posture of Stendhal may be said to look ahead, and to ground itself, on bases resembling those of the Romantic poets I have been discussing. At its most sublime, when it pervades an achieved work, irony involves a sort of infinite regress, and for that reason, as Schlegel asserted, it suggests the infinite. Schlegel as a theoretician saw both early and late the powerful possibilities for expression that lay to hand in the ironic procedure.[1] The relation between the infinite regress and ironic procedure may imply, and the persistent indefiniteness of the bearing in an ironic work neatly capitulate and articulate, the Romantic connection between the infinite and the indefinite.[2]

As de Man well says, irony is the trope of tropes, comprising as it does a conflation of the relations between the topological and the performative systems.[3] We need not, however, rest with de Man's genius for stressing the deconstructive dimension of literary procedures; Schlegel's "eine permanente Parekbase," subjecting irony to temporality, need not be taken, as Schlegel would not have taken it, in an exclusively negative way. Rather, in its positive dimension it permits the sort of dialectic in which Stendhal implicitly engages. We may side with Starobinski and Peter Szondi, as against de Man, and see that irony in such as Stendhal, or for that matter in Hoffman and Kierkegaard, is a "preliminary movement towards a recovered unity, as a reconciliation of the self with the world by means of art." The death through illusion of Julien Sorel, through Stendhal's ironic interplay, is made to expand at once the sympathy and the distance of the reader. Locking into that temporal series of interactive disillusionments also affords a key to the lock.[4] The procedure at its best is comprehensive enough to resist metaphoric containment, as in René Bourgeois's notion of 'theatre.'[5]

"Trope of tropes" though it be, irony does not just present the limits of a self-trapping dialectic of assertion against counter-assertion. By moving the quick of linguistic expression into this constant tension, by triggering an "absolute comedy,"[6] it contains its own self-transcendence. Such a movement is explicit in Blake, who again and again transmutes ironic postures and leaves them behind. He has moved to another plane, as the constant hyperbole of his allegorical beings, themselves in constant transmutation, constantly advertises: irony, as Beda Allemann says, contains the capacity of broadening itself and elevating itself into a poetic withness-to-the-world (dichterisches In-der-Welt-Sein).[7]

2

All this was very new at the beginning of the nineteenth century. Plato's ironic practice, comparably profound, is aimed clearly at abstract questions only.[8] Not Schlegel, not Kierkegaard, and not Nietzsche, can turn Plato to Romantic uses without markedly distorting him.

Stendhal's ultimate rapidity of narration and nervous collocation of events betray a tense urgency to reconcile what in the deep currents of the time were opposed feelings. He finally learned, after many efforts, to tauten a narrative so that it could at once analyze and enhance the trembling on the brink felt by a protagonist who is both a lover and a highly risking aspirant. The gradualness of Stendhal's development well points up his transition from a sort of eighteenth-century wit-dominated dilettantism to the full play of his self-discovered version of Romantic Irony.

It did take Stendhal a long time, not only to hit his stride but to feel it at all. Novelists are often late starters, and yet when the brilliant school mathematician came to Paris with the ambition of becoming a great world writer, it was not the novel especially that led him on. Anything but. Then it was the drama, and a plethora of false starts in criticism, in this or that autobiographical attempt, in travel writing, and at last in a treatise on love. He arrived in Paris, as he repeatedly tells us, on the eve of the Eighteenth Brumaire in 1799; if we count most of his work of the late twenties as still practice; it was a good thirty years till he hit his full stride in *Le Rouge et le noir,* completing that novel with his finally characteristic speed while the Revolution of 1830 was coming to a head.

What enabled Stendhal at last to attain his characteristic expression, I should like to show, was marshalling his ideological conflicts to produce a powerful and dominant ironic interplay. In the process of this demonstration, having analyzed elsewhere the contrastive force of his irony of event and its implicit ability to generate potentially infinite pairs of contradictions,[9] I should like to take a long look at the range of ideals and feelings that the irony he thereby discovered can be made to cover, and at the implications in the contrasts his irony engenders. It is in *Le Rouge et le noir* that Stendhal's irony enters into full interplay, harnessing a dazzling capacity to hold incommensurables uneasily but lucidly in the same purview while deploying them along the temporal sequences of a narrative line. ("Le roman, c'est un miroir qu'on promène le long d'un chemin" — an epigraph used precisely in this novel.)

Take the point at which Julien Sorel has just been locked in his death cell. He continues all his speculations full-blast, exhibiting a strangely languid suspension over his motives for the murder attempt upon his motherly mistress, between love and ambition, and also between that earlier mistress and the younger, aristocratic one whom he had, he convinced himself, approached coldly out of calculating ambition. The irony moves easily over the at once momentous and trivial disproportionateness of fantasizing a last interview with the beloved he will shortly lose in the guillotine: he is imagining what he can say to Madame de Rênal to explain shooting her in the church. "After such an act, how to persuade her that I love her alone? For finally I have wished to kill her from ambition, or from love for Mathilde." ("Après une telle action, comment lui persuader que je l'aime uniquement? Car enfin j'ai voulu la tuer par ambition ou par amour pour Mathilde.") Three incommensurable alternatives are here held in ironic suspension. From them he moves idly on not just to thoughts of the guillotine, but to Danton's joke about the lack of a first person past tense for the verb *guillotiner.* The implicit and disproportionate comparison between this impulsive provincial admirer of Napoleon and the great revolutionary statesman is itself framed in another set of values by being recalled as part of a conversation between Julien and a Count Altamira whose title and Italianate name suggest at once the trivial salons where Mathilde de la Mole was an opportunity and the whole world of proportionate *ancien régime* witticism. That world is itself primed on a callousness that belies its elegance, as Julien is repeatedly made to observe. This is notably the case for the actual character Count Altamira, who is the victim of that world; he is a tall, pious, liberal Jansenist heedless of religious-hypocritical money-grubbing and condemned to death in his own country. In fact, it was while assiduously eavesdropping at a ballroom conversation between the condemned Altamira and a Julien in whom she senses the air of future condemnation that Mathilde, seeking relief from her boring marital prospects of endless aristocratic pleasure, had first pointedly fixed on Julien. The ironic interplay keeps suggesting the possibility of resolving all these contradictions by its very exuberance in producing fresh ones.

This former seminarian had earlier fantasized the priesthood as the proper post-Napoleonic route and had been shipped into training for it by the revelation of his first affair. Now he goes on to reflect that one might well in the afterlife be able to say "j'ai été guillotiné." Then he contrasts the despotic "Christian" God with that of Fénelon, the pre-Enlightenment sentimentalist admired by the Napoleonic apologist for Christianity, Chateaubriand, whom Stendhal himself found *ridicule*:[10]

> But if I meet the God of Fénelon! He will say to me perhaps: Much shall be pardoned thee, because thou hast loved much. . . .
> Have I loved much? Ah! I did love Madame de Rênal, but my conduct has been atrocious. There, as elsewhere, I abandoned a simple and modest merit for what is brilliant. . . .
> But then too, what a prospect! Colonel of Hussars, should we go to war; Secretary of Legation in time of peace; after that, Ambassador . . . for I should soon have learned the business . . . and had I been a mere fool, need the son-in-law of the Marquis de la Mole fear any rival? All my foolish actions would have been forgiven me, or rather counted to me as merits. A man of distinction, enjoying the most splendid existence in Vienna or London. . . .
> Not precisely that, Sir, to be guillotined in three days' time.
> Julien laughed heartily at this sally of his own wit. In truth, man has two different beings in him, he thought. Who the devil dreamt up that malicious reflection?[11] (Translation mine, based on that of Moncrieff)

In imagining that Fénelon would say "tu as beaucoup aimé," Julien is not only bringing his love or loves into the perspective of a soft religion by vague Biblical echoes of the "woman who loved much" (Luke 7.47), a woman traditionally identified with Mary Magdalene. Since Julien repeatedly shows that he knows the New Testament literally by heart, he may be thought of as himself making the analogy, and thereby continuing his extravagance. Yet he belies the analogy at once here by career speculations whereby a Romantic-Napoleonic career dimly blends with a pre-Revolutionary tinge of "jouissant de la plus grande existence à Vienne ou à Londres." Such a high-living aristocratic *jouissance* is not exactly coordinate with the Napoleonic glory. But both are ironically belied by the circumstances at which he immediately laughs—not at his foolishness but at his inventiveness. The laugh thereby blends self-mockery with self-adulation, and leads to the quasi-Goethean reflection "l'homme a deux êtres en lui."[12] All this is qualified by the overweening "Great Expectations" of which he half accuses himself. Julien, a brilliantly correct calculator in a ridiculously inappropriate situation, is subjected to an interplay in which mockery and admiration are ironically played off against each other. "Le mérite simple et modeste" and "ce qui est brillant" comment on each other, and Stendhal's own tone plays fast and loose with a comment on those comments, as well as on their contradiction.

The flow of thoughts, returning always to execution, exhausts Julien. On awakening (less than half a page further on), he is brought up short by seeing Mathilde instead of the executioner, the very apparition that had started the flow of thoughts. This time she is really there. Taking comfort in her *incomprehension*, he is off again, and they ride a series of small but contradictory responses, between incomprehension and love, fury and being dry-eyed, and so on, as indicated by the italics:

> A good answer, he thought, and fell asleep. Someone woke him in the morning by shaking him violently.
>
> What, already! said Julien, opening a haggard eye. He imagined himself to be in the hands of the executioner.
>
> It was Mathilde. *Fortunately, she did not understand me. This reflection restored all his calm.* He found Mathilde changed as though after six months of illness: she was positively unrecognizable.
>
> That wretch Frilair has betrayed me, she said to him, wringing her hands; *rage prevented her from crying.*
>
> Was I not fine yesterday when I rose to speak? replied Julien. I was improvising, and for the first time in my life! It is true that there is reason to fear it may also be the last.
>
> *At this moment Julien was playing upon Mathilde's nature with all the calm of a skilled pianist touching the keys of a piano.* . . . The advantage of noble birth I lack, it is true, he went on, but the great soul of Mathilde has raised her lover to her own level. Do you suppose that Boniface de La Mole cut a better figure before his judges?
>
> Mathilde, that day, was tender without affectation, like any poor girl dwelling in an attic; but she could not win from him any simpler speech. *He paid her back, unconsciously, for the torment that she had often inflicted on him.*
>
> We do not know the sources of the Nile, Julien said to himself; it has not been granted to the eye of man to behold the King of Rivers in the form of a simple brook: so no human eye shall ever see

Julien weak, if only because he is not weak. But I have a heart that is easily moved; the most commonplace words, if they are uttered with an accent of truth, may soften my voice and even make my tears flow. How often have not the dry hearts despised me for this defect! They believed that I was begging for mercy: that is what I cannot endure . . . one may become learned, one may become skillful, but the heart! . . . The heart cannot be taught.[13]

Both lovers are carried along by reactions to the dominant but at once erroneous and impulsive ideas of Julien, whose very coldness leads him to congratulate himself on his susceptibility. Here and earlier we are notably shown the randomness with which he exploits the eighteenth-century Laclos-like calculations that a Russian prince had schooled him in. The randomness of these calculations takes from them all but their naked incongruity before Romantic impulsiveness. This process keeps breaking down the very class barriers, in her and in himself, that he imagines he has been skirting. In truth "Le coeur ne s'apprend pas," and in one sense there has been no *Bildung* in this *Bildungsroman*; in another sense, nothing else. Its experience offers, to Julien and to us, a perpetual threshold. This relationship, so tenuously and conflictingly sustained, will finally break down as at the end Mathilde's presence becomes an intrusive annoyance before his last prison visits from the older, earlier mistress.

To the very end Julien is made ironically to teeter in confusion between codes that are somehow interfused here, though Stendhal had kept them rigorously separate, and rationalistically codified in themselves, in *De l'amour*: the *amour-goût* and also the *amour-vanité*, which may be associated with the eighteenth-century world view of aristocratic Epicureanism, as against the *amour-passion* of the nineteenth-century Romantic exaltation of the infinite. The former codes Stendhal, like Julien, admired; to the latter he was subjected through much of his life. While Stendhal was struck by his encounter with the aged General Laclos, whom he ran across one evening in the Milan opera,[14] he at no point tried to reproduce the achievement of *Liaisons dangereuses*; such control was within the reach of his admiration, but not of his temperament. He could use the eighteenth-century vanity-calculus of pleasure only as a whole element for recombination; its ironies had to be resubjected to a further, transcendent irony. And the heady mix of the combination, first fully exemplified in his work in *Le Rouge et le noir*, causes him to create what Balzac characterizes as a literature of ideas,[15] something beyond the abstract distinction-maintenance of the *idéologie* of the philosopher Destutt de Tracy, whom Stendhal admired and from whom he borrowed the term to characterize the enterprise of *De l'amour*.

Le Rouge et le noir, the title, offers a simple antithesis in expression. The terms schematize as well as emblematize one set of contradictory elements, the religion (black) and the politics (red) that serve contradictorily both to further and to undo Julien. Since the hazard of the Stendhalian plot's open direction[16] is involved, red and black may also signify a roulette wheel, and possibly also love and death. But all these ironic antitheses are themselves ironically skewed from the central ones with which the novel really concerns itself: ambition versus love, *amour-goût* versus the *amour-passion* into which it changes, the provincial, maternal, adulterous beloved versus the aristocratic, Parisian, obsessive one, over whom she prevails but against whom she does not win out.

The eighteenth-century code of love amounts to the formulation of Mathilde's father to Julien, "One should amuse oneself. . . . That's the only real thing in life,"[17] a statement that tries to draw a metaphysical conclusion as well as to enunciate a premise. This code of *amour-goût* founds itself on pride, on caste, and on the dexterities of experience; whereas the nineteenth-century code of the grand passion, of course, glories in just the opposite of these qualities: in self-sacrifice, in equality, and in the sublimity of innocence.

Almost all Stendhal's Romantic predecessors and contemporaries either retire in despair before the impossibility of the romantic life, like the authors of *Werther, Confessions d'un enfant du siècle, La Nouvelle Héloise,* and *Wuthering Heights,*[18] or else they extend a version of eighteenth-century analytic codification into the slightly different shadings of passion, like Benjamin Constant, Jane Austen, and (a bit later) Trollope. Stendhal, who aimed his *Souvenirs d'egotisme* at "un être tel que Mme. Roland ou M. Gros, le géomètre"[19] — at a sublime lover embroiled in politics or at a liberal mathematician who also figures as a minor character in *Le Rouge et le noir* — manages to keep the fine-meshed sequences of *marivaudage* in balance with the delineated passion of his lover. He lays bare, as a follower of Laclos, the laws of power and jealousy, all the while activating a set of Romantic laws at once weaker than the others and predominant over them. The force of his irony constantly acts to suspend the incommensurability of the two systems, while letting them interact so as to generate the explosive and decisive events of his novel.

Such an interplay is too complex for the novelist's analysis, but not for his presentation. The irony keeps it going by shifting viewpoint, like a mirror along a highway. It would oversimplify just as much to divorce Stendhal from his characters as to identify him with them. M. de la Mole's pleasure principle, "il faut s'amuser," is not rejected; indeed, Julien's fate may be said to confirm it. M. de la Mole is a sort of Count Mosca without the Achilles heel of love. And yet, at the same time, the fate of his own daughter undermines his pleasure principle, as do the political intrigues, at once daring and small-mindedly sordid, with which he occupies himself, earning at once the contempt and the admiration of the ex-seminarian crypto-Bonapartist in his household. This post of secretary, indeed, like Julien's earlier post of tutor, at once affirms the caste system of the eighteenth century by assigning Julien a hierarchical place and undermines it with implicit nineteenth-century egalitarianism. Someone who is not by blood a member of the family or by birth a member of its caste is introduced into the family on terms that, with the help of eighteenth-as well as nineteenth-century ideals, will serve to activate a Freudian dynamic of identification that plays fast and loose with the exclusion-inclusion of the interloper-member.

"For Julien, as for posterity, there was nothing between Arcoli, Saint Helena, and Malmaison."[20] The reference to posterity makes this a judgment on Stendhal's part as well as an observation; he at once mocks and shares Julien's exaltation of Napoleon. At the same time, it is while borrowing volumes of Voltaire on the sly from her father's library that Mathilde first encounters the Julien whose special privilege of quasi-adoption is marked by his being permitted to work there, as the other secretary, who unsuccessfully jockeys for this same advantage, is not.

Byron, who often serves to provide epigraphs here, in fact falls short of so dexterous and comprehensive a combination. The jaunty cynicism of *Don Juan* carries him away towards *amour-vanité* and *amour-goût*. This aristocrat's romanticism is more a self-indulgence, seducing the world by its narcissism, than a clarification. In Stendhal the ironic balance works to clarify as well as to suspend everything. Even provinciality has two sides, not only in the nineteenth-century code, where innocence takes on positive value, but even by the kind of analysis that intensifies love by delaying it. At Paris the position of Madame de Rênal and Julien would have been *simplified* (not complicated) — thanks to novels. Stendhal's irony opens possibilities and balances divergences, unlike the "froide ironie" of the imaginary Parisian[21] whose act of definition would have awakened Julien and so excluded him from the joys of *amour-passion*.

3

Without speculating on the reasons, we can see the results developing in Stendhal over the very decade he singles out as crucial in the *Souvenirs d'egotisme* (1832), 1821–1830, as he successfully returns to autobiographical writing — after several false starts from 1822 on — once his special and capital literary development has confirmed itself without his conscious inspection.

The massive shift of the decade was triggered by his break with Métilde Dembrowska, on the heels of which in 1819 he abandoned his beloved Milan, gravitating towards Paris, abandoning also the journal he had been keeping for twenty years, closing its thousand pages with a reference to her in English ("you love not me") and to the shame of garrulity ("Hier, trop parlé, beaucoup trop").[22]

His first literary project thereupon, a novel aimed at as well as titled for her, the *Roman de Métilde*, while it already contained both his characteristic subject matter and his preoccupations of attitude, lacked, as his writing would continue for some time to lack, the splendid ironic interplay without which he would be a mere miniaturist chronicler of particular social shadings. As though to repeat the self-accusation of garrulity, substantiated by the doodle-like notes scribbled every which way on the manuscript title page, he stopped it short, inscribing "fin du roman" on the unfinished work, whose linearity is lucid without special distinctiveness:

> And yet this victim, this Poloski who was so envied, was almost as unhappy as the duchess. Only for an instant had he been near the young Bianca. He was always before her in a violent state: plunged into silence; and then it seemed to him that all eyes were reading his love in his eyes—, or, if he wanted to say something, the fire that was devouring him passed into his words and gave them almost the traits of madness. It was that, of all traits, that was most designed to shock the countess.[23]

Here we have all his later elements — the faintly ridiculous melancholy lover (described elsewhere as an admirer of Napoleon), silent before his equally melancholy beloved in a crowded salon, later described as acting the madman in a way that would most shock the woman he most wanted to impress. The irony operates in the portrayal, and in such terms as *victime*. But it has not learned to harness any interplay; there is no crackling of incongruities, only the fixed attitude of the narrator. Only Beylists, the already committed, could find in such narration what they would have brought to it before the fact, the coruscations of the later great writer.

What he abruptly abandoned this trial run for was something again aimed explicitly at Métilde, in the critical vein he had already practiced and was to launch himself in Paris with, an abstract treatise on love punctuated with anecdotes: *De l'amour*. Early on in this work, too, he devotes a whole, short chapter to the desirability of that quality of dryness, of being *sec*, which in the prison passage quoted above he ironically has Julien blame on the *coeurs secs* who would blame him. As yet Stendhal just brings it to bear on the inexpressibility of what he feels crowding in on him for expression:

> I make every possible effort to be *dry* [*sec* — his emphasis]. I want to impose silence on my heart, which believes it has much to say. I am always trembling that I may have written down only a sigh when I believe I have registered a truth.[24]

This (quite accurate) sense of insufficiency in expression continues to plague him. Rereading the work in the middle, he registers that he has given a very poor idea of love (p. 137). He imagines (p. 180) that one kills reverie and imagination by noting them down. And he asks his steady correspondent early on to eradicate from the work that which is *"ridicule* [his italics]. . . . le faux, l'exagéré, l'obscur."[25]

The anecdotes he incorporates, even when he amplifies them, do not manage to start the play he can retrospectively be said to be desperately seeking. A whole chapter devoted to it (52) does not rescue from dryness the troubadour story of Cabestan and the beloved who dashed herself to death rather than eat again after her husband had fed her the lover's heart. In the anecdotes of *De l'amour* observation is occasionally present:

> Miss Cornel, a famous London actress, saw the rich colonel who was helpful to her enter her salon unexpectedly one day. She happened to be in the company of a small-scale (*petit*) lover whom she found only pleasant. Mr. X, she said, all flustered, to the colonel, came to look at the pony I have for sale. I am here for an entirely different reason, answered proudly this small-scale lover who was beginning to bore her and with whom after this reply she fell furiously in love all over again.[26]

But the observation cannot operate for combinatory revelation: it immediately detaches itself for illustration before it can take over the irony and stretch the perspective. This is true even as late as 1825, in *Ernestine,* a tale that remains merely illustrative. This is in fact the purpose Stendhal announces at the end of the tale, that it has shown us a soul who has run through the seven steps of *De l'amour* from indifference to passion (p. 500). Irony serves merely to trigger a surprise ending: the lover-suitor is declared to be prevented by the author from marrying the beloved for abandoning an overripe mistress. Again, in the thick of Stendhalian concerns, no livening comes about:

> He went there thirty-three days in a row without seeing Ernestine; she appeared at the church no more; they said mass at the castle; he approached in disguise, and twice he had the pleasure of

seeing Ernestine. In his eyes nothing could equal the expression of her features, at once noble and naive. He said to himself: "With such a woman I would never experience surfeit." That which touched Astézan most was Ernestine's extreme pallor and her ailing air. I could write ten volumes like Richardson if I were to undertake to register all the ways a man—who, it should be said, did not lack sense and experience—explained Ernestine's swooning and her sadness.[27]

But the eighteenth-century sentimentalism of Richardson, even elaborated into "dix volumes," could never catch the interplay on which Stendhal is still only verging. Once again the circumstances are all there, and the attitude seems fully formed. All that is missing—it is everything—is the interaction of the elements.

It is, I am asserting, the juxtaposition of ideological contraries, which are prior to tone and style, and not the other way around, insofar as one can assign priorities. Something like proof resides in passages like these, where the tone and the style by which we recognize, or believe we recognize, Stendhal, are present, but to no avail. One can say of him here what he says of himself, "Mes jugements ne sont que des aperçus."[28]

Soon a discovered angling of his narrative will give a judgmental force to the *aperçus*. Till then, he can only react, back to the love affair rather than ahead to the achievement that will finally transcend it by incorporating it fully: he will merely have tears in his eyes while correcting the proofs of *De l'amour*[29] or else all but go mad correcting them.[30] Only when he strikes his keynote can he find a place in his plot for the beloved clutching the severed head, the final vision of Julien's head in the hands of Mathilde echoing his own persistent vision of Métilde: he saw her features in the Salome with the head of John the Baptist of Luini's that he believed to be Leonardo's. Until then, as he much later says with only partial retrospective truth, "On gâte des sentiments si tendres à les raconter en détail."[31]

Les Souvenirs d'un gentilhomme italien (1826), his first published novella (if indeed it is his), sets a religio-political intrigue comparable to that of *La Chartreuse de Parme* in an Enlightenment perspective, where irony merely serves to underscore skepticism and the tone remains much like that of Diderot. As late as 1829, in *Vanina Vanini*, he subjects the love story too rigorously and earnestly to the political involvements of the Carbonari for any interplay to get under way between love and the social milieu.

At last in *Armance* (1827), for the first time, he clearly and distinctly launches the ironic interplay. He does so, first of all, through the enabling aspects of a *sujet* that, in turn, he must be reckoned to have been seeking. Octave, indeed, is the most extremely incapacitated of Stendhal's heroes—not an impulsive, gifted peasant like Lucien. Rather, Octave is in love and at the same time impotent, a situation that in the first few pages Stendhal hints at most deliberately and also most tenuously. Banking those fires, Stendhal is soon banking his central fire. Here the function of Stendhal's particular kind of plot may be seen not just as a causal organization or a characteristic signature of the novelist, but rather as a device that releases him for organizing ideological complexity along a dilatory time line. So it is with other novelists too: even the fictional moralist always codes the moral considerations more complexly into a story than a disquisition could permit, as a jokester, in Freud's reading, packs social cathexes into his wit.

Stendhal, of course, once he had at long last learned to release himself by becoming one, is something of a jokester too:

> Making these sad reflections, Octave found himself seated on a divan facing a little chair occupied by his cousin Armance de Zohlihoff, and by chance his eyes settled on her. He noticed she had not addressed a word to him all evening. Armance was fairly poor, the niece of Mme. de Malivert, about Octave's age; and as these two beings had only indifference for one another, they spoke with complete frankness. For three quarters of an hour Octave's heart was slaked with bitterness; (then) he was seized with this idea: Armance pays me no compliments, she alone is a stranger to this increase of interest that I owe to money, she alone has some nobility of soul. And it was a consolation for him just to look at Armance. There is a being worthy of esteem, he said to himself, and as the evening wore on, he noticed with a pleasure equal to the chagrin that had at first flooded his heart that she continued to address him no word whatever.[32]

Stendhal is having a great deal of fun here. The 1825 law of indemnity has been passed, and Octave, though already a graduate of the Polytechnique, is so callow that he is astonished that the two millions his family will get are easing his own way into society. His mother is so depressed over her son's mysterious, melancholy-breeding ailment that she cannot even think of the two millions. He himself is silenced, as we see him here, to such a degree that his wounded vanity makes him forget the ailment enough to relax and fall in love—not only through his own silence, but also that of the only other silent person, Armance. Her silence, which in a social context must usually be read as a blank indifference and the opposite of the studied neglect that Octave prizes, turns out to be just that opposite: a sign of melancholic temperament like his own. Here we do have the interplay between the verifiable facts of social intercourse and the equally verifiable, contradictory hazards of amorous development. Among the latter is the puzzlingly incidental (and essen-

tial) character of the physical capacity to make love. Stendhal the diplo-
mat has found a way to make that knowledge interact with that which
he codifies in *De l'amour.* The ironist has been born at the same moment, and in the same stroke, as the visionary. Archness has broadened
his horizon.

Stendhal has got himself firmly beyond the doctrinal bind of Rousseau, towards whom he is able to formulate his ambivalence as early as
1810: "A man who, if he had been able to abstain from a hapless pedan-
try, would have been the Mozart of the French language and would have
produced a greater effect than Mozart on the hearts of men. But he wanted
to be their legislator and not to ravish them."[33] This is at once conventional and obscure: and yet it is clear that *pédanterie* would have something to do with both the Tracy-like classification of *De l'amour* and the
historical astigmatism of *Vanina Vanini.* And it took him some fifteen
years more to learn to leaven the Rousseauism he had set himself the task
of shaking off five years earlier still, coding the injunction in the Italian
of his most secret and summary thoughts: "Ma perciò più di tenerezza
alla R——" ("No more softness in the manner of R[ousseau]"), leaving
the name blank.[34] Nor is the converse exactly true that he declares of
himself somewhat later: "I am the opposite of J. J. Rousseau in many
things, no doubt."[35] When he had at last learned to come to terms with
the Rousseau in himself, and to provide it with the foil of countervailing
difference, his ironic interplay did make him a kind of Mozart, with a
consequent ability to *ravir.*

Stendhal's irony, thus rippling through the plot, is consequently more
than simply a tone of eighteenth-century "dry mock." Ordinary irony harnesses for special verbal emphasis the contradiction between the sign and
its referent: "It's a *fine* day" indicates displeasure at the fact that it is
actually raining out the window. The base of reference is firm in reality
(we can see the rain) and in principle (we have a standard of what a fine
day would be). For Stendhal the reality expands in complexity while the
principle becomes obscure. It is not just that Enlightenment and Romantic views of love and personal destiny are set against one another in the
sort of dead-heat contradiction by which the classicist and the roman-
ticist are set up for dialogue in his *Racine et Shakespeare.* These artifacts
are not self-consuming (if any successful literary ones ever truly are). Here
psychological displacements, the operation of what later came to be called
the unconscious, do not incapacitate: it is felt to be a charm, an inducement, and a deepening of both their similarity and their love that Mme. de
Rênal and Julien should — as it ironically happens, alternately — mistake
the persistence of love for a simple remorse. Octave and Armance continue the charming silence of their first meeting, which unites them more

than it separates them, until his ultimate suicide, left in a sort of unexplained silence, separates them finally. The achieved fact of their love hangs in the atmosphere, for all his incapacity and her unawareness. Romantic attitudes are presented as at once sillier and sublimer than Enlightenment attitudes. Rousseau is purged (so to speak) by Diderot or Voltaire and also valued over them. As Beda Allemann says generally,

> The question of an ironic truth remains banal, so long as the movement of presentation stays in the compass of the logical contradiction between something said in the foreground and something meant in the background. In a more genuine sense even the background and the thing meant are also included in the thing ironically said, for without this background it would be senseless to speak of irony at all.[36]

And Allemann goes on to speak of the *Spielraum*, the room for play or interplay that irony accords itself when it would become transcendent, as in Stendhal's finally discovered practice it has supremely become. The dialectical openness Stendhal achieves, by thus setting frames of reference into play against one another, liberates him from the classic and neoclassic "theory of genres" distinction, even as later systematized by Northrop Frye, between an irony whose understatement makes it somehow less than lifesize and a prior epic larger than lifesize. As it happens, though, this liberation had already been achieved differently by Plato in his presentation of the first *eiron*, Socrates, where an open-ended and gently self-deprecating modesty subserves an idealism not shrunk in values, though altered, from the epic universe it is replacing.

"Floating" (Allemann's term is *schweben*) along the line of the plot, the irony at once releases and qualifies the sense of time, to become an "irony of irony," in the phrase of the Schlegel whom Stendhal admired. Schlegel, too, makes the connection between irony and time that Stendhal may be said to have activated. In Stendhal's own work, indeed, we may trace the giant steps that he declares have been taken since 1721—though he attributes them to the simple realization of a sincere egotism: "egotism, though a sincere one, is a way to depict this human heart we have made giant strides in learning about since 1721, the time of the *Lettres Persanes* of that great man I have studied so much, Montesquieu."[37] Irony is the time-activating dialectic that puts him beyond Montesquieu. The sense of self-conscious play set into time-progression may, indeed, be paralleled with that of his close contemporary, Hegel.

In the complication of narrative form, Stendhal is to Diderot as Hegel is to Montesquieu.

He achieves a fusion of what Allemann (p. 135) describes as Nietzsche's two types of irony, the one that is weary of the past and the other that activates a gaiety (*Heiterkeit*) about the future. One of Nietzsche's few direct uses of the word *Ironie* links an "ironische Selbstbewusstsein" to a foreboding sense of historical lateness and irreconcilability that could be taken as a characterization of Stendhal, and one that Stendhal's *énergie* could be seen to be seeking.[38]

Without a complete metafictional self-reference (if such an activity were possible), playing fast and loose with the statement and silence of irony along a time line raises, by the very fact of such verbal interplay, the deep question of the relation between time and signification. It is this aspect of irony in general that explains, for Paul de Man, the tendency in early Romantic discourse for irony and allegory to be linked, "a structure shared by irony and allegory in that, in both cases, the relationship between sign and meaning is discontinuous, involving an extraneous principle that determines the point and the manner at and in which the relationship is articulated."[39] For allegory, however, the very structure implies a spatialization of the relationship: it remains, however richly or discontinuously, one-for-one and lexical — and this would also be the case for the "synecdoche" of the symbolism often opposed to it. The time-energized irony of Stendhal, by contrast, is syntactic. Allegory cannot achieve, at once simultaneously and successively, Stendhal's "realité voilée et dévoilée par les faits," to repeat the phrase Merleau-Ponty (in a lecture) attributed to him.[40]

In the very spiritedness of the progressive, deliberate, and also rapid presentation of events, the ironic interplay, by suspending judgment among its alternatives, and at the same time by coming down on the side of Romantic exaltation, makes that sentiment somehow seem to include at least the possibility of all the calculations that are set in opposition to it. Therefore, and thereby, two limited and conflicting systems, to follow further along Schlegel's line of speculation,[41] are made, as they are embodied in sequenced events, to seem to resolve conflicts and then to open something like an unlimited perspective. The nostalgia for the infinite in such fictions takes on not a symbolic character, embodying itself synecdochally in an object. Rather, it hovers over the very impossibility of fully defining just what a set of events adds up to. And at the same time, because sets of systems are being applied to the events, the irony emphasizes that the addition of meaning is both crucial and conceivable for these events. Such a sense it is the fiction's final achievement to have the ironic interplay bring about.

7

Pushkin
The Balance of Irony

1

The paradoxical effect of Stendhal's irony is to reassure. The bewilderments of the tale are organized to mock bewilderment. Such irony provides a tone of resignation it has made indistinguishable from a sensitive alertness. The perpetual discovery of incongruities is harmonized into a sense of world-wisdom. And the reader *is* reassured; he is included among the elect, the "happy few" in Stendhal's phrase, more powerfully but in the same way that a friend is when he is gladdened by an ironic statement. "He was a charmer," you say to a friend on the departure of some odious person, and friendship is solidified. As Schlegel says, without applying the term in this specific fashion, "Irony is a clear consciousness of the eternal agility of chaos that is endlessly full."[1] The reader has been brought beyond the sterile mental agility of, say, the detective story, about which Genette's formula for Stendhal — or Pushkin — would be equally true: "The reader is led to incessant comparisons between situations, personages, sentiments, and actions, instinctively disengaging the correspondences by superposition and perspectival adjustment."[2] True: but in Stendhal, though not in the detective story, the very failure to clear up incongruities produces, through the novelist's constant control, a tonic wakefulness that will not resign from politics and freeze up at love. Rather, Stendhal gives the reader the marked impression that detachment need not entail resignation, and that the world would be well lost for something so precious as love. He sustains the reader in the perception of the sort of threshold quite opposed to the detective story reader's satisfaction with terminal neatness.

The arbitrariness and complexities of love add to its desirability and glory. Love is an island of selflessness in a selfish world.

Pushkin in *Eugene Onegin* manages a similar effect, though through very different means.[3] Pushkin's means have been wrought, as were Stendhal's, by a profound transmutation of eighteenth-century attitudes and procedures. And these means are still ironic, the balancing off of inequalities among two men and two women, through the self-defeating but enlightened reactions of a protagonist who is selfish from the very first stanza, which recounts his frustrated boredom at the sickbed of the dying uncle from whom he will inherit. The woman he loses gives him an ultimate lesson in selflessness as she bids him farewell forever. The effect of the narrator's irony is paradoxical throughout, while our sense of the hero's irony is not so. A larger irony tests the smaller. The exquisite control of the poetry, the logic that the novel causes to be derived from seemingly random incident, bring personal loss into focus with personal fulfillment in the balance by which the narrator tests the relation between the two.

2

Pushkin provides his balance of irony, in a splendid undertone, with an exalted simplicity. Much has been made of Pushkin's simplicity,[4] a quality that lends his style an air of almost foreshortened directness, so that even his *skazki*, simple in their plots and artfully naive in their presentation, gain a patness not found so markedly even in the folklore materials for which he shared his contemporaries' enthusiasm.[5] "Simplicity," indeed, was a favorite word with him in its various forms.[6] Both simplicity and clarity are enjoined upon the reader in the very first stanza of the Preface to *Eugene Onegin*:

> Poezii zhivoi i yasnoi,
> Visokikh dum i prostoty.

> Of live and limpid poetry,
> of high thoughts and simplicity.
> (Translated by Vladimir Nabokov)[7]

The simplicity of Pushkin's style is such that it curbs his verse from the metaphors and rhetorical figures by which we are often tempted to characterize so formal a poetry. Before Pushkin's relative paucity of such figurative devices, we are brought up to the question of how the poetry comes to seem so formal, especially as a sense of a play of mind runs constantly through his verse, notably in *Eugene Onegin*, the work that stood on his desk throughout his entire mature career, begun when he was twenty-four, with gaps left to be completed in the edition published the year of his death.

This play of mind can be defined as another quality, the "irony" that defines at once the protagonist and the author of *Eugene Onegin*, though the word was one that Pushkin used rarely, and then only of the drawing room attitude of an aristocratic *désinvolture*, an attitude recognizably akin to Onegin's but distinct from Pushkin's.[8] How does so complex and supple an irony come through so simple a style? To begin with, Pushkin's rigorous understatement, his common practice of drawing subjects from legendary life (*Ruslan and Lyudmila*) or humble existence (*The Cottage in Kolomna*), of centering on the events of a prior century (*The Bronze Horseman, The Moor of Peter the Great, The Captain's Daughter*), all amount to his setting up an alien formal element in his work to neutralize the emotion that is an important, if not the chief, concern there. This enacts what amounts to a philosophy of the feeling. The same may be said for the high degree of control maintained by intricately rhymed and numbered stanzas over the freely detailed contemporary material that he uses for his "novel in verses," *Eugene Onegin.*

What exactly is neutralized and centralized in *Eugene Onegin*? Certainly not the easy Byronic world-weariness and cynicism of his immediate model, even filtered through French.[9]

Pushkin's plots, to begin with, tend to set up a fundamental recursion that characteristically checks, and also fulfills, the characters: he offers no titanic, damned Manfreds, and also no cynical, sentient Don Juans slipping sideways through their adventures. Even after his disillusionment, Onegin still holds to Byron (VII, xxii, 4–5). Yet he wants to repent his slighting of Tatyana, and it is too late; she will be faithful to her husband, while never ceasing to love Eugene; her pining is neutralized by her intent, and her forgiveness of the truculence that has killed Lenski leaves no opening for the furthering of a trivial erotic intrigue.

It is a natural catastrophe, a flood on the Neva, that drives the young man in *The Bronze Horseman* to go mad and then to expire on the islet where the flood has cast up the hut of his beloved. The protagonist of *The Queen of Spades* ruthlessly takes over the heart of a ward in order to get at her aged protectress' card secret. He makes a fatal mistake that turns a woman to the deadly losing center, and it is the very same aged woman whom his midnight rustlings have literally frightened to death. The ward marries, while the manipulative protagonist goes mad. A profound lesson on forgiving adultery is read to the young exogamic Russian husband by his father-in-law, who banishes him forever from the forgiving gypsy band after he has murdered his gypsy wife and her lover. Ruslan is simply devoted to Lyudmila, seeking her across distances. The "Prisoner of the Caucasus" earns freedom through the love of a Caucasian maid who is willing to lose him to give him that freedom.

In all these plots circularity of event relativizes unfulfillment against a moral absolute derived from, but never identified with, love. They hold strongly in check the events that are presented against profoundly evocative backgrounds. The steppes of *Gypsies*, the winter of *Eugene Onegin*, the flood-breaking Neva waters of *The Bronze Horseman*, keep grandeur and irrelevant distance in close proximity.

"Roll on, thou deep and dark blue ocean, roll" is an invocation whose tone is not easy to parallel in this imitator of Byron; he is rarely so direct, and never personal at the length of *Childe Harold*, whose hero Onegin imitates in bearing (I, xxvii, 9–10). As Eikhenbaum[10] says, where Lermontov adopts the philosophy of Byron, Pushkin leaves the world-view behind and seeks only the "lyricism," by which must be meant the associative and conversational manipulation of the subject. Even there, he trims the vulgarity or extravagance out of the plots, which he rarely if ever parallels, while he tightens the English poet's exaggeration of statement into calm understatement, his slipshod measures into an exact music. The literary references in *Eugene Onegin*, if they find their closest parallels and perhaps also a legitimization by convention in those of *Don Juan*, are never allowed the distancing of parody. Tatyana's reading of Richardson or Eugene's of Gibbon, Rousseau, and Bayle (VII, xxxv, 1–8) is a stage in development, something less lofty in the first case and less selective in the second than the taste of the author; it is a stage in the development towards a condition he neither rejects nor sneers at. The fulfillment of the function damps the irony of the moment, and the cited title is immobilized between function and fact:

> Creations by the happy power
> of dreaming animated
> the lover of Julie Wolmar,
> Malek-Adhel, and de Linar
> and Werther, restless meetings
> and the inimitable man Grandison
> Who brings upon us somnolence.   (III, ix, 5–11)

Pushkin's distancing from Richardson here is only a passing turn, one that his admiration for Tatyana keeps in focus. Byron's literary rejections, on the other hand, are meant to issue from the same fund of worldliness as his sexual wisdom:

> Thou shall believe in Milton, Dryden, Pope,
> > Thou shalt not set up Wordsworth, Coleridge, Southey;
> > The second drunk, the third so quaint and mouthy.
> > > (*Don Juan*, I, ccv, 1–4)

The slapdash effect of *Don Juan* is at best merely cumulative:

And if she met him though she smiled not more,
　　She look'd a sadness sweeter than her smile,
　　As if her heart had deeper thoughts in store
　　She must not own, but cherish'd more the while
　　For that compression in its burning core;
　　Even innocence itself has many a wile,
　　And will not dare to trust itself with truth,
　　And love is taught hypocrisy from youth.

But passion most dissembles, yet betrays
　　Even by its darkness; as the blackest sky
　　Foretells the heaviest tempest, it displays
　　Its workings through the vainly guarded eye,
　　And in whatever aspect it arrays
　　Itself, 'tis still the same hypocrisy:
　　Coldness or anger, even disdain or hate,
　　Are masks it often wears, and still too late.

Then there were sighs, the deeper for suppression,
　　And stolen glances, sweeter for the theft,
　　And burning blushes, though for no transgression,
　　Tremblings when met, and restlessness when left;
　　All these are little preludes to possession,
　　Of which young passion cannot be bereft,
　　And merely tend to show how greatly love is
　　Embarrass'd at first starting with a novice.
　　　　　　　　　　　　　　　　(I, xxii–xxiv)

"Novice" in the last line expends its superior indulgence in a static worldly wisdom of the obvious; "hypocrisy" is simply the "novice's" concealment of her passion from herself, the effect of which is to promote it rather than to inhibit it. No sequence of events, no combination of purposes, no fathomings of passion, serve to qualify this psychology or place it in any other perspective. Pushkin's tale of thwarted adultery, *Graf Nulin*, in far shorter compass, is far more subtle.

For Pushkin Byron is "the poet of pride," a vice that he associates with the narcissism of self-portraiture (I, lvi, 10–11).

We must look at a passage of some length to compare the import of Pushkin's flow to that of Byron and to see the fine-tuned open-endedness of the emotions on whose threshold he sets his characters.

Amidst obedient admirers,
other odd females I have seen,
conceitedly indifferent
to sighs impassioned and to praise.
But what, to my amazement, did I find?

While, by austere demeanor,
they frightened timid love,
they had the knack of winning it again,
at least by their condolence;
at least the sound of spoken words
sometimes would seem more tender,
and with credulous blindness
again the youthful lover
pursued sweet vanity.

Why is Tatyana, then, more guilty?
Is it because in sweet simplicity
deceit she knows not and believes
in her elected dream?
Is it because she loves without art, being
obedient to the bent of feeling?
Is it because she is so trustful
and is endowed by heaven
with a restless imagination,
intelligence, and a live will,
and headstrongness,
and a flaming and tender heart?
Are you not going to forgive her
the thoughtlessness of passion?

The coquette reasons coolly;
Tatyana in dead earnest loves
and unconditionally yields
to love like a sweet child.
She does not say: Let us defer;
thereby we shall augment love's value,
inveigle into toils more surely;
let us first prick vainglory
with hope; then with perplexity
exhaust a heart, and then
revive it with a jealous fire,
for otherwise, cloyed with delight,
the cunning captive from his shackles
hourly is ready to escape.   (III, xxiii–xxv)

In these lines Pushkin manages at once to praise Tatyana and to be distanced from her. It is Onegin—"a Childe Harold"—who will shortly fail to bridge the distance between Byronic sophistication and the supreme value of this "simplicity." The irony of the almost exactly contemporary *Le Rouge et le noir*[11] offers an interplay between Enlightenment objectivity and a foolish Romantic exaltation, so that only by reshuffling and recombining his characters' attitudes can one derive Stendhal's own. Pushkin's irony towards his character shades into the tenderness of indulgence, creating the "simple" sense of a single limpid view, a view reinforced by the exact, even progressions of a formal meter. Into that view all the splendid particulars of the poem are transparently assimilated.

It is the long sweep of the plot, and the plot alone, that creates a sense of the narrator's distance from Tatyana. His direct statements lock his verse into the fullness of the moment, as the sonnetlike Onegin stanza preserves that fullness by standing usually in numbered distinctness (whereas Byron, characteristically, as above, overflows his stanza units). Though the contrast here amplifies a sentiment of Parny's, Pushkin adds to Parny precisely the distinction of his own attitudes, and his own tempo.[12]

Instead of Byron's prolix and random comments on a single law, overflowing the stanza in subject as elsewhere in rhythm too, Pushkin offers three separate and distinct units of subject, as of rhythm, in these stanzas. And each unit coordinates a powerful series of events. In the first an attitude of "indifference" produces an interaction—"austere demeanor," "timid love." This gives way to a "condolence" about this very opposition, in turn producing the pursuit of "sweet vanity." (*Suetoi*, the final word, suggests the "bustle" of pursuit, or of the ball's turmoil, as well as the attitude that keeps it going.) Set against this series is a persistence that offers a quality, "simplicity," that gets the same adjective, "sweet," as the *suetoi* itself, something between an attitude and an activity. These distinct phases ride, as it were, the deep current of possible loves in Tatyana and Onegin, a possibility never actualized, as on a succession of thresholds.

There is movement not only from feeling to feeling, but from one type of actualization to another. The poem celebrates this possibility by an exactness in depicting the codes and mechanisms that cause it to remain unfulfilled. Where stanza xxiii offers a series, stanza xxiv offers a solid and steady position ("trustful"), which consequently has a number of simultaneous attributes: "restless imagination," "intelligence," "live will," "headstrongness," "flaming," and "tender heart."[13] Thus in the last attribute the warmth of the susceptibility is linked to the steadiness that implies fidelity, and the conditions have already been delineated that make merely rhetorical the final question whether the reader will forgive her "the thoughtlessness of passion."

Stanza xxv draws the conclusion of making the contrast explicit, setting against Tatyana's "dead earnest" (*liubit ne shutia*) still another version of the coquette's series—a version that could be different from that offered in stanza xxiii or could alternatively be another aspect of the same: "prick vainglory with hope," then "with perplexity exhaust a heart," then "revive it with jealous fire" to prevent its being "cloyed with delight."

The presentation in these three stanzas is such that the two identifiable alternative ways of putting love through its paces are already stalled, and as it were shamed, by the presence of a third possibility, one that already admits of no conceivable progression other than simple success or simple failure. So it adumbrates in feeling-tone the end of the whole poem, the final result of the plot. The narrator steadily sees the coquette as against Tatyana. Eugene, remaining a little like Childe Harold (I, xxxiii, 9; IV, xliv, i), sees the coquette with too much boredom — she is the sort of woman he has left behind in St. Petersburg — and he will continue to see Tatyana with too much condescension. For the narrator the clarity of his presentation undermines the possibility of a Byron-like condescension, while at the same time it harnesses and coordinates the knowledge on which condescension would be based. In being at once identified with and distanced from Tatyana, he damps the irony of his presentation into a not quite opposing pathos. A rhythmic corollary of his control is offered in the closed worlds of the separate stanzas as well as in the exactly counted syllables that are so distinctive a mark of his style, "each syllable ranked and in order."[14]

Onegin, half-noble and half-cowardly in this way, is suspended by his own attitudes. These lead directly to the confrontation on which the plot hinges, Onegin's vicious play for Olga, which leads to Lenski's death and the dispersal of the three who survive. It is Tatyana's demeanor on their meeting after their discussion of her letter — itself provoked by the attitudes here analyzed — that discomfits Onegin to the point where:

> noting
> that languid maid's tremulous impulse,
> out of vexation lowering his gaze,
> he went into a huff and, fuming,
> swore he would madden Lenski,
> and thoroughly, in fact, avenge himself.
>
> (V, xxxi, 6–11)

There is a symmetry of couples here: the sensitive, experienced Onegin and the sensitive, inexperienced Tatyana, versus the jejunely idealistic, inexperienced Lenski and the hedonistic, experience-eager Olga. But playing up to Olga out of "revenge," Onegin does "madden" (*vzbesit*) Lenski enough to provoke the duel that kills Lenski and forces Onegin into an abrupt departure. His action suspends Tatyana enough for her to be packed off to Moscow, where she meets the husband who will forever block her from the Onegin she will forever love.

How complex a world of emotional possibility is expressed by these developments may be measured by comparing Pushkin's "novel in verses" not only with Byron but also with Goethe's *Die Wahlverwandschaften*, which Pushkin's two-couples symmetry quite surpasses. Goethe's novel is finally rather superficial. His Ottilie literally pines to death as she maintains the honor of her bearing towards Charlotte, who in turn sends away the Major without any true reconciliation, and the feeling of Eduard is really left hanging, till he also dies. Mere pathos dominates; the last paragraph of the novel tells how the lovers are buried side by side.[15] However, it would be hard, in fact, to parallel the symmetry of Pushkin's plot. A still deeper asymmetry lurks at the heart of *Eugene Onegin*, to generate constant ironies, in the tumult of the fine detail in the duel scene and elsewhere. Tender and seemingly responsive to one another, the characters at the same time are prevented by the play of their passions from truly responding in a way that would reproduce in furthered action the symmetry of their schematized match. *Otomstit*, "avenge," is a curious word here. This word stands at the heart of the asymmetry, as it just fails to name the complex of Onegin's motives. Lenski has done Onegin no injury. And so why "revenge"? Onegin has tagged along to this name-day party only because the young poet swept him up in the gladness he should, if anything, have been half-glad to share. *Otomstit* must imply "hurt because of Lenski's blind happiness," or "get even because Onegin cannot break free of his own fated disassociation from the evening," or "punish because Onegin feels powerless either to marry Tatyana against his disinclination or to ignore the obvious power of her own response to him." These motives are not equivalent to one another, nor has any sibling rivalry or psychic schematism of ordinary jealousy begun to manifest itself. Onegin is suffering from the lacerations of a pure melancholy, one that reveals an asymmetry at the heart of this moment, and with direct consequence also for the total sequence of events. We must go beyond the silence of the poem to provide these explanations; Pushkin offers for them only colloquial terms: "the old chap was cross" (*chudak serdit*), "vexation" (*dosady*), "went into a huff" (*nadulsia*), "fuming" (*negoduia*). Tatyana, who has already had a predictive dream about Lenski's death at Onegin's hands, is immobilized, while Olga is curiously liberated into what will be the lifelong career of a coquette.

An asymmetry produced by time on human responsiveness serves to close the novel with a symmetry more than despairing. It is not just that Onegin and Tatyana are tragically in love and tragically separated:

> All ages are to love submissive;
> but to young virgin hearts

its impulses are beneficial. . . .
But at a late and barren age,
at the turn of our years,
sad is the trace of a dead passion.
(VIII, xxix, 1–3, 8–10)

Onegin is spoken of here, on the threshold of his final, checking encounter.[16]

3

Controlled by a sort of underlying principle of ironic contradiction is the backdrop of landscape "in nature" for Pushkin's characters. They never skate over its surface or confront it by casual impression, as Childe Harold apostrophizes the "deep and dark blue ocean." Pushkin's landscape does not open out as a source of Proustian dialectic, like Wordsworth's, though it reproduces some of the "spirit" of the poet whose *Excursion* he set himself the task of translating. Nor does it possess the "contraries" of Coleridge's persistent idea. Yet its motions are more interactive than the correspondence of inner state and outer sight in "The Rime of the Ancient Mariner."

Instead of providing a Blakean system for landscape or a Wordsworthian dialectical system, Pushkin sets the traits against one another: the Bessarabia of *Gypsies* possesses at once a Burkean sublimity of rock and torrent and a quite unsublime simplicity. The ice-locked Neva breaks up in *The Bronze Horseman* for an interseason between winter and spring. Tatyana's dream is preceded by the bright hush of the midwinter "holy days," and traits of gaiety confusedly infuse the winter, as traits of sadness do the spring:

gay magpies outside,
and the hills softly overspread
with winter's brilliant carpeting.
All's bright, all's white around.   (V, i, 11–14)

Rime in the sun upon a frosty day,
and sleighs, and, at late dawn,
the radiance of the rosy snows,
and gloam of Twelfthtide eves.   (V, iv, 5–8)

The night is frosty; the whole sky is clear;
the splendid choir of heavenly luminaries
so gently, so unisonally flows. . . .
she trains a mirror on the moon;
but in the dark glass only
the sad moon trembles.   (V, ix, 1–3, 6–8)

This effect of winter joy-sadness resembles in combination what it differs from in emphasis, the sadness-joy of spring:

> How sad your apparition is to me,
> Spring, spring, season of love. . . .
> With what oppressive tenderness
> I revel in the whiff
> Of spring fanning me free,
> in the lap of the rural stillness!
> Or is enjoyment strange to me . . .
>
> (VII, ii, 1–2, 4–9)

The staple attitude and vocabulary of French elegiac,[17] in the more conventional poetry of the time, does not achieve such combinations, any more than do the verses that are confected here as Lenski's (VI, xx, 14): "Whither, Ah whither are ye fled / my springtime, golden days?" (VI, xxi, 3–4).

Again the control by which the brightness of the winter landscape and its sadness are made to interfuse is exercised in such a way that it cannot be differentiated from the way in which the landscape sets off and interfuses with the feelings of Tatyana. The narrator's distance from her is equivalent to his presentational objectivity towards the landscape, and a faint but pervasive ironic effect is carried off, through this high control, without any explicit irony. The irony is, as it were, damped by something in the overall procedure of the poem.[18]

In Pushkin's prose, too, the control acts as a sort of damper, and there is a faintly ironic effect easy to identify but hard to define. An even, flat style of near-reportage recounts events of highly charged emotional content: the loss of trust and love in *The Moor of Peter the Great*, the possibilities of death and injustice in *The Captain's Daughter*, of betrayal in *The Stationmaster*. The first two offer an implied contrast to begin with, by giving a historical setting to their essentially personal stories, and by making the personal seem, in some suspended assertion, to illustrate the period as well as to serve for a fable of human events. The same, to a lesser extent, is true of *The Queen of Spades*, since the expiring dowager has brought the card secret from eighteenth-century Paris to nineteenth-century St. Petersburg. Pogov[19] shows how Pushkin adapts Golikov's original study of Peter the Great, breaking a complex style down into "short utterances," and *The Captain's Daughter* has a parallel and contrast in Pushkin's own history of the Pugachov Rebellion. In addition to the objectivized style and the distancing by large, mostly unmentioned events of a public character, in *The Queen of Spades* all the relationships are ironized. They are given an air of mystery by the disproportion between the urgency of loves and deaths and the triviality of a card trick, or even of the money that its successful performance is supposed to bring.

In all this the effect of Pushkin's prose does not have a different ironic bearing from that of the poetry.[20] In the verse itself, there is a superbly manipulated symmetry of sound that counterpoints, especially in the free-seeming conversationlike flow of *Eugene Onegin*, an asymmetry of sense. Correspondingly, in both prose and verse narrative, there is an unusually balanced symmetry of plot counterbalanced by a disproportionateness of feeling in Eugene Onegin himself. In the prose tales there is a disproportion either between the feelings of the characters and the shifts to which they are subjected or between the large historical public picture and the lucidly presented private events.

"Romanticism" might serve as a cover term for the narrator's distance in *Eugene Onegin*, and for the understated proportionateness in its intricate manipulation of represented feelings. It is the term Pushkin raises and drops[21] in characterizing Lenski's verses, written on the eve of the duel in which he is to die. Yet usually[22] Pushkin himself uses "romanticism" as a foil for "classicism," and his longest critical statement on the opposition between the two merely defines romanticism as the introduction of genres not used by the ancients. The term "classicism," indeed, in our own critical vocabulary, might apply to the equipoise and control of Pushkin's presentational strategy, but he never uses the term in that sense.

Nor is the problematic cancelled attribution of "romanticism" to Lenski so simply detached as its simple attribution in the narrative might make it seem. On the one hand, Lenski's verses (VI, xxi, 3, xxii, 14) do lack all the contrastive richness of the rhetorically similar feeling-in-landscape stretches Pushkin elsewhere gives in his own voice. Yet on the other hand, these verses, since they express a sense that their author might perish (VI, xxii, 1–4), constitute a premonition as correct as Tatyana's dream of the disaster shortly to occur. They also serve as an epitaph on the fictional poet. If Pushkin's conveyed attitude to Lenski is closer to Onegin's attitude than to Lenski's sense of himself, still we cannot merge Pushkin's attitude and Onegin's. The complication of these postures around the "romanticism" of Lenski would forbid our applying Pushkin's irony as just a version of Onegin's indulgent, and mortally dangerous, slighting *hauteur*. (This is pointedly carried out right through the duel by the choice of a servant as a second and by the carelessness with which the mortal shot is fired.)

But Pushkin offers us no Stendhalian dialectic to thread through the feelings. Equipoise and proportion do the whole job. This peerless strategy accords with the supreme literary value that Pushkin repeatedly adduces: verisimilitude (*pravdopodobie*).[23] Indeed, his plea for the avoidance of periphrasis, for saying "friendship" instead of "a feeling whose flame is blest,"[24] may be equated to a plea for *pravdopodobie* in linguistic expression, and so his search for verisimilitude can be seen as an aspect of his simplicity.

There is a proportion of successiveness in the mere direct naming of feeling, as in the account of Lenski's last meeting with Olga:

> "Why did you vanish yesternight so early?"
> was Olinka's first question.
> In Lenski all the senses clouded,
> and silently he hung his head.
> Jealousy and vexation disappeared
> before this clarity of glance,
> before this soft simplicity,
> before this sprightly soul . . .
> He gazes with sweet tenderness;
> he sees: he is still loved.
> Already, by remorse beset,
> he is prepared to beg her pardon,
> he quivers, can't find words:
> he's happy, he is almost well . . .   (VI, xiv)

While an individual term may have a rich range of reference in Pushkin, this range is buried in the word; it is subjected to no Wordsworthian analysis. Here sequence, held in the proportion of the simple schematic plot and the calibrated meters, does duty for analysis. We have "all the senses clouded," and then the reported results of an interaction (rather than a fictional representation of the interaction): "jealousy and vexation disappeared . . . before this (soft simplicity)." Every ensuing line here gives us a single further feeling, a feeling that the meter and the paralleling of noun or verb begin to divide into two (and so to analyze) in lines 10, 12, 13, and 14.

The presentation of Onegin's feelings and Tatyana's is much lengthier, much more complex; we measure each couple by the other. But that presentation, too, is funded into mere attributive abstractions, as well as into the particulars of scene and gesture and furnishing. The "novel in verses" combines abstraction and gesture, thereby anticipating the practice of the post-Flaubertian novel, as the controlling, semi-detached, marginally participating narrator anticipates James. No novel in prose of Pushkin's time or earlier can be shown to do either.

But this is to look ahead, and also to overemphasize the "novel" of his title, which is in *verses* that purify and normalize attitudes so standard as to be easily recognizable. The tone of elegy and the tone of irony are both to be found in eighteenth-century practice generally. Byron's "pride," to use Pushkin's repeated term for him, unites elegy and irony in the unreflective and overpersonalized mix of self-pity and contempt for the world. By normalizing and depersonalizing both the pity and the irony, Pushkin turns both into a proportionately represented and objectivized feeling that surpasses even the complex but sensibility-bound posturing of *Hero of Our Time*. Shklovsky, looking backward, finds that Pushkin resembles Sterne in having the detail of his presentation contrasted (*protivopostavleno*) with the action.[25]

And yet though Pushkin is "close to the manner of Sterne," there is a difference: he does not parody. This difference is crucial. To carry off irony without parody is to damp it so that it exactly covers, and enriches rather than diminishes, the objects in view. Romanticism at its best generalizes and universalizes feeling. Pushkin found, and uniquely exemplifies, a way to make a properly controlled irony at once universalize and generalize feeling, by holding the particulars in a proportionate and contrastive view that qualifies them without undercutting them, even in Stendhal's extravagant and indulgent manner. The threshold of feeling is controlled in its very expansiveness.

8

Baudelaire
The Assessment of Incapacity

1

"Tout pour moi devient allégorie," Baudelaire says (82).[1] All becomes allegory for him in his centering effort to give full credit to a sense of loss and fault. In that perspective, his doctrine of correspondences, turning nature into a "forest of symbols," provides a firm set of dimensions within which the pillars of the temple of nature can let their voices be confounded and confused from afar. Yet his figures are seen sharply. Confusion and clarity coexist on the threshold of a perception awake to the spiritual dimensions of time and vision. The opening of "Le Voyage" balances the two in terms of scale:

> Pour l'enfant amoureux de cartes et d'estampes,
> L'univers est égal à son vaste appétit.
> Ah! que le monde est grand à la clarté des lampes!
> Aux yeux du souvenir que le monde est petit!   (122)

> For the child who loves maps and engravings
> The universe is equal to his vast appetite.
> Ah how large is the world in the clarity of lamps!
> In the eyes of memory how small is the world!

Not a theologian, Baudelaire takes a theological principle and gives it full play as he focuses an individual poem, usually, on an individual image or figure. Into the poem do allegorical figures enter — Death, Venus, Beatrice, Anguish, Hope. Figures like the drunkard or the negress are easily allegorized. But while the language of abstracting such figures draws on the Renaissance emblem, the subject at hand is handled so as to assess the somber feelings of the speaker. Allegory is, so to speak, the other face

139

of caricature, an activity that for Baudelaire brings to expression in its various manifestations the deep, fallen nature of man.

Baudelaire, who inveighed against eclecticism, felt that a profundity that would avoid eclecticism could be attained only by a sacrifice (929–30). It is against the odds, of which he retains a persistent critical awareness, that he holds his vision in place to carry off the profound, single perspective of his work.

The title *Les Fleurs du mal*, appropriated with the same finesse and genius for proportionate truth-telling as the book itself, balances between the scandal of its presentation — they are fleurs du *mal* — and the assertion of its aesthetic yield: they are *fleurs* du mal. *Mal* is itself a nascent allegory, one by which incidental allegories are measured. Baudelaire, having opted for the less sensational and more comprehensive title he quickly borrowed from the friend who suggested it (*Les Lesbiennes* and *Les Damnées* had been his first thoughts, then *Les Limbes*), kept the title, evidently deciding as time went on that it would serve to cover his life's output of poetry.

The earlier titles all involved women whose damnation turned them away from men, human beings whose gestures of self-evasion and self-annihilation might also summarize what the poet and the "hypocrite lecteur" were finally up to: the last line of "Les Femmes damnées" might be the daring and despairing injunction of any sinner to himself: "Et fuyez l'infini que vous portez en vous! " (139).[2] The women turned towards the poet also, as well as these inverts of whom he speaks, present an "âpre stérilité" of "jouissance." A man who faces them, too, cannot avoid finding that "le vent furibond de la concupiscence / Fait claquer votre chair ainsi qu'un vieux drapeau" ("The furious wind of concupiscence / Makes your flesh clack like an old flag"). Seen from inside their own psyches, these women are human beings fully equal to men in their subjection to distortion and loss. Seen from outside as objects, they are frozen into the familiar types of "object choice" (though not entirely). Their allegorical clarity of outline and intensity of focus make them escape the stereotypes of automatic nineteenth-century male response. So, indeed, does Baudelaire's radical categorization of his own dominant stereotypes about the figures of women as sinful obsession, or what amounts to that. He trenchantly detaches his thinking from what his emotions cannot modify.

Baudelaire's candor in the ironic assessment of human incapacity allows him a wide spectrum for depicting the female figure who as an object of attention fuses the allegorical and the personal. The woman can be a Cruel Mother ("La Bénédiction"), or something like a Muse ("La Muse malade," "La Muse Vénale," "La Beauté") or something like a transfixing and cruel mistress, a "Vampire." The "chat," the *très chère* of rich and obsessing nudity, stands apart from the speaker in a mobile pose, to be adored and measured. In "Portraits de Maîtresses," the only perfect woman of those described is also for that very reason intolerable, and her husband kills her (296). Baudelaire's "Béatrice" laughs at him while caressing dwarf demons, in a notably allegorical tableau (111).

Here, characteristically, Baudelaire insists on a kind of tonic wakefulness and delicate balance as he reverses the benign Romantic stereotypes of the Mother and the Beloved, while still he retains the mere masochism mystique of the "Belle Dame Sans Merci." Here the speaking poet is something more than a victim. Baudelaire offers a scheme wherein the question of Keats, "What can ail thee, Knight-at-Arms?" gets an answer that begins but does not end with a firm theological perception of sin. "All voluptuousness is found in evil" (1250), and woman is spoken of in a census of "modern subjects" as a sort of supreme allegory, "this being terrible and incommunicative like God" (1181) (though there is the difference that God is infinite and in a sense has at once nothing and everything to tell). Such a notion could lead directly for Baudelaire to the observation that is psychological, historical, and etymological all at once: "The femininity of the Church as a reason for its omnipotence" (1248).

Woman transfixes the persona of the speaker powerfully enough to reverse the common Baudelairean oblivion, a depiction that makes him a kind of anti-Wordsworth and anti-Proust. "Your memory shines in me like a monstrance" (45), but we are meant neither to rest on the easy, and deeply traditional, fusion of the beloved and the divine, nor ironically to reject it. The hint of irony here simply contributes to the wakefulness that defines, and thereby "confesses" through the power of an erotic fixation, the extreme situation in which this putative *homme moyen spirituel* finds himself. "But sadness in me rises like the sea" (54). This common Romantic image of infinity is put at the service of defining what would deny such a feeling: not release but sadness, thanks to the beauty who as a "scourge of souls" acts as a sort of infernal and fitful John the Baptist ("O Beauté, dur fléau des âmes, tu le veux!"—54). Beauty here is allegorized, but at the same time she is not wholly distinct either from the woman whose "claw" and "fierce tooth" are a less purgative version of the "scourge" of *la Beauté*. In this "Causerie" which puts Baudelaire's consistently ultimate vision in the perspective of an everyday conversation, he has the speaker declare that, having reacted so fully, he can no longer be acted upon: "Don't look for my heart any more; the beasts have eaten it." Here the word *coeur*, frequent in Baudelaire as in poetry since the Middle Ages, stands for something more complex than just the love relationship. "La Beauté" is at once inaccessible and absorbing to contemplation: "My eyes, my wide eyes of eternal clarities" (20).

The insistence on a perverse element of "vice" locks the Romantic agony into an all-but-Nietzschean falling-short. It is in a context where Baudelaire enumerates varieties of attitudes towards a mistress (473) that he declares, "The vices of a great nation are its greatest treasure." And with respect to Laclos, by contrast to the commoner romantic adorations, he says, "Fucking and the glory of fucking—were they more immoral than this modern manner of *adoring* and of mixing the holy with the profane?" (640). He sets a Sade-like diagnostic of interaction between the public and the sexual towards the future—rather than towards a self-contained and class-structured present, like Sade. "The Revolution was made by voluptuaries" (639). (Does he mean Danton, whom he quotes [1317] and also allegorizes [1318]? Would he exclude the Madame Roland whom he does not mention?)

In his early story "La Fanfarlo," Baudelaire has a journalistically embroiled alter ego, Samuel Cramer, seduce, by the upstaging hauteur of his bad reviews, the actress-mistress of his ideal beloved's husband. He does so on the promise that the beloved will reward him with the possession of herself. Samuel is more profoundly indolent and more diverse in background than the sort of Balzacian character on whom he is modeled, Lucien de Rubempré or Félix de Vandenesse. Cramer is half Chilean and half German, of a nature "lazy and enterprising at the same time—fertile in difficult projects and laughable abortings" (485). And nowhere in Balzac—in the comprehensive *Illusions perdues,* say, the sensationally cynical *Sarrazine,* or *Les Secrets de la Princesse de Cadignan*—could the concision of this fable be paralleled, where the virtuous wife becomes a scheming cheat, the adoring poet an ensnared lover, the strayed husband a chastened exemplar of fidelity, and the powerful, manipulated La Fanfarlo herself a domesticated helpmeet ambitious for the husband who must now grub to support her and her offspring. One could almost capitalize all the nouns in the last sentence, so characteristically close to allegory does Baudelaire here remain. Yet La Fanfarlo retains a distinct personal presence. Her beauty takes on a cast of the "fat, clean, shiny, and canny" (512), so that she becomes a sort of "ministerial call girl." The temper of these sexual evolutions would grace a still more urban Pushkin. Laclos and Sade have been called to put Balzac, briefly, through more strenuous paces than his own, thanks to a despairingly clear-eyed, yet abstracting, view of the extreme possibilities to which the extremity of human desire tends to lead.

2

A person incapacitated by extremity is felt to be in the grip of neurosis, and yet the whole of mankind lives under the shadow of universal neurosis — in Baudelaire's theological terms, of sin. To apply his sense of universal incapacity to Baudelaire himself will result in the more or less skillful psychoanalytic exposition of what he himself saw, in Sartre, or Blin, or Butor (or, contrariwise, in Feuillerat).[3] Yet Freud's "common type of object choice" will not exhaust Baudelaire's scheme of enrapturement with Jeanne Duval or Mme. Sabatier — it will not exhaust "La Fanfarlo" — as it can easily do for the gestures codified into Manon Lescaut, or for that matter into the elegies of Propertius.[4] The woman of his poems is too unpredictable, too self-possessed, too incommunicative, and at the same time too consistently held in an abstraction, to play the role of the girlish, plebeian flirt. Nor does she especially present the threat of infidelity; Baudelaire is quasi-conjugal, and her subjection to the oppressiveness of evil makes her resemble the poet as an exemplary figure. As Baudelaire quotes from Poe, "There is a mysterious force in man . . . these actions hold the fascination of the abyss . . . natural perversity."[5] At this margin original sin and the limits of perception are versions of each other.

Baudelaire's gesture of "tell all" is the gesture of Rousseau, without either Rousseau's doctrinal optimism or the liberating benefits. Nor does Baudelaire offer a comprehensive doctrine of *rêve*, wherein Nerval attenuates a century of German theoreticians.[6] "The ghost in broad daylight buttonholes the passerby" (83), and the crucial step has been taken that will lead to the surrealist reading of the dream life into the waking life. For Baudelaire dream and waking merely hover together, but also apart. Each is on the threshold of the other. They cannot be surrealized because they are set too definitely into their generalizing, allegorical function. In his view of the relation between dream and waking, Baudelaire remains, as in everything else, sturdily and heroically proportionate, in order to remain singleminded. He begins with the revealed fact of incapacity rather than a Rousseau-like nostalgia for an Elysium of capacity (a vision he also includes). This gives Baudelaire the means whereby he can take the measure of a pre-psychoanalytic universe for which the same *horreur* does not induce a mere blanking of rejection: "Where all, even horror, leads to enchantments" (85). "We are all more or less mad" (102), but "As sin is everywhere, redemption is everywhere, the myth everywhere. Nothing more cosmopolitan than the eternal" (1229).

Baudelaire's very representation of physical impressions, Richard shows us,[7] opens into a view of *profondeur*, a depth that at the same time tends to recede. When this spatial perception is applied to time, it differs from its Platonic prototype. "The previous life" stands under the pathos of something that cannot shed its air of distance, where "j'ai vécu dans les voluptés calmes, / Au milieu de l'azur, des vagues, des splendeurs" ("I have lived in calm delights / Amid azure, waves, and splendors," 17). Yet the end of this "refreshment" is a dolorous *profoundeur*: "to deepen / the sad secret that made me languish." Moreover, the poem stands under the same rubric as all, *Les Fleurs du mal,* and it is fixedly placed and numbered between "Le Guignon" and the "Bohémiens en Voyage," for whom the future, like the past, sheds a gloom: "The familiar empire of future shadows" (18). And even in such pieces as "L'Invitation au voyage" and "Le Balcon," the Watteauesque atmosphere does not firmly locate the poem either in a figurative past or in a pastoral present. The allegory permits only the defining demarcations it provides.

The dominance of time in Baudelaire, described by Poulet,[8] results in, and corresponds to, the radical human incapacity, which it is the task and the triumph of this poetry to measure. "Et le Temps m'engloutit minute par minute" ("And Time is swallowing me minute by minute," 72). Memory does not get recaptured in Baudelaire, though the first step of a Proustian yearning is endemic to his sensibility. Rather, memory shrinks experience: "Aux yeux du souvenir que le monde est petit!" (122). "To particularize too much and to generalize too much both block memory . . . nature gives nothing that is absolute or even complete. It is above all in the human race that the infinity of variety is manifested in a frightening manner." A sort of anti-Proust or anti-Wordsworth, Baudelaire depicts himself as standing back fortified before the shrinking of the human body itself, whereby the coffin of an aged person is finally no larger than a child's ("Les Petites Vieilles," a poem much admired by Proust). Before eternity the physical similarity of old woman and child allows their allegorical assimilation to each other. It is significantly of old *women* that Baudelaire notices this process. And woman, too, acts to shrink the world: "You put the universe in your alcove / Foul woman!" (26). In "La Cloché fêlée" (68), the poet's soul is cracked like a bell; he finds it at once bitter and sweet, while the bell sounds, to hear slowly rise the memories that at the same time are *lointains.* The very accumulation of memories operates not to coordinate experience, as in Proust, or even to effectuate Balzacian disillusionment, but rather to render everything into shrunken, flat equivalence. Allegorizations serve as a counterweight of defining expression, against which a feeling of horror or boredom can measure itself. "J'ai plus de souvenirs que si j'avais mille ans" ("I have more memories than if I were a thousand years old") occasions a feeling of "Spleen" (69). The memories come to a bare list of bric-a-brac, where the savor of his most powerful experiences, "De vers, de billets doux, de procès, de romances," is sapped into the equivalence of verbiage written on papers thrown into a drawer "encumbered" with them. The next "Spleen" depicts a prince in whose veins, the last line tells us, runs "the green water of Lethe" instead of blood (70). The last of the "Spleen" poems has a black day sadder than night cast upon collective humanity, and Angoisse triumphs over Espoir. In this whole section of "Spleen et Idéal"—the first, and by far the longest, of the sections—the "spleen" holds the "idéal" constantly in check, measured by a strong repertoire of allegorized figures. After some years Baudelaire gave the title "Spleen de Paris" to the "petits poèmes en prose," allowing the name of an overall response and condition, momentary and all-embracing, to surface as the single mark in feeling of all the perceptions he marshals. Spleen heightens melancholy, transcends satire, activates an *ennui* from which it is not wholly to be differentiated, generalizes a mood, and raises the pitch of *le cafard*.

The process of arriving at what may be defined as Spleen is exemplified in the narrative course of individual poems, as in "Une Charogne" (28), which appears under the rubric "Spleen et Idéal." Of the four poems given that title individually, the first "Spleen," in the poised formality of a sonnet, runs a course backwards, as it were, in time, but consistently in allegorization from the name of the Revolutionary month (Pluviose) to a Laclos-like set piece of conversation between eighteenth-century playing card figures (68–69):

LXXV

SPLEEN

Pluviose, irrité contre la ville entière,
De son urne à grands flots verse un froid ténébreux
Aux pâles habitants du voisin cimetière
Et la mortalité sur les faubourgs brumeux.

Mon chat sur le carreau cherchant une litière
Agite sans repos son corps maigre et galeux;
L'âme d'un vieux poète erre dans la gouttière
Avec la triste voix d'un fantôme frileux.

Le bourdon se lamente, et la buche enfumée
Accompagne en fausset la pendule enrhumée,
Cependant, qu'en un jeu plein de sales parfums,

Héritage fatal d'une vieille hydropique,
Le beau valet de coeur et la dame de pique
Causent sinistrement de leurs amours défunts.

Pluviose, provoked against the whole city,
From his urn pours in great floods a gloomy cold
On the pale denizens of the graveyard nearby
And on the foggy suburbs pours mortality.

My cat seeking a litter on the tiles
Stirs restlessly his lean and scaly body;
The soul of an old poet strays in the rainspout
With the sad voice of a touchy phantom.

The bumblebee whines, and the smoky log
Sings falsetto with the clock that has a cold,
While in a card deck full of filthy smells,

Fatal legacy of a dropsical crone,
The handsome Jack of Hearts and the Queen of Spades
Chat ominously of their expired loves.

Loss, occasioning spleen, is suggested in the first two lines: the month
Pluviose (a name formed on "rains"), the tipping of urns, and the verb
verse — all predict furious rains, but instead we have "un froid ténébreux,"
a presence-in-absence. Spleen, too, is here a sort of presence-in-absence
because *irrité* names a feeling that does not rise to *spleen* and does not
even have that capacity (and the irritation of Pluviose is causeless, a pathetic fallacy with the pathos unnamed).

In the second quatrain what should carry water carries instead the
disembodied voice of an old poet. The humble, present, visible detail gives
way to a supernatural manifestation out of the past. In the first tercet
of the sestet, the water, again, enters only in the metaphor (a sharp definition of a clock that strikes more faintly than one might think) of "la pendule enrhumée," and in the possible liquidity of the "sales parfums," which
turn out to be the legacy of someone who died because she was super-
saturated, the "vieille hydropique," to whom the "jeu plein de sales parfums" is appended. The *causerie* about "amours défunts" is contained
in the *mortalité* of the first quatrain, and a defunct love confounds its
two possibilities — loves of dead persons, or loves that have run their term.
The process from weather to love, from above the whole city to the apart-
ment, from strangely dry to fatally wet, involves diminution, and the
whole triggers what it stands for, the named feeling, "Spleen," caught
in these exemplary and emblematic circumstances that begin and end
with figures allegorical enough to get capital letters for their names. The
next three poems, however, do not repeat this complex sequence. We get,
instead, a miscellany in couplets, a languid king described in couplets,
and a set of quatrains beginning with a *ciel* that "pours a black daylight
sadder than the nights" (70), recalling the action of Pluviose and diminishing it by offering a less metaphoric manipulation. The final sequence,
too, is even more markedly allegorical.

"Spleen et idéal" could be an alternation, or a scale, or a set of equivalents. In the process of feeling that the poems represent and occasionally
mime, the "spleen" operates, so to speak, to translate the ideal into a restlessness of voyage, something for which in the pure state there is no con-
tingent motive: "Les vrais voyageurs sont ceux-là seuls qui partent /
pour partir" ("True voyagers are those alone who leave / For the sake of leav-

ing," 122). The impulse is easily universalized and compounded: "This life is a hospital where every sick person is possessed with a desire to change his bed" (303) — not only sick, but restless in the hospital itself.

"L'Irréparable" is not simply a given set of circumstances (52–53). It "gnaws with its cursed tooth / . . . And often it attacks / as the termite does / At the base of the building" ("Ronge avec sa dent maudite . . . Et souvent il attaque, ainsi que le termite / Par la base le bâtiment"). Another name for this condition is "L'Irrémediable," under which an idea-form or a being that starts out in l'azur falls into a "muddy, leaden Styx" (75). The "sole solace and glory" is a perception of the defining condition itself, "consciousness in Evil" (976). The angel of "Réversibilité" (42) is invoked not because he[9] offers hope but simply because he offers a contrast in his gaiety, goodness, health, and beauty to the anguish, hate, fever, and wrinkles that humankind cannot avoid. The angel, however, may perceive these, as the poet does, and possibly pray for the universally afflicted.[10]

One of Baudelaire's literary projects was to substitute the "essence divine du cercle vicieux" (517).[11] In his vision, do alternation, reversibility, permutation, lead back to the same repetition: "Nous imitons, horreur! la toupie et la boule" ("We imitate, o horror! the top and the ball," 123). "De la vaporisation à la centralisation du *moi*. Tout est là" (1271). This is a psychological alternation in which each term undoes rather than completes or even simply alters the other. So "Cruelty and voluptuousness" are "identical sensations, like extreme heat and extreme cold" (1278). And, more generally, "Even as a child I felt in my heart two contradictory feelings, the horror of life and the ecstasy of life" (1296). Naming them by such abstractions allows firm placement, proportionate relations, and ultimate reference to the felt condition of loss.

It takes hashish to bring a man to the sentiment that Rousseau attributes to the natural man. "I am the most virtuous of all men" (381) is for Baudelaire a reflection induced by a debilitating, will-sapping drug, the maxim of "paradis artificiel." Man is naturally a Swedenborgian devil as he approaches remorse (380), and even the philosophizing of the human spirit closes a circle (386). In the second "Spleen," he says, "je suis un cimitière" and "je suis un vieux boudoir" (69). Laurent Jenny[12] notices the rhetorical, and by implication the perceptual, deflections implied in these attributions: "I am he . . . the antinomy between the intimate body of the self and these receptacles of absence." Such deflections work to abstract the speaker, too, into the allegorical schema.

The strategies of escape tend to become self-defeating, in need of constant renewal. Hence the need for intoxication, and "Le Vin" occupies a whole section of *Les Fleurs du mal*. Wine is called a *fleur* in the last word of "L'âme du Vin" (100) — a "fleur du mal," of course. The term is on the way to converting metaphor into allegory. "De vin, de poésie ou de vertu, à votre guise," Baudelaire says at the end of "Enivrez-vous" (286). "Il faut être toujours ivre" is the self-mocking injunction of the Romantic élan that will later emerge, unironically, as Pater's "To burn always with this hard, gem-like flame is success in life."

To couple *poésie* and *vertu* is already a Renaissance topos. The addition of *vin*, given the prominence of first place in the list, extends the identification by threatening to undo it. The abstract equalization of the three constitutes, in effect, a warning that there is no escape from the deep human incapacity — of which another inescapable sign is the very longing to escape. For Baudelaire the merely aesthetic is not possible, even in the physical delectation of wine, and *Les Paradis artificiels* opens with a scornful rejection of the quintessential gastronome, Brillat-Savarin (323–25).

Baudelaire carries much further than the Poe of the *Eureka* he praises the application of a quasi-theological conception of the function of poetry. His subject matter becomes so obsessive that the doctrine of correspondences itself, while somewhat transcendent in its ability to define disturbances of perception ("fixer des vertiges" is Rimbaud's later phrase), still also partakes of the necessarily failed quest. As Richard says (p. 102), "La loi de l'universelle analogie peut donc s'interpréter comme une sorte de perpetuelle *invitation au voyage*" ("The law of universal analogy can thus be interpreted as a perpetual invitation to the voyage"). The *gouffre* opens everywhere in Baudelaire's physical and spiritual perceptions, as Richard (p. 93) and others have pointed out:

> Pascal avait son gouffre, avec lui se mouvant.
> Hélas! Tout est abîme, — action, désir, rêve,
> Parole! . . .
> J'ai peur du sommeil comme on a peur d'un grand trou.
>
> Pascal had his gulf, moving on with him.
> Alas! All is abyss — action, desire, dreams,
> Speech! . . .
> I fear sleep as one fears a big hole.   ("Le Gouffre," 172)

And in the "Hygiène" of *Fusées* he enumerates various *gouffres* that effectually identify them with his several preoccupations of thought and feeling.[13]

Poetry itself, then, is a two-edged instrument. It possesses a capacity for delivering a view of ultimate moral verities and aesthetic correspondences, but it all adds up to a giddy awareness of incapacity. The most fully aware tends to be the most deprived, a Romantic notion Baudelaire sternly refrains from romanticizing. Indeed, it has a Biblical analogue in the publicans and sinners who have attained the first step of divesting themselves from hypocrisy. One would say of Baudelaire what he says of a composer: "Beethoven began with stirring up the worlds of melancholy and incurable despair amassed like clouds in man's interior sky!" (739). The *lectuer* is a *semblable* in all ways but that he conceals it from himself as a *hypocrite*. Baudelaire places at the very beginning of *Les Fleurs du mal*, after this invocation, the "Bénédiction" (I), which recounts the origin of the poet's psyche in the curses of a mother, so convincingly that a century of readers was led astray from appreciating the positive aspects of Mme. Aupick herself, who was somewhat sensitive to her son's needs (and infirmities). To her he sent *Mon coeur mis à nu*.[14].

The very next poem in this sequence, insisting on the role before he proceeds further to exercise it, offers a correspondence for the poet in imagined anecdote, "L'Albatross" (II). This allegorized figure serves as a sort of anti-type to the angels in the poems, who are full of joy and beauty wherever they may turn. The wings of the trapped albatross are a curse on the deck where he is mocked. "His giant wings prevent him from walking" (10). The inarticulateness of the bird, as well as his entrapment, bar him from any "Cain"-like or "Manfred"-like countermotions. Baudelaire, as characteristically, has transformed the topos variously represented in Romantic times by the still dominant Byron and by the Chatterton who had served de Vigny as a protagonist. (Moreover, Baudelaire does *not* play up the *poète maudit* side of Poe.)

Seen as a proposition, the poem's transcendence of what is perceived cancels itself: its proper function is to state the obsession and incapacity of the speaker. Seen as an act, however, it stands achieved, its perception a final distillate of Goethe's "Wer immer strebend sich bemüht, / Den können wir erlösen" ("He who always strivingly bestirs himself, / Him can we redeem," *Faust*, 11936–37). As Baudelaire says of Daumier:

> C'est un satirique, un moqueur;
> Mais l'énergie avec laquelle
> Il peint le Mal et sa séquelle,
> Prouve la beauté de son coeur.   (151)

> He is a satirist, a mocker,
> But the energy with which
> He paints Evil and its result
> Proves the beauty of his heart.

In "Un Voyage à Cythère," the hope of a *locus amoenus* gives way to a desert where a rotting corpse is picked to pieces on a gibbet, and the poet declares that he has "a heart buried in this allegory" as in a "thick sudarium." The term of literary definition, *allégorie*, and the final in-junction hold him in a gesture that involves fixity, since he can contem-plate only Cythère. But also it involves reparation, since he wishes "De contempler mon coeur et mon corps sans dégout!" (113).

In this final injunction there is no state beyond good and evil. Nor could his contemplation, if achieved, realize the inarticulate innocence that persists in a woman given over to debauchery. The poem's title, "Allégorie," gives us the cue to extend it beyond portraiture; she is imag-ined finally to face death "like a newborn babe—without hate and with-out remorse" (110). Baudelaire himself would not dispense with remorse. Rather he would absolutize it, so that it could wholly operate without bringing in its train the ultimately self-indulgent responses of *dégout*. Baudelaire modifies the Christian maxim that rain falls alike on the just and the unjust to expand, in "Le Soleil" (79), on how the sun shines on the sick and the well equally.

And yet there are expansive possibilities in the very power of human perversity. "The vices of man, which are as full of horror as one supposes them to be, contain the proof (unless this be only their infinite expan-sion!) of his taste for the infinite" (348).

3

"Tout pour moi devient allégorie." The immediate occasion of Bau-delaire's saying this is his comparison, powerful just because forced, be-tween the Seine and not the real Simois but its counterfeit in Andro-mache's exile. So that in a double sense is the Seine "this lying Simois." It is the spectacle of a city's change that suddenly fecundates his memory and makes him realize that "my dear memories are heavier than the rocks" (82).

The special equilibrium of Baudelaire centers the personal self of his poems in a city that is not merely a focus for satire. It too is at once an allegorical figure and a matrix for allegory. For the Roman poets, as for Johnson and Pope, the city is a finite, perhaps entropic, entity. For Baudelaire, however, the city partakes of a sort of infinity. "There is noth-ing more cosmopolitan than the Eternal" (1229). In "Rêve Parisien" he dedicates to Constantin Guys a poem that offers an image strikingly apoca-lyptic, quite beyond those in the graphic work of this "peintre de la vie moderne." A Venice-like Paris is extended in a vision where "all, even the color black / Seemed polished, clear, rainbowed" (98). And the distances of this dream must be reckoned in the millions of leagues as they stretch infinitely outward:

Des nappes d'eau s'épanchaient, bleues,
Entre des quais roses et verts,
Pendant des millions de lieus
Vers les confins de l'univers.   (97)

Sheets of water spread out, blue
Among the quays of rose and green,
All through millions of leagues
To the confines of the universe.

The Romantic poet who turns away to the sublimities of solitude leaves the city behind him in his dream. So Hölderlin and Nerval. For Wordsworth the city is a sleeping panorama, a presence in a fog, or a sort of jumble-shop. He is "long in populous city pent." Baudelaire manages to subsume a comparable solitude and turn it squarely to the city, which serves at once as a vehicle for solitude and a block against it. The urban debilities of Villon's Paris, by contrast, depend on the fixed definitions of role to which, time and again, an object corresponds that is being transferred by the testamentary will of the speaker. Villon's bird-pecked corpses are not an allegory for love, as in Baudelaire's "Un Voyage à Cythère" (III), but actual criminals, and his aging beauty is defined by the loss of her beautiful attributes, item by item. Baudelaire's *petites vièilles* are set explicitly in the "Tableaux Parisiens," and the first line of that poem reestablishes that frame:

Dans les plis sinueux des vieilles capitales,
Où tout, même l'horreur, tourne aux enchantements.   (85)

In the sinuous folds of the old capitals,
Where all, even horror, turns into enchantment.

The city, as a chimerical vehicle for psychic expansion, provides a continuum along which attraction and repulsion merge into each other, a motion impossible for Villon. "It is above all from frequenting enormous cities, it is from the crossing of their innumerable relations (*rapports*), that this obsessive ideal is born" (229). The city provides an occasion for a gawker, a *guetteur* with the urban-endowed idleness of the perfect *flâneur*, to spot, along the lines of his own floating but fixed desires ("obeying my fatal impulses"), beings who are "singular, decrepit, and charming."[15]

Baudelaire's own perceptions make the city itself a vast engine for interactions. He locates his women in an urban setting as condensations of the city's force rather than as types exercising a function, or as the eloquent symbols into which Wordsworth turns the sufferers he encounters on his country excursions. The perfect *flâneur* to whom Baudelaire refers, as Benjamin reminds us, only becomes possible when an industrial society operates at so abstract a remove in its assignment of social tasks that such a functionless observer may emerge, at once totally incapacitated and panoramically aware. For such a *flâneur* Paris can be a *tableau*, whereas through the eighteenth century the idle gentry or nobility of country and city are locked into the role as part of the tableau. Baudelaire, to be sure, has not clearly marked his protagonist with the lifelong, revelatory idleness of Flaubert's Frédéric Moreau, whose education for lack of a well-defined and progressive social role, may be the more purely *sentimentale*.[16] Nor does Baudelaire offer the memory-dialectic wherein the lifelong idler Marcel recaptures the casual events of his drifting life for a transcendent recapitulation. Rather, his persona easily enters a "Spleen" induced by uninterrupted converse with the city, a "Spleen de Paris."

Over an urban landscape, the twilight, that favorite of Romantics from Kaspar David Friedrich to Lamartine,[17] loses it calming and blurring function. In "Le Crépuscule du soir" (262), twilight serves, rather, as a stimulant: "twilight excites madmen." These madmen are men at whose extremity the usual reactions are reversed and whom the poet therefore singles out, just as he remarks that debauchery and idleness exact more of their devotees than ordinary labor would: "The debauchees returned, broken by their labors" (99).

At twilight there is a slow and imperceptible transition between two Baudelairean states—the alertness in which the object that is penetratingly perceived takes on an illusory cast (as in "Les Sept Vieillards," also part of the "Tableaux Parisiens") and the oblivion that the fierce pace of the city's physical transformation brings: "La forme d'une ville / Change plus vite, hélas! que le coeur d'un mortel" ("A city's form / Changes more quickly, alas, than a mortal's heart," 81). "Sous le noir présent transperce le délicieux passé" ("Under the black present pierces the delicious past"). So he draws to the end of "Le Crépuscule du soir," rounding out the extravagant comparison of the stars over the city to a transparent dress over a dazzling petticoat worn by the sort of dancer one would only see in a metropolis (262). The city's illusion of visible change resembles the elaborate dress of the woman (touching on the old topos, "city equals woman"). On this transparent dress, the stars, like the stars over the city, "represent the fires of a fantasy that only lights up well in the profound mourning of night." Here we are far from Haussmann's Boulevards, though above them. And we are also far from the galleries that more precisely marked the Paris in which Baudelaire wandered. The architectural achievements of which the rebuilding of the area around the Pont du

Carroussel was part ("Le Cygne") only serve to extend the psychological alertness and desolation of the poet. He notices in them not what is congruous but what is incongruous, the swan, trailing in mud, escaped from his cage, which reminds him of a negress caught in the city fogs far from her native Africa and from the tropical splendor she hankers back to and he evokes.

Incongruity, memory, dream, and always incapacity are levitated into interfusion by the city itself, whose very surplus of persons leads to the erasure of boundaries and the access of fantasy:

> Fourmillante cité, cité pleine de rêves,
> Où le spectre en plein jour raccroche le passant!   (83)

> Teeming city, city full of dreams,
> Where the ghost in broad daylight buttonholes the passerby.

4

In his direct confrontation of the city, as in other aspects of his vision, Baudelaire comes to realization and focus by profoundly modifying the earlier Romantic assumptions. Valéry emphasizes the abrupt disjunction of Baudelaire's situation by saying that he faced the question of how to be a great poet and not be Lamartine, Hugo, or Musset, as though he cast about and found evil an unworked subject: "je ferai donc autre chose" ("so I'll do something else").[18] In his apologetic posture Baudelaire did indeed express something like this attitude. Still, he stays within recognizable distance of the registers these other poets worked, though his means are more profound. Like Hugo, who was writing *La Légende des siècles* while *Les Fleurs du mal* was being composed, like de Vigny and Lamartine, Baudelaire draws heavily on theological motifs. Putting these motifs on a par with everyday tragic losses, he filters them through something like the consciousness of a Chateaubriand, to ascertain afresh wherein consists "le génie du christianisme."[19] A nostalgia not unlike that of Lamartine permeates Baudelaire's poetry, and "Le Lac" would only have to darken a bit to take on the coloration of Baudelaire.[20]

The "blue devils" of de Vigny's Stello already amount to the "spleen" of Baudelaire, and they also carry the muted and heavy exoticism of the British temper. De Vigny's sense that the poet is cursed, and particularly by his parents, has a Baudelairean ring.[21] By translating him in 1828, Musset brought attention to de Quincey and to opium eating much earlier than Baudelaire did. Poe himself served as a condensed, foreign vehicle for attitudes that Baudelaire could have found (and presumably did find) in these writers, or in Nerval. Yet in them there is no dialectical suppleness to the posture. For example, instead of Baudelaire's rigorous self-examination of his obsessive infatuation, Musset (whom Baudelaire disdained) gives us an easy self-pity when he dwells on a first abandonment by an unfaithful mistress (this is also the theme of *Confessions d'un enfant du siècle*, which insists rather imposingly on its historical significations). Musset's meditation takes place not by the lake, as for the Lamartine to whom these verses are addressed, but

> De cet immense égout qu'on appele Paris;
> Autour de moi criait cette foule railleuse
> Qui des infortunés n'entend jamais les cris.
> Sur le páve noirci les blafardes lanternes
> Versaient un jour douteux plus triste que la nuit.

> In this immense sewer they call Paris;
> About me there cried that jeering crowd
> That never heeds the cries of unfortunates.
> On the blackened pavement the bleary lanterns
> Shed a doubtful light sadder than the night.[22]

Here we are given something like the Baudelairean melancholy and view of the city, without either the trenchant self-criticism or the visual transformation. Baudelaire imitates the last line in his final "Spleen" poem — "Il nous verse un jour plus triste que la nuit"— but he expands it.

As Valéry goes on to say, Baudelaire brings corrections and contradiction to the "Romanticism" (in the narrower, French sense) that dominated the literary horizon against which he came of age. It was the most formal of these writers, Gautier, rather than the closest in spirit to him, Nerval, who drew his attention. And it is in relation to Gautier that he most vividly defines the others — Balzac, de Vigny, Hugo, Sainte-Beuve, and the Chateaubriand who "sang the dolorous glory of melancholy and boredom" (689). This last phrase, indeed, applies without alteration to himself.

Like Stendhal, Baudelaire assumes the posture of someone who masters the Romantic heritage by at once acknowledging it and applying to it a relentless irony and candor. The candor, indeed, is so relentless that it tends to reverse its heritage. For Rousseau's free man and for Goethe's striving man, Baudelaire substitutes not a Hegelian "servant" (*Knecht*) and not someone who will successfully undergo purgation, but rather a man whose freedom consists in honestly refusing hypocrisy and acknowledging his subjection to a process of original sin. "Mais le riche métal de notre volonté / Est tout vaporisé par ce savant chimiste" ("But the rich metal of our will / Is all vaporized by this learned chemist," 9). Satan himself here acts in the Faustian laboratory of elective affinities and repulsions. The term "riche métal" gives a faintly Rousseauist cast to the orthodox theology in these lines, and the term "vaporisé" suggests a process that Wordsworth or Blake could have described but no eighteenth-century theologian or Faculty psychologist would have understood. Here a Romantic imagination operates on a definition of the original sin that is resolutely restored to a central position.

Rousseau, in effect, makes man an "homme-dieu," and such Romantic poems as Lermontov's *Demon* and Lamartine's *La Chute de l'ange* (put on the Index shortly after its publication) make capital of obscuring the difference between man and god. "L'homme-dieu," however, is the title of a section of *Les Paradis artificiels*. The artificial element, the perversely illusory character of the term, leaves Baudelaire's candor with a constant irony that does *not* offer an infinite regress of perception, as does that of E. T. A. Hoffman, or even the Rousseau presented by Paul de Man. In this place Baudelaire speaks unequivocally of the "moral ravage caused by this dangerous and delicious gymnastics" (374). He goes on, in the more deliberate dialectic of his own discussion, to *polariser* the man who is his subject, one given like de Quincey to hashish.

It is with such topoi in mind as Byron's "Roll on, thou deep and dark blue ocean, roll"[23] — though elsewhere Baudelaire draws on the sea as a chief symbol — that he says "je te hais, Océan" (71). He declares (183ff.), contrary to the Romantic mystique and anticipating the "nature red in tooth and claw" of Tennyson's Darwinism, that nature is cruel and virtue artificial.

Baudelaire can draw only dialectically on Romantic sublimity or nostalgia to carry the mood of his expression. There is nothing automatic about Baudelaire's poetic productions. A strong indication of how slowly he eked out his expression is the marked paucity of his output vis-à-vis that of all his contemporaries. And they were busy men besides, while he had no other occupation than the literary. His unity of tone, then, on the evidence at once of the slenderness and the power of his work, has been derived not from the automatic stance or set attitude of the speaker, as it might seem. Rather, it has been exacted, dialectically, out of the very attitudes it at once contraverts and transcends. Poetry is conceived of — at its best, it goes without saying — as producing, and alone producing, such singleminded unity of mood and figural aptness. "The heart contains passion, the heart contains devotion and crime; only the imagination contains poetry" (687).

"Romanticism" resides in "la manière de sentir," in a mood. In this notion Baudelaire echoes Heine's essay on Romanticism. It is to be found not in the "exécution parfaite" but, again and finally, in "une conception analogue à la morale du siècle" (879). Romanticism is a rare achievement: "if there are few romantics, it is because few among them have found romanticism" (878). And Baudelaire goes on in a list at once comprehensive and suggestive of the gamut he has himself learned to run, "intimité, spiritualité, couleur, aspiration vers l'infini."

The obligation that the writer takes on to tell the truth squarely would seem to go without saying. And yet the gesture that says, "Look in thy heart and write" is for Sir Philip Sidney only a momentary one, a rhetorical resource among others. In this primary instance, as generally, Romantic attitudes exponentialize Renaissance ones.[24] The confessional impulse of Rousseau, the fidelity to an unconscious dream universe of the large tradition discussed by Béguin,[25] and the long resurrection of the naive through such as Herder, Wordsworth, and Schiller — all testify to the elaborate and thoroughgoing mechanisms necessary to bring to light what might seem to be *prima facie* present in the literary act, some true state of affairs. In philosophy, correspondingly, the establishment of the verity of the consciousness Descartes had by implication estranged may be seen to parallel Rousseau's introspective establishment of a ground in feeling for conduct.[26] And even the Marquis de Sade, in his finally unreflective extreme of universal perversion, has at least the merit (and has been credited for it beyond his strict due) of thereby following as well as contraverting Rousseau, of unflinchingly facing the dark side of sexuality, a universal "sadism" or masochism later unfolding, as implied in the idea of universal neurosis. Baudelaire himself praises Sade in a context where he is planning novels whose possible power, at least of plot, we might imagine from the strong sample of "La Fanfarlo." "We must always return to Sade," he says, with an arrestingly irrational capitalization of *Revenir*, "in other words to the Natural Man, to explain evil" (521). This is the element he finds lacking even in a painter, even in Corot, who he finds "N'a pas assez souvent le diable au corps" (1079).

But Baudelaire is no Sade. Sade plus Rousseau equals Baudelaire (one could go further and say Rousseau plus Baudelaire equals Proust). It is the hypocrisy of her *contremorale* that makes Baudelaire so severe at such length with George Sand. And it is what he praises in the Romantic school, which "called us back to truth of image," having destroyed the "academic cliche . . . *l'art pour l'art*, art for art's sake [which] excluding morality, and often even passion [is] necessarily sterile" (605). Baudelaire's own vision of sterility here is not itself sterile (and he is, of course, far from espousing the doctrine that evil should be embraced for its incitement to artistic discovery). At the same time, he does not cease to excoriate "the childish excesses of the school called romantic" (617). And he expresses contempt for a Hugo who plays the Prometheus, putting an imaginary vulture to a breast "that is torn only by the mustard plasters of vanity" (1262). He discerns the *sentiment* betrayed by absurdity in his admired

Gautier (722). And he compares Hugo unfavorably, as using "trickery," with the creative power of Delacroix. The comparison implies what he states elsewhere, the union of visionary tasks in all the arts, whether in poetry, in painting, or in such music as Wagner's.

"Make your life hang on the truth" ("Vitam impendere vero"). Baudelaire (899) quotes this "austère devise" approvingly and says only three have followed it: Jean Jacques, Louis Blanc, and George Sand. The last in the list, as we know from his other statements about her, already implies what he then quotes Joseph de Maistre as generally saying: that if a writer adopts this device, "there is a good chance he is a liar."

5

Byron, Tennyson, Poe and Company. Sorrowful (*mélancolique*) sky of modern poetry. Stars of first magnitude. (805)

Baudelaire here would seem to single out melancholy as the defining quality making a poet a star of the first order. Beyond these names, and just in the light of this defining temper, realizing melancholy as a sort of metaphysical state, we would add Baudelaire's own name (along with many others). But of all these poets Baudelaire alone adopts a critical posture, a constant near-irony, yielding a melancholy of generalizable power. (Wordsworth goes through the motions of self-criticism but is not radically *self*-critical.) The pity of Baudelaire's melancholy, and the pitilessness of his irony, are two aspects of the same large gesture of poetic understanding. "Two fundamental literary attributes," he says, "supernaturalism and irony" (1256). And because his *mélancolie* constantly implies *surnaturalisme*, it becomes ironic. He embraces both qualities and balances them in the evenness of his figural presentation.

The presence of a melancholic tone, indeed, controls the irony of Baudelaire, preventing it on the one hand from abutting into a satiric miscellany, and on the other hand from expanding into the infinite regress of a Stendhal, the self-canceling or self-inspiriting mordancy of E. T. A. Hoffman, whom Baudelaire himself finds exemplary (991–92). His irony, however, contained within or combined with his melancholy, does admit of some sense of expansion, not the easy expansiveness of Lamartine, but the regretted, rigorously examined possibility of expansion, feeling the infinite at the very moment of seeking it.[27]

In structure the Baudelairean human situation undergoes ironic self-definition even when in the turns of rhetoric no specific ironies of statement or even of event have been called upon. There is, so to speak, a prior hypotyposis to each of these poems, which the title, *Les Fleurs du mal*, effectually announces. "Human laughter," he says—thus assimilating that subject to his own vision—"is intimately limited in the action of an ancient fall" (978). A limit is felt always to be present, a *gouffre* that yawns and must be perceived for any true assessment of a condition. "Vertigo," he says, "is absolute comedy" (990). This is apropos of the Pierrot "full of a high aesthetic," and of pantomime in general. "Pantomime is the purging of comedy," he says, and it is as though this condition led to his own work—where all the beings are strangely silent, seen and faced in their allegorical posture, and even obsessively addressed, but never heard to answer. The perception becomes not comedy again so much as melancholy, though Pierrot is melancholic, a fact on which Laforgue will construct a whole emotional poetics. And here in Baudelaire's context it is Pierrot's end under the guillotine—not exactly a comic event—that is being discussed.

The "vertige" of the "comique absolu" is produced by a situation akin to a common stance of Baudelaire's, the fairy's silent wand waving promise to Harlequin and the others—after which they all act because "La destinée nous précipite" ("destiny rushes us on," 991), again much like the persons in Baudelaire's poems. As Baudelaire says in "De l'essence du rire," "The artist is only an artist on the condition of being double and of overlooking no phenomenon of his double nature" (993). He is writing, he has begun by saying, about caricature, and he does not want to do a treatise on it (975). The essay, like his poems, is informed by a "doubleness" of seeing mankind as a distortion of its ideal possibility and as a realized entity striking to observe in the fated extremity of its course of behavior: "Nous imiton, horreur! la toupie et la boule" ("We imitate —horrors!—the top and the ball," 123). In this light, "The sage only laughs with a tremble" (976). His allegory transcends caricature in a third way, beyond normal distortion or the "absolute" inflation residing in the grotesque.

In this light it is not surprising that for Baudelaire, earnestness, melancholy, a comic absolute, and reductive critical definition converge into a single tone. "Woman is the opposite of the dandy. So she should inspire horror" (1271). Should we feel horror or its opposite at the opposite of what inspires horror? There is something missing here, once we are not told to be horrified, or reassured, by the dandy himself. He is exalted as a stance but not definitely distinguished in his lack of naturalness or vulgarity (traits listed for *la femme*) from the Baudelairean speaker, whose reaction may be described variously as *horreur, vertige, spleen*, or *ennui*. Indeed, Baudelaire asserts a continuity between such emotions and the pervasive neglect that amounts to an indolent, all-embracing sadism:

Il ferait volontiers de la terre un débris
Et dans un bâillement avalerait le monde;

C'est L'Ennui! — l'oeil chargé d'un pleur involontaire
Il rêve d'échafauds en fumant son houka.
Tu le connais, lecteur, ce monstre délicat —
Hypocrite lecteur, mon semblable, mon frere.   (6)

He would willingly make the earth a shambles
And in a yawn would swallow up the world;

That's Boredom! Eye charged with an involuntary tear
He dreams of scaffolds while smoking his hookah,
You know him, reader, this delicate monster —
Hypocrite reader, my likeness, my brother.

At the culminating point of this liminal poem, a vice is characterized by a strange oxymoron as a "monstre délicat." The balance of the poet, no less than cosmic, is poised to a point where dandy and anti-dandy would no longer be discernible. In the book, as in the trail-off lines of individual poems within it,[28] there is an anticlimactic drift from the high-pitched, often exclamatory "Au Lecteur" and "Bénédiction" (with its scathingly ironic title) to the low-keyed summary descriptions of "Le Voyage." It is a movement from "Spleen et Idéal" to "La Mort," the "Tableaux Parisiens" taking a middle position in the sequence. "Révolte," which so revolted his contemporaries, is placed penultimately as a sort of desperate gasp rather than being grouped with "Bénédiction," which it most resembles in tone.

Throughout *Les Fleurs du mal* we are made aware of what Valéry calls "the plenitude and the singular exactness of his ring."[29] The Racinian formal line controls an equanimity of definition so potentially at odds with the appalling matter to be defined that it can allow itself none of the headier *correspondances*, doctrine or no, which Nerval had already demonstrated as possible for poetry. We are beyond modulation, and Baudelaire cannot speak of himself, like Nerval, as "modulant tour à tour sur la lyre d'Orphée / Les soupirs de la Sainte et les cris de la Fée" ("modulating in turn on Orpheus' lyre / The signs of the saint and the fairy's cries,").[30] Nowhere in Baudelaire are the *correspondances* more than *échos de loin*. The allegorical evenness is itself too dominant. In his work we do not find anything like "un pur esprit s'accroît sous l'écorce des pierres" ("a pure spirit grows under the bark of stones").[31] Among Baudelaire's most conflated images are the allegorical descriptions of painters in "Les Phares," where the colon after each name insists on the precision and formality of the equivalence. The principle of disorder — of what I have elsewhere called diffusion[32] — appears in the randomness with which the swan enters and leaves the poem called "Le Cygne." The randomness underscores the allegorical function of the swan, while displacing it from such squarely formal symbolization as Mallarmé (and later Valéry and Rilke) endowed it with.

Another step and we are in the completely opposite mode, the prose poem, which Baudelaire cuts back rigorously from the vaguely sublimating and highly anaphorized register of Aloysius Bertrand's *Gaspard de la nuit,* even more than did Mallarmé, who also made a point of mulling over Bertrand.[33]

Baudelaire hovers between the extremes of order and randomness. As he says (311) in his projects for the *Petits poèmes en prose,* they are at once "without head or tail" and "all head and tail." In the elaborately rhymed and highly structured poem "La Chevelure" (25), with the usual French preponderance of end-stopped lines, the object stands synecdochally for the enrapturing woman, and also for the universe of which she is part, including possible voyages:

> Tu contiens, mer d'ébène, un éblouissant rève
> De voiles, de rameurs, de flammes et de mâts.
>
> You hold, o ebony sea, a dazzling dream
> Of sails, of rowers, of flames and of masts.

The fall of hair is also, finally, the source of remembrance for the poet:

> N'est tu pas l'oasis où je rêve, et la gourde
> Où je hume à longs traits le vin du Souvenir?
>
> Are you not the oasis where I dream, and the gourd
> Where I savor in long draughts the wine of memory?

In the title of the corresponding prose poem in *Spleen de Paris,* "Un Hémisphère dans une chevelure" (252), Baudelaire makes the whole idea more arbitrary. The lack of rhyme is made to give the separate assertions about the *chevelure* an anecdotal randomness, since they are not swept up together in the rhetoric of a Bertrand. There are, besides, distancing statements, and the conclusion is merely: "When I bite your hair, elastic and rebellious, it seems I am eating memories." This is not an assertion about *souvenirs* but an anecdote about the possible illusion of eating something abstract as the counterpart of a small perverse act.

Baudelaire applies to both poetry and art Emerson's dictum "the hero is he who is immovably centered" (1127). He himself consistently exalts a singlemindedness difficult to sustain against such cross-currents. The threshold of heroism, as for Nietzsche, exacts a constant effort. The prose poem, in his hands, freed of rhetorical afflatus, of more than incidental argumentative structure, and of interwoven narrative line, boldly exemplifies and produces an utterance where the expectation of *poème* converges upon a nakedness lacking any other marking features than *prose.* The poet here becomes indistinguishable from the cynical anecdotalist, the proto-scripturalist, the moralist, the *causeur*, and the ethnographic traveler, all of whom find a voice in *Spleen de Paris.*

As Baudelaire says, "J'invente une langue," and the matter-of-factness of the prose may be seen to carry the *spleen.* A high point is aimed for through fixity of time: "The supreme point of art would consist in remaining glacial and closed. That way the effect of horror would have been increased."[34]

To imagine the speaker of such poems is, of course, to reinvent something in the nature of poetry by making explicit the foundation of poetry in dominant feelings out of which such intimations of vision may arise. Baudelaire enables the young Rimbaud to amplify and reinfuse these elements. The infernal voyage of Baudelaire now becomes historicized, and it is given the episodic suspension of an expanded series of *petits poèmes en prose* in *Une Saison en Enfer.* Is this season a lifetime or a purgatorial stint to be followed by other, different seasons? It is at once a threshold and a disastrous goal; as in *Spleen de Paris,* we are not told which. And in *Les Illuminations* the process holds whereby the *luxe, calme, et volupté* of "Invitation au Voyage" stands under the rubric of *Les Fleurs du mal,* while the paradises of "Le Voyage" are more treacherous, because their loss is not realized. Baudelaire, indeed, provides the principle as well as the elements for such transformations by his immovable insistence on the gravity of the poetic task, and by the calm abstractness of the figures in which he casts his visions of the depths.

9

Mallarmé
The Deepening Occasion

1

Mallarmé, as it were, liberated the allegorical entities of Baudelaire, co-ordinated them, elevated them, and invested them in common objects of his "symbolic universe" by returning them to the language of the tribe. Thus terms like "fold," "whiteness," "abolished," "feather," "urn," "nude," "swan," "sunset," ride buoyantly on a poetry that manages, by algebraizing a Romantic symbology, to be at once periphrastic and epigrammatic. The polysemous and the simple are brought to a convergence in a self-generating abstractness that accords the named objects a plenitude of hovering-through-absence. "Absence" is Mallarmé's own term, but a large presence also obtains: "I say: a flower! and, aside from the oblivion into which my voice relegates every contour, insofar as it is something other than the known calices, there arises musically—the very idea and soft, the absent one of all bouquets."[1] The "I" to speak so is the "I" of Mallarmé. The speaker centers himself as the self-effacing and self-glorying aesthete who produces a new version of Baudelaire's "comique absolu." Baudelaire found this attitude in the mime of Pierrot, and Mallarmé's own comments on mime can be made, in Derrida's impressive reading, to define much of his own practice.[2] His words, especially in their inter-action with the calculated white spaces of *Un Coup de dés*, converge on wordlessness; his self-presentation finds an analogue in the common dream of self-mocking idolatry—almost the chastised clown of his poem ("Le Pitre Châtié"). Pierrot, his murdered wife Columbine, and her lover Harlequin are liberated from the specificity of a folk origin and personal catastrophe. Plot has disappeared, except for its Hamlet-like vestiges, in *Un Coup de dés*. Or else it has been hyperbolically allegorized, at the beginning of this poet's career, in figures drawn more directly from classical and Biblical legend—*L'Après-midi d'un faune, Hérodiade*.

Though "solitary and autonomous," in the words of the Valéry who knew and revered him,[3] Mallarmé angled the artificiality of that solitude, the solitude whose literary power he had learned from Baudelaire, to test it without self-indulgence. In his work he tests it by its opposite, taking a quietly liminal posture that allows him to deprecate the momentary social nature of an occasion. The achieved Baudelairean balance is carried a step further by being divested of special attitudes and ingrained into a common staple of images.

Mallarmé is said on the same authority to have abhorred his métier — though he persistently kept on it the notes of "Les Mots Anglais" that can be given lines of connection to his poetry. And unlike Baudelaire he did have a métier, not that of the professional man of letters, to which he rose, characteristically, on festive and ceremonial occasions, but the rather humble métier of the lycée teacher. Such a métier could never serve to launch someone to the exalted official posts of a Hugo and a Lamartine before, a Claudel or a Perse afterwards; rather it provided a neutral basis, a steady ground, upon whose social circumstances Mallarmé could project not only the regularity of his "Mardis" but, surprisingly, an armature for the scintillations of his austere poetics.

The austerity has so impressed his successors that the basis in an ordinary setting, and often an ordinary occasion, for his algebralike poetry has become obscured. We have not properly pondered the weights of his splendid balance. Yet we should find arresting, to begin with, the fact that, perhaps uniquely in the *oeuvre* of so important a writer, something over half the verses that have come down to us take as their form and occasion the most momentary of trivia: address poems, poems for birthdays, poems written to accompany Easter eggs or glazed fruits for the New Year, Honfleur cakes or crocks of Calvados, poems to be written on fans, poems to go with teapots, books, mirrors, handkerchiefs, and kazoos (*mirlitons*).

The occasional leads to the hermetic, merges with it, gets adapted for it, or is redefined in its context. "La Déclaration foraine" culminates in an impromptu incident on an afternoon excursion with his mistress, Méry, when she impulsively gets up on the small stage in a park, a "vivante allégorie." This prose poem, as a centerpiece of description to explain the attraction Méry would have for spectators, quotes the late sonnet "La chevelure vol d'une flamme à l'extrême." Then the sonnet is shifted to the *Poésies* to take on in separation a more emblematic ring; the references to the single occasion thereby become more obscure, but they do not vanish. This prose poem itself was published twice in periodicals before it was included in first one collection of prose poems and then another one, with the significant title *Divagations* (1560). Accordingly, segments of Mallarmé's column in the *Revue Blanche*, "Variations sur un sujet," were sometimes detached and printed separately as prose poems, while his first column was prefaced by the poem "Petit Air"— thereby giving that poem a critical dimension.

Baudelaire's urbanite, by another twist, could be free in his personal solitude, for all his fixity in a bureaucatic occupation. He could be free, in fact, to move into (and out of) what in a less cosmopolitan society might have seemed to be the opposite of that freedom, the sort of sociable and festive participation in the stream of public leisure that introduced him to Méry in Manet's studio. The eighteenth-century London of Pope and Collins, for all its being a prototypical compendium of the modern city, could not have afforded such freedom. The public writer could not attain the register of the private one, or vice versa. But Baudelaire, or Mallarmé, so to speak, could be Pope and Collins both — or at once Diderot and Rousseau.

On his arrival for a teaching assignment to Paris, Mallarme's first literary-commercial enterprise, and his most protracted public one, was to undertake singlehanded the production of a monthly fashion magazine. And in the numbers of *La Dernière Mode* he offers, with equal aplomb under varying pseudonyms, a guide to the theatrical season along with advice on children's fashions, festive menus along with answers to questions about fashion, an essay on jewels following recommendations about costume ensembles. That the self-projection of so solitary a writer found itself so fully absorbed in this polyptych of worldly transience indicates the profound harmony he was willing to invest, and to discover, in the momentary.[4] Steeped progressively in such transience, he was able to recast its elements into purged visions or a sort of poised, idealized permanence.[5] While for Baudelaire "tout devient allégorie," for Mallarmé the significance was already vested in an object and its occasion, the poem only deepening and revealing it. This is the "world" side of his exaltation of the book: "Tout, au monde, existe pour aboutir à un livre" ("Everything in the world exists to end in a book," 378).

Mallarmé was implicitly released for such possibilities by the Romantic transcendence in general, and Baudelaire's in particular, of a distinction between the transitory and the momentous.[6] He found a way to bring the transitory and the momentous perilously close to identification, thereby also annulling, as even Baudelaire and Rimbaud had not, the classical scale of gravity for poetry, the fixed scale ranging from the light verse of epigram to the grand diapason of epic.

Take the late poem that he himself chose as the first and introductory item of his ultimate collection: "Salut."

Rien, cette écume, vierge vers
À ne désigner que la coupe;
Telle loin se noie une troupe
De sirènes mainte à l'envers.

Nous naviguons, ô mes divers
Amis, moi déjà sur la poupe
Vous l'avant fastueux qui coupe
Le flot de foudres et d'hivers;

Une ivresse belle m'engage
Sans craindre même son tangage
De porter debout ce salut

Solitude, récif, étoile
À n'importe ce qui valut
Le blanc souci de notre toile.   (27)

Nothing, this foam, virgin verse
To designate only the cup;
Such far off there drowns a troop
Of many sirens upside down.

We navigate, my diverse
Friends, I already on the poop
You the splendid prow which cuts
The flood of lightnings and of winters;

A fine drunkenness engages me
Without fear of its rolling
To carry upright this toast

Solitude, reef, star
To whatever it was that was worth
The white care of our sail.
                    (Translation mine, based on that of Roger Fry)

  Baudelaire's "Le Voyage"—which comes last, rather than first, in *Les Fleurs du mal*—has here been returned to something like the pastoral mode. Baudelaire's long, culminating poem is a meditation on the Death underlying the motives of a series of solitary voyages. It begins by contemplating the difference between childhood and the narrowing world of adulthood. Sublating Baudelaire's symbology, Mallarmé's tonic invocation celebrates what it couches in loaded images, a single, collective, allegorizable voyage. Eros (the sirens) and Thanatos (the lightnings and winters) are neutralized in the act of accounting for them by displacing and abstracting them into images. They become the "absent flower" of the verbal bouquet that presents them in a sprightly arrangement. Stoic resolution and Epicurean delectation have been levitated into a single encompassing attitude.

Here the navigation of the "divers amis" refers initially to the poetic enterprise (it is read at a banquet of poets). The "ivresse belle" has lost all the bitterness of Baudelaire's "Vins" without entirely abandoning the psychological theory behind them. The canvas remains blank and white, or leaves some white blank as a core. The equivalence of value holds, though it be among incommensurables:

> Solitude, récif, étoile
> À n'importe ce qui valut
> Le blanc souci de notre toile.

"Le flot de foudres et d'hivers," for all its literariness, is not entirely to be divorced from what is in fact its primary reference, the weathers and seasons of a mortal life abstracted enough for death itself to be a mere object of contemplation. "Sea," "life," "poetic afflatus," here enter into a union neither uneasy nor quite sublime.[7]

The ineliminable lightness of tone here fastens this poem to the immediacy of its felt occasion, even if we quickly abstract it by widening its reference beyond the circumstances of its first delivery. Originally entitled "Toast," it was recited by Mallarmé at the annual banquet of a literary society whose president he was (1406).[8] Social modesty blends with a flight of nearly mathematicized metalinguistic speculation in the persistent negatives or near negatives, from the initial *Rien* to the *blanc* of the last line (*ne que, à l'envers, sans, n'importe*).

And, contrariwise, the play of Mallarmé at his lightest touches on abstraction, and even on a solemnity, unknown in so subtle a combination to the writers of such epigrams in the long tradition begun by the poets of the Greek Anthology. The note of the tiny and transitory "Don de fruits glacés au Nouvel An" (126) is in a register close to that of "Salut":

> Se souvenir désaltère
> Comme un fruit tard enfermant
> L'émoi de notre parterre
> Avec Madame Normant.
>
> Remembering slakes
> Like a late fruit enclosing
> The bustle of our lobby
> With Madame Normant.

Neither Baudelaire nor Wordsworth would have disavowed that first line, suddenly deepening the occasion it lightly refreshes. To describe the

sort of poetic process he devised, Mallarmé invents a word oddly negative in its prefix-qualification: "Alors en nous *l'impersonnabilité* des grandes
occasions" (320).

Approached from the side of the specific and public occasion that would
seem to counter the general and intimately private expression in lyric
poetry, Mallarmé in some of his most urgently declarative and solemn
poems, the *Tombeaux* and the *Toasts Funèbres* he wrote for the dead,
touches on the lightness of mode he used for the "*toasts*" he composed
in prose for delivery to the living (862–65).

These testimonial poems have the fixity that tributes to the dead usually do. The inscrutability of the whole life so unites with the commonplace of the solemnity in contemplating it that the act of the poem, harnessing the solemnity and embracing the occasion, charms away the
discrepancy between the *jeu d'esprit* and the Delphic utterance, as between celebration and mourning, platitude and discovery.[9] On this high,
simple plane there is no longer any room for *correspondances* identifiable
as such. A high aesthetic abstraction comes to seem like de-aestheticization.
Gautier is a "fatal emblême" in "Toast Funèbre"— of "notre bonheur"
(54–55). Nothing like the actual poetry of Gautier enters this poem, though
the *Tombeaux* attempt to characterize Baudelaire and Poe by assembling
images most commonly associated with those writers. "Le splendide génie
éternel n'a pas d'ombre" ("The splendid eternal genius has no shadow"),
and Mallarmé punctiliously avoids adding any shading to his portrait to
displace the commonplace of the poet who triumphs over the mortality
that engulfs him. Death rises as

> Le sépulcre solide ou gît tout ce qui nuit,
> et l'avare silence et la massive nuit.

> The solid tomb where lies all that does harm,
> And miserly silence and the massive night.

The poem chooses to close on this identical rhyme, perforce a *rime riche*,
to close complicated sentences of the platitudes about the silence and the
imposing permanence of death.

The meditations follow much the same line in the *Tombeaux* of Poe,
Baudelaire, and Verlaine, the *Hommages* to Wagner and Puvis de Chavannes. The poet's fullest identifications and most committed responses
return us via the funeral occasion to the common humanity distilled in
the formal mastery of these utterances. Supreme in their very denial, they
do not permit themselves the incidental beauties and Orphic identifications usually associated with lyric poetry. In this connection Mallarmé's
words about Baudelaire apply with much greater appropriateness to him-

self: "Qu'advient-il de cette absence de mystère? Comme tout ce qui est absolument beau, la poésie force l'admiration; mais cette admiration sera lointaine, vague — bête, elle sort de la foule" ("What happened with that absence of mystery? Like everything that is absolutely beautiful, poetry forces admiration; but that admiration will be distant, vague — stupid, it comes from the crowd," 257).

The highest mystery is to refrain from mystery. When the dialect of the tribe is purified, the crowd must (*force*) admire, but vaguely and from afar. Indifference as to particulars, instant exhibition, and the persistence of sight are linked in Mallarmé's summary of such a process, "l'exhibition prompte, sous toutes les façettes, de quoi que ce soit et notre vue adamantine." The route from the pagan sexuality of *L'Après-midi d'un faune* and the quasi-Christian agony of *Hérodiade* leads to an identified condensation-improvisation so fluid, and so finally commonplace, that it cannot be separated by any other elements than the simplest and most final ones like life and death.

2

Mallarmé's distance from the crowd provides the culture, in his time and our own, with the type he represents, the type of the "difficult" writer that Valéry declares him to have established.[10] Yet the emotional and intellectual force of what that distance mediated does bring Mallarmé into a focus that restores the assertiveness of idea to the words from which he supposedly said poems were made, doing so by putting a word and its idea into "vibratory" interaction.[11]

For Mallarmé difficulty was a mediation that would permit the platitude at once a weight and a freshness, much as the term "rose," by being absent from all bouquets, permits the most conventional and typically poetic of all flowers to be understood as present. And even the most ordinary gracious presentation to a hostess could perform an abstract leverage on ideas via poetry.[12] Separated from the "idée même et suave," the word that stands for it provides a mode of access to the idea and its dialectical combination, a mode only refined by later linguistic theories of signification. The word in Mallarmé is a sort of depth charge that carries along with it the soothing countercharge of its inseparable lexical platitudinousness: it remains the language of the tribe, though purified. In him the new popularity of the Romantic experience, and the still newer Modernist hermeticism, converge as on a threshold. Where Baudelaire's self looks at its horizon to spot the accident of a swan in "Le Cygne," Mallarmé's swan, set in the resplendently curved mirror of "Le vierge, le vivace, et le bel aujourd'hui" (67), rises to its culminating name in the last word of the last line, centered while immobilized in a sort of phantom state:

> Fantôme qu'à ce lieu son pur éclat assigne,
> Il s'immobilise au songe froid de mépris
> Que vêt parmi l'exil inutile le Cygne.

> Phantom that in this place his pure dazzling assigns,
> He is stilled in the cold dream of contempt
> That clothes among a useless exile the Swan.

The object enters a contemplative, and emotional, order by being provided with an occasion so strong it can survive the dialectical negations against which the poet makes his language test it.

The object taken by itself tends towards an undialectical void of precision:

> Exclus-en si tu commences
> Le Réel parce que vil

> Le sens trop précis rature
> Ta vague littérature.   (73)

> Exclude if you begin
> The real because too vile

> Sense too precise erases
> Your vague literature.

The Mallarméan contemplation, however, while facing *inanité*, masters the Baudelairean *gouffre* in its most dominant objects. "L'Horloge" concludes the "Spleen et Idéal" section of *Les Fleurs du mal*, and it ends by invoking the "Horloge! dieu sinistre" by having it join in the whole process of declination: "Le gouffre a toujours soif; la clepsydre se vide. . . . Meurs, vieux lache! il est trop tard!" (The gulf is always thirsty; the waterclock empties itself. . . . Die, old coward! It is too late!")[13] For Mallarmé, however, "L'horloge me fait souvent grand bien" ("The clock often does a lot for me") — a statement that holds, in effect, for the precise hour, *minuit*, of the sonnet "Ses purs ongles," and the time of *Igitur*.

Totally enmeshed in the dialectic of its occasion for Mallarmé, the object may be seen to move in either direction, from occasion to object or from object to occasion. As Mallarmé says (869), "C'est le parfait usage de ce mystère qui constitue le symbole: évoquer petit à petit un objet pour montrer un état d' âme, ou, inversement, choisir un objet et en dégager un état d'âme, par une série de déchiffrements" ("It is the perfect use of this mystery that constitutes the symbol: to evoke an object little by little in order to show a state of the soul, or inversely, to choose an object

and disengage from it a state of the soul by a series of decipherments.")
And the first draft of "Ses purs ongles," written in 1868, nineteen years
before publication, was entitled "Sonnet allégorique de lui-même" (1488).
In explaining his first draft, Mallarmé characterized it as at once extracted
from "une étude projetée sur la parole" ("a study projected upon speech"),
lending itself to "une eau-forte pleine de rêve et de vide" ("an etching
full of dream and emptiness") and "représentant, comme elle [mon oeuvre]
peut, l'univers" ("representing, as far as [my work] can, the universe").

In the light of the interaction between the psychic life and the external object, or between the height of the poet and the distant crowd whose
commonplaces he elevates by giving them voice, the "difficult" poet is
difficult because only by being so can he bring over the essence of a common perception, can he "purifier les mots de la tribu" ("purify the words
of the tribe"). In this sense one can read from book to world in Mallarmé,
as well as (more usually) from world to book, the seeming aestheticism
of his repeated statement "le monde est fait pour aboutir à un beau livre"
(872). Made in an interview — and therefore a trifle scandalously but
withal firmly rooted in a conversational occasion — this version of the statement offers tribute to the connection between world and supreme letters
as much as it asserts the primacy of the Book. As elsewhere in his writing, Mallarmé is claiming a triumph as much philosophical as it is aesthetic; the function of even Zola (as against Proust's disdain for realists
in general) is "non à montrer la forme extérieure des choses, mais à dis-
sequer les motifs de l'âme humaine" ("not to show the exterior form of
things but to dissect the motifs of the human soul," 871).

Un Coup de dés introduces a principle of perpetual hazard ("jamais
un coup de dés n'abolira le hasard") to serve as a "tetrapolar"[14] grid for a
selected number of objects. These objects are then purified in perception
by being isolated in the white spaces and disjunct syntax of the poem.

Now preeminently here, but generally, the poet renders the verbal circumstances of his occasion difficult by stripping them of their normal
attributes. His verse attends more markedly to inter-echoes within a line
than to the onrushing and cumulative cadence of line after line: it does
not sing. It adopts a sort of hyperbaton, of word order reversal, as a standard rhetorical device. Hyperbaton is even more than a device in Mallarmé; it is a constant compositional principle, forcing the sequential to
reflect the constantly escaping possibility of the simultaneous.[15] His prose,
too, markedly resists the spoken flow of conversation and the expected
pattern-bends of syntax: it does not lend itself to being spoken. At the
height where the distinction between prose and verse has been attenuated away — in *Un Coup de dés* — there seems to be a kind of rhythmic
suspension, even though Valéry tells us that Mallarmé recited this poem
to him in an "absence d'artifice": "D'une voix basse, égale, sans le moindre

'effet,' presque si à soi-même" ("In a low, even voice, without the least 'effect,' almost to himself").[16] So complete was his mastery, we may say, of the conversational occasion that he could repose in it under the most trying of conditions.

Mallarmé's procedure scuttles the profound and complex connections, persisting in Baudelaire and Rimbaud, verse and prose poems alike, between the canons of classical rhetoric and the literary effects of someone who puts on the French mantle of "writer." Classical rhetoric sets its objects into a complex, rational order, resisting at once the extreme singularization and the fetishistic engulfment of the object, on both of which Mallarmé verges. His prose poems take a figure and work over it with meditations that keep it from coming even to Baudelaire's anecdotal terms. He creates an echolalia of process in sound and in the speaking mind, wherein there is no chiming to claim that the analogies carry out fully their correspondences. The "Démon de l'analogie" (272) is characterized by "lambeaux maudits d'une phrase absurde" ("cursed tatters of an absurd phrase"). The suspensions, in sound and idea, are dampened by the constant small wrenches of syntax. Events are slowed, displaced, and yet not covered by hyperboles and other rhetorical figures. "Par conséquence," Valéry says,[17] "La Syntaxe, qui est calcul, reprenait rang de Muse" ("Consequently, Syntax, which is mathematics, assumed the rank of a Muse"). So in the prose poem "Un Spectacle Interrompu," the popular spectacle of a clown dancing with a bear, interrupted as it were by the feeding of the bear, is itself recounted in interrupted phrases of condensed attribution, a constant hyperbaton, where a "loque substituée saignant" is a piece of meat, without structure or hyperbolic correspondences in rhetoric and therefore without the Gongorism that the detached phrase would suggest. What insists is a violence to syntax, since present participle does not often follow past and all three words are without benefit of article or other demonstrative label. Moreover, the whole is a noun phrase with "understood" verb, appended to the previous sentence.

Each word, taken by itself, is passably literal. The torn meat is a rag in an extended lexical sense. It has been substituted. It is *saignant* in both the anatomical and the culinary senses:[18]

> Loque substituée saignant auprès de l'ours qui, ses instincts retrouvés antérieurement à une curiosite plus haute dont le dotait le rayonnement théatrical, retomba à quatre pattes et, comme emportant parmi soi le Silence, alla de la marche étouffée de l'espèce, flairer, pour y appliquer les dents, cette proie. (278)

Since this passage begins as a suspended noun phrase appended to the phrase "un morceau de chair" early in the previous sentence, and since the last phrase, "cette proie," stands also in neat apposition to both, all eight phrases in this series, set off by commas, come to undergo the attraction of a sort of substitute nominalization. This is also a phantom nominalization, for of them all only the first and the last are actually noun phrases. The suspension of syntax has the effect of making the other phrases sound as though they ought to be assimilated (nominalized) to the first phrase and the last. And of them all only the last phrase lacks some verb form, buoying it up as though each phrase were pressing to become a separate sentence.[19]

The late sonnets build heavily on such counter-movements, as in "La chevelure vol d'une flamme à l'extreme / Occident"—itself first quoted, and suspending its suspensions, in the prose poem "La Déclaration foraine" (282). The effect is one of slowing towards, around, and away from the gradually unveiled object of the poem. With respect to the utterance, it teases the sequence into a semblance of total artificiality—"pour charmer un esprit ouvert à la compréhension multiple" ("to charm a spirit open to multiple comprehension," 283), as he says in the same poem. Here, and in "Le Nénuphar blanc," the syntax keeps the feminine figures set in a dialogue form too nebulous to conform wholly to their originals, the etched archetypes of Baudelaire. In *Un Coup de dés* these suspensions of semi-apposition become a main armature to the poem. It is they, we may say, that activate the white spaces whose role Mallarmé stresses into "subdivisions prismatiques de l'Idée" (455).

Looking back at Keats's injunction to Shelley, we may say that Mallarmé "loads every rift with ore," not only by leaving no syllable of a verse line unworked, but by forcing his speech instances thus to halt and "scintillate." The interactive verbal ordonnance of the Horatian and Vergilian ideal has been accommodated within the limpidities of traditional French verse. In *L'Après-midi d'un faune*, pastoral (the subtitle is *églogue*) is pushed to a breaking point of subjectivity, and the syntactic disjunctions already begin to help:

> Si clair
> Leur incarnat léger, qu'il voltige dans l'air
> Assoupi de sommeils touffus. (50)

> So clear
> Their light incarnation that it flutters in air
> Drugged with tufted sleeps.

As he says not much later in the letter about the early draft of "Ses purs ongles," he wishes to create "un mirage interne des mots mêmes" (1489), a mirage that incorporates the sense, even the idea, of the poem, and poises it in a tragic lightness of verbal gesture.[20] So Mallarmé's Pierrot does not, like Baudelaire's, envision an "absolute." Rather, he offers a process, "un tourbillon de raisons naives ou neuves" ("a whirlwind of reasons naive or new," 310). Always in view, and contributing to the sense of sublime tentativeness, is the "scène à ne pas faire" (343), instead of the "scène à faire" of well-made boulevard drama.

Mallarmé's term for Baudelaire's central incapacity is the *impuissance* that he reads (projectively, as it were) into Baudelaire's rhythms, transposing them into his own. "Muse de l'Impuissance qui taris le rhythme et me forces de relire" ("Muse of impotence who dries up the rhythm and forces me to reread," 261, 1547). Of his own rhythms he may be said to be implicitly speaking in the reworked "Le Démon de l'analogie," since that prose poem centers on a kind of dead syllable beat extended to a philosophical time: "*La Pénultième* / finit le vers / et *Est morte* / se détacha de la suspension fatidique plus inutilement en le vide de signification. Je fis des pas dans la rue et reconnus en le son *nul* de la corde tendu de l'instrument de musique" ("*La Pénultième* / finishes the verse / and *Est morte* detached itself from the soothsaying suspension more uselessly in the void of signification. I took some steps in the street and recognized in the sound *nul* of the stretched string of the musical instrument," 272). Within the line of the alexandrine, Mallarmé posits a greater rhythmic interplay among the twelve syllables when the metronomic regularity ("compteur factice") is broken: "l'oreille, affranchie d'un compteur factice, connait une jouissance à discerner, seule, toutes les combinaisons possibles entre eux, de douze timbres" ("the ear, freed from an artificial metronome, experiences pleasure in discerning, by itself, all the combinations possible among them, of twelve timbres," 362).

To the play of rising movement against falling movement, which permits the interplay of these "douze timbres," there corresponds Mallarmé's notion of a double state for speech. Both states are located in a single instance of speaking (so that he is not offering an early version of Saussure's distinction between *langue* and *parole*): "Un désir indéniable à mon temps est de séparer comme en vue d'attributions différentes le double état de la parole, brut ou immédiat ici, là essentiel" ("An undeniable desire in my time is to separate as in view of different attributions the double state of speech, here raw or immediate, there essential," 368).[21] Mallarmé himself, we may say, wants to deny this desire of separating the two states while in the act of fulfilling it: he wants the "brut ou immédiat" of a fulfilled occasion — one whose fulfillment incorporates and releases the "essentiel."

In *Un Coup de dés* the very white of the paper, by being spaced in irregular intervals, serves not as a neutral background but rather as a kind of silent replay of the rhythmic interactions: "Le papier intervient chaque fois qu'une image, d'elle-même, cesse ou rentre" ("The paper in-

tervenes each time an image, by itself, ceases or returns," 455). Throughout all these rhythmic tensions the tone remains light: the emotion strives
towards an effect of profound casualness. The privacy of the Romantic
visionary and the public posture of the Romantic revolutionary have both
been transcended. Even the portentous trans-Hamlet of *Igitur* can dwell
on the detail that the protagonist's mother forbade him to slide down
the banister, and he did it anyway (450). The Baudelairean solemnity
has been sabotaged by being suffused with pleasureableness:

> "Je me mire et me vois ange! et je meurs et j'aime." (33)

This is the early "Fenêtres," written before Baudelaire's poem of the
same title. The still earlier "L'Enfant Prodigue" subverts the Baudelairean
infinity and gulf-in-a-woman that it adopts, and subverts it through the
mechanism of a single adjective *fraîche*: "J'endormirai mon mal sur votre
fraîche chair" (15). Mallarmé's poet is born not mother-cursed, like the
one of *Les Fleurs du mal*, but as the by-blow of an accidental coupling
(22). Even the speaking, severed head of St. Jean in *Hérodiade* expresses
in his *cantique* a kind of exaltation, and the notion of an ideal — as central for Mallarmé as is the notion of fault for Baudelaire — has often the
effect of releasing melancholy in the direction of pleasure: "Mendieurs
. . . / Mordant au citron d'or de l'idéal amer" ("Alms-seekers . . . / Biting
on the gold lemon of the bitter ideal," 28). The figures, and their gesture,
are Baudelairean. But the honorific attached to the lemon, "citron d'or,"
anticipates and exceeds *l'idéal*, even though *amer* is the last word. The
"Nourrice" and "Hérodiade" in their dialogue turn the desperation of the
"femmes damnées" (whom they surely echo) towards a contemplation
so active and orchestrated in its idealizations that it almost seems to deny
the dominant perversity (providing a note that permits the later trivialization of Oscar Wilde's *Salome*). This same process happens in the handling of single images, as in Mallarmé's somewhat abstracted, repeated
use of the *chevelure* he adopts from Baudelaire.[22]

In such procedures, Mallarmé tends to level off as well as to abstract
all differences of semiological strategy, not just those that mark a difference between verse and prose. Only the utimate matters for him, though
the term *dandysme* derives from Baudelaire and accords with the editor
of *La Dernière Mode*: "Mais où point, je l'exhibe avec dandysme, mon
incompétence, sur autre chose que l'absolu." ("But where does there appear, I exhibit it with dandyism, my incompetence, on anything else than
the absolute," 330).

Signification — in all its byways — is always the aim: "que n'existe . . .
qu'un compte exact de purs motifs rhythmiques de l'être, qui en sont les
reconnaissables signes; il me plaît de les partout déchiffrer" ("that there

exist . . . only an exact count of pure rhythmic motifs of being, which are its recognizable signs; it pleases me to decipher them everywhere," 345). The function of the interrupted rhythms is to release a clarity — of perception, since one of expression is not yet there: "Dites, comme si une clarté, à jet continu, ou qu'elle ne tire d'interruptions le caractère momentané, de délivrance." ("Speak as if a clarity at steady blast, or one that draws from interruptions their momentary character, deliverance," 384). The process, by virtue of being subjected to the emotions of the moment, pitches its ultimates on randomness, on *Un Coup de dés*. Or as he puts it in *Igitur*: "'Vous avez tort' nulle emotion. L'infini sort du hasard, que vous avez nie." ("'You are wrong' no emotion. The infinite comes from chance, which you have denied," 434). "Nulle emotion" is to the fullness of emotion as the act of saying "rose" is to triggering an idea of "l'absente de tous bouquets."

In this way Mallarmé achieves a liminal state of wondering what it can mean for feelings and perceptions, identified in time-honored Romantic fashion, to be at once abstracted and totally given over to randomness. This state is evoked by the carefully maintained insistence on the portentousness of all the tentative gestures in these poems. Their aim is *not* to create an inter-referring labyrinth of verbalizations, though such must be their byproduct, as so many critics of Mallarmé have inferred, overstressing his deconstructive dimension. On the other hand, as he anyway asserts, "Quoiqu'y confiné une suprematie ou déchirement de voile et lucidité, le Verbe reste, de sujects, de moyens, plus massivement lié à la nature" ("Though confined there, a supremacy or ripping up of veil and lucidity, the Word remains with subjects, with means, more massively linked to nature," 522). And, going in the other direction, not from word to nature but from nature (*fait*) to the significance of word (*idéal*), "La divine transposition, pour l'accomplissement de quoi existe l'homme, *va du fait à l'idéal*" ("The divine transposition to accomplish which man exists, *goes from the fact to the ideal*," 522 — italics Mallarmé's). This is a post-Kantianism that realigns Kant in the direction of Plato — all this ideation standing at the service of the generalized world, which it defines, or moves towards defining, while building into itself an absence from definition.

3

The *idée même* of Mallarmé, then, whether it be taken to fix on and transform some particular object like a rose, or to embrace his whole conception of the poetic act, involves more — it is worth asserting for what it implies, though it is well-known — than the loose, common doctrine

of "art for art's sake," that distillation of the Romantic valuation of poetry. Something like this older idea was held by his friends Barbey d'Aurevilly, Villiers de l'Isle Adam, and Huysmans, whom he admired. But he
also admired Zola, not to speak of that dominant mythologizer of the
passions, Wagner, to whom he would seem to have recurred as much as
did Baudelaire.

The *Prose pour des Esseintes,* addressed to Huysmans' archetypical
protagonist, reminds that imaginary aesthete that it is perceptions that
artists are participating in:

> Oui, dans une île que l'air charge
> De vue et non de visions
> Toute fleur s'étalait plus large
> Sans que nous en devisions.   (56)
>
> Yes, in an isle the air charges
> With view and not with visions
> Every flower spread out more large
> Without our devising from it.

Mallarmé had already said here that the excess of perception over assess-
ing guesswork will have had some effect in that dominance over all aspects of the real world for which the term *autorité* may be taken to stand:

> L'ère de autorité se trouble
> Lorsque, sans nul motif, on dit
> De ce midi que notre double
> Inconscience approfondit.
>
> Authority's era is troubled
> When, with no motive, it is said
> Of this noon that our double
> Non-consciousness deepens.

The very gratuitousness of the poetic task, in this view, does not separate itself from common perception. Rather it sets up an interaction in
which a historical moment (*l'ère*) receives trouble and profundity at once.
As it happens, this extravagant claim is true for Mallarmé, if not for the
less profound Huysmans.[23]

> Cette foule hagarde! elle annonce: Nous sommes
> La triste opacité de nos spectres futurs.   (54)
>
> This haggard crowd! It announces: we are
> The sad opacity of our future ghosts.

Mallarmé reads the sad opacity of these future specters, chooses to read
it, and thereby finds a form where the haggard crowd and the poised

poet, by being linked in the common ritual act of a funeral commemoration, get an emotion into play that can serve as a dialectic for a sense of history. Richard stresses Mallarmé's early discovery of Hegel, arguing for his incorporation of a comparable ontology into the dialectic of his poetry.[24] While it would exaggerate Mallarmé's use of *ère* to attribute a Hegelian sense of history to it, the collective consciousness of the "foule hagarde" is only imaginable after the *Phänomenologie*. And the personalization of the process in Mallarme's implication takes it beyond Hegel: it is as though Hegel had been asked to become Nietzsche.

There is a persistent, though rudimentary, metahistorical side to this metapoetry:

> Quand l'ombre menaça de la fatale loi
> Tel vieux Rêve, désir et mal de mes vertèbres.   (67)

> When the shade menaced with the fatal law
> Some old Dream, desire and ill of my vertebrae.

The poet, too, is subject to an authority for which "la fatale loi" is another name. His dream, allegorized by a capital letter, is only commonplace: it is a "vieux Rêve." This is a Baudelairean dream, "désir et mal" of his inmost structure. That dream itself, however, is subjected through the process to redefinition, and the moral "ennui" is put at the service of an awakened sensibility. The end of this scene sets out a public and even a cosmic environment: "Que s'est d'un astre en fête allumé le génie" ("That the genius of a festive star has been lit up").

In this light it is not surprising that Mallarmé should say of a friend and minor writer: "On sent que l'auteur a vécu son oeuvre" ("One feels the author has lived his work," 251). And he sets down a comparable condition for his apocalyptic project: "Oui, le Livre . . . suffit avec maints procédés si neufs analogues en raréfaction à ce qu'a de subtil la vie" ("Yes, the Book . . . suffices with many a procedure quite new, analogous in rarefaction to that which is subtle in life," 318). It could be said that Mallarmé himself presents a serene obverse and a "brutal" reverse, like the ancient coin he describes: "La pièce de monnaie exhumée aux arènes, présente, face, une figure sereine et, pile, le chiffre brutal universel" ("The piece of money excavated from the Arena presents on its obverse a serene face and on its reverse a figure brutal and universal," 415).[25] Or, similarly, "La transparence de pensé s'unifie, entre public et causeur, comme une glace, qui se fend, la voix tue" ("The transparence of thought is unified, between public and conversationalist, like a mirror that breaks, the voice silent)."

The state refined by these poems accommodates and idealizes Baudelaire's incapacity. If Baudelaire is a counter-Romantic, making ennui yield what exaltation does for his predecessors, Mallarmé is a counter-Baudelaire, restoring a finality and ideality to such feelings: "Ici: névrose, ennui (ou Absolu!)" ("Here neurosis, ennui [or Absolute!]"— 439). As the last sentence of *Igitur* puts it, "Le Néant parti, reste le chateau de la pureté" ("Nothingness gone, there remains the castle of purity," 443).

Here, in a series of noted equations (428–29), drama, hero, mystery, hymn, act, and idea verge towards an identity that proposes to reassemble the essence of prior literary forms and gestures into a comprehensive, abstracted state.[26] The heavy slumber Mallarmé curiously ascribes to such a state (438) makes the solitude of the poet in the modern city into a version of his identity with a universe of other solitaries: he names his sleep; they live theirs. In the separation he accepts for himself, there is a kind of identity, we may infer, through the focus on mortality, which is a chief subject of these poems: "le cas d'un poéte en cette société qui ne lui permet pas de vivre, c'est le cas d'un homme qui s'isole pour sculpter son propre tombeau" ("the case of a poet in this society that does not permit him to live is the case of a man who isolates himself to sculpt his tomb," 869) — his own tomb and that of others.

The comprehensive power of a sensibility in solitude to project a society in time leads one way, to Proust. In *Un Coup de dés* words with depth charges set so as to schematize a macrohistorical view lead the other way, to *Finnegans Wake*.

In this absoluteness of role that Mallarmé filled out and invented, the modern poet, for the first time in the austerity of this vision, escapes the relativity of a role. The Romantic dream of the universalized poet has been achieved in a way that Blake and Whitman would not have recognized. Of the modern poet's very individuality Mallarmé says, "Pour la première fois, depuis le commencement, les poètes ne chantent plus au lutrin" ("For the first time since the beginning, poets no longer sing at the lectern" 866). The last word both ties him in with a seventeenth-century literary dictator. Boileau, author of *Le Lutrin*, and abjures the connection. The double role kept him poised.

10

Emily Dickinson's White Exploits

1

"I dwell in Possibility," Emily Dickinson says, "A fairer House than Prose" (657).[1] A state of perpetual liminality is named in the word "Possibility" and given the emphasis, frequent in her work, of capitalization. "Possibility" is not a true opposite for "Prose," and the ellipsis between the two terms acts verbally to exemplify the preferred state by forcing the reader to mediate in a way the language does not. Thus the language, without any irony, offers a dramatized mediation between deficiency and excess. Yet in no way does it subvert its own procedures.

Instead, the notion of possibility can easily be extended to more specific, if all-embracing human concerns, to the love and the death that as topics dominate her poems.

Preponderantly it is death, with a monumental series of ratiocinations about what death implies, that locates these poems on a giant threshold. Emily Dickinson, in a formulation as tentative as Hölderlin's, as philosophical as Blake's, and as singleminded as Baudelaire's, turned her powers on the aspects of transcience and death that Leopardi both mourned and celebrated. She brought herself to the pitch of calling death a "White Exploit" in a relatively late poem (922). What justifies the term "exploit" and the qualifier "white" is that she had reasoned her way through a psychic and intellectual series of steps leading at all moments to death.[2] Her work is eschatological in its final ground and for its ultimate horizon. Over half her poems deal in some way with that other side of mortal life. Emily Dickinson took personal note of the new profession of "undertaker" in a society that previously had prepared within the family the bodies of the dead for burial. And she insisted on a private funeral for herself.[3]

Through Christian doctrine and through romanticized perception alike, she discovers a depth and definition for mortal life only in the face of death. Heidegger could well have gone to her for a deep and manifold sense of the *Sein zum Tod*.[4] One must, she keeps declaring, "come / to that odd Fork in Being's Road— / Eternity—by Term—" (615). At that point, as the poem concludes, there is "Behind—a Sealed Route—Eternity's White Flag—Before— / And God—at every Gate—." The poem trails off in one of her dashes—the stubborn indeterminacies or lacunae of imperception. The dashes punctuate her work, as though to counterbalance the emergence of not one but, here, all the entities into the hypostatization of quasi-allegorical capital letters. "Before—were Cities—but Between— / The Forest of the Dead—." We are shown a strange geography, where death stands not as a future on this journey but, subverting space by making this life co-present with an afterlife, an enfilading wood of qualified growth, "The Forest of the Dead." Cemeteries occupy all of this physical space but only some of this psychological space. There is a perceptible but indomitable difference between human and divine with regard to the time when they intersect in death, "too late for Man— / But early, yet, for God—." The process undergone, hospitality emerges: "How hospitable—then—the face / of our Old Neighbor—God—" (623).

For Dickinson the function of the poem is to discover the omnipresence of this hospitality by working out the psychological consequences of death's omnipresence. Death locates the psyche: "Behind Me—dips Eternity— / Before Me—Immortality— / Myself—The Term between—" (721). This abstractness shades at once into a reassuring identification of Death with a change in the sky reminiscent of sunrise: "Death but the Drift of Eastern Gray, / Dissolving into Dawn away, / Before the West begin." And the resolution is the identity of everything previously named, through the action of God to "Himself diversify— / In Duplicate divine— / ". . . 'Tis Miracle before Me—then— / 'Tis Miracle behind—between . . . / And Maelstrom—in the Sky—." The final, more savage image of something like a sunset remains reassuring, for all the transformation of its softness into intensity, through the process that the poem recommends, infers, and embodies. Music itself vaguely graces the afterworld of the redeemed (503).

To such a center does each life converge, given the qualifier of indefiniteness in the poem making that assertion: "Each Life converges to some Centre— / Expressed—or still—" (680). Here death is only implicit. The term is "A Goal." Whether success or failure—"Ungained—it may be— by a Life's low Venture—" there is still the encompassing help of that which will bring what is unstated here, the resolution and end: "But then— / Eternity enable the endeavoring / Again." Death is defined, effectually, as a drink for the thirsty, and the giver of the cup may have to take the drink too when she "awakes" into what amounts to death: "And so I always bear the cup / If, haply, any say to me / 'Unto the little, unto me' / When I at last awake" (132). So the quotation of a kindly gesture of Christ's is assimilated and embedded in the eschatological lightness of welcome.

In her declaration against the whole process of bringing her utterances before the public, "Publication— is the Auction / Of the Mind of Man—," Dickinson adduces the transition into an afterlife as a justification: "We— would rather / From Our Garret go / White— Unto the White Creator— / Than invest— Our Snow" (709). Here she brings into an identity the three plenitudes of being: the person at the end of life and the God who made her and the written expressions of herself. All three are white, and that term can be taken either for the absence of all colors or the presence of all colors, so that the plenitude partakes of an absence that signifies it. The snow will stay white if it is regarded as priceless, valueless, infinitely precious. The Creator is inescapably white; the person will be so only if what he has created is allowed to remain so, held back from "so foul a thing" as changing the snow from white, by fouling it. Natural beauty, emblematic purity, unreal blanketing, cold, and here a pricelessness in two senses are signified by the snow, as all these attributes are at one or another time invested by the poet in death.

The act of naming everything from a star to a butterfly, and of renaming "Heaven" as "Zenith," is shown as a long learning process (70); the user of language never gets beyond the liminal. But "When Time's brief masquerade was done," these learned names may be reversed: "What if the poles should frisk about / And stand upon their heads?" And the boundary between earth and heaven, as though to substantiate the change, has a name at once strange and familiar, called "pearl" for a certain kind of light or by a kind of analogy in an existence when analogies will have dropped away:

> Perhaps the "Kingdom of Heaven's" changed—
> I hope the "Children" there
> Won't be "new fashioned" when I come—
> And laugh at me— and stare—
>
> I hope the Father in the skies
> Will lift his little girl—
> Old fashioned— naughty— everything—
> Over the stile of "Pearl."

The familiar has here been estranged, since death is colloquially called "the Pearly Gates." Key familiar terms are put in quotation marks, insisting on their analogic force. In naming herself, as she has reverted to her status as a child of God, the list of the dying person's attributes is quickly curtailed by the admission that any adjective may be applied: "everything." The reassurance that the difficult transition will survive the bepuzzlement of naming, indicated by the three terms placed between quotes in the first stanza here, is affirmed by the quotes around the intensity and loveliness of the analogic last term, "Pearl."

So the awareness in this world is really an awareness leading to that in the next. Natural thirst, she declares, "intimates the finer want" (726) that can only be fed, not just by belief, as in the abounding waters of the New Testament analogy, but by actually crossing over, into the realm of the afterlife. Its "adequate supply / Is that Great Water in the West— / Termed Immortality—."

The very horror that may accompany death is a sort of induction (281). "The Cordiality of Death— / Who drills his Welcome in—" (286). An elision of boundaries takes place at the crossing of the boundary: one is suddenly in a realm that has no exit, a realm to be entered through the source of light itself: "Doom is the House without the Door— / 'Tis entered from the Sun—" (475). In this condition, the alternative is still provided, though the "Ladder's thrown away" and "Escape—is done—," of meditating on nature from the new vantage: "'Tis varied by the Dream / Of what they do outside— / Where Squirrels play—and Berries die— / And Hemlocks—bow—to God."

The capitalization of "Dream" here comes to make it seem total rather than intermittent in a realm where terms like "day" and "night" have lost their significance. And at the same time it may be glossed weakly as an imagination or memory rather than as an actual sleeping vision. Actual dreaming—rather than sleeping—is likened to death (531), and at any time of waking we may discover that "the Phantasm—prove the Mistake— / And the livid Surprise / Cool us to Shafts of Granite— / With just an Age—and Name— / And perhaps a phrase in Egyptian—." Death impinges on the perception of loneliness (532) and is "potential" between friends when otherwise "unconspicuous" (548). A full perception even of a sunset makes us "start—as if detected / in Immortality" (552)—a state that by that very fact makes it indifferent whether we are in this life or the other. Death brings an exhilaration, and the verbless poem that celebrates the speaker's "White Election!" has six terminal exclamation points in its nine lines (528). The "Resurrection" has no "Parallel . . . Significance," gathering a crowd of unparalleled size and brightness: "All Multitudes that were / Efface in the Comparison— / As Suns— dissolve a star—" (515).

Emily Dickinson is no more just specifically Puritan in her poetic dramatization of a Christian bearing towards death than Kierkegaard is specifically Lutheran. To typify her movements of statement and image as Puritan, even more to typify them as somehow implicitly anti-Puritan, would have the comparably unfortunate result of obscuring the powerful generality with which she contemplates and centralizes these last things. Terms like "White Election" never seem to imply a Calvinist predestination for the chosen soul, though the term itself must be given a Calvinist definition.[5]

It is as though the Romantic sensibility towards wakening consciousness in nature had been rethought in Christian terms and imputed to humankind as a given attribute, or as though Blake's and Whitman's messianic hopes for the development of human consciousness were already implicit in the eschatological bearing of human life. "God can summon every face / On his Repealless—List" (409): this well expresses the balance in her doctrine between the Calvinist election ("List") and the ecumenical spirit ("every"), the latter emphasized by the inclusiveness, as well as the exclusiveness, of "Repealless." The dash after this penultimate adjective underscores its theological force.

The experience of death, at the same time, is inescapably singular: "The Grave is strict— / Tickets admit / Just two—the Bearer / And the Borne / And seat—just One" (408). Such arithmetic, however, itself is superseded in the transcendence of the afterlife, and in the analogous three-in-one of the Trinity:

> One and One—are One—
> Two—be finished using—
> Well enough for Schools—
> But for Minor Choosing—
>
> Life—just—Or Death—
> Or the Everlasting—
> More—would be too vast
> For the Soul's Comprising—   (769)

The green of the "Outer Grave" in summer, the white in winter, and the elusive color within are all effectually at once evidences and concealments of the kinds of perceptions the dead may be imagined to have (411; see also 876). A series of religious verdicts on the self prepares the soul to meet death "tranquilly, as friends" (412). But in another aspect there is a turbulence in death, and so an equivalent preparation: "'Twas like a Maelstrom with a notch" (414). Terms like "happy," "conscious," and "homesick" become strangely inapplicable (417). Nightfall itself trains the mind to the acceptance of death (419).

What a person perpetually possesses may be taken, seen in an eschatological light, to transcend the categories life and death:

> Always Mine!
> No more Vacation!
> Term of Light this Day begun!
> Failless as the fair rotation
> Of the Seasons and the Sun.
>
> Old the Grace, but new the Subjects—
> Old, indeed, the East,
> Yet upon His Purple Programme
> Every Dawn, is first.   (839)

The purple of this life resembles that of the other (980), as do perceptions of nature (East) and the spirit (Grace). Here the slightly submerged metaphor of eternity as a school makes itself recognized by no property other than the lack of intermittence ("No more Vacation!"). A curriculum remains, but "new the Subjects," and the place is recognized by its being comparable to the progression of the seasons and the common attribute of Light.

"Each Life Converges to some Centre—" (680) only by virtue of what "Eternity enable." Dickinson's center is this very process: "The Only News I know / Is Bulletins all Day / From Immortality" (827). Death provides, abidingly, the assessment for life through a "Compound Vision" that takes the power of Wordsworthian retrospection, so to speak, and transposes it from the present's look at the past to an absolute future's look after death at a simultaneous present:

> The Admirations—and Contempts—of time—
> Show justest—through an Open Tomb—
> The Dying—as it were a Height
> Reorganizes Estimate
> And what We saw not
> We distinguish clear—
> And mostly—see not
> What We saw before—
>
> 'Tis Compound Vision—
> Light—enabling Light—
> The Finite—furnished—
> With the Infinite—
> Convex—and Concave Witness—

>   Back—toward Time—
>   And forward—
>   Toward the God of Him—   (906)[6]

Only after this process has been gone through does the newly enabled person discern what he must. The process can be described as heading either "back" or "forward" but always "toward" that essence of the "Him" he would have to have worshipped to be able to name, and for which term "God and Son" would itself already be too definitive.

Size may always be implied by references like these to finite and infinite, especially since an alternate spatial metaphor is given of quasi-equivalence—"Convex—and Concave"—though it is not clear which term is to be paired with "Finite" and which with "Infinite." As in space, so in emotions, "Magnitude / Reverses Modesty" (914). There is, on the one hand, "a finished feeling / Experienced at Graves— / A leisure of the Future— / A Wilderness of Size" (856). But, on the other hand, this chaos, in the same poem, permits a focus: "By Death's Bold Exhibition / Preciser what we are / And the Eternal function—Enabled to infer."[7]

Only eternity, oddly, permits an assimilation to the vastness of time, when God will "prepare / by Processes of Size / For the Stupendous Vision / Of His diameters" (802). So perceived, a grave may be seen either as very restricted or as "ampler than the Sun" (943). And the principle stands at hand in the soul for such a surpassing act of measurement: "My Faith is larger than the Hills—" (766). Language and perceptions in this life, then, may be mustered to render an account of this imagined process by treating the remote posthumous future as a present:

>   Because I could not stop for Death—
>   He kindly stopped for me—
>   The Carriage held but just Ourselves—
>   And Immortality.
>
>   We slowly drove—He knew no haste
>   And I had put away
>   My labor and my leisure too,
>   For His Civility—
>
>   We passed the School, where Children strove
>   At Recess—in the Ring—
>   We passed the Fields of Gazing Grain—
>   We passed the Setting Sun—
>
>   Or rather—He passed Us—
>   The Dews drew quivering and chill—
>   For only Gossamer, my Gown
>   My Tippet—only Tulle—

> We paused before a House that seemed
> A swelling of the Ground—
> The Roof was scarcely visible—
> The Cornice—in the Ground—
>
> Since then—'tis Centuries—and yet
> Feels shorter than the Day
> I first surmised the Horses' Heads
> Were toward Eternity—   (712)

Here the process of recognizing one's location in the afterlife is rendered as a gradual census of dissimilarities-in-similarity. The speaker drives, but in a strange way that dismisses into equivalence the two manners of handling human time ("my labor and my leisure too") in the face of a social reception recognized as "Civility," but more powerful if it has this effect. The distantly seen children keep at their normal activities, and the sun sets as before, but a third visible entity has an attribute that endows growing food with the sight that only those who eat it possess, caught in a fixity that could be taken as an extreme sketch of the visual look of wheat spikes: the "grain" is "gazing." The rider wears garments, but thinner ones than those that give the gown and the tippet their earthly names. The house has fused, or sunk, with the earth itself, and its architectural features, "scarcely visible," are scarcely namable.[8]

The very failures in perception are here enlisted for inference, as the inadequacies of language sometimes are; in Poem 949 "over" and "under" may indifferently be applied to the grave. Learning to approach death resembles learning to speak and name (426). In a later, more abstract version of the surmising chariot ride through the afterlife, it is spoken of as "a quiet way" (1053). The grave shows "another way to see" (627). It only seems to the living that "In dying—'tis as if Our Souls / Absconded —suddenly—" (645).

Dickinson evens out and at once universalizes and palliates the Romantic identification of love and death. "Forgive me if to stroke thy frost / Outvisions Paradise!" (577). Love, too, is assessed against the supervening eschatological imperatives: "The Test of Love—is Death—" (573). In that light, even love undergoes some of the puzzling "compound vision" that affects physical nature, space, and time before the afterlife. "Love— is anterior to Life— / Posterior—to Death—" (917). Here the term "love" embraces indifferently the human and the divine. It is at once Eros and Agape, beyond the need for the sublimations, and even for the repressions, to which the individual recluse Emily Dickinson seems emphatically to have been subject. "Love—is that later Thing than Death— / More previous—than Life," she says, slightly rephrasing this (924). Love stands by in the afterlife diminished before God here: "Then hovers — an inferior Guard— / Lest this Beloved Charge / Need — once in an Eternity— / A smaller than the Large—."

However, the special, universalizing function of love is validated by its unique resistance to the principle of analogy: "Itself is all the like it has" (826). This attribute it alone, perhaps, shares with the "One" that can or cannot become two indifferently. However, it takes two for love (453), and love is at once necessary to and a sort of joking equivalent for the realm of God: "Bliss — were an Oddity — without thee — / Nicknamed by God — / Eternity." In a more conflated, less qualified formulation:

> For Love is Immortality
> Nay, It is Deity
> Unable they that love — to die
> Unable are the Loved to die
> For Love reforms Vitality
> Into Divinity.   (809)

This astonishing psychological perception, whereby an oceanic feeling is created by the lovers, takes the principle of life and transposes it into what governs the afterlife: "Vitality" into "Divinity." "Love is like Life" and also "Love is like Death" (491). If from another angle love does not partake of this eternity, we outgrow it. In a common, more prudential perception, "We outgrow love, like other things / And put it in the Drawer" (887).

Death may be a variably lowered temperature (422), a stronger Light (692), "A Clemency so common" (694), something less than suspense (705), or alternately corruption or salvation (432). In any case, in Emily Dickinson's explanation of its Christian implications, death is a sort of contradiction in terms (432).[9]

2

The tradition of English poetry from Shakespeare through Keats directs the rhetoric, and especially the rhythms, of Emily Dickinson's poetry less forcefully than do the tradition of hymnody and the quatrains of the popular poetry of the time, leavened by Emerson.[10] These two traditions, the sacred one of hymnody and the secular one of occasional verse, are fused and transformed. She attains an utterance proper, complete, and modestly laconic on the threshold of the beyond. Hymnody, instead of being a skillful phrasing of standard doctrine, becomes in her work the rhythmic setting for theological probes. Occasional verse, instead of prettifying or sentimentalizing love and nature, takes both love

and nature precisely as the chief elements in an act of theological quest-
ing. The earlier Romantics either declared what amounted to the theological function or service of poetry, like Coleridge, Wordsworth, and
Hölderlin (and to a lesser degree Novalis) or tried to make poetry substitute for theology entirely, like the "atheist" Shelley and Poe the theoretician of *Eureka*. Dickinson, on the other hand, in a tremendous and private act of vision so fully achieved it seems effortless, simply turned a
humble and direct form of poetry to theological use, thereby eliding a
possible distinction between the sacred and the secular. She carries out
Schlegel's assertion and program that poetry is philosophy. Her poems
are indifferently versified records of theological speculation, analogous
to the lifelong philosophical notebooks of such as Novalis, Leopardi, and
Valéry; or they are shapely verses that happen to take eschatological concerns as their dominant subject.

In the rhythms of these simple stanzas, in her characteristic quatrains
at least, there is little room for the periodic or even for the kind of subtle
modulation afforded by everything from the Spenserian stanza to the lyrics
of Blake. Instead of rhythmic modulation Dickinson breaks her stanza,
and powerfully, by the constant and intermittent super-caesura of her
dashes. The jinglelike rhythms of the quatrains are suspended, by dashes,
often to and through the very end of a poem, which she will often conclude with a dash. The quatrains are made to accommodate, and to conform to, the rudimentary thrust of the thought as it issues into words
jot by jot. This is not exactly the phrasal or breath movement of later
poets; the units are too varied for that. What governs them is not just
the breath but also the increment of each meditation, added with unre-
mitting linearity to the prior meditation. The dashes preserve the equivalence of these thought units while the quatrains, usually, herd all the
statements together into an overall utterance.

"One and One—are One—" has five dashes in addition to the ones
at the ends of lines, twelve altogether in eight lines. In "Because I could
not stop for Death," eighteen of the twenty-four lines have no such break;
there is therefore a prevailing linearity reinforcing the quatrain, making
the process of inference both deliberate and casual. Still, there are points
of more sharply emerging reflection to be marked in rhythm, as in the
pause of "Or rather—He passed Us—." The odd capital of "Us" reinforces
the process of fusion that the reflections, underscored by the rhythms,
are bringing to awareness. The prior break inside a line had been an especially marked one, "—in the Ring—," set off after a very long run, "We
passed the School, where Children strove / At recess." The thought is
calmly but brokenly projected ahead. If it gets more broken, the quatrain may disappear, as in a poem like "Her—'last Poems'— / Poets—
ended— / Silver—perished—with her Tongue—" (312).

Often the initial integer in these series of thoughts within a poem will be a keen act of natural perception. Such a perception can on occasion occupy an entire poem, a rendering of an object like a bee (416), or a sunset (628), a sunrise (318), or the moon (629) or the gentian (331), an oriole (1466) or a bat (1575) or an umbrella (1747), rain (1426) or water (1528). In a poem about the wind, "No bone had He to bind him — / His Speech was like the Push / Of numerous Humming Birds at once / From a superior Bush—" (436). Even this poem, occupied entirely with the wind, cannot be divorced from hints of theology, given Dickinson's sense of humming as joining in the heavenly chorus, and given her revising the term for this particular bird into a generalized activity. The two capitals and the splitting of "hummingbird" into two words immerse identification in universalizing inference. Items in nature always reveal the supernatural. "The Robin is a Gabriel / In humble circumstance" (1438).

On the other hand, it may be said that her poems get more abstract, and less accessible to imagery, as she progresses through her career. In one sense this happens not because her inspiration diminished but because it refined to the point where all she needed was the inferences. "I am alive — I guess — / The Branches on my Hand / Are full of Morning Glory — / And at my finger's end—" (470). The gesture of capitalizing "Morning Glory" implies that at some point in the movement of thought it may cease to be a flower without losing its poetic force. The process must hold, indeed, in her doctrine, or it will be nearly irrecoverably lost:

> The Brain, within its Groove
> Runs evenly — and true —
> But let a Splinter swerve —
> 'Twere easier for You —
>
> To put a Current back —
> When Floods have slit the Hills —
> And scooped a Turnpike for Themselves —
> And trodden out the Mills —   (556)

The dashes aid her own thought to "run evenly" and indicate that it is doing so. Just one perception in nature may do, on occasion. The one perception works because it is held firmly in place by the demarcating dashes, to effectuate the crucial eschatological inference:

> I heard a Fly buzz — when I died —
> The Stillness in the Room
> Was like the Stillness in the Air —
> Between the Heaves of Storm —
>
> The Eyes around — had wrung them dry —
> And breaths were gathering firm

> For that last Onset—when the King
> Be witnessed—in the Room—
>
> I willed my Keepsakes—Signed away
> What portion of me be
> Assignable—and then it was
> There interposed a Fly—
>
> With Blue—uncertain stumbling Buzz—
> Between the light—and me—
> And then the Windows failed—and then
> I could not see to see—   (465)

The buzz of the fly preserves the nuance and the indirection of threshold perception while the speaker is performing the direct act of making a will. The disproportion between perception and act is preserved, and yet it is also lost. The narrative progress of a death moves implacably forward to elide them. The buzz gets three of the only five adjectives in the poem, and one of those adjectives—its strangeness reinforced by a dash—serves also as a powerfully nascent noun, "With Blue—."

The indirection is a matter of principle, "Tell all the Truth but tell it slant—" (1129), or otherwise it will not be seen: "The Truth must dazzle gradually / Or every man be blind—." As she here says, "Success in Circuit lies," and the term "Circuit" is a rough equivalent for the "Circumference" she frequently names. Given such indirection between individual acts of inference, the relationship may be puzzling, resolved only by some circuit. As, for example, in this poem:

> Are Friends Delight or Pain?
> Could Bounty but remain
> Riches were good—
>
> But if they only stay
> Ampler to fly away
> Riches are sad.   (1199)

Here the alternatives add up to an enthymeme of implied resolution of such earthly contradiction in the heaven she has hinted at.

There is consequently an open symbology in many of Dickinson's poems, a trait to be noticed in the seeming incoherence of her metaphors. And in the little poem just quoted, even though the metaphor is coherently phrased among "bounty," "ampler," and "riches," the propositions pointedly are not.

Another step, and we reach the verbal form of posing a puzzle for a solution, the riddle. Dickinson's poems are occasionally almost riddles.[11]

They usually differ, however, in that the description makes the object so obvious that the puzzle is a transparent veil, as in the poem about a snake (986) and the one about a train (585). And in a common rhetorical progression she first describes the object and then reveals its name, as in one poem about a bee (916) and another about a butterfly (173).

That one is dead oneself is to be inferred through a mighty and total riddle in the narrative of "Because I could not stop for Death." And death itself has so overwhelming a repertoire of attributes that it may be deduced from alternate series of inferences, in poem 559 and differently in poem 560. "Alas, that Wisdom is so large— / And Truth—so manifold!" (568). So manifold, indeed, that the process may be reversed; then what puzzles is not the name of the object but the terms, equivalent to poetic kenning, which may phrase it:

> Who is the East?
> The Yellow Man
> Who may be Purple if He can
> That carries in the Sun.
>
> Who is the West?
> The Purple Man
> Who may be Yellow if He can
> That lets Him out again.   (1032)

Sunrise and sunset, then, are alike as to their elements but different as to their modality and their order. So to name them is to produce a reassuring litany, to run through a validating circuit, in which the terms are the purple that for Emily Dickinson is royal and the yellow that she says is rare in nature. Riddle itself is a sort of inducement, or else a falling short:

> Further than Guess can gallop
> Further than Riddle ride—
> Oh for a Disc to Distance
> Between Ourselves and the Dead!   (949)

This is the last stanza of a poem that presents not so much a riddle about death as a puzzle about how to handle a state that can be successively described as "under," "further," and "over" in each of a series of three introductory stanzas. This final one sighs at the impossibility of resolution rather than offering a resolving answer.

Since this death makes all in life a mystery, a census of objects in nature will produce, unfailingly and somehow reassuringly, a comparable puzzle or contrariety of propositions:

> Some things that fly there be —
> Birds — Hours — the Bumblebee —
> Of these no Elegy.
>
> Some things that stay there be —
> Grief — Hills — Eternity —
> Nor this behooveth me.
>
> There are that resting, rise.
> Can I expound the skies?
> How still the Riddle lies!   (89)

In still another strategy, echoing the Voice from the Whirlwind in Job, a series of rhetorical questions to which the answer is God alternates with a series of praising commands about nature (128).

Of "the Infinite" she says, "His fingers are the size of fists" (350), a statement that must be taken for a deliberately failed approximation, where failure brings one back to a reverential posture towards the initial question. The process of testing the self will produce the same result (351). And in the face of the Infinite even the measurable size has the capacity to produce a paradox:

> My Basket holds — just — Firmaments —
> Those — dangle easy — on my arm,
> But smaller bundles — Cram.   (352)

Here the dashes surrounding "just" and "dangle easy" function logically as a notation combining a plus sign and an equals sign. Tonally the dashes function as a kind of phonetic equivalent for a hesitation comprising doubt and awe and effort and relief at getting out a single word of adequate precision, and resignation at being able to say no more, a dynamized "inexpressibility trope."

Mood and definition, anyway, both reinforce each other and open each other up in the natural-supernatural experience of mortal life:

> There's a certain Slant of light,
> Winter Afternoons —
> That oppresses, like the Heft
> Of Cathedral Tunes —
>
> Heavenly Hurt, it gives us —
> We can find no scar,
> But internal difference,
> Where the meanings, are —
>
> None may teach it — Any —
> 'Tis the Seal Despair —

An imperial affliction
Sent us of the Air —

When it comes, the Landscape listens —
Shadows — hold their breath —
When it goes, 'tis like the Distance
On the look of Death —   (258)

This poem proceeds very rapidly from the description of a very particular kind of sunlight to evoking the theological side of metalinguistic conditions. And it also mimes and evokes a restful way to do what shadows do, "hold their breath," as before "The Fact that Earth is Heaven — / Whether Heaven is Heaven or not" (1408). This faces radical doubt and also faces it down.

Physical nature serves in Emily Dickinson's view for a subsistent source of revelatory inferences while it offers itself for Wordsworthian sublimities of reaction. The latter, when they happen, are valuable chiefly as inducements and guarantees of the former.

And yet how still the Landscape stands!
How nonchalant the Hedge!
As if the "Resurrection"
Were nothing very strange!   (74)

Beside all this rush of experience from all sides, naming is best used for praising; the inadequacies of language cannot be trusted themselves to yield inference; "Going to Heaven! / How dim it sounds! / And yet it will be done" (79). Direct statement itself is roundabout in the face of the circuit or circumference of supernaturally charged natural events: "We — prone to periphrasis — / Remark that Birds have fled!" (45). The dead enjoin trust on the living who, as they once did, pass the graveyard on the way to school (51).

The function of the poet is to disengage, at a slant or angle, inferential series from all these intimations. The poet takes a standard lexicon and makes it do startling things, the ordinary made to yield the amazing:

This was a Poet — It is That
Distills amazing sense
From ordinary Meanings —
And Attar so immense

From the familiar species
That perished by the Door —
We wonder it was not Ourselves
Arrested it — before —   (448)

That poet, having brought the amazing into expression out of the ordinary, is transfigured into neutrality. He or she is named as "That," the sex of the poet hypostatized and obscured into pronominal and relational indistinguishability. The speaker of another poem (449) must die for beauty to discover the kinship of beauty and truth. She (?) becomes garrulous over the fact as she finds a friend in one who died for truth: "Until the Moss had reached our lips— / And covered up—our names—."

Plenitude is reestablished only gradually in this poetry. To shorten the process would result in a surrealism and make its emotional objectivity too automatic to sustain. Moreover, surrealism exalts dream, begun in a *dérèglement* such as that of Rimbaud.[12] Here there is no room for dream; reality is too vast, and too seamless in its very discordances.

3

Indirection for Emily Dickinson is not only an inescapable condition of human life. It is an emotional necessity, and markedly for "The Redoubtablest" of subjects, "Where go we—" (1417):

> How Human Nature dotes
> On what it can't detect.
> The moment that a Plot is plumbed
> Prospective is extinct—

Gradualness holds for man's relationship to God:

> The Stimulus beyond the Grave
> His Countenance to see
> Supports me like imperial Drams
> Afforded Day by Day.   (1001)

Here to be assimilated gradually and to be put out of sight are two aspects of the same crucial goal. Ideals themselves are a "Fairy Oil," provisional and preliminary: "But when the Vital Axle turns / The Eye rejects the Oil" (983). A psychological process must go through its inferential stages, and must look ahead (904). Only then can it achieve "Circumference." As Emily Dickinson says, emphasizing the surprise and reverence of the accompanying emotion, "Circumference thou Bride of Awe" (1620).

The application of this principle to perceptions in physical nature provides the link of similarity with the other life. Even assimilating birdsong passes through three stages:

> At Half past Three, a single Bird
> Unto a silent Sky

Propounded but a single term
Of cautious melody.

At Half past Four, Experiment
Had subjugated test
And lo, Her silver Principle
Supplanted all the rest.

At Half past Seven, Element
Nor Implement, be seen —
And Place was where the Presence was
Circumference between.   (1084)

The metaphor here of a logical progression through experiment, proof, and something like a totally assimilated law exhibits its figurativeness, and it does so progressively. The first stage has one term "Propounded." At the second stage there are two terms that rise to the generality of capital letters, "Experiment" and "Principle." At the third stage, in the third stanza, there are five: "Element," "Implement," "Place," "Presence," and "Circumference."

The three stages of tentative single song, fullness of song, and "presence" or recapitulative silence after the song has ceased resemble the three stages of Wordsworth's perception, except that his middle stage rather than his final stage involves the silence of a blank in a consciousness.[13] And in another poem about birdsong at sunrise, Emily Dickinson makes not remembrance but forgetfulness the final stage: "The Miracle that introduced / Forgotten, as fulfilled" (783). The Wordsworthian perspective is for her only one possible modality:

Looking back is best that is left
Or if it be — before —
Retrospection is Prospect's half,
Sometimes, almost more.   (995)

"What triple Lenses burn upon / The Escapade from God —" (894), she says in a poem about consciousness that imagines human perception as secret "Behind the Eyes of God."[14] As she says in a formula that anticipates Proust, "Perception of an object costs / Precise the Object's loss" (1071). This is, of course, not true of the divine object, about whose distance she complains in the second stanza here: "The Object Absolute — is nought —."

The accessibility of her multiple and far-fetched images may be derived from the complications involved in this process of perception. Her whimsicality, too, functions as an attempt to retain the right mood to receive indirection without being overwhelmed by the urgency of the truth it conceals.

Dickinson frequently names emotions, and she subjects them to progressive action even in the compass of a brief poem:

> A darting fear—a pomp—a tear—
> A waking on a morn
> To find that what one waked for,
> Inhales the different dawn.   (87)

Fear, pomp, tear, and waking precede a perception that is as natural and invigorating as to inhale not air but light. Such possibilities bear the aspect of urgency; one poem (754) makes the speaker a loaded gun, with moral inferences derived from what amounts to apprehension. In another poem (761) the speaker shuts her eyes because " 'Twas lighter— to be Blind—." In the onrush of perceptions to her "quick" ear she seems herself as much object as subject (891): "Creation seemed a mighty Crack— / To make me visible—."

For a perpetual receptiveness "The Soul should always stand ajar" (1055). The state of readiness may be defined in one way as a kind of impassivity: "As far from pity, as complaint— / As cool to speech—as stone— / As numb to Revelation / As if my Trade were Bone" (496). So the person as he stands either towards death or in death. "Pain—has an Element of Blank / It cannot recollect" (650), and this stroke of penetrating pyschology assimilates feeling to absence in the face of the perpetual presence of ultimates, another name for which is "The Loneliness One dare not sound—" (777), solitude become feeling before the eternal.

At its "loudest" the Spirit is still (1225). And a sequence of feeling, in this realm where sequences are everywhere, can be fraught with mysterious attributions:

> Her spirit rose to such a height
> Her countenance it did inflate
> Like one that fed on awe.
> More prudent to assault the dawn
> Than merit the ethereal scorn
> That effervesced from her.   (1486)

To be too elevated is akin to being overfed. And yet "her" perceptions, fed on the deep rightness of a praiseworthy attitude, "Awe," have a justice that makes them unassailable; it would be more prudent to assault the dawn than to stand indicted under her scorn, to merit it. The scorn on the one hand partakes of an astral quality: it is ethereal. On the other hand it effervesces; it bubbles up and is quickly over (the verb is in the past tense). The feelings engendered here enact their apocalyptic correlatives confusedly. "The mob within the heart / Police cannot suppress"

(1745). Grief may be defined, with a stanza given to each definition, as a mouse, as a thief, as a juggler, and as tongueless (793). Suffering and sickness, once over, empower the soul to question them (957). "After great pain, a formal feeling comes—" (341). Even in this sequence, leading to "A Quartz contentment, like a stone—," there is another sequence lurking: "First-Chill—then Stupor—then the letting go—."

Such acuteness leads continually to discriminations. "I cried at Pity—not at Pain—" (588), again from the vantage point of a dead person, allows the discriminating response to become a "Lullaby—." "Arid Pleasure" is "As different from Joy— / As Frost is different from Dew—" (782). "Time is a Test of Trouble— / But not a Remedy" (686). Since Joy has more "push" than Grief, a speaker is able to "wade . . . Whole Pools of it—," whereas the "least push of Joy / Breaks up my feet—" (252). Horror brings its contrary to pass: after it "my soul is giggling still" (410). "A Hairbreadth 'scape / . . . tingles in the Mind" (1175). "Pang is good / As near as Memory" (1133).

Not just patience but "Transports of Patience" lead to Bliss (1153). The contemplation of her life as though it were finished induces not death but something that "tasted" like death, night, frost, and fire (510). Horror is a perpetually restored presence after other feelings (512). Even "Delight" has a "Despair" that it is less than a "Longing" (1299). Sequence is subtle enough, in this poem, to produce a common error:

> Enchantment's Perihelion
> Mistaken oft has been
> For the Authentic orbit
> Of its Anterior Sun.

In such a process bliss and despair may be taken for each other (756). Bliss, a term of her frequent usage, is different for child, man, and courting couple, impervious to rebuke (1553). It may be wasted or increased (1057). Something like it, "happiness" may reverse its usual function of fulfillment and be an atonement for a reversed function of suffering: "For miseries so halcyon / The happiness atone" (1449). Here a psychology of pleasure-in-anticipation is broken into elements and inverted so that it may be theologized. A comparable adjudication is applied (1720) to the stages of bliss, and to the alternatives of handling anger: "Anger as soon as fed is dead— / 'Tis starving makes it fat—" (1509). Despair itself is a "White Sustenance" (640). And in an astonishing set of inferences that anticipates certain aphorisms of Kafka, Emily Dickinson declares that Love could raise the dead, except that it gets tired (1731). The force of happiness or Joy is strong enough to afford a transition to the afterlife (787, 788). Despair, too, has the advantage of resembling death (799).

Anguish may be so slow as to be imperceptible (584). But the perception of delight through its opposite pain does not merge the two. Rather it is more clearly seen for being like a sort of landscape, "Delight—become pictorial— / When viewed through Pain—" (572).

Such feelings connect to others because they train the soul for its future life:

> The hallowing of Pain
> Like hallowing of Heaven,
> Obtains at a corporeal cost—
> The Summit is not given
>
> To Him who strives severe
> At middle of the Hill—
> But He who has achieved the Top—
> All—is the price of All—   (772)

Correspondingly, "A lonesome glee . . . sanctifies the Mind" (774). This process may exceed expression, as with "The Moments of Dominion / That happen on the Soul / And Leave it with a Discontent / Too exquisite —to tell—" (627). It does not exceed naming the emotional residue of its inexpressibility. Heaven is mental (370) and endows a wakeful person, through its very absence, with his wakefulness to particulars: "The Missing All—prevented Me / From missing minor Things" (985). In another poem (1653) "Nothing" is the force that renovates the world. In this light feelings may find their definitions by being set in a perspective of time: "Remorse—is Memory—awake" (744); "Expectation—is Contentment" (807); "When Death lit all the shortness up / It made the hurry plain—" (795). A reference to the divine explains this process: "Apprehensions— are God's introductions— / To be hallowed accordingly" (797). Thus the acceptance, the definition, and the awareness of emotional stages converge in a single disposition of the spirit: "Strong Draughts of their refreshing minds / To drink—enables Mine / . . . To go elastic" (711). And space opens out as well as time: "Affliction cannot stay / In Acres—Its Location / Is Illocality" (963). "That awful stranger Consciousness" (1323) works to throw feelings into a seemingly haphazard sequence. So one poem puts satisfaction, satiety, want, and joy into a sort of jumble (1936). "Hope," too, "is a strange invention" (1391). Yet, if it is properly heeded, a religious emotion, awe before "Peril" or "Danger," "searches Human Nature's creases / As clean as Fire" (1678).

The self, consequently, is "columnar" (789). In another poem the self is a plaything not to be put away (423). It is as though the Biblical injunction to enter the Kingdom of Heaven as a little child were invoked to govern one's disposition towards oneself. "It is easy to work when the soul is at play—" (244). In such a way will awareness come of an innermost being, the heart inside the heart (217). Or, treating the language as the sort of plaything that should not be put away, it is also called "this little Hound within the Heart" (186).

4

What is the instrumentality of a poetry that exercises a function so determinedly theological? Unlike many poets of the time, Emily Dickinson never asks herself this question. She serenely takes the function of poetry almost for granted in its mode of religious discovery, as though she were a conscious heir of the German Romantics who asserted as much. She is, to be sure, an heir of the Emerson who was open to the German Romantics. When she does ask, in effect, what the difference is between the Bible and Orpheus, the heaviness of her irony betrays her uneasiness at separating them (1545).

Without ado Dickinson takes the poetic instruments that stand easily to hand for her. Then she brings their language to bear on her perceptions in such a way that the ensuing meditations will work philosophically to extend theological principles, to push them to an ultimate. In this she does not follow Blake's way. She does not build the language and a view of it into a philosophical system that also integrates metrical invention while deploying a free relation to visual accompaniment. Nor does she produce poised lyrics that are grounded on expansive philosophical speculation, as Leopardi does. In her work it is as though the poems of Leopardi had somehow been fused with the *Zibaldone*. Emerson stands behind her, but she is a more powerful *thinker* than Emerson. So her poems do not have the post-philosophical ring of Hölderlin's. Nor of course does she force the instruments of verse and language themselves to yield a universalizing and normative vision, like Mallarmé. Each of these fusions of poetry with philosophy has its own distinctness. Hers is to centralize poetry and philosophy on a base that is at once common in its meter and its diction while idiosyncratic in its dash-marked rhythms and in the predicative power and open sequence of its statements.

A poem is a public act: its features of recurrence that are superadded to the ordinary language of its sentences (meter, rhyme, and the like) can only be understood as calling attention to themselves. A personal letter is private, a communication between one person and another. A prayer, too, is private. Theological speculation is public, part of a common discourse. Emily Dickinson's poems, sharing something of the prayer and something of theological speculation, may be said thereby to exist midway between the public and the private, as her hesitations before publication also indicate. And her poems, curiously but understandably, operate also at times as rough equivalents for letters, their public character as poems subverted at their origin into a private communication. One of her first poems (4), about sailing to eternity, emerges suddenly after a number of lonely, passionate effusions to her future sister-in-law Susan Gilbert, letters so exuberant and demanding in their statement that not even the convention of amorous banter between unmarried women may fully explain them.[15] The poem is prefaced by a single line: "Write! Comrade, write!" This statement, in the same meter as the poem, directs the poem, ambiguously, towards a gesture of appeal, raising the ante to an eschatological assertion. Is the poem an evasive reference to common mortality? An exhibition of the skills, and desirability, of the appealing writer? A diversionary amusement? An incitement for the talented Susan Gilbert to respond in kind and therefore to respond? It is all of these. This poem-substituted-for-a-letter would seem to have helped inaugurate Emily Dickinson's writing of poetry by validating a homely and private context for it. She continues in this vein throughout most of her writing career, her "Letter to the World" becoming intermittently a letter to a chosen individual, her brother or the Reverend Samuel Bowles or Thomas Wentworth Higginson, the poem offered as at once a heightening of ordinary communication and a substitute for it.

Though in a general Romantic strain she compares poets to lamps (883) and poetry to love (1247), Emily Dickinson's poems are not artifacts so much as notes, records of a spiritual self-definition. One could not subsume her speaker under a particular philosophical or theological category because she rises to engage in radical philosophizing and theologizing at every turn, a sort of optimistic Nietzsche. When she compares poetry to love, in the same poem she is writing about something like a Last Judgment. She almost prefers the act of perception to the ability to communicate it (505): "Nor would I be a Poet— / It's finer—Own the Ear— / Enamoured—impotent—content." In this poem she goes on to imagine, by a kind of preterition, what some such poetry as she in fact writes would do to her, as though it were a possibility and not an actuality:

> A privilege so awful
> What would the Dower be,
> Had I the Art to stun myself
> With Bolts of Melody!

Language for Emily Dickinson is always a pressing of limits, as Guthrie points out.[16] The "covered vision" and the "compound vision" remain in unstable struggle. In a poem about a poet's attempt to choose a word that will fit his vision, she denies speech with a command: "Not into nomination / The Cherubim reveal—" (1126).

The relation in these poems between the metaphoric and the literal is potentially to be superseded by a heavenly perspective and its concomitants of different rules for signification. And so for such definitions of the "piercing Virtue," "Renunciation":

> Renunciation—is the Choosing
> Against itself—
> Itself to justify
> Unto itself—
> When larger function—
> Make that appear—
> Smaller—that Covered Vision—Here   (745)

The vision becomes covered when "Day's Great Progenitor— / Outvie." "Creation" is "but the Gambol / Of His Authority" (724). In the language she learns to exercise as a human being, the sacred and the secular blur; her poem about a carpenter (488) could apply to herself or to Jesus equally. She frames one poem in the rhetorical form of a protest against specific alternate metaphors for defining heaven (1270). "This Compound Frame" is "As manifold for Anguish— / As Species—be—for name—" (264).

The surprised "I" does not want to lock itself into a public posture. Dickinson draws on the poems for inclusion in letters, wanting from Thomas Wentworth Higginson as much validation that the poems "live" as she wants publication, a desire quickly and easily deflected. This woman lived in a house with nineteen Bibles[17] but never joined the church; whimsicality and privacy protected her. It would seem that she could only preserve her unique mode of creating prayers as poems by equating the silence of the uptake of a prayer—about which she wrote a whole poem (437)—by not putting into institutions for definition and reception her "Letter to the World" (441). In addressing the "Savior" she invokes a logic of excess and lost contingency before concluding:

> Defeat—whets Victory—they say—
> The Reefs—in old Gethsemane—
> Endear the Coast—beyond!
> 'Tis Beggars-Banquet—can define—
> 'Tis Parching—vitalizes Wine—
> "Faith" bleats to understand!   (313)

For such a sheep even the word "Faith" must be put in the quotation marks of approximation. Before "Avalanches," "lives . . . look cautious for their Breath — / But make no syllable — like Death — / Who only shows his Marble Disc — / Sublimer sort — than Speech —" (310).

11

Dostoevsky
The Apocalypse of Anguish

Money is the nearest form for the terrible hope of freedom, sexuality
is the most interior form, and murder is the climactic form.
—R. P. Blackmur

1

The novel as an expansive, open form serves well to set forth the hesitations and contradictions of the interior life, and also to depict a society
of persons rising to actions that crystallize the impulses of the interior
life.[1] Dostoevsky's first writings almost immediately conflate Dickens,
Balzac, and Gogol both psychologically and socially, through a language
that carries traces of its effort to assess the spiritual life. In his identification with deep suffering, he brought his writing past a document carrying some features of a novel (*From the House of the Dead*) and past a
large series of disquisitions on social problems with a spiritual side (*The
Diary of a Writer*) to the crux of the spiritual life in major novels centering on crime. In *From the House of the Dead*, Dostoevsky shows the terror of punishment as it coexists with the prisoner's sense that he needs
it for expiation, and the energy of these major novels draws on the thresh-
oldlike equivocation of the narrator between identification with the judge
and identification with the sinner. These novels, we have come to see,
are remarkable for tonal fusions that show in their very language the orientation towards a future redemption for characters who stand on this
threshold as the narration comes to a close.

In the notes for the beginning of *Crime and Punishment*, Dostoevsky
stresses tone. Bakhtin[2] has shown at convincing length how he fuses voices
and styles into a sort of Menippean satire, so that, for example, "dia-
tribe," "confession," and "sermon" blend in *The Dream of a Ridiculous*

Man. Dostoevsky, however, transforms Menippean satire. He aims not at denial, or some mixture of denial and delicate resignation, like Lucian, but at an affirmation that will face the deepest difficulties and look forward to possibilities, as though Baudelaire's vision had been heavily tempered by the aspiration of Rousseau. This is so even for the strong satiric undercurrent of the short story "Bobok" ("Bean"), where accommodations are assessed and finally sexuality addressed through the voices in a cemetery. "Bobok" mocks human frailty in the light of its failing before redemptive possibilities, not simply in the light of its illusions. The elaborate repertoire of voices classified by Bakhtin—stylization, *récit*, *Icherzählung*, and the rest[3]—for Dostoevsky becomes a sort of chorus blending into harmonies and not discords. If the laughter of carnival is ambivalent in celebrating both death and resurrection, in Dostoevsky the laughter is purifying, not just in a human but also in a specifically religious sense. The oxymoron does not just cancel out, and no multiple "point counterpoint" of views is permitted finally to predominate.

Dostoevsky refers, in fact, to "the demon of irony" (*Devils*—called *The Possessed* in English—Part One, V, VI). We must hear the ring of earnestness through all the psychological framing: Barbara Petrovna uses the phrase at one explosive moment, quoting Stepan Trofimovich to his son Pyotr, applying it apprehensively to her own son, Stavrogin. The Karamazov brothers have differences of ethos, different temperaments, different purposes, different views. However these differences may be schematized, the schematic sets fall into secondary status before their fundamental erotic-religious, filial aspirations and failings. These are the measure of everything, the ground base for all stylistic effusions, from a casual remark to the "poem" of "The Grand Inquisitor," which has within itself its own "dissonances."[4]

Grossman, Bakhtin, and Joseph Frank have all remarked on Dostoevsky's affinity for the style of the *feuilleton*, which "fitted him like a glove."[5] The Dostoevsky who turned away from the quasi-*feuilleton* of *A Writer's Diary* for the novel assigns such separable ruminations on church and state to a single character, Ivan, in a single aspect of his existence. The newspaper serves to make the link between public and private more evident, Dostoevsky said.[6] The novel serves, in his hands, to provide transcendent sequences of word-clouded action where what is evident is also what is obscure. Kirpotin remarks that in the notes for *Crime and Punishment* it is stipulated that there be no word about love between Raskolnikov and Sonia:[7] the love is a silent common denominator, a culminating *argumentum ex silentio* for the characters. After terrible events, after long suffering, the silence wins out over all the verbalizations.

The intertwining dialectic of multiple voices is brought powerfully by Dostoevsky to a convergence; the gradual attunement of language becomes the means whereby the future is adumbrated at every moment, even under extreme pressure. The beginning of *Crime and Punishment* marshals the pressure through a sort of *erlebte Rede* that stays close to Raskolnikov and his thoughts. This "indirect free style" gets attenuated away; the end is direct. It makes the realization of the future explicit, at a charitable distance from Raskolnikov:

> But at this point already there begins a new story, the story of the gradual renewal of a man, the story of his gradual regeneration (*pererozhdenie*) of his gradual transition (*perechod*) from one world to another, his acquaintance with a new, hitherto completely unglimpsed actuality. That could constitute the theme of a new tale, but our present tale is ended.   (Coulson 527; 6.422)[8]

The inner "regeneration"— literally "trans-generation"— accompanies and causes an outer "transition," a possibility already incorporated in the rich fusions of the narrative style.

The voices have merged into a single tone by the end of *The Brothers Karamazov*, too, where Alyosha leads the happy boys off to the funeral of Ilusha. This last episode offers a sort of event-litotes: the ordinary death of a child for the murder of an old man, the mild future of the boys and Alyosha for the agonized futures of Dmitri and Ivan, the sex-free band for the sex-strains of Katerina and Grushenka. The narrative leans heavily on the word "eternal," repeated six times; on "rapture" (*vostorg*), four times; on "fine," "see," "remember," "death," "love," "rise again," and "live." All these ordinary locutions through their repetition[9] verge on a litany of sorrowful celebration:

> Well, and who has united us in this fine, good feeling, which we shall remember all our lives? Who if not Ilyushka, the good boy, the dear (*mily*) boy, precious to us for ever and ever. Let us never forget him. May his fine memory live eternally in our hearts for ever and ever from this time forth. "Yes, yes, eternally, eternally," the boys cried in their ringing voices, with faces rendered soft with emotion (*umilěnny*, "touched"). "Let us remember his face and his clothes and his poor little boots, his coffin and his unhappy, sinful father, and how boldly he stood up for him alone against the whole school."
>
> "We will remember, we will remember," cried the boys.
>
> "He was brave, he was good!"
>
> "Ah, how I loved him!" exclaimed Kolya.
>
> "Ah, children, ah, dear friends, don't be afraid of life!"

"How fine life is when one does something fine and just."

"Yes, yes," the boys repeated rapturously.

"Karamazov, we love you!" a voice, probably Kartashov's, cried irrepressibly.

"We love you, we love you!" they all caught it up. There were tears in the eyes of many of them.

"And may the dead boy's memory live eternally!" Alyosha added again with feeling.

"Live eternally!" the boys chimed in again.

"Karamazov," cried Kolya, "Is it really true what religion says, that we shall all rise again from the dead and shall live and see each other again, all, Ilyushechka too?"

"Certainly we shall all rise again, certainly we shall see each other and shall tell each other with joy and gladness all that has happened!" Alyosha answered, half laughing, half rapturously.

"Ah, how fine it will be," broke from Kolya.

"Well, now we will finish talking and go to his funeral dinner. Don't be embarrassed at our eating pancakes, it's an old custom, eternal, and there's something fine in that!" laughed Alyosha.

"Well, let us go! And now we go hand in hand."

"And eternally so, all our lives hand in hand! Hurrah for Karamazov!" Kolya cried once more rapturously, and once more all the boys repeated his exclamation.

(Translation mine, based on that of Garnett-Matlaw; 15. 196–97)

Sorrow intrudes here only in the abjured gesture of embarrassment before eating *bliny* at the wake. All the complications of parricide have been transformed into the dead boy's remembered act of defending (rather than attacking) a sinful father. The verbal repetitions drown out everything else in the uniform impetus to tender emotion, an *umilenie* of confident rapture. That word, too, repeats: Ilyosha was *mily* ("dear," "tender"); the faces of his friends are *umilënny*. Not Dmitri or Ivan or the dead Karamazov father and son, but only the tender Karamazov, is signified in the repeated salute, "Hurrah for Karamazov." The last word of the novel is a metalinguistic one, a word describing celebratory words: "exclamation."

The "polyphony" in Dostoevsky's novels works energetically to transform the characters. When a transformation has taken place, the voice can straighten into direct, simple narrative (*Crime and Punishment*) or trail off into raptures (*The Brothers Karamazov*). In the meantime the events also register the strange self-transcendences of the persons in these novels, stressed by Ortega and Romano Guardini.[10] The verbalization of psychological pressures is momentarily haphazard, but in the long range it turns out to be self-revelatory.

2

For Dostoevsky the depth-psychological is the moral.[11] The anguished, fluctuating states of his characters, over a long span, may yield a mysterious redemptive state of being where the psychological reinforces the moral. Otherwise the psychological undermines the moral, and only in the second phase of his Siberian existence does Raskolnikov begin to redeem himself. Svidrigailov, split between ambiguous acts of financial generosity and satiric justification of his lust, dreams that a five-year-old girl leered at him like a whore. In the aftermath of the dream he shoots himself with the pistol Dunia had fired at him. Earlier, when she was still governess in his family, he had presented Dunia with the standard Utopian proposal of adulterous unions from Romantic times on — they would run away together and begin a new life in Europe. Raskolnikov's sister, ambiguously lured, overcomes her state of bothering about Svidrigailov, and the psychological no longer undermines the moral. She marries Razumikhin, the psychological reinforcing the moral for him as for her: he is no longer the untrustworthy "drunkard," and his provident side takes over wholly under her influence.

"The Drunkards" was to have been the title and subject of his novel, but the conception of Raskolnikov puts the psychological on a deeper plane, the moral into a less cyclical pattern. Drunkards move to the second level of action; it is through his generosity to the drunkard Marmeladov that Raskolnikov meets the man's daughter Sonia, the sacrificial prostitute.

Raskolnikov has decided to kill the pawnbroker Alyona Ivanovna before the novel opens. Yet the first word Dostoevsky uses to characterize him is "indecision." His oscillation between decision and indecision, first before the crime and then before the implicit or explicit confession that will lead to punishment, provides him always with a fluid set of emotional responses. These are often mysterious to those around him and not simply obvious even to the reader who knows he has committed the crime. The act of confession puts an end to this sequence: the bearing down of the necessity to confess carries with it so much anguish that it may be reckoned the "punishment." Siberia is characterized as an "epilogue," and that final segment has its own sequence of first stiffness and then yielding under the influence of Sonia.

Changing his initial first person narrative to the third person, as he did, allowed Dostoevsky to bring his universe of characters into like responsiveness. His is the perspective, the voice, that coordinates and unifies their voices. Raskolnikov's thoughts about superior people and the justified murder are expressed not in dialogue but in the published arti-

cle that we hear about only midway through the novel. These thoughts
are echoed in the conversation of a student and an officer in one of the
taverns his restlessness drives him to enter. Even Alyona Ivanovna is not
entirely free of this anguish: as the widow of a government official she
has presumably become usurious to stave off a slow descent not unlike
the one that threatens Raskolnikov. Her compulsions are centered on
money, as Raskolnikov's have persistently been, though in a different way.
Indeed, she has pressed her handicapped sister into service night and day,
a circumstance that catches this Lizaveta in the network of the murder.
Raskolnikov's mother, comparably, has been trying to arrange her daughter Dunia's marriage so as to benefit Raskolnikov financially. Dunia is
threatened with what is called a sort of legalized prostitution to Luzhin
on the one hand, and by seduction from Svidrigailov on the other. The
handicapped Lizaveta is mysteriously pregnant, as we learn from joking
young people in a tavern.

Dostoevsky at every point explicitly indicates his protagonist's emotional response, mysterious and as though random, in this overheated July
of sad urban drift. The first chapter establishes and comments on Raskolnikov's oscillation between depression and elation, his orbiting from
the solitude of his room to the crowds of the beer shops. This process only
intensifies his mood, as drink does for Marmeladov, who says he drinks
the more because he feels the more (6.15).

The pitch of anguish in the beginning of the novel remains steady. The
sufferings of Marmeladov recall those of *From the House of the Dead*,
the book Dostoevsky had finally got off his chest not long beforehand.
Marmeladov's gladness (1, 2) that his wife pommels him cannot be as-
cribed to mere masochism; it expresses a true sense of guilt reaching for
expiation. Its emotional complex parallels and recalls the terrible beat-
ings in *From the House of the Dead*.

The flow of the novel gives us the fine, complex turnings of Raskolnikov's own reactions. This passage about his reaction to his mother's letter
is typical:

> Thus he teased and tormented himself with these questions, and even
> found a kind of pleasure in doing so. These questions were not new,
> however; they did not confront him unexpectedly but were an old,
> painful story of long standing. It was a long time since they had be-
> gun to lacerate and torture his feelings. Long, long ago his present
> anguish (*toska*, also "yearning" and "melancholy")[12] had first stirred
> within him, and it had grown and accumulated until of late it had
> come to a head and concentrated itself into the form of a wild, fan-
> tastic, and terrible question that tormented his heart and mind, ir-
> resistibly demanding resolution. Now his mother's letter had struck

him like a thunderbolt. It was clear that now the time had come,
not to languish (*toskovat*, the verb of *toska*) or suffer passively, arguing that the questions were unresolvable, but to act at once, to
do something now and with speed. He must resolve on something
or other, or . . .   (Coulson, revised, 42–43; 6.391)

Slowly, out of a long welter of such closely sequenced feelings, does
Raskolnikov come first to crime and then to punishment. As in Dostoevsky's work from the beginning—in *Poor Folk*, *The Double*, *Mr. Prochar-
kin*, among others—the solitude of the urban dweller intensifies his capacity for feeling while exposing him to uncertainties and the desperate
need for sociability. *Poor Folk* locates a love sacrifice amid crowding, early
deaths, meaningless work, and scattered families. The people here are
already caught in a trans-Dickensian clinging together. Poverty opens a
tutor into responding to the poor, and the pressure of poverty releases
a stream of feeling in Barbara towards her sick mother (1. 87). For the
troubled spirit a solitude of near-strangers hangs over the events as a persistent charitable possibility. *Crime and Punishment* transforms these conditions by widening and destabilizing the class base, and by making the
erotic-psychological a version of the theological-moral, all through the
central means of delineating the thrust of feeling. This feeling gathers
the past, looks to the future, harrows the present. The feeling in its flow
may take several names or series of names: finally it is characterized as
either guilty or redemptive, whatever intermediate name it may bear.
It is judged morally in the process of being depicted psychologically. And
there is no other possibility for action, no resting place from the energetic servitude to guilt or freedom in redemption; the process permeates
the active universe of persons in their purgatorial metropolis.

3

What should be logically calculable in a society is what Dostoevsky
shows as deeply subject to such spiritual pressures: the money that the
characters handle. Money is often mentioned in his novels, and all cluster around it, but usually no social class can rest comfortably on it. As
R. P. Blackmur says of *The Brothers Karamazov*, "Money is the nearest
form for the terrible hope of freedom, sexuality is the most interior form,
and murder is the climactic form."[13] As Dostoevsky himself says in the
notebooks for *Devils* (*The Possessed*), "Although money does give him a
terribly *steady* focus and provides him with an answer to *all* his questions, this very *focus* vacillates on occasion (poetry and a good many other
things), and he sees no way out. It is precisely this *vacillating* condition
that gives substance to this novel."[14] Here, too, either way there is no rest-

ing place. To be poor lays one open to insult and injury; to be rich gives one means to tempt others and oneself. A calculating meanness of spirit produces a seediness in the landladies of Raskolnikov and the Marmeladovs.

We learn late that Raskolnikov, who murdered for the ancillary reason of using the pawnbroker's money, never even counted the money he put under the stone, a sum ten times that at his disposal. He compensates by a series of small, charitable distributions that get swallowed up in the morass, helping to pay for the Marmeladov funeral. We hear of money often; he throws money in the water (6.90); there are reports about lots of counterfeiters (6.126). Raskolnikov's plea of poverty is at once a fact and a screen: "I am a poor, sick student depressed by poverty" (6.80).

His mother strains the resources of her pension to send him part of the sum he is half-distractedly distributing. She will virtually sell Dunia to Luzhin. Luzhin himself through money provides an X-ray of his malice. He gives ten rubles to Sonia, then frames her with the additional hundred rubles he thrusts in her pocket, then publicly accuses her of theft. Svidrigailov himself never goes so far; he, in fact, uses his riches as an opposite trap, to seduce and not to shame. So money shades over into sexuality.

Love itself is treacherous for those who lack money, the poor. In *Poor Folk* the rich seducer walks off with the girl, who has a hapless poor lover already. In *The Insulted and Injured* the pampered son abandons his first love for a young, rich girl. In *Christmas Tree* and *Wedding* money provides the extra lure for an older man successfully to court a girl in her teens. The fifty-year-old Svidrigailov has been using his money to set up a similar betrothal. So money, overempowering sexual choice, is comparably treacherous for the rich; it tempts them to tempt others.

The money floats, surfaces, disappears, lures. In *The Gambler* Dostoevsky declares that all Russians have something in them of the gambler (5.317). And Dostoevsky in a letter compares *The Gambler* to *From the House of the Dead*.[15]

Nastasya in *The Idiot* and Grushenka in *The Brothers Karamazov* begin as protégées whose financial dependency becomes a sexual dependency. Ripened, they both become money managers and at the same time sexual free agents. Money is burned in a fireplace in *The Idiot*, then pulled out of the fireplace, a temptation. In *The Village of Stepanchikovo* it is trampled underfoot (3.84).

Hidden sums, fleetingly publicized, run all through *The Brothers Karamazov*. These sums are pretext, lure, concretization, screen, and a constant focus for disturbing incidents. Dmitri jokingly jumps at Alyosha from under a tree on a dark night and shouts, "Your purse or your life"

(14.141). He replaces the 4,500 rubles that Katerina's father has embez-
zled from his regiment on condition that she will come to his rooms;
when he does not take advantage, she falls in love. She entrusts 3,000
rubles to him to mail, which he supposedly squanders on Grushenka.
Actually he has kept 1,500 in a bundle around his neck.

Katerina gives 200 rubles via Alyosha to the insulted officer Snegiryov,
who throws them away. Dmitri has come home in the first place to seek
the inheritance his father is refusing. Instead the calculating Fyodor has
put 3,000 rubles in an envelope as a present for Grushenka if she comes
to his room — a pattern crucially different from his son Dmitri's, since
Fyodor obviously would take advantage of Grushenka. Dmitri is accused
of having taken these 3,000 rubles; they are confused with the ones he
has been squandering and/or concealing. But it turns out that the father's
rubles sealed in the envelope were taken by Smerdyakov at the time of
the parricide; Ivan produces them.

Dmitri, on his spree, asks Grushenka's protector Samsonov for money,
then Madame Hohlakov. He is refused both times. He offers the Poles
3,000 rubles to leave the Grushenka one of them had seduced, but they
refuse haughtily. Later they are reduced to begging for the small sums
that Grushenka doles out. Nor is Dmitri able to complete the sale of the
forest that his father has offered Ivan as a substitute for an inheritance.

Indeed, no one of these many transactions is cleanly completed. All
are torn awry by the spiritual forces they at once displace, complicate,
and exemplify.

4

In this way the events keep disrupting any semblance of a stable exchange pattern. The spirit predominates. If this condition holds for something so common and seemingly neutral as money, it holds all the more
for the deep personal exchange of sexuality. In these novels sexuality is
subjected to the full range of yearnings, humiliations, sacrifices, and social sufferings; it runs into them and fades into them and takes its color
from them. Netochka in *Netochka Nezvanovna* finds life in an adoptive
family to be a temporary salvation and a permanent curse. Her infatuation with the daughter of one family forces her into the midst of another,
where she is falsely accused of corrupting the wife after discovering a
lover's letter.

A match can only come about between Razumikhin and Dunia, between Raskolnikov and Sonia, after a full range of events has had its play
upon their spirits. The same is true for the final unions in *The Brothers
Karamazov*. Often a match is merely perverse, as the marriage of Stav-

rogin, or a false realization, as the marriage of Aglaia in *The Idiot*. Myshkin is eclipsed between Aglaia's bad marriage to a Pole and Rogozhin's fruition with Nastasya in not marriage but murder. Dissolute sexual arrangements, the fact of his illegitimacy, plague the "raw youth" in the novel of that title. Fyodor Karamazov is harried by the three sons born from his two divergent, troubled marriages; he is killed by the one illegitimate son sired as a result of a predatory, drunken sexual episode.

Dostoevsky sketched but did not write a simple novel about a love affair (*Marriage*, 5.319). In *Devils* he cut back Granovski's (Stepan Trofimovich's) endless plans about marriages. The exchange patterns of love that Dostoevsky brings to realization are ridden by an unrealizable ambiguity. As Dmitri says (7.122), "falling in love is not the same as loving." Even where, as characteristically, the love relations are split into triangles, Dostoevsky nowhere closes his events in a simple Racinian pathos where *A* loves *B* who loves *C* who loves *A*. Prior erotic commitment may supervene, as in *White Nights*. Or the terrible superior force of money carries the day, as in *Poor Folk* and *The Insulted and Injured*. Most profoundly, a preference for evil over good emerges in an appealing, troubled woman: in *The Landlady*, in Nastasya's submission to Roghozhin.

Mochulsky[16] neatly summarizes the oscillations:

> In *Crime and Punishment* we have before us the triangle: Svirdrigailov-Dunya-Razumikhin. In *The Idiot* the triangles: Myshkin-Nastasya Filippovna-Rogozhin, and Nastasya Filippovna-Myshkin-Aglaia. In *A Raw Youth* Versilov is between his wife and Akhmatova; in *The Devils* Stavrogin is between Liza and Dasha and Liza between Stavrogin and Mavriky Nikolayevich. Finally, in *The Brothers Karamazov* we find three triangles: Mitya between Grushenka and Katerina Ivanovna, Katerina Ivanovna between Mitya and Ivan, Grushenka between Mitya and Fyodor Pavlovich.

There is, in each instance, much to qualify these already complex erotic interactions. Luzhin also bears upon Dunia, and his strange overtures to Sonia put the two into corresponding sets, as Raskolnikov has observed. Indeed, Dunia's relation to her brother bears upon each of these men; she not only meets Razumikhin as Raskolnikov's friend but marries him, we may say, as a result of the purgative series. And there is more to the gallery—Marmeladov's marriage out of pity to Katerina, who marries him out of desperation, the girl suicide whom Svidrigailov seduced or violated, Raskolnikov's dead fiancee.

It is the erotic life that makes every axis of the triangle set every other axis to trembling. There the energetic nexus keeps working. The career of Rozanov, who began as a critic of Dostoevsky and ended as a sort of

Russian D. H. Lawrence, substantiates the erotic program for which these novels could be utilized. So in *The Idiot* Myshkin's relation to Aglaia not only polarizes his relation to Nastasya and brings her to impulsive outbursts. It also is affected by, and affects, his relations to Ganya and to Rogozhin. In the communal spiritual possibility away from which these characters fail, a term like "jealousy" is far too simple. In *Crime and Punishment* Sonia's degrading profession removes jealousy because it is sacrificial; it purges almost directly the erotic into the redemptive. Dostoevsky revised out of his drafts of the novel the places where a jealous Raskolnikov rages with obscenities against Sonia. As he realizes these characters, they move more energetically, more in harmony with a vision of good and evil. Sexuality serves at once as an impetus and a figure for good and evil, never an end in itself, never merely a means.

In *Devils* many of the relationships are past-and money-bound: Stepan Trofimovich has two dead wives and a female employer whose sexuality he has refused. The political murk of the novel keeps Liza and Shatov's wife and Stavrogin, who has also driven a girl to suicide, from even an intimation of erotic realization. In *The Brothers Karamazov*, however, all three legitimate brothers act in such a way that erotic realization would be possible. Even Smerdyakov has a fiancee. They are new men in the light either of a debauched natural father or of a chaste spiritual father, Zossima. Beyond these sexually mature brothers are those who have not yet entered the sphere of Eros, the boys whose band finds celebration even in the conclusion of a funeral for one of their number.

Thus the end of a long series in *The Brothers Karamazov* is a celebration joyous but inconclusive, one centered on the generation to come. The Utopianism of Dostoevsky's fiction centers on a future, or on the elsewhere of the Switzerland from which Myshkin has come and to which Stavrogin aspires. In his journalism it centers on the deep, unrealized community whose visible form is the Russian Orthodox Church. Dostoevsky's theological originality not only locates "Madonna" and "Sodom" in the same breast, as Dmitri Karamazov regrets. It also moves both Madonna and Sodom through events that fall away from Utopia unremittingly while irrepressibly aspiring to it. The whole process takes place in an energized past, present, and future, which gain their meaning, as sexuality and money and everything else does, from the aspiration and at the same time from the failure to realize it. Dostoevsky, it may be said, combines the analysis of Baudelaire with the will of Nietzsche — and with the tough-grained hope of Emily Dickinson.

As Dostoevsky said in a letter, "The present does not exhaust reality — it merely exists under the future secret Word not yet spoken."[17] In its sexual form, the Utopia of this "Word" would be a marriage like that of

Sonia and Raskolnikov or Grushenka and Dmitri, realized in a sketched future. In its political form it would be community—an undefinable, "not yet spoken" one, sadly traduced by Stavrogin's group in their forced efforts at definition. Instead of creating a community, they bring in their wake failure and murder, if not the sort of silly ideas about dissolving the family and sexual loyalty mouthed on the sidelines of *Crime and Punishment* by Lebedniazikov. In its form of religious social action, the tender feeling that might be Utopian either withdraws, in the person of Father Zossima, or is crucified by the action, in the person of Myshkin.

In Dostoevsky every act is a free act, as Bakhtin notes.[18] Ortega and Romano Guardini have emphasized how this freedom opens up the individual character into unpredictability. I have elsewhere discussed how the represented freedom of these characters opens up the plots of Dostoevsky's novels.[19] From his protagonists, echoing their freedom, the society stirs outward in the anguish of its unrealized freedom. Raskolnikov passes the drowning girl (6.130–32). She is struck, much as he has been, by the dream of the horse beaten across the eyes. A given event points many ways; Ganya's defense of Myshkin in *The Idiot* shows both generosity towards Myshkin and a priggish spite towards Burdovski and his other auditors; the event encapsulates positive and negative possibilities. The same may be said for Aglaia's sympathy towards Myshkin, which at once teases and evades, while seeking fulfillment. In her meeting with Nastasya Fillipovna, generosity and sadistic self-assertion interact in an uneasy mixture.

The social code, in its resistance to Utopianizing responses, induces the withdrawal of Father Ferapont, a rivalry on a different plane but in some ways similar to that in the regiment that Zossima abandoned, unwilling to insist on masculine rivalry. Alyosha is loved by everybody and moves easily to the possibility of reconciliations, but he is young, aimed towards the future.

The Utopian response always lurks in the consciousness as a possibility for all but those who set themselves to keep denying it—Svidrigailov, the Prince of *The Insulted and Injured,* Stavrogin. Stepan Trofimovich in *Devils* may be wallowing in inconsequentiality as a "dependent," but the fact of his so defining himself, and the very stutter with which he does so, contains the possibility that he will become a religious wanderer, merging into old Russian folkways. His counterpart in *The Village of Stepanchikovo,* the literary hanger-on Foma Fomitch, retires to a monastery and prays day and night (3.12). In "An Unpleasant Anecdote," the drunken overseer passes out and is put to sleep in the sole available bed, that of his impoverished employee's daughter, newly wed to a rake. Around these events there hovers the constant possibility of the employee's courtesy and evasion; society, in its lowliest members, preserves this trace of the Utopian possibility.

The characters in Dostoevsky's novels are set in a schematic relationship of correspondences that does not fully issue into the plot: Raskolnikov and Svidrigailov are pairs; so are Raskolnikov and Razumikhin, Luzhin and Svidrigailov, Lizaveta and Sonya, Pulcheria and Alyona, Raskolnikov and Alyona.[20] This sort of schematism becomes elaborate in *The Brothers Karamazov*, where the psyches of the brothers meet as they dispose of a paternal pair, the natural and evil Fyodor corresponding to the spiritual and virtuous Zossima. The brothers' psyches meet, in turn, through the crisscrossing of their relationships to the two dominant women, who themselves are in a sort of alternating correspondence, Katerina and Grushenka.

Their ideas are schematized too, and with all the force that the journalistic pamphleteer of *A Writer's Diary* put into the novel after abandoning that serial to write it. Not just in the section with that title, but at every point, we are faced with "Pro and Contra," so much so that Golosovker can assert that a still deeper underlying schematization, that of the Kantian antinomies, will obtain for the ideas here.[21]

However, the antinomies are constantly transcended. The plot weaves its connections between the schematism of the characters' relations and that of their freedom of salience beyond our expectation. The plot also offers a continuing undercurrent of demonstration that freedom remains open to Utopian possibility while continually going under to the domination of perverse disintegrations, of the "lacerations" (*nadryvy*) that tear people and their purposes apart. The disproportion between schematic characters and open plot keeps the view steadily spiritualized while the progress of the action stays uncertain. The guilt of parricide schematizes as a certain fact over Smerdyakov; it reverberates as a multiple possibility over the other brothers.

The interaction of characters in these novels trembles towards an intimacy. The intimacy is based on response and not just on any nexus of relations: it forces the language to extravagant dialogic turns. The largeness of the city also randomizes and spiritualizes these encounters. Even as early as *Poor Folk*, the epistolary novel is infused with an intimacy quite different from the round robin of letters in Richardson's novels. Two people write back and forth; they reveal their inmost thoughts; they are random neighbors, and the pressures are such that their sympathies cannot become effectuated as love.

In all Dostoevsky's early work, through *Netochka Nezvanovna*, characters steady in their sorrow distantly glimpse freedom through the workings of dangerous but inescapable intimacy. This is true even in *The*

Double, which Dostoevsky valued enough to work it over in the sixties after writing it in the forties. There, however, the intimacy is hallucinatory, between parts of a personality or else occultly identical persons: it is never clear. Golyadkin's excessive politeness to his double masks and combats the uncanniness of their relation, different from Golyadkin's "sense of oppression" before the doctor who peers at him leaving the office or the officials he imagines are slighting him. At one point (1.157) he confesses to the double. Their blocked intimacy differs, too, from the double's almost magical attainment of conviviality in Golyadkin's own circles.

The "hollowness" of Golyadkin comes to a rhetorical climax. It carries rhetoric with it (1.143) as an approximation and evasion of the intimate *feuilleton*-confession-narrative "garrulity" of Dostoevsky's mature manner. Raskolnikov puts the imagined statements of his mother through the ironization of his own voice.[22] This irony does not just imply that the son rejects the limitations of the mother; he also seeks, and deplores his distance from, the steady reassurance of her attention. He imagines her seeing him as extraordinary; but that is the way he envisions himself in his article about extraordinary men.

At an unexpected climax, the other side of doubleness comes to the fore: Raskolnikov confesses, Smerdyakov kills, Nastasya abandons Myshkin for Rogozhin, Rogozhin murders her. But as Shestov says of Dostoevsky's characters, no one enters tragedy voluntarily.[23] Though Dostoevsky had addressed himself at the very beginning to "the insulted and injured," and though he had depicted an "honest thief," a mysteriously attractive gang accomplice ("The Landlady"), and a sadistically fraudulent prince (*The Insulted and Injured*), it took him over twenty years of his writing career, as weil as five years among felons in Siberia, to put a crime at the center of a novel. Once he had done this in *Crime and Punishment*, his longer writings, except for *A Raw Youth*, kept crime at the center, staying with murder as the most revelatory of the pathetic realizations of the Herculean forces at work in the people he conceived: *The Idiot, Devils, The Brothers Karamazov.*

A capital crime brings to grievous and sharply specific realization what it is that the insulted and injured are suffering from: the failure of society to become the sort of charitable mutuality that Christianity envisages and Soloviev depicts.[24] The man who commits that crime unleashes in himself tremendous forces, and these operate over a long stretch of time: crime is shorter than punishment, punishment than the full expiation, if it ever comes. It comes for Raskolnikov, who commits his crime fairly early in the novel. It does not come for Rogozhin, who commits his at the end. It may or may not come for Dmitri or Ivan Karamazov, who suffer only a tangential spiritual guilt for their complicity of wish and omission in a crime that happens in the middle of a novel.

The opposite of crime is sacrifice, again a leading conception for Dostoevsky's friend, the theologian Soloviev. Fear or dread (*strach*) he claims to be the first religious feeling,[25] a feeling that well characterizes either Raskolnikov or Sonia, in whose union crime meets sacrifice and is purged. The next step of religious feeling in Soloviev's scheme is a reverence that enlists the reason. Only at a third step does love express religious feeling — a step that Raskolnikov is just barely reaching at the end of the novel. This step is accessible to Alyosha and the boys, difficult for Father Zossima, and a distant goal for Dmitri and Ivan once it has proved an impossibility for their father.

The redemptive process of love is long, silent, and full of strange turnings. Arrest these, take away the time of sequenced development, and a schematism results: the controversy between faith and reason in the first debate between Aloysha and Ivan, the schematized "miracle, mystery, and authority" of the Grand Inquisitor's social analysis. This is an accurate picture of the human state while it falls far short of Dostoevsky's vision of the full human process. And symbolically the Inquisitor's discussion takes place over the flower-decked coffin of one child, while more fully the novel will take its unexpected, muted end in a celebration before the coffin of another. For Golosovker the subtext of the schematism is the antinomies of Kant's *Critique of Pure Reason*, one position contraverting another without dialectical sublation. Yet Dostoevsky sent from Siberia, in his own process of unjust suffering rendered as atonement, not for anything of Kant's but for Hegel's *Philosophy of History*, the discussion of a process that rises out of and above static schematism.

The schematism of the later novels stretches the capacities of the characters who would find escape in them. From *The Insulted and Injured* on, Dostoevsky's very titles tend towards abstractness. Rhetorically, self-accusation is indeed self-justification in *Crime and Punishment*, but the paradoxical identification between the two serves as a preliminary screen for Raskolnikov, a giant verbal "acting-out" of a stage in his development.[26] For the Underground Man, who concludes with the paradox of a scene of sympathy that he drowns in sado-masochistic rejection, there is no development. He remains underground in the wilderness of verbal paradox.

Raskolnikov wants to murder the old woman so that he can use her money to do good in the world, and he repeats this sterile contradiction as he keeps asserting the value of life in his conversations with the abandoned woman (6.123), as well as in his many small charitable donations. Caught in an oscillation between serving as the nurse of Ordinov and the masochistic mistress of her fatherly lover Murin, the "Landlady" is lost. Kirpotin quotes Glivenko[27] on the contradiction between Raskolnikov's two desires: to be a good citizen and to be an extraordinary man. Only in the purgative extremities of the entire action does this contradiction get resolved. In the Utopia of Dostoevsky's Christian Nietzschean-ism, as one may call it, only the extraordinary man is truly the good citizen.

In the light of the dominant and protracted process he represents, the increase of description in Dostoevsky's later novels takes on urgency and mystery, and the "polyphonic" drift of the style swirls steadily, with all its many eddies, towards the kind of resolution that the simple language of the conclusions quoted above exemplifies. So the cruelly dying child does not just arrest the reader into pathos, as in the work of the Dickens whom Dostoevsky intently read, nor does the bad dream just figure events as they stand: they are part of the process, purgative. Already the air of the detective story[28] hangs over the crimes of these novels without the detective story's intent interest in solving the crime. Their intent interest lies on another plane, that of somehow making absolution accessible to the criminal. There tends to be a "secret" as well as a "Mystery."[29] A giant hidden cause underlies the many proximate causes that Zosimov summa-rizes for Raskolnikov's "illness." "He had found his patient, he said, in a very satisfactory condition. According to his observations, the illness had some psychological causes in addition to the bad material conditions the patient had been living in for the past few months; 'it is, so to say, a product of many complex moral and material influences, anxieties, ap-prehensions, worries, certain ideas . . . and other things'" (Coulson 198; 5.159).

The past is deeper and more flagrant, the future more pregnant with possibility, than such accounts can assess—and the account itself will be enmeshed in the purposes of personal life or career. Here Zosimov wishes to make a good impression on Dunia; the investigators in this novel and the prosecutors in *The Brothers Karamazov* all have their own axes to grind.

Rozanov emphasizes the importance of the future in Dostoevsky's novels.[30] The "laceration," taken by itself, wishes to arrest the process, and it is therefore perverse, except in the exalted Biblical image of Ra-chel mourning for her lost children and refusing to be comforted. Eros struggles towards and away from laceration, yearning for a future and at the same time undermining a future.[31]

The future, however, itself opens into many dimensions. At the end of *The Brothers Karamazov*, there is the certain condemnation of Dmitri and the punishment possibly to be justifiably avoided by escape to Amer-ica. The guilt diffuses over the suicide brother Smerdyakov and the an-guished brother Dmitri and the implicated logical brother Ivan. The guilt is still further diffused by having the novel conclude on a now largely unrelated future, that of Alyosha and the youths. Theirs is a proximate future of Utopian participation, *bliny* at the wake in a few minutes. Beyond that is the distant future, the promised meeting with Dmitri after thirty years in Siberia. And over all is the ultimate future, the salvation and grace for the injured Alyosha, a possibly "rapturous" present partaking somewhat of all. This is made possible through the continuation in Alyosha of the vicariousness that Zossima had begun. Zossima himself cut off one future to find another. He came to his death after resolutely disappointing any expectations of miracle, mystery, and authority. These novels express the possibility of deeper expectations, without ever taking the shortcut into mere piety.

12

The Moment of
Nietzsche

Das Denken beginnt erst dann, wenn wir erfahren haben, dass die seit
Jahrhunderten verherrlichte Vernunft die hartnäckigste Widersacherin
des Denkens ist.

Thinking begins when we learn that reason, which has been glorified
for centuries, is the most stubborn opponent of thinking.

Heidegger on Nietzsche

1

Nietzsche is a poet and composer as well as an aphorist like Coleridge,
a moralist like Baudelaire, a theologian like Emily Dickinson, a classical
scholar like Leopardi, and a philosopher whose later writings have con-
tours that more resemble the *Zibaldone* of Leopardi than they do the
comprehensive and systematic works of the philosophers from Kant
through Schopenhauer in whose tradition he was writing. Unlike theirs,
and in some ways to a still greater degree than Kierkegaard's, his writings deeply bear the marks of a perpetual striving, a struggling sense of
the emotional and intellectual threshold that also serves them as a recurrent and endlessly puzzling subject.

Thinking finds in reason its most stubborn opponent, as Heidegger
rightly assesses the role in Nietzsche's work of the philosopher's indispensable faculty. Reason, however, is also indispensable for Nietzsche.
Without ever succumbing to the infinite regress of some equivalent for
Kierkegaard's paradoxes, Nietzsche places himself, and his language, at
a zero point of survival strategy. He assails the reason he will be enlisting. To do so automatically ironizes a discourse that at the same time
struggles beyond irony. The pseudo-scripture of *Also sprach Zarathustra*

is an anti-irony, a survival tactic of throwing together for an imagined desert a rhapsodic series of stunted myths and severe warnings. Kierkegaard abounds in preliminary ironies too, in interlocking pseudonyms and the alternating whole theories of *Either/Or*. Nietzsche also carries Rousseau further by putting himself, the developing speaker and encouraging leader, at the center of his discourse. But Zarathustra is a mask, compounded of a real figure from a primitive religion, ironically displaced from the Christianity of Nietzsche's own culture while retaining theological speculation as at every point an implied central topic. The name can intend no less.

Not the history of the world is subject to dialectical manipulation, as with Hegel, but the psycho-history of the self as by reaching to the future it discovers in itself the nearly ineradicable traces of the past. The future finds its deepest patterns and most significant ground of meditation in the movements of the past. The moment, in its quick and implications, was a vast threshold for Nietzsche, as it was for Blake.

Deeply aware of the moment in its reach to the future and out of the past, Nietzsche intensifies both his prospective concerns and his retrospective ones. These two concerns, prospective and retrospective, already converge in *The Birth of Tragedy*, which both offers an account of a major shift in the attention of the Greeks and proposes a model for directing the artist's attention — *Zukunftsphilologie* indeed, to alter Wilamowitz's pejorative.

That model still follows Rousseau's emphasis on the emotions,[1] though in a way that makes Nietzsche, thanks partly to Hegel, more of a depth-historian, one who reads depth-psychological patterns in history, than Rousseau or even Vico had tried to be. *Rausch* is a state of feeling, *Traum* another: both the Dionysian state and the Apollonian organize the emotions around a coherent attitude prior to any utterance. And they are fluid enough to intermingle; tragedy itself combines the two.

Nietzsche, however, dynamizes the relationship between the past and the present by locating and identifying those attitudes in a somewhat alien, exemplary society, the Greek. Where Rousseau brings in anthropological data and constructions about origins to buttress a present, universalized psychology, Nietzsche leaves problematic, or rules out entirely, the question of universality. He attacks such notions directly, and indirectly the intense tendentiousness of his language glories in subverting its propositional character. Nor does Nietzsche allow for Hegel's completion of a stage in history at the moment when it is to be superseded by another stage. Nietzsche's moment is also dynamized: the bearing of Greece on the future, of a present Dionysiac perception on its origins and its destiny, hovers in the will of the thinker. The very title "The Birth of Tragedy from the Spirit of Music" indicates a time progression, the painful issuance of something in time, tragedy, out of something generalized, the spirit of music. Philosophy itself, he declares, occupies no privileged position, but rather is subject to such a sequence; from it the emphasis of Socrates is only a further birth.

It is not hard to see Nietzsche's obscure doctrine of the Eternal Return in a psychological light as a way of resolving the intensity of the moment (in later fiction, Joyce's epiphanies), and the balanced unity of past and present in a grand recapitulation (Proust's mémoire involuntaire). *The Birth of Tragedy* itself offers a grand recapitulation; it is only possible, so to speak, if the doctrine it implies be allowed to have preceded it. The transvaluation of *all* values, his later program, implies much time, and an interaction of time, if it would take whole generations to create just one generous custom.[2] Testing values is not a merely logical exercise; it, too, enters the dynamic progression of time, a progression in which the potential lockstep of the Hegelian dialectic has itself been wholly *aufgehoben*,[3] as it already has partially in Hegel.

Slightly displaced in time Nietzsche calls himself, somewhat ironically: *Untimely Reflections* is the title of his next book, and yet "untimely," *unzeitgemässig*, like many key terms in Nietzsche, is not simple. It is self-qualifying without being ironic. "Independent" and "old-fashioned" are relevant lexical senses of the word, and those senses combine. Nietzsche displaces himself in time so as to provide a radical critique of views about history that are insufficiently dynamic. To hark back in time—to look at the Greeks, say, for an explanation of Wagner—and to persist in an old mode, will lead to the settling of accounts from which the will may be purged. Thus it can find its realization in a deep time that has little to do with mere timeliness. Timeliness is the parody of time, not its realization; and after *The Birth of Tragedy* this book turns to those whose investigations into the past lack a proper focus and weight: David Strauss and even Schopenhauer; to considerations of the pros and cons of history as an aid (*Vom Nutzen und Nachteil der Historie für das Leben*); and finally to Wagner's success in the *Ring* at setting forth a model for the *Volk* and expressing the past by liberation from the past, so as to comprise the key of the past and the true orientation of the future in one empowered moment.

Before any of this, Nietzsche had begun by writing about a historian of philosophy, Diogenes Laertius. Soon impelled beyond such antiquarianism, and even beyond the prolonged focus on a single culture of *The Birth of Tragedy*, Nietzsche became conscious of the whole past working in him:

Ich habe für mich *entdeckt,* dass die alte Mensch- und Tierheit, ja
die gesamte Urzeit und Vergangenheit alles empfindenden Seins in
mir fortdichtet, fortlieb, forthässt, fortschliesst . . .

I have discovered for myself that the old state of man and beast —
yea, the whole primeval time and the past of all perceptive beings,
keeps on in me, poeticizes on, loves on, hates on, concludes on . . .[4]

Each of these verbs qualifies and stretches the others.

It is waking up to such concerns that he declares gives him access to
the "Dream." It also obliges him — he concludes this segment with the
phrase and italicizes it —"to sustain the duration of the dream" along
with his place among the dreamers: "die Dauer des Traumes aufrecht-
zuerhalten."

It is in this sense that only the strong can endure.[5] The past is an oracle;
it can only be understood as an architect and component of the future.[6]
Even Hegel implicitly fails when he brings all history too simply to converge on his present Berlin.[7] History implies, and permits a measurement
of, progress; we are different from the Greeks and surpass them in our
knowledge of humankind.[8]

The sense of progress and the urgency towards a history-oriented ca-
pitulation lie at the heart of Nietzsche's most sensational and most persistent themes, the indictment of Christianity and the abandonment of
"values" or "morality." Usually he defines these as entailing a fatally un-
free constriction within a particular historical setting. Morality in general,
the Kantian imperative, must be abandoned as anti-developmental, anti-
historical, and therefore both a hindrance to self-realization and a falsification of the complicated human situation.

The relation between history and morality is, indeed, a puzzle, whether
one goes from morality to history or the other way around. Nietzsche
only keeps broaching a solution; he does not offer one:

Die Gebiets-Verkleinerung der Moral: ein Zeichen ihres Fort-
schritts. Überall, wo man noch nicht causal zu denken vermocht
hat, dachte man moralisch.

The area-*diminution of morality*: a sign of its progress everywhere;
where man has not yet managed to think causally he has thought
morally.[9]

This at once follows Rousseau and turns him on his head: it declares the
cause of morality to be an atavistic trait, not a civilized one, whose cause
is the failure to think causally. There is, by contrast, a "Sittlichkeit der
Sitte," an essence referred, again, to a supreme history: "als die *wirkliche*

*und entscheidende Hauptgeschichte welche den Charakter der Mensch-
heit festgestellt* hat ("as the *real and decisive chief history that has established the character of mankind*").[10]

The Eternal Return itself also has a historical aspect; it derives from
the urgency towards repetition of a human fulfillment, "dieses Stück
Menschheitsgeschichte w i r d und muss sich ewig wiederholen,"[11] a notion oddly connected with the desire to re-experience a work of art.[12]
Congruently, Nietzsche proposes an anthropological investigation as a
prelude to the study of moralistic matters.[13] In this perspective he enjoins
an abstention from judgment about social corruption, which is flagrant
in manner while neutralizing in tone and historicizing in assumption.
"Korruption ist nur ein Schimpfwort für die *Herbstzeiten* eines Volkes"
("Corruption is only an invidious term for the autumn of a people"),[14]
a notion in harmony with his later assertion that there is no morality,
only interpretation, itself of extramoral origin.[15]

In the light of Nietzsche's insistence on the dominance of history, "God
is dead" is less an abstract proposition than a challenge to assess what
the moment in history adds up to. The assertion historicizes and drama-
tizes an inspiring moment of perception.[16]

Reason itself is subject to historical process, rather than the other way
around: "Die Vernunft ist ein langsam sich entwickelndes Hilfsorgan"
("Reason is an auxiliary organ that develops slowly").[17]

Both the unhistorical and the historical are said to be necessary for
a culture.[18] Past and present are one and the same.[19] In such assertions
as these Nietzsche links his principles to a permutation of Hegel's devel-
opmental historicism with Kant's categorical ethics, and vice versa. Nietzsche, for his assertion of the primacy of history as well as for his attention
to the logic of the passions, may be thought of as historicizing the depth
morality of Kierkegaard (though he did not read him) much as Hegel
historicizes Kant's phenomenology of perception.

"Der Tausendkünstler der Selbstüberwindung"— so, in Erwin Rohde's
suggestive phrase, is Nietzsche characterized, and he himself quotes the
formulation in the stress of his breakup with Lou von Salomé and Paul
Rée.[20] "A versatile juggler of self-overcoming" presupposes a person oriented to the future, and it is the future where Nietzsche located the manifold justification for the lapses of the present. Those very lapses he accords
a charm, the "charm of incompleteness" ("Reiz der Unvollkommenheit.")[21]
Here to register as attractive that which elsewhere he deplores must be
taken to imply the paramount role of the future in any assessment of being and activity. Those two terms, being and activity, may be thought
of as converging in his cataclysmic image for humankind, an image whose
realization is located in the future, "waxing volcanoes": "Wir sind Alle

wachsende Vulkane, die ihre Stunde der Eruption haben werden,"[22] itself here an alternative image for "hidden gardens."

The morality that transcends good and evil is a morality of development, a development that includes play in its future orientation. "Wir sollen auch *über* der Moral stehen können; und nicht nur stehen . . . sondern auch über ihr schweben und spielen!" ("We should be able to *overcome* the moral — not only stand over it . . . but float and play over it.")[23] Such a notion of futurity lies at the heart of any program for betterment; and any system of ethics indeed may be taken to imply a set towards the future to be realized. Nietzsche, however, pushed that implication to the extreme, so as to clear the terrain for development. And as Jaspers insists,[24] his anti-morality is to be seen in the light of his future orientation. All his polemics, including those against Christianity (probably by count his most persistent), were at the service of readying for the future, cutting the tie to the present and standing in a properly open frame of mind before "das Umgreifende der Möglichkeit," "possibility" rather than actuality being given the feature of "encompassing." The solution to world problems, including Nihilism, appears for Nietzsche once the problem is linked to the future.

His three categories of society, the Alexandrine, the Hellenic, and the Buddhist,[25] could be redefined as those oriented towards the past, the present, and the future respectively. The Alexandrianism he excoriates in his contemporaries functions not only as a preoccupation with the past — something he himself exemplifies — but more significantly as a closing of the future. Settling into a philosophical position entails the same danger, through a present-orientation. He sees the function of philosophy, in a manner not so different from the "love" of St. Paul, not as bringing mankind into one organism but rather as allowing men their particular differentiation.[26] "The Philosophy of the Future" is the subtitle of *Beyond Good and Evil*. Indeed, his notion of the certain superiority of the future[27] implicitly qualifies even the doctrine of the Eternal Return, which if taken in a cosmological sense would render the future an exact recapitulation of the present, not a transcendence.

Philosophy aims at a transformation, in his view. It too, chiefly, finds justification in its service towards the art of realization, towards "becoming what you are" in the phrase of Pindar's Second Pythian that Nietzsche was fond of quoting. Philosophy is instrumental; it serves to aid self-transcendence: "Er *kann* eben nicht anders, als seinen Zustand jedesmal in die geistigste Form und Ferne umzusetzen — diese Kunst der Transfiguration *ist* eben Philosophie" ("He *can* [thus] not do otherwise than transpose his condition each time into the spiritual form and distance — this art of transfiguration *is* indeed philosophy.")[28] Seen thus, all philosophy strives towards the condition that Nietzsche's own philosophy exemplifies: it moves rather than defines. Its relation to the future makes it something that partakes of scripture and art work, like the poems of Blake, but coded more definitively and severely into abstract statements.

Again, instead of offering a definition of Romanticism, for example, Nietzsche claims that in the light of a dominance of all intellectual activities by an orientation of the future, it too cannot be other than such an orientation. "Was ist Romantik? Jede Kunst, jede Philosophie darf als Heil- und Hilfsmittel im Dienste des wachsenden, kämpfenden Lebens angesehen werden." ("What is Romanticism? Every art, every philosophy must be regarded as a means of healing and helping in the service of growing, struggling life.")[29] The oscillation between a sense of morality and a sense of causality ("Gegenbewegung zwischen Sinn der Sittlichkeit und Sinn der Kausalität")[30] would have to be resolved, like everything else, by the transcendence at whose service it must be construed as being.

The persistent perspectivism and recurrent paradoxes in Nietzsche's writings emerge, through their relation to a complexity of development, merely as a means to realization, rather than as the predicated assertions that Nietzsche keeps insisting are a temptation for the philosopher. It is the will that unifies — as well as distinguishes — all bearings towards the future, that "Wille zur Macht" which is not a single force, like the "will" of Schopenhauer, but something whose complexity corresponds to the complexity of the elements its dynamism is bringing together; "Wollen scheint mir vor allem etwas *Kompliziertes*" ("Willing appears to me most of all something *complicated*"), he says, italicizing the predicate.[31] Will for Nietzsche is at once something cosmic and something personal, a blind force and a resource for the aspiring person. As such it combines in a single term a whole spectrum of Romantic attitudes, turning the historical dialectic of Hegel back to the psyche of the individual without releasing the individual entirely from a historical dialectic.

Nietzsche drafted many plans, as well as hundreds of scattered pages, for the last and culminating work he never wrote, *Wille zur Macht*. One such draft typically offers a conspectus of psychology, history, and epistemology under the aegis of will:

> Im ersten Buch: der Nihilism als Consequenz
> der idealen Werthe
> Problem der Civilisation
> das 19. Jahrhundert, seine
> Zweideutigkeit:
> Es fehlt bisher die Freiheit von der Moral.
> Pessimisten sind Revolter
> des moralischen Pathos

Die Moral als Ursache des Pessimismus
Der Pessimismus als Vorform des Nihilism

Im zweiten Buch:
    Geschichte der Vermoralisirung wie man die Tugend
      zur Herrschaft bring
    Moral als Circe der Philosophen

Im dritten Buch: Das Problem der
    Wahrheit

Im vierten Buch: Geschichte der höheren Typen,
    nachdem wir die Welt entgottet haben
    die Mittel, um eine Kluft auf zu reissen:
      Rangordnung
      Ideal der weltbejahendsten Lehre
      das tragische Zeitalter.
die psychologische Naivität in dem Ideale Gott

1. Nihilism as a consequence of ideal values. The problem of the 19th century and its ambiguity . . .
2. The history of demoralization . . . morality as the Circe of philosophers.
3. The problem of truth.
4. A history of higher types.[32]

The very elusiveness of the will relieves Nietzsche of the necessity of arguing out fully the connections among these large areas. His impulse is not to define but rather to offer a perception, one that can substitute impetus for definition and will for truth. Or as Deleuze says, Nietzsche substitutes the connection between the phenomenon and sense for that between effect and cause. The "Wille zur Macht" may have a cosmological comprehensiveness, and it may release a thinker for the merely reactive stances into which the primacy of interpretation in thought tempts him.[33] For all that, as an idea it places a striving at the center of all human perception: the exaltation of "becoming," the ideal of the Übermensch, re-renders, as a single, exclusive future moment, the essence of Goethe's Faust principle: "He who, always striving, bestirs himself, / him can we absolve" ("Wer immer strebend sich bemüht, / den können wir erlösen"). Here clarity and intricacy are both retained. The need to adjudicate between pluralism and Dionysiac affirmation is bypassed.[34] The willed text exemplifies the self-transcendence of the doctrine about will that it promulgates, permitting a flexibility towards less final categories. Thus the pessimism of the Greeks[35] is taken not as a sign of fatigue—the way Nietzsche reads modern pessimism—but of strength.

And the single term "will" opens to constant permutation the other terms for which he finally substitutes it. Still another outline, for example, expands it into a typology of eight alternatives for human behavior. These are called indifferently the typical self-formations (*Selbstgestaltungen*) or eight main questions:

Die typischen Selbstgestaltungen
Oder: die acht Hauptfragen
1) Ob man sich vielfacher haben will oder einfacher.
2) Ob man glücklicher werden will oder gleichgültiger gegen Glück und Unglück.
ob man zufriedner mit sich werden will oder anspruchsvoller und unerbittlicher?
4) ob man weicher, nachgebender, menschlicher werden will oder "unmenschlicher".
5) ob man klüger werden will oder rücksichtsloser.
6) ob man ein Ziel erreichen will oder allen Zielen ausweichen (—wie es zum Beispiel der Philosoph thut, der in jedem Ziel eine Grenze, einen Winkel, ein Gefängniss, eine Dummheit riecht . . .)
7) ob man geachteter werden will oder gefürchteter? Oder verachteter!
8) ob man Tyrann oder Verführer oder Heerdenthier werden will?

1. Whether one wants to hold himself more manifold or simpler;
2. to become happier or more indifferent;
3. to become more content or more demanding;
4. to become more human or more "inhuman";
5. to become wiser or more inconsiderate;
6. to attain a goal or avoid all goals;
7. to become more esteemed or more feared or more despised;
8. to become tyrant or seducer; shepherd or beast of the herd.[36]

Will measures and defines these alternatives. As their underlying motive it at once subjects them to judgment and provides a principle whereby they may transcend it.[37] The will to truth itself is the will to power.

The term "will" is made to carry more than its lexical possibilities by Nietzsche, and it may be said to fuse in his implications, and in such a character as Zarathustra, with the feeling or emotion that he also accords a leading role in his psychodynamics.[38] Nietzsche brings the Romantic emphasis on the primacy of emotion to a pitch where it informs a broad unconscious and inspirits the very act of knowing with gaiety—a *fröhliche Wissenschaft*. This gaiety, again, is not easily distinguishable from the élan of the will's impulse.

Thought, as well as will, connects easily with emotion, again as in many early Romantic writers,[39] though Nietzsche forces the connection more energetically, and oddly insists more peremptorily on the philosophical deduction needed to make the connection:

Gesetzt dass nichts anderes als real "gegeben" ist als unsre Welt der
Begierden und Leidenschaften, dass wir zu keiner anderen "Realität"
hinab oder hinauf können als gerade zur Realität unsrer Triebe—
denn Denken ist nur ein Verhalten dieser Triebe zueinander . . .

Granting that nothing else is given as real than our world of desires
and passions, that we can go up and down to no other reality than
the reality of our drives (*Triebe*)—then thinking is only the disposition of these drives towards one another.[40]

The linking term here is one Freud will later use, "drive"—a term implying both will and emotion—but the connection is not a simple one.
Elsewhere he calls drive a basic form of will, "Triebe als Grundform des
Willens."[41] The relation between drive and thought, too, is complex, in
that "thinking is only the disposition of these drives towards one another";
the drives stand in an uneasy equilibrium that is equivalent to a thought
process.

Arthur Danto correctly, if perhaps too simply, says that for Nietzsche
every problem is reduced to a problem of psychology.[42] One could as well
say that it expands to a problem of psychology, but the emphasis either
way leaves the dynamized psyche at the center of a universe whose changes
it may empower itself to command. One returns to psychology, Nietzsche insists, as the means for solving the basic problems: "Denn Psychologie ist nunmehr der Weg zu den Grundproblemen."[43] A way is envisaged
here as elsewhere—a relation between past, present, and future. And in
this light through a principle of contradiction too unstable to be called
Heraclitean, Nietzsche elsewhere speaks of drives that are transformed
by moral judgments, reversing the priority: "Die Triebe durch die moral-
ischen Urteile umgestaltet."[44]

The self-generating power that he predicates for the human psyche,
applied to his own procedures as a philosopher-sage, enables Nietzsche
to enter into such shifts of emphasis without providing either a Hegelian
system for contradictions or an Emersonian ease with such a possibility.
Idea comes to seem like play, a momentary play, a *fröhliche Wissenschaft*. In this way, too, it derives from emotion and easily shades from
play to earnest, again without "irony," a term little used by Nietzsche.
While he may be enlisted for later deconstructions,[45] he offers no models
for deconstructionism because he never rests at a particular point in the
continuum between thought and feeling, never offers the philosopher's
structure of predications. So he speaks of "moralische Gefühle und moralische Begriffe," moral feelings and moral concepts, as it were inter-
changeably.[46] In a further causal reversal, he assigns a priority of judgments to feelings: "Gefühle und deren Abkunft von Urteilen" ("feelings
and their derivation from judgments").[47] Nor is his Zarathustra either

just a philosopher, or just a prophet, or just a poetic fantasy, but a figure whose feelings are made possible by his encompassing all three roles without fully embodying any. The conception of Zarathustra is "literary" on the surface, philosophical in its separate assertions and its overall bearing. This "latecomer" (the word is Nietzsche's) has moved the Romantic fusion of poetry and philosophy onto the ground of philosophy itself.

"Aus den *Leidenschaften* wachsen die Meinungen"[48] — from *passions* grow the meanings or opinions. This declaration, Rousseauist in origin, may be taken to dynamize Rousseau by obscuring the difference between nature and culture, person and society, distinctions that Rousseau always keeps fixed. Nietzsche's statement cannot be taken as recommending a reversion to an earlier and primitive social condition; nor does it dissociate itself therefrom. It is a general proposition about a development in time between the passions and the union of subjective opinion and objective meaning, a range of senses that the German word *Meinung* allows. Emotion *an sich* offers much that is difficult to understand in his view,[49] as it would not in Rousseau's, who proposes to flood it with clarity.

In an application of a Christian term that by implication he sets himself the task of cleansing and revitalizing, Nietzsche measures Wagner by the notion of "redemption" (*Erlösung*).[50] Wagner envisages both love and revolution in the figure of Siegfried. Yet Nietzsche declares Siegfried to be a false superman because Wagner has shown him to be simply subject to what Nietzsche elsewhere calls "grosse Leidenschaft."[51] Nietzsche, at a given moment, glimpses the possibility of "procedures so tender they would best be overwhelmed by something coarser" ("Es gibt Vorgänge so zarter Art, dass man gut tut, sie durch eine Grobheit zu verschütten").[52] Siegfried, we may presume, is lost to this distinction; we cannot characterize his feeling as either fine or coarse. He offers no access, therefore, to the *fröhliche*, to the *Heiterkeit*, that Nietzsche has discerned in *Oedipus at Colonus*, and also, strangely, in *Oedipus Rex*,[53] and that he declares must be kept upright since there is nothing more "necessary."[54]

Wagner's passion is also too enveloping, whereas for Nietzsche the feelings are creative as a result of their capacity for flowing into one another. His list of "die Jasagende Affekte" in the notes for *Wille zur Macht*[55] includes pride, joy, and health, but also sexual love, war, a strong will, a will to power, and thankfulness towards earth and life. Here he offers the conventional high Romantic transposition between joy and sorrow: "*Verlangen nach Schönheit* . . . aus Entbehrung, aus Melancholie, aus Schmerz erwachsen ist."[56] Sympathy (*Mitleid*) occasions an elaborate description.[57] And every single pleasure is characterized as "complicated," the way will had been: "Jede Lust und Unlust ist jetzt bei uns ein höchst kompliziertes Ergebnis, so plötzlich es auftritt." ("For us every pleasure and displeasure is a highly complicated event, however suddenly it may appear.")[58] The complication appears at the sudden moment that the feeling comes on stage. Then it will undergo the sorts of metamorphosis for which Nietzsche often provides a sketched plan. In the feelings he allows for subtle effects of seeming contradiction, like "the extreme rest of certain intoxicated feelings" ("Die *extreme Ruhe gewisser Rauschempfindungen*").[59] Such surface contradictions do not lend themselves to true opposition: "Lust und Schmerz kein Gegensatz" ("Pleasure and pain are not an opposition").[60] The highest man, indeed, is one who is defined as having the greatest multiplicity of drives.[61]

In the history of moral feelings, the counterbalance to sympathy, compassion, and sacrificial devotion (*Mitleiden, Barmherzigkeit,* und *Aufopferung*) is *not*, as one might expect, cruelty and selfishness, but rather, staying still within what is desirable from a quasi-Christian point of view, good nature, friendliness, and courtesy (*Gutmütigkeit, Freundlichkeit, Höflichkeit*).[62] Nietzsche excoriates the more sensational Christian accesses of feeling not just to eradicate them, we may then infer, but rather to purge them of potentially stultifying postures, of the merely self-deceiving, or even the merely reactive, the *ressentiment* whose secondary and self-defeating nature he continually lays bare. Pain itself, harnessed to the moment of growth, offers advantage[63] — another Christian derivative in his thought. And madness may lead to discovery.[64]

The last notion is buttressed with anthropological references, a Rousseauist procedure, and in this passage he cites Rousseau. But Rousseau in Nietzsche's schema involves a typology of men defined according to what amounts to feeling. This Rousseau looks not to the past but to the future; he is the revolutionary. Nietzsche as it were emphasizes the Nietzschean side of Rousseau, complementing him by the "Goethe," who offers the quieting corrective to revolution. The third type is the "Schopenhauersche Mensch," "who takes upon himself the free-will suffering of truth" as a sort of Christ of truth, a truth attained through suffering, and not a truth fixed into place, a *Wahrheit*, but a disposition to truth, a *Wahrhaftigkeit*.[65]

2

The philosopher, the artist-aphorist, the tendentious would-be reformer, and the depth-historian meet in Nietzsche. By a kind of instinct for the play he praises, he allows these stances to interfuse. To define such near-improvisation and inconclusiveness as irony, or as the Heraclitean antithesis he himself praises, would deprive it of the dimension of tentativeness, in Nietzschean terms of aspiration, that essentially characterizes it.

There is not only interaction for Nietzsche between *Vernunft* and *Leidenschaft*, but whole stages of interaction.[66]

As for the philosopher, Nietzsche can be described, with Heidegger,[67] as the last of the classical philosophers, touching base on their most persistent problems. He only touches base, however, and one could assimilate him to Vico, in his role as depth-historian, as easily as to Kant.

He characterizes as naive the uses of cognition that serve to further happiness or virtue or a nihilistic stance (*Erkenntnis*): "die drei grossen Naivetäten:"

> Erkenntnis als Mittel zum Glück (als ob . . .
> als Mittel zur Tugend (als ob . . .
> als Mittel zur "Verneinung des Lebens"—insofern sie
> ein Mittel zur Enttäuschung ist—(als ob . . .)[68]

> Cognition as means to happiness (as if . . .
> as means to virtue (as if . . .
> as means to "denial of life"—in so far as it
> is a means to disillusion—(as if . . .)

Such naiveté is a more complex version of Blake's diabolical reason, but Nietzsche's initial gambit is the same as Blake's: the insistence on an arresting contradiction in order to force the attention towards some higher desideratum. As for ethical virtue, Nietzsche reduces it to a contradiction of principles and motives, or logic and psychology, or, in Schopenhauer's terms, will and idea, *Wille* and *Vorstellung*: "Die *Motive* zu dieser Moral stehen im Gegensatz zu ihrem *Prinzip!*" ("The *motives* of this morality stand in opposition to its *principle!*")[69] Taking it from another angle, the "virtuous" man is seen anthropologically and historically as failing to achieve an identity; he is of a lower species because he is no "person": "Ein tugendhafter Mensch ist schon deshalb eine niedrigere species, weil er keine 'Person' ist."[70] In a declaration that finds a more rigorous exposition in the practice of the late Wittgenstein, Nietzsche reduces the contradiction between representation (*Vorstellung*) and existence, the problem of Kant,[71] to a simple assertion that *Vorstellung* is a condition of being, one that includes the crucial properties of feeling and will:

> Vorstellen selber ist kein Gegensatz der Eigenschaften des esse: sondern nur sein Inhalt und dessen Gesetz. —Gefühl und Wille sind uns nur als Vorstellung bekannt, somit ist ihre Existenz nicht bewiesen.

> Representation itself is in *no* opposition to the properties of being: but only its content and the law of that. —Feeling and will are known to us only as representation, and therewith is their existence *not* proved.[72]

In such a passage as this we do not have the sort of closed aphorism that Heraclitus almost surely offers us:[73] the italics alone push its emphasis beyond such neatness. We cannot, therefore, translate it into an irreducible contradiction between "law" ("Gesetz") on the one hand and "lack of proof" ("nicht beweisen") on the other. The assertion is irreducibly aspectual — a glance of the intelligence thinking on the question and offering quasi-solutions to be taken as incitements. Belief in the categories of reason is for Nietzsche the cause of Nihilism.[74] Where Kierkegaard turns the Hegelian dialectic to an absolute irony,[75] Nietzsche transvalues it by simply loosening its connections.

To pursue the reasoning, as the philosopher in him urges us to do, would lead us to the "laughable overestimation and misunderstanding of consciousness" that he deplores.[76] Logic is a kind of optimism,[77] and it "bites its own tail."[78] The Philistine sees reality as reason[79] — a poor instrument with which to measure what is "glorious" (*herrlich*) in Hölderlin. In speaking of the origin of cognition Nietzsche links "truth" to a weak form of it, and he declares, as a limit rather than an attainment, that within cognition itself such propositions as he too has been offering may be put through a set of exhaustive logical paces: "jene Sätze wurden selbst innherhalb der Erkenntnis zu den Normen, nach denen man 'wahr' und 'unwahr' bemass — bis hinein in die entlegendsten Gegenden der reinen Logik" ("those propositions belong themselves inside cognition to the norms by which they are ascertained as 'true' and 'untrue'— all the way to the furthest regions of pure logic").[80] The furthest regions of pure logic here are a kind of distraction, not a hope for the balance that must be personalized and spirited, *fröhlich.* "Absolute truth" allows the aesthetic to be transferred into the moral: "Sobald es die absolute Wahrheit in Anspruch nimmt, schlägt das aesthetische Urtheil in die moralische Forderungen um." But the transfer can go the other way too: "Reduktion der Moral auf Aesthetik!"[81] Nor does Nietzsche confine himself to either of these transfers, since on the one hand he considers "art for art's sake" as effectually immoral,[82] and on the other hand he proposes taste as a basis for *Meinung.*[83] He names three errors. One, which he associates with Newton, is that science-knowledge (*Wissenschaft*) will make us understand the goodness and wisdom of God; a second, associated with Voltaire, is that it will bring about a union of the moral and the happy; and a third, associated with Spinoza, is that it is harmless. All three are errors of excessive expectation of this particular faculty, coupled by implication with insufficient expectation of the whole self.

The philosophical enterprise, then, takes on the dimension of personal striving, and of problematic historical development, as it is qualified by history: "Definierbar ist nur das, was keine Geschichte hat."[84] Philosophy cannot be disentangled from these two conditions, nor can the strong assertions that can be made with the aid of a philosophical process, the affirmation of Nihilism,[85] or all the theological caveats that Nietzsche offers, including and most especially "God is dead." As Heidegger says, this assertion "is no atheistic proposition (*Lehrsatz*) but the formula for the basic experience of an event in Western history."[86] The assertion is further, in Deleuze's characterization, dramatic,[87] a challenge rather than a bare proposition.

A late note on the origin (*Herkunft*) of the ideal posits a series of relationships between Christianity and deification (*Vergöttlichung*),[88] and Nietzsche throughout his career returns to the task of disallowing shortcuts, especially those that have been sanctified by the institutionalized religion of the milieu in which this pastor's son grew up. Like Blake again, or Kierkegaard, he wants to establish something like Christian principles by driving out what is endemically debasing in institutional Christianity. And as with Blake, the relation of this enterprise to the philosophical task of getting things straight remains fluid and uncertain. Decadence must be fought off, in the person of Wagner, who only plays with these ultimate feelings. Consequently, he says of him that "'good and evil' is only a variety of that problem" ("'Gut und Böse' ist nur eine Spielart jenes Problemes").[89]

Nietzsche addresses directly what he calls the distress of the soul:

> Was die Noth der Seele aber betrifft, so sehe ich mir jetzt jeden Menschen darauf an, ob er sie aus Erfahrung oder Beschreibung kennt, ob er diese Kenntnis zu heucheln doch noch für nötig hält, etwa als ein Zeichen der feineren Bildung, oder ob er überhaupt an grosse Seelenschmerzen im Grunde seiner Seele nicht glaubt und es ihm bei Nennung derselben ähnlich ergeht wie bei Nennung grosser körperlicher Erduldungen.

> But as for what concerns the need of the soul, I now regard each man in that connection, whether he knows it from experience or description; whether he considers it necessary to pretend this knowledge, as a sort of sign of finer education, or whether generally he does not believe in great soul-pains at the base of his soul and the naming of these strikes him the same way as naming great endurances of the body.[90]

Description and experience are two means of knowledge, both faulty —like all means, especially that which claims faultlessness, or logic. For elsewhere he declares that there is no name for where language leaves off and existence (*Dasein*)begins, by the same rule determining that we have names for extreme feelings but not, he claims, for intermediate ones.[91] Style is defined as "eine innere Spannung von Pathos durch Zeichen" ("an inner tension of pathos through signs").[92]

Indeed, Nietzsche describes his own historical situation as the conviction that we do not have the truth, whereas all earlier men "possessed the truth" ("hatten die Wahrheit"), even the skeptics.[93] The feeling we have is one of that infinity that is like a sea where we are shipwrecked; so Nietzsche reproduces and effectually cites, without quoting it, the last line of Leopardi's "L'Infinito."[94] There are no facts or *Tatsachen*, only interpretations,[95] and yet by interpreting the emotion behind a belief Nietzsche arguably provides a means to avoid the neutrality of all later relativistic skepticisms: his focus is finally on something more steadfast than the intellectual positions that can be set against one another.

Nietzsche, in the last analysis, enjoins a Romantic version of religiosity, not by the scholarship of Renan and Strauss that he qualified to the point of mockery, and not by disengaging contemporary uses from orthodox doctrine like Chateaubriand and others, but by radicalizing the gesture of a religiosity he declares to be related to underlying conviction:

> Der Glaube ist eine Eselsbrücke. Der Hintergrund ist eine tiefe Überzeugung, das instinktive Bewusstsein ebenso, Luthers und seines Gleichen von ihrer Unfähigkeit zu christlichen Werken . . . : so dass der Werth der Existenz auf einzelne hochgespannte Zustände der Unthätigkeit fällt (Gebet, Effusion, usw.) — Zuletzt hätte er Recht: die Instinkte, welche sich im ganzen Thun der Reformatoren ausdrücken, sind die brutalsten, die es giebt. Nur in der absoluten Wegwendung von sich, in der Versenkung in den Gegensatz, nur als Illusion ("Glaube") war ihnen das Dasein auszuhalten.

> Belief is a bridge of asses. The background is a deep conviction, instinctive consciousness even, of Luther and his like of their incapacity of Christian deeds, so that the worth of existence falls on individual high-tension states of *inactivity* (prayer, effusion, etc.) — finally he is right, the instincts . . . are the most brutal things there are. Only in the absolute *turning away* from oneself, in a sinking into the *opposite*, only as *illusion* ("belief"), could they bear existence.[96]

The urgency of such a passage makes it bypass the contradictions it encompasses. Nietzsche, at this same late time, defines himself as finally having bestowed a new charm on virtue ("der Tugend einen neuen Reiz ertheilt").[97] He would honor the "redemption" in the great religions, while leaving the term *Erlösung* in the quotation marks of quizzical qualification.[98] Jesus is singled out as speaking from a bare, inner experience ("bloss vom Innersten, von Erlebnissen"), and everything else has "the sense of a sign and of a means of speech" ("den Sinn eines Zeichens und eines Sprachmittels").[99]

Not just in the main conception of *Ecce Homo*, with its daring and blasphemous Scriptural citation-identification between the author and the savior, but throughout his work, Nietzsche echoes Scriptural phrases,[100] and in *Also sprach Zarathustra* he echoes a Scriptural style and tonality. "What is done out of love happens always beyond good and evil," he finally says in the treatise of that title,[101] allowing it to be oriented towards religiosity and not towards amorality.

If religion remains questionable for Nietzsche, so does everything else in his "experiment of the person knowing."[102] He early asserts the necessity of myth and its relation to abstract thought, anticipating the later systematization of Cassirer, who defines myth as a realm to which the categories truth and falsehood do not apply. All the formulations of Nietzsche's final doctrine, the "eternal return," are themselves posed as questions, not answers.[103]

The big question for Nietzsche is the direction of existence, of persons in general, and of himself. His stance towards truth and belief, more saliently in his Romantic embodiment of it than is usually the case, leads almost directly to his stance of questioning, and then to the form the questioning took in his work: the negative and critical stance towards such deep elements in himself as religious-ethical striving and historical-philosophical definition of the past; the reliance of disjunct, broken units in the manner of a sort of super-Coleridge; the headily questionable mask of the Persian cult figure turned into a mouthpiece for a doctrine embedded in a wandering-narrative; the use of a single problematic myth-image, Dionysus, to resume all that is desirable; the glances at a problematic fusion between Dionysus and the Christ in whom he wishes to reject much.

We cannot refer that fusion to the later, simpler ones of Frazer and others, which Nietzsche anticipates: he is much less reliant on seasonal and fertility patterns than they, much more insistent on a dynamics of emotion. Dionysus finds expression, for Greece and in his own work, through art, an art conceived of "metaphysically, in the widest and deepest sense."[104] *Rausch* is necessary for art. Socrates' "influence perpetually completes the transformation (*Neuschaffung*) of art," and, itself infinite, validates the infinity of art.[105]

The very principle of resolution between art and philosophy incapacitates a formal act of resolution between them, while empowering the feat Nietzsche brings off of achieving an adaptable balance between them, what Heidegger calls "Der erregende Zwiespalt zwischen Wahrheit und Kunst"[106] ("The exciting split between thought and art"). When the tension relaxes into form, in his poetry and presumably in his music too, Nietzsche is at his weakest. Music for him serves not only as an ultimate example—in Wagner's achievement and in Greek tragedy, "born from the spirit of music"[107]—but also as a sort of realization or soporific. He is attracted in music by a "poor fragmentary quality," not by its strength, when through it he "can forget my poor fragmentary philosophy."[108]

The poems in *Die fröhliche Wissenschaft*, written under psychological pressure, offer no Menippean satire of juxtaposition to the central prose document. Rather, they allow the points of philosophical discourse to escape into metered jots of feeling. They simplify, as Nietzsche's reading of Spinoza's formulation, and its incorporation in his own philosophical practice do not. "'Non ridere, non lugere, neque detestari, sed intelligere' sagt Spinoza. . . . Indessen: was ist dies *intelligere* im letzten Grunde anderes als die Form, in der uns eben jene drei auf einmal fühlbar werden?" "'Don't laugh, grieve, or hate, but think' says Spinoza. . . . What else is this 'intelligere' in the last analysis but the form in which just these three at one moment become feeling?").[109]

The indeterminacy of thought, for Nietzsche, finds expression in the overdeterminacy of words: "Jedes Wort ist ein Vorurteil" ("Every word is a prejudice").[110] We are kept, however, from enlisting him as a sponsor of modern atomistic and radically decentralizing notions of communication by the persistence and abundance of his confidence in utterances that might seem curtailed. He is clearly not willing to consider them fragmentary. "Sayings are to be peaks," he proclaims. ("Sprüche sollen Gipfel sein.")[111] He praises Fontenelle and Chamfort.[112] "Sprüche—Vermischte Meinungen und Sprüche" ("Opinions and Sayings Mixed") is the title of a major section, and also in the subtitle of *Menschliches, Allzumenschliches*. Speech and consciousness are not only linked; the discovery of signs sharpens consciousness.[113] The artist deals with ever smaller units in Greece.[114] If the masters of prose are masters of poetry,[115] and if the very lie of art accords it power,[116] then the forms stand unstably but powerfully at hand for appropriation or analogy. The "dithyrambs" he occasionally mentions assimilate him to the verbal worship of Dionysus and the "old and new tables" of *Also sprach Zarathustra* to scripture.[117]

Nietzsche is a sort of dynamized Rousseau, never allowing himself the easy hide-and-seek of the *Dialogues*. His presentation is too strenuous in its drive for immediacy—and also too many-faceted in its individual units: "Dies Mosaik von Worten, wo jedes Wort als Klang, als Ort, als Begriff, nach rechts und links und über das Ganze hin seine Kraft ausströmt, dies Minimum in Umfang und Zahl der Zeichen, dies damit erzielte Maximum in der Energie der Zeichen" ("This mosaic of words, where every word streams forth its force, as sound, as place, as concept, left and right and over the whole—this minimum in compass and number of signs, this maximum, attained thereby, in the energy of signs").[118]

Nietzsche posits the possibility of two speakers, one who leaves passion behind and another who brings it forward.[119] The two operate in tandem for his writing: the lie of art seduces while it stimulates and enables.[120] His conception of the situation of the writer pushes his aphorism beyond aphorisms: as his longer utterances do, they become probes, "peaks" for the mountain climber of thought.

We cannot align Nietzsche's texts without oversimplification either on the side of a quasi-mythic fictional assay at presenting the thinking man or on the side of thought-propositions that call for coordination and decipherment. Correspondingly, by thus poising his utterance in what amounts to so provisional a position, Nietzsche's act of statement forces the very consideration the statements themselves have been enjoining, the sort of man they will aid to reveal himself by coming into being. We are thrown back, by the sort of *ad hominem* principle Nietzsche applies to historians and philosophers, upon Nietzsche himself. The *ad hominem* becomes an *ad se*; the personalist individualism of Romanticism becomes transfigured. It also remains so provisional that we cannot without falsification either applaud the heroism of Nietzsche in risking madness or deplore the foolhardiness that drove itself mad in him.[121]

The ego, or self, or persona—Nietzsche puts the term "Ich" in his characteristic quotation marks, which themselves hover between qualification and italicization—"subordinates and kills" while it "organizes and dominates": "Das "Ich" unterjocht und tötet: es arbeitet wie eine organische Zelle: es raubt und ist gewalttätig. Es will sich regenerieren— Schwangerschaft. Es will seinen Gott gebären und alle Menschheit ihm zu Füssen sehen." (. . . it works like an organic cell. . . . It will regenerate itself—pregnancy. It wants to give birth to its God and see all mankind at his feet")[122] From such a vantage point of strenuous self-definition, other formulations, however internally consistent, are made to seem inadequate. Other careers, not obviously similar, can be equated, as Hegel is approximated to Goethe.[123]

Dionysus provides the positive measure, and Christianity the negative. Dionysus for Nietzsche is the name for forces to be identified with a process in the depth history of Greece but not fully with any of the attributions we may resurrect as specifically applying to the God himself in the context of Greek mythology. Dionysus begins as a way of explaining the rise and transformation of Greek tragedy.[124] and then moves to the center of the system in such a way that at the end Nietzsche identifies himself with Dionysus—at the very moment when he is beginning effectually to identify Dionysus with Christ, in the last words of *Ecce Homo*, offered as an ultimate explanation:

> Hat man mich verstanden?—
> *Dionysus gegen den Gekreuzigten.*
>
> Am I understood?
> *Dionysus against the crucified.*[125]

And he is shortly to sign the last, mad letters both "Dionysus" and "The Crucified." "Ich bin ein Doppelgänger," he says.[126] And Dionysus himself is "ambiguous and seductive" ("jene grosse Zweideutige und Versucher-Gott")[127] — Dionysus who, as Deleuze reminds us,[128] must be seen for Nietzsche in at least four relationships: towards Apollo, towards Socrates, towards Christ, and towards Ariadne. He is a "labyrinth" for Ariadne in her "Klage" among the dithyrambs of Dionysus, just as Wagner is a "Labyrinth" for the modern soul.[129] Under Dionysus, Nietzsche early says, "Der Mensch ist nicht mehr Künstler, er ist Kunstwerk geworden" ("Man is no longer an artist, he has become a work of art").[130] Dionysus sponsors intoxication, a *Rausch* not distinguishable from the chaos a man must have within him in *Also sprach Zarathustra* to dance on a rope — and man himself is a rope over an abyss.[131]

Following the Blakean strategy of blaming something in what is praiseworthy so as to purify it, Nietzsche also does the converse and praises what normally he blames. While Apollo is opposed to Dionysus as the fixed to the growing,[132] Nietzsche allows *Rausch* to Apollo as well as to Dionysus.[133] So what opposes transformation is assimilated to transformation, and vice versa: Dionysus objectifies himself in the Apollonian appearances.[134] By identifying himself with his work and sacrificing himself to it — by "writing with his own blood"[135] in accord with the principle that "blood is spirit" for the only kind of writing he professes to value, Nietzsche manages a transformation that aligns history with depth history, with the sort of new sacred history analogous, again, to what Blake aimed at: "Alle Geschichte wird zur Heilsgeschichte" ("All history becomes sacred history") in Heidegger's ascription.[136] In the person of Zarathustra, Nietzsche can imagine the future as already there. Man becomes what he is through what might be called art. For art, in turn, is defined as enabling man to enjoy himself in a perfection that it at once strives for and somehow fulfills. ("Dies Verwandeln-müssen ins Vollkommne ist — Kunst . . . in der Kunst geniesst sich der Mensch als Vollkommenheit.")[137]

Nor can Nietzsche's ideal be defined simply as the heroic; he writes against the cult of heroes.[138] As Deleuze acutely shows, one may derive the hero as an opposite of Dionysus, as a false preliminary to him.[139] He is finally himself; the exhibit he offers of his thinking is unmasked and remasked as the person behind the thinking. The whole future is declared a threshold.

In *Ecce Homo* Nietzsche converts his *ad hominem* principle into a spiritual *Autobiographia Literaria*. He turns it on himself, advertises himself, complains about his sufferings, identifying himself with the Christ exposed to the multitudes. The turn of his *Ecce Homo* will shortly get a counterturn in *Der Antichrist*. But, as often, the counterturn is not full face, and not definite enough for one text to ironize the other. Christ is implicit in *Ecce Homo*, a faint but persistent overtone set into a sort of polyphonic counterpoint with the texts it quotes, the long stretches of *Also sprach Zarathustra*.

As it goes on to discuss *Also sprach Zarathustra*, *Ecce Homo* becomes heavy with quotation, retrospect taking over from prospect. This procedure leads him to quote "The Night Song" from the earlier work, making a claim that is at once boast for the future and lament for the past: "Und auch meine Seele ist das Lied eines Liebenden" ("And my soul too is the song of one who loves"). This declaration concludes a long lament of how hard it is to be one who gives light like a sun.

He continues to turn up the boast side of the register, though lament is still present to torment the voice into italicized emphasis:

> Dergleichen ist nie gedichtet, nie gefühlt, nie *gelitten* worden: so leidet ein Gott, ein Dionysos. Die Antwort auf einen solchen Dithyrambus der Sonnen-Vereinsamung im Lichte wäre *Ariadne* . . . Wer weiss ausser mir, was *Ariadne* ist! . . . Von allen solchen Rätseln hatte niemand bisher die Lösung, ich zweifle, dass jemand hier auch nur Rätsel sah.—Zarathustra bestimmt einmal, mit Strenge, seine Aufgabe—es ist auch die meine—, dass man sich über den *Sinn* nicht vergreifen kann: er ist *jasagend* bis zur Rechtfertigung, bis zur Erlösung auch alles Vergangenen.
>
> Ich wandle unter Menschen als unter Bruchstücken der Zukunft: jener Zukunft, die ich schaue.
>
> Und das ist all mein Dichten und Trachten, dass ich in eins dichte und zusammentrage, was Bruchstück ist und grauser Zufall.[140]

> The like has never been poeticized, never felt, never *suffered*. Thus does a god suffer, a Dionysos. The answer to such a dithyramb of sun-isolation would be *Ariadne* . . .
>
> . . . Who besides me knows what *Ariadne* is! . . . Of all such riddles no one till now had the solution; I doubt that anyone here ever saw a riddle—Zarathustra decided once, with power, his task—it is also mine—that man cannot transgress beyond the *sense*: he is

yea-saying to the point of justification, even to the resolution of the whole past.

I wander among men as under fragments of the future, the future that I see.
And that is all my poeticizing and striving, that I poeticize into unity and bring together what is fragment and riddle and grim chance.

The quotation about wandering is continued. It illustrates, amplifies, qualifies, and at the same time displaces the critical comments that include it. The running comment defines, but is meant to be fulfilled by, the quotation. The whole texts of Nietzsche's past become fragments to be put together for the future. The quotation from Zarathustra claims to be putting them together, but as quoted it is itself the fragment it defines its activity as being occupied with. It is held in the crepitations of "yea-saying," the comprehensive boast of the voice of *Ecce Homo* that forces mythological figures to yield a meaning declared rather than explicated.

The italics also force an order upon disparate entities that make philosophy and mythology define each other by being compressed into the high notes of a strenuous cry: *suffered, Ariadne, yea-saying, sense. Sinn* ("sense"), the last, is the most comprehensive, carrying the whole body and the whole mind. Ariadne is the most mysterious, and the one repeated in italics. Ariadne is presented as a riddle in the form of a dare, a solution withdrawn into the assertion of a personal secret. Dionysus is defined by that which he seeks, and what he seeks is the Great Mother as Lost Daughter. Ariadne, we may say, is for Dionysus at once Demeter and Persephone, while at the same time she is a dynastic Cretan with her own particular story. The fertility goddess permutes with the princess abandoned by Theseus and then restored to a greater figure, Dionysus— a figure whom her complexities are here taken to explain. We may say it, but Nietzsche does not. He relies here wholly on the condensed hint, the bare name thrown up in the context of interpretable and intermittently self-interpreting self-revelation. The energy of onward movement in the words revealing thought is identified with a mythic entity, but that energy is not deflected into lesser details of the story. Dionysus is wholly deflected: the classical scholar become a reviver of myth defines the mythic riddle, Dionysus, by its counterpart, by the woman whose story is itself a riddle. One riddles deserves another, and both riddles meld into the emphatic rhythms of strong assertion. The myth loses any modernizing gesture of irony in a pure allusiveness that at the same time pronounces a comprehensive view too compact for us to take it beyond a powerful suggestiveness. Ariadne, in the assertive name, hovers between the evocation of myth and the intellectualizing of myth through interpretation. She is both and neither, where the bare Dionysus of *The Birth of Tragedy* attempts to release the power of myth by interpreting what it might evoke. Ariadne is not opposed to Dionysus, as Apollo is to Dionysus in the earlier book; but neither is she some "emanation" of equivalent for him. She is a being important because her mystery cannot be resolved, while at the same time it is offered as resolution: the riddle of the riddle that is its own solution.

"Ariadne" is repeated. In the normal voice there are other repetitions: *dichten, leiden, Rätsel.* There are also oppositions: past and future, whole and fragment. The repetitions cross the boundary between comment and quotation , but they may be modified. Both the hieratic text and its commentary turn abstract, philosophical terms to "poetic" uses by imposing upon them at once metaphors and the running metalinguistic qualifications of the speaker. Affirmation, in the tonality, overrides all the fragmentations: assertion is followed by assertion. And the assertions will not rest as propositions, though the theoretical nature of the assertions and some of their language makes them seem like propositions. Here Nietzsche is straining his style to a breaking point of complication. The voice is at a high pitch, as though he were the white-haired Zarathustra at the end of *Also sprach Zarathustra* whose lion frightens "children" away from his cave.

And still he modulates into a kind of innocent posture, as though he were a child, one of the children who join Zarathustra.

At this extreme Nietzsche impresses upon all the problems he has raised a reselection brought about by his insistence on the centrality of his own life. He is and is not, in his declaration, a Dionysus-Christ, as the Zarathustra he is and is not has been relegated to a past here resurrected. Time and sacrifice are involved in the self-exposure of this declared self-realization. And the self-exposure of the human typicality comprised in his extraordinary utterance has become the only way to advance thought. The literary remanipulation of this philosophy ends in an *Ecce Homo*, a typological identification with the humanity of the suffering Christ presented by Pilate to the multitudes.

Nietzsche, like all the writers whom I have discussed here, could have signed the angled quotation from Goethe that I quoted at the beginning of my discussion: *Gefühl ist alles.* And in fact long before Goethe brought *Faust* to completion, Hegel, whose concerns Nietzsche may be said to transpose, stressed feeling, while also stressing the centrality of the subject and rooting it in a process of becoming (*Werden*), just as Nietzsche might have done—and did in his own way.[141] And all of these writers, in their various ways, question such terms as well, posing themselves on the threshold of their utterance to make question and affirmation modify each other, so that a regenerative cycle is set up between *Gefühl ist alles* and *Ecce Homo*. These are the utterances that we are still pondering, responding to, and incorporating for the still further regenerations that the heroic expressions of such writers have empowered us to address.

Notes

Preface

1 Jacques Derrida, *D'un ton apocalyptique adopté naguère en philosophie*, Paris: Galilée, 1983, translated in *Semeia 23, Derrida and Biblical Studies*, New York: Scholars Press, 1982. Derrida here begins from, and translates in his title, Kant's *Von einem neuerdings erhobenen vornehmen Ton in der Philosophie* (1796). It is the extensibility of tone that licenses Derrida's using the term "apocalyptic" to translate Kant's *erhobenen*, "elevated," a participle whose adjectival form, *erhaben*, "lofty, sublime," has an important history in Kant's writings from his early discussions of Burke's sublime through the *Critique of Aesthetic Judgment*.

Introduction

1 For the literary application of van Gennep's "threshold," I should state my indebtedness to my former colleague Angus Fletcher, though his own emphases in using the term differ somewhat from my own. So the terms of his title indicate: "'Positive Negation': Threshold, Sequence, and Personification in Coleridge" (in Geoffrey H. Hartman, ed., *New Perspectives on Coleridge and Wordsworth*, New York: Columbia University Press, 1972, 133–64). In this title none of the terms used except "threshold" would well accord with my emphases. Fletcher applies "thresholds" to Spenser and Milton as well as to the Romantics: "If temple and labyrinth provide the models of sacred stillness and profane movement, the threshold is the model of the transitional phase that links these two fundamental modes of being" (135). My somewhat more metaphorical "thresholds" are not transitional but permanent. As such, they would not lend themselves to another of Fletcher's interesting angles of vision: "the poetics of threshold require an inversion of the ideal of epic containment. . . . the tradition is thus one of brevity, wit, and metaphysical conceit" (149). These assertions lead Fletcher to quite a different side of Coleridge from that of my approach here. And Blake, in my presentation, transmutes rather than inverts "the ideal of epic containment."

2 The *Neveu de Rameau*, too, looks to the future as well as to the past. I emphasize its rootedness in a past age, not its modernity, as Trilling does (*Sincerity and Authenticity*, Cambridge: Harvard University Press, 1971, 27–34, 44–47).

3 Jean-Jacques Rousseau, *Les Confessions, Oeuvres Complètes*, Paris: Pléiade, 1964, I, 236.

4 Jean Starobinski, *J. J. Rousseau: La transparence et l'obstacle*, Paris: Gallimard, 1971.

5 Paul de Man, *Allegories of Reading*, New Haven: Yale University Press, 1979, 135–301.

6 Rousseau, "Premier Dialogue," *Oeuvres*, I, 668.

Rousseau is a locus classicus, of course, for the interaction of feeling and "nature." Again with Goethe, we are already on the way to such a perspective as Hegel's or Lenau's when he says somewhere that religion is nature's attempt to heal a wound in itself. "Nature," in turn, may designate a tangle. (Arthur O. Lovejoy, "'Nature' as Aesthetic Norm," *Modern Language Notes*, 42, 1927, 444–50.) And consciousness, set to examine itself in a historical spirit, quickly becomes an infinite regress. Still, both nature and consciousness may expand as ideas in perception under the dominance of feeling, a feeling deeply understood and allowed a complexity proper for such motions of the mind. Hegel's focus in the *Phänomenologie des Geistes* on gradually cumulative and culminating historicity may thus, conversely, be taken for a guide to, say, the fluidity of feeling in Shelley. (I owe to Terence des Pres and Jonathan Arac the suggestion that Hegel's *Phänomenologie des Geistes* might be applied specifically to Shelley.) As Hegel says of humankind generally, it can only come to truth through a process of remodeling: "Der Mensch ist nicht von Natur, wie er sein soll; er kommt erst durch den Prozess der Umbildung zur Wahrheit" (Hegel, *Philosophie der Geschichte*, Stuttgart: Reklam, 1961, 567).

Lenau, too, historicizes the "Zwei Seelen wohnen ach! in meiner Brust" of Goethe:

> Vielleicht ist unser unerforschtes Ich
> Vor scharfen Augen nur ein dunkler Strich
> In dem sich wunderbar zwei Welten schneiden.

(Nikolaus Lenau, *Sämtliche Werke*, Frankfurt: Insel, 1971, I, 289.) The title of this poem is "Doppelheimweh"— even nostalgia is intensified by the notion of repetition.

7 Christopher Ricks (*Keats and Embarrassment*, Oxford: Oxford University Press, 1974) demonstrates how rich and sensitive a resource was embarrassment as a notion or principle of response for Keats.

8 Mario Praz, *La Carne, la morte, e il diavolo nella letteratura romantica*, Florence: Sansone, 1966 (1942) (*The Romantic Agony*, Oxford: Oxford University Press, 1951). Praz points out (40) how the site of melancholy changes from intellect to sensibility in the shift from the eighteenth century to Romantic times.

9 Quotations are from John Keats, *Poetical Works*, Oxford: Oxford University Press, 1956.

10 Geoffrey Hartman, "Poem and Ideology: A Study of Keats' 'To Autumn,'" in *The Fate of Reading*, Chicago: University of Chicago Press, 1975, 124–46.

11 Walter Jackson Bate says (*John Keats*, Cambridge: Harvard University Press, 1963, 598–99), "Now one of Keats' basic premises, deepening with every half year of his development, is the inseparability of joy and pain to the awake and honest consciousness (the Shakespearean 'bittersweet' mentioned in the sonnet on Lear). The song of Apollo, representing the new poetry, the more discerning world to come, had made Clymene, in the first Hyperion, 'sick / Of joy and grief at once'; in the yet undiscovered regions mentioned in the 'Ode to Psyche,' the branching thoughts will bring new pleasure and pain simultaneously; the interplay of joy and pain is used dramatically in the 'Nightingale' and as a central theme in 'Melancholy.' Finally, Lamia's magic ability to 'unperplex bliss from its neighbor pain' underlies much of the illusory happiness she inspires: it is exactly this divorce between joy and pain that the outright 'dreamer,' Lycius, craves most and believes he is finding."

As John Baker expands Keats's implications into a theory of poetry, the contradictions recede, especially in the "Ode to a Nightingale," to secondary status: "The contest which the ode's dramatic presentation [offers] takes place on a purely internal plane of the speaker's consciousness. A kind of *epoche* or suspension of normal belief in presences is spontaneously performed. . . . its dramatic contest of intra-mental tendencies (or drives) is articulated in the difference between 'mythicizing' language in which a surrender of consciousness to object states is contemplated and a critical or reflexive language in which the difference between consciousness and object states is reconfirmed." ("Poem and Metalanguage: Emergence of the Silent Subject," manuscript study).

12 Such conditions accompany, if they do not help to cause, profoundly changed social attitudes towards the individual, of which the obverse is a Romantic emphasis on the individual and his feelings. The capitalist sees the individual as an economic being, an exploitable cog in a machine, while the Communist program of Marx casts him, comparably, as a constituent in a new impersonal social order. The turn of the eighteenth century saw the first general census (1801) in England, the invention of military conscription by Napoleon, and the demographic theories of Malthus. All imply a view of the individual that treats him as a statistical entity. Malthus brought questions of economic management to bear theoretically — they had always been brought to bear practically — on questions of sexual arrangement.

The totalitarian perversity of the Marquis de Sade, coming to literary expression at the time of Malthus and Napoleon, anticipates not only Freud but the Marxist-Capitalist reduction of the person to serviceable entity. So Roland Barthes (*Sade, Fourier, Loyola*, Paris: Seuil, 1971, 146–57) analyzes an episode in which sexual victims are tagged with colored ribbons indicating to whom they are assigned and for what part of the body: "[The tag] is in a single movement an index of property (like a cattle brand), an act

of identification (like a soldier's serial number), and a fetishistic gesture that
cuts the body up."

13 Mary Moorman, *William Wordsworth: A Biography*, London: Oxford University Press, 1957, I, 288.

14 Kathleen Coburn, ed., *The Notebooks of Samuel Taylor Coleridge*, Princeton: Princeton University Press, 1957–73, III, 288.

15 Karl Schlechta, ed., *Nietzsches Werke*, Munich: Hanser, 1966, II, 911.

16 Theodor Adorno, *Versuch über Wagner*, Munich: Knaur, 1962 (1952): "It turns into tautology, into permanent overtuning" (109); "The mythical music drama is secular and magical at once: thus is solved the rebus of phantasmagoria" (124); "Siegfried . . . transforms himself into an 'individual,' and as such immediately into the illusory image of a history-pure immediate and essential human being. From the revolutionary comes the rebel. All his opposition remains in the compulsive system of bourgeois society because it itself did not develop from the social process; rather it is opposed to the latter apparently from without and then shoved into the mix" (140–41).

17 Sartre, *L'Idiot de la famille*, Paris: Gallimard, 1971, I, 700ff. See Peter L. Thorslev, "Incest as Romantic Symbol," *Comparative Literature Studies* 2, 1965. Thorslev cites Grillparzer's *Die Ahnfrau*, Schiller's *Die Braut von Messina*, the last chapter of *Wilhelm Meisters Lehrjahre*, Walpole's *The Mysterious Mother*, Lewis' *The Monk*, and Tieck's *Der Blonde Eckbert*. The Cain and Manfred of Byron, like Byron himself, are haunted by incest. Later actual incestuous relations may well have involved Nietzsche and Trakl.

18 E. H. Carr (*The Romantic Exiles*, Harmondsworth: Penguin, 1968 [1933]) gives the details of this relationship, as of several others among those given over to "adultery and revolution," in the catchphrase of Robert Hass (personal communication). The saga begins with the near-incest of near-orphans: the marriage of Herzen and his wife, first cousins who are both illegitimate children.

19 Max Wickert, "Orpheus Dismembered: Operatic Myth Goes Underground," in *Salmagundi*, 38–39, Summer–Fall 1977, 118–36.

20 Charles Percy Sanger ("The Structure of Wuthering Heights," *Bronte Society Transactions*, part LXII, 1952, 100–105, as reprinted in William Sale, ed., *Wuthering Heights, A Critical Edition*, New York: Norton, 1963, 286–98) trenchantly lays out the legal and genealogical facts derivable in great precision from *Wuthering Heights*. A lawyer who wrote a treatise on wills, Sanger was well qualified to observe the extraordinary symmetry of family relations in the novel, as well as their considerable complexity: "In actual life I have never come across a pedigree of such absolute symmetry. . . . It is a remarkable piece of symmetry in a tempestuous book." Remarkable indeed, since the symmetry is therefore as imagined as the tempestuousness, and thus the pedigree is a counter-fantasy to the love.

21 Peter Quennell, *Byron: The Years of Fame*, London: Collins, 1967 (1936), 200–208.

22 Julian Moynahan ("Pastoralism as Culture and Counter-Culture in English Fiction 1800–1928: From a View to a Death," *Novel*, 6, Fall 1972, 20–35)

points out the element of recreative and nostalgic fantasy in the persistent emphasis on and devotion to country life among the industrialized British.

23 Werner Sombart, *Liebe, Luxus und Kapitalismus*, Munich: Deutsche Taschenbuch Verlag, 1967 (1922). Sombart (62ff.) derives the particular emphases of love after the Industrial Revolution, as against the practices of the cavalier-lover in Renaissance times, from the Calvinist emphasis on propriety (*Wohlanständigkeit*).

24 Novalis, "Die Lehrlinge zu Sais," in Carl Seilig, ed., *Gesammelte Werke*, Zurich: Bühl, 1945, I, 382–83. "Das Denken ist nur ein Traum des Fühlens, ein erstorbenes Fühlen, ein blassgraues, schwaches Leben."

25 "Gefühl ist gebildete (organisierte) Bewegung." Ibid., III, 189, no. 1376.

26 Friedrich Schlegel, "Philosophische Vorlesungen insbesonderes über Philosophie der Sprache und des Wortes," in Ernst Behler, Jean-Jacques Anstett, Hans Eichner, eds., *Kritische Friedrich-Schlegel Ausgabe*, Munich: Verlag Ferdinand Schöningh, 1958–   , XV, 20: "Das Gefühl ist von scheinbar indifferente, eigentlich aber fruchtbar volle Mitte des Bewusstseins," and, further, "wo die einzelnen Regungen aller anderen isolierten Kräfte sich begegnen, zusammentreffen, durchkreuzen und sich gegenseitig neutralisieren oder auch zu einem neuen Leben einander durchdringen und harmonisch vereinigen" ("Feeling is the full measure of consciousness, apparently indifferent but actually fruitful, . . . where the single impulses of all other isolated forces meet, coincide, cross, and mutually neutralize themselves or even penetrate to a new life and unite harmoniously." In "Über dramatische Kunst und Literatur" (vol. VI), "Das ganze Spiel lebendiger Bewegung beruht auf Einstimmung und Gegensatz" may be translated as "the entire play of living movement rests on concord and opposition."

27 Jean-Jacques Rousseau, *Essai sur l'origine des langues*, ed. A. Belin, 1817, 505.

28 E. P. Thompson, book in progress on Blake, read as a lecture series at Brown University, November 1980.

The German stage remained a place where demonstrations of abstract virtue could take place, in Schiller's *Maria Stuart* or Lessing's *Nathan der Weise*, though Emil Staiger has shown (*Stilwandel*, Zurich: Atlantis, 1963) how even there the *Sturm und Drang* gradually subverted the neoclassical shaping of imitation. As it did so, he shows, it opened language powerfully in the direction of feeling (as the name of the movement implies), notably and traceably in the gradual access to emotion through the speeches of raging women. This process becomes apparent in such plays as Lessing's *Emilia Galotti*, which Goethe has Werther reading just before he dies.

29 "Song of Myself," 26, 599–603, in Harold W. Blodgett and Sculley Bradley, eds., *Leaves of Grass: Comprehensive Reader's Edition*, New York: Norton, 1965.

30 Robert D. Faner, *Walt Whitman and Opera*, Philadelphia: University of Pennsylvania Press, 1951.

31 In Gerhard Stenzel, ed., *Die Deutsche Romantiker*, Salzburg: Bergland, 1954, 592–93.

32 "Phantasien über die Kunst," ibid., 586.

33 This remark is quoted by Lucien Stryk in *American Poets in 1976*, Indianapolis: Bobbs-Merrill, 1976, 392. Balzac attributes comparable ideas to the musician Pons and his friend Schmucke: "They believed firmly that music, the language of heaven, was to the ideas and the feelings (*sentiments*) that which the ideas and the feelings are to speech" (Paris: *Pléiade*, 1951, VI, 539). See also Kierkegaard on music and the musical in *Either/Or*, New York: Anchor, 1959, I, 63.

34 Michael Hamburger, ed., *Beethoven: Letters, Journals and Conversations*, New York: Anchor, 1960, 53 and 76.

35 Gerhard Stenzel, *Die Deutsche Romantiker*, 144. "Wenige verstehen welch ein Thron der Leidenschaft jeglicher einzelner Musiksatz ist — und wenige wissen dass die Leidenschaft selbst der Thron der Musik ist."

36 Lionel Trilling, *Sincerity and Authenticity*, 5.

37 Paul de Man, *Allegories of Reading*, 278–301.

38 Emil Staiger, *Stilwandel*, 80.

39 Werner Hoffman, *Das Irdische Paradies: Motive und Ideen des 19. Jahrhunderts*, Munich: Prestel, 1974, 16.

40 Rousseau, *Oeuvres*, I, 382.

41 How the internality of feeling comes to embrace nature may be exemplified in the persistently spiritualized use of birds by Romantic and post-Romantic writers. In this particular instance, as in others, the role of the natural creature has been powerfully refined and complicated. For Coleridge, who saw nature in terms of forms and energies, starlings are a metaphor for thoughts; he observed the actual birds in nature so as to catch some impetus to particularity (Coburn, *Notebooks*, I, 1589, as cited and discussed in Samuel Beer, *Coleridge's Poetic Intelligence*, London: Macmillan, 1977, 230, 255). "Ich wünscht ich wär ein Vöglein," says the folk song — and, to be sure, the sentiment is familiar at least since Euripides. Goethe need only translate Alcman's poem about birds to locate them in a landscape that is an exemplum more general than Alcman's: "Über allen Gipfeln ist Ruh" ("Over all peaks there is peace"). Shelley's skylark represents a new spiritualization. Tieck's bird in the forest (Ludwig Tieck, "Der Blonde Eckbert," in *Schriften*, Berlin, 1828, IV, 144–72), a forerunner of the one whom Wagner's Siegfried hears, links the evanescent, the quickly responsive, and the magical: "Waldeinsamkeit, / Die mich erfreut," the bird sings before the girl betrays it in the forest. We are left with the haunting question of why loneliness should bring joy — to which the answer is the Romantic pleasure in the very depth of the forest, in "wood-loneliness / that brings me joy." When the girl betrays the bird, it rues the wood-loneliness as its only pleasure, now lost:

> Waldeinsamkeit,
> Wie liegst Du weit!
> Oh, dir gereut
> Einst mit der Zeit.

Ach, einz'ge Freud,
Waldeinsamkeit.

Wood-loneliness,
How far you lie!
Oh you will rue it
One fine time.

Ah, single joy,
Wood-loneliness.

The finale of Keats's "Ode to Autumn" locates birds at the margin of what is effectually both perception and event: "And gathering swallows twitter in the skies." Chateaubriand in *Mémoires d'outre-tombe* finds in the sight of swallows something that compasses both Keats's fullness and Tiecks's pleasure-in-loneliness. As Irving Massey says of these lines (*The Uncreating Word*, Bloomington: Indiana University Press, 1970, 47), "for all his 'tristesse' in the autumn, Chateaubriand sees the return of the birds of passage with the autumn storms 'with inexpressible pleasure.' In his unhappiness, then, he must be finding happiness."

Tennyson has recourse to such mutely significant birdsong in the climactic image of "Tears, Idle Tears":

Ah, sad and strange as in dark summer dawns
The earliest pipe of half-awaken'd birds
To dying ears, when unto dying eyes
The casement slowly grows a glimmering square.

The melting of sight into blurring throws distant attention onto sound, and so onto a wakefulness towards what is sad and strange in the emotion of various fusions. The dawns are dark, the listener is dying, and tears at perceiving the whole situation come to his eyes. For the tears of that dying man, song serves as screen, vehicle, condensation, displacement, and inadequate signal. For another discussion of bird topoi as connected to internality and imagination, see Thomas McFarland, *Originality and Imagination*, Baltimore: Johns Hopkins University Press, 1985, and Fred V. Randel, "Coleridge and the Contentiousness of Romantic Nightingales," *Studies in Romanticism*, 21, 1982, 33–56, with references.

42 Mikhail Bakhtin, *La Poétique de Dostoevsky*, Paris: Seuil, 1970.

43 Irving Massey, *The Uncreating Word*.

44 A virtual theory of literary representation is built up by Charles Olson on the implied tensions in Melville's style. As Olson puts it, "Melville's prose does things which its rhetoric would seem to contradict" ("Equal, That Is, to the Real Itself," in *Selected Writings*, New York: New Directions, 1966, 49). Robert Caserio persuasively extends this practice to include Melville's sense of plot, and thereby his whole vision of experience (*Plot, Story, and the Novel*, Princeton: Princeton University Press, 1979). John Seelye (*Melville: The Ironic Diagram*, Evanston: Northwestern University Press, 1970) maintains that

Melville begins with German "Romantic irony" and develops to a point where "most of [his] structures involve a planetary balance of forces, in which the narrative thrust — the forward movement of quest — is countered by a system of paradoxical contrasts" (9).

45 Marshall Brown has shown ("Mozart and After: The Revolution in Musical Consciousness," *Critical Inquiry*, 7, 1981, 689–706) how the fantasia developed between 1780 and 1800 as an important vehicle of musical expression.

46 Albert Béguin, *L'Âme romantique et le rêve*, Paris: José Corti, 1967 (1939), surveys the vast German literature expounding the visionary validity of dreams and its derivatives in French poetry from Nerval through the surrealists. He, interestingly, characterizes the limitations in this regard of French "Romantic" poetry in the narrower sense: "The French romantics, on the contrary, seem to perceive no beyond for their pure subjectivism: a confessional literature in lyric did not pretend to overturn the traditional laws and consecrated forms of the art of writing so as to give free reign to the expression of the feelings, the torments, the uncertainties, of the poet himself" (328).

47 Michel Foucault, *Les mots et les choses*, Paris: Gallimard, 1966, 312.

48 Edward Ahearn expands on this point in *Rimbaud*, Berkeley and Los Angeles: University of California Press, 1983.

49 The matter is discussed in *Wordsworth's Poetical Works*, ed. Ernest de Selincourt and Helen Darbyshire, Oxford: Oxford University Press, 1940, I, 361.

50 Geoffrey Hartman, *Beyond Formalism*, New Haven: Yale University Press, 1970, 226–27.

51 Geoffrey Hartman, "Wordsworth and Goethe in Literary History," in *The Fate of Reading*, 179–202.

52 Richard Ohmann attributes such effects to rhetorical sleights ("Speech, Action, and Style," in Seymour Chatman, ed., *Literary Style: A Symposium*, London: Oxford University Press, 1971, 241–62): "A poem, too, moves on a rhythm of illocutionary acts; and that rhythm is often telling, as in Blake's 'Ah, Sunflower, weary of time . . .' where the illocutionary act that encases all the rest is an *apostrophe*, so that the poem avoids *assertion* (indeed, predication of any sort), and thus hangs suspended, as it were, in an almost actionless state, which accords well with its content, or Wordsworth's Immortality Ode, in which tension builds through the first sixty lines between the acts of *rejoicing* and *lamenting*, until it is resolved in the explanation — a kind of lawlike fiction for the nonce — that begins 'Our birth is but a sleep and a forgetting'" (249). I have benefited from the discussion of this poem by E. D. Hirsch (*Validity in Interpretation*, New Haven: Yale University Press, 1967, 230f.), though I am asserting a "hovering" meaning beyond his interpretation. I also assert a special "dream" effect that would disallow the general hermeneutic suspension that Max Black, in a lecture, has argued that this poem exemplifies; nor can it be assimilated to allegory, as Paul de Man tries to do ("The Rhetoric of Temporality" in *Blindness and Insight* [expanded ed.], Minneapolis: University of Minnesota Press, 1982), though it shares some of the sense of discontinuity for which allegory and irony are

brought forward. In "Shelley Disfigured" (*The Rhetoric of Romanticism*, New York: Columbia University Press, 1984, 93–123), he reasons that the various slippages of this sort in Shelley's *The Triumph of Life* are evidence for Shelley's control of such slippages, and even for Shelley's promulgation of a figural infinite regress not so different from that for which de Man nearly always argues.

53 F. W. Bateson (*Wordsworth: A Re-Interpretation*, London: Longmans, 1956) quotes Arnold and expounds various divisions in Wordsworth's approach to poetry (8ff.). He is sensitive but too negative; what Arnold meant by "no style" is clearly the plain style towards which Wordsworth aspired, a style that in the "Lucy" poems takes on a tonality strangely vague for the plain style; a dream-empowered vagueness is brought into being.

54 Geoffrey Hartman, *The Fate of Reading*, 291.

55 John Jones, *The Egotistical Sublime: A History of Wordsworth's Imagination*, London: Chatto and Windus, 1954, 32–34.

56 Ibid., 356.

57 *Wordsworth's Poetical Works*, II, 395. Preface to the 1800 "Lyrical Ballads."

58 The term is Donald Davie's, adapting ideas of Perse and Valéry. As Davie says (*Articulate Energy*, London: Routledge and Kegan Paul, 1955, 107ff.), "We can make a start by pointing out that Wordsworth's world is not preeminently a world of 'things.' His language has not, in St. John Perse's sense, 'weight and mass.' It is not concrete. . . . In those passages of *The Prelude* where Wordsworth is trying to convey most exactly the effect of the natural world upon himself, his words ('ties' and 'bonds' and 'influences' and 'powers') will carry the reader only (as Valéry says) so long as he does not loiter, so long as they are taken, as coins are taken, 'as values of monetary-exchange.'"

59 Perhaps the culminating instance in his work of the confrontation with expression-in-inarticulateness is the doubly deprived image of the blind beggar with the sign around his neck:

> 'twas my chance
> Abruptly to be smitten with the view
> Of a blind Beggar, who, with upright face,
> Stood, propped against a wall, upon his chest
> Wearing a written paper, to explain
> The story of the man, and who he was.
> My mind did at this spectacle turn round
> As with the might of waters, and it seemed
> To me that in this label was a type,
> Or emblem, of the utmost that we know,
> Both of ourselves and of the universe.
>
> (1805 *Prelude*, VII, 609–19)

60 As often with such passages of summary definition, there are virtually no variants between the 1805 version and the 1850 version of these lines. (In 1850 "they must" in line 534 and "then" in line 550 are italicized; that is all.)

61 In a very different register, Lautréamont mixes conscious and unconscious

by describing outlandish conjunctions in sternly classical prose, as Maurice Blanchot says (*La part du feu*, Paris: Gallimard, 1949, 166–79). Jacques Derrida expands on the self-fantasizing character of the *Chants de Maldoror (La Dissémination*, Paris: Seuil, 1972, 40ff.): "Having recourse, so he might play with them, to the opposition of two modes of mathematical demonstrations, analysis and synthesis, Lautréamont in a parody inverts the positions and rediscovers, to struggle like Descartes, the constraints and the topos of the 'vicious circle'" (44).

62 *Wordsworth's Poetical Works*, II, 399.

63 Herbert Read isolates this central role of meter in Wordsworth's theory (*The True Voice of Feeling*, London: Faber, 1968 [1947], 41): "Wordsworth is pointing out that the recollection of emotion in tranquillity produces by reaction a spontaneous overflow of feelings, and that this overflow must be controlled by some means if poetry is to be composed. This means is metre—a veil of harmony drawn over the description of the deeper passions. . . . The specific quality of poetry is the 'complex delight' produced by this interplay of the reality- and the pleasure-principle."

The Prelude begins in the indirection of incapacity, a long idling over the question "What shall I write about?" It proceeds by feeling its way from one traditional topic to another until it bursts out in the invocation:

> Was it for this
> That one, the fairest of all rivers, loved
> To blend his murmurs with my nurse's song,
> And, from his alder shades and rocky falls,
> And from his fords and shallows, sent a voice
> That flowed along my dreams?   (I, 272–77)

Now structured as an enabling interruption, this passage about "a voice / That flowed along my dreams" began as the very first impulse for his unnamed long poem; it begins the "JJ" manuscript of 1798–99, and it remains virtually unchanged till 1850—except that "intertwined" originally stood for "flowed." "Intertwined" emphasizes the intricacy of the poet's perceptions, and commas are added to break the flow.

The invocation lets him by the back door into the crucial subject of boyhood. In the poem's finally settled rhetoric, the inexpressibility-preterition frames the rising note of Invocation and omniscience.

64 As such it is in theory infinitely extensible: one could add hundreds of further lines of invocation without altering the conception, something that would be impossible with, say, the *Divine Comedy* or *Paradise Lost*. In the "Was it for this" passage, the commas are added to the original manuscript draft, we may say, to indicate the associative character of the rumination. And Wordsworth's rhythmic pattern, unlike Milton's, is additive. Where Milton offers highly wrought periodic sentences, those of Wordsworth keep adding, rhythmically, as though in afterthought or dreamy free association. Again and again, one could put a full stop before he continues, whereas in a periodic style the full stop can usually come only at the end of the actual sentence.

65 Edward E. Bostetter, *The Romantic Ventriloquists*, Seattle: University of Washington Press, 1975, 48–49.

66 Terence Ogden in "The Power of Distance in Wordsworth's *Prelude*" (*PMLA*, 88, 1973, 246–59) details the background of Wordsworth's precise perceptual depictions. The idea of "objects larger than mist" (VIII, 262–67) is to be found in the works of Le Cat, *Traité des sens*, Amsterdam, 1744, as reported by Joseph Priestley, 1774. The "rocking moon" (IV, 87–92) is to be found in William Porterfield's *Treatise on the Eye*. Wordsworth also discusses the afterimage and the projected apparent motion in his treatment of the visual side of "the fluxes and refluxes of the mind."

67 Geoffrey Hartman, *Wordsworth's Poetry 1787–1814*, New Haven: Yale University Press, 1964, 287.

68 Herbert Lindenberger, *On Wordsworth's Prelude*, Princeton: Princeton University Press, 1963, 51.

69 Clint Goodson, "Kubla's Construct," *Studies in Romanticism*, 18, 1979, 405–25. Goodson effectively redresses the exaggerations of the "intertextual" critics who would enclose the poem wholly in its interreferences to itself and other poems, and also the persistent New Critical countertendency, nominalist in implication, to have "representation . . . remain the first poetic function." As he well says, "The case of Coleridge shows that anti-nominalism does not in itself entail a critical view of the representational function." Goodson's book in progress on Coleridge's theory of language should richly flesh out these assertions.

70 Albert Cook, "The Language of Fiction," in *The Meaning of Fiction*, Detroit: Wayne State University Press, 1960, 77–87.

71 As John Baker says ("Situating the Mind of Keats," unpublished manuscript), "What Keats thought is, for better or worse, identical with the forms of discourse, or 'discursive formations,' to which he repeatedly had recourse. That is, an articulation of what he thought cannot begin with the things most resembling propositional statements—often, when taken in themselves, Keats's weakest remarks—but rather with the way in which Keats groped somewhat uncertainly towards thought. . . . mixed discourse, that peculiar romantic juggling of possible perspectives which both denies and fears conclusion, the philosophical-doctrinal pinning down, is exactly what Keats's romantic mind demanded. . . . The 'Psyche,' 'Nightingale,' and 'Urn' odes are all dramatizations of ways in which the imagination vies with and challenges the contending world in which it finds itself."

72 For a discussion of the implications of the Romantic use of myth in a larger historical context, see Albert Cook, *Myth and Language*, Bloomington: Indiana University Press, 1980, especially chap. 2, 37–66.

73 Gary Handwerk (*Irony and the Ethics of Intersubjectivity*, New Haven: Yale University Press, 1985) demonstrates complexly how Schlegel made irony so comprehensive a term that he was able to substitute for it the terms *Gewissen* ("conscience") and *Bewusstsein* ("consciousness") in his later writings. Handwerk also shows how these philosophical concerns carry through and define deep attitudes right up to those found in Lacan and Beckett.

Blake: The Exaltation of Fluidity

1 Roman Jakobson, "Linguistics and Poetics," in Seymour Chatman and Samuel R. Levin, eds., *Essays on the Language of Literature*, Boston: Houghton Mifflin, 1967, 296–322.

2 Robert Scholes, *Semiotics of Interpretation*, New Haven: Yale University Press, 1983.

3 John Baker in a study in progress analyzes the underlying philosophical implications of the poetic practice of Keats and Hölderlin in this regard.

4 Albert Cook, *Myth and Language*, Bloomington: Indiana University Press, 1980, 69–106.

5 Irving Massey, "Words and Images: Harmony and Dissonance," *Georgia Review*, 34, 1980, 375–95.

6 See Introduction, section 6.

7 Albert Cook, *Myth and Language*, 60–62.

8 Martin Heidegger, *Erläuterungen zu Hölderlins Dichtung*, Frankfurt: Klostermann, 1951.

9 The phrase is Irving Massey's ("Literature and Contradiction," mimeographed, SUNY–Buffalo, 1974). As he puts it, "Coleridge's argument that in metaphor, and in the work of art as a whole, difference is reconciled in unity, gradually came to appear unconvincing and finally boring. The parts of a metaphor maintain their independence and in their contrast they continue to reverberate against each other, they do not simply merge, even in a new reality. As an alternative to what I am inclined to call Coleridge's wishbone theory of metaphor, in which the parts, separate to begin with, join at the peak, I decided to propose a tuning-fork theory; that the parts begin together as a whole and subsequently separate under the stress of the aesthetic experience. They are still together, but at the base, not at the summit. Difference, not resemblance, is the principle of metaphor; resemblance is at least in part a pretext for emphasizing difference."

10 This notion is discussed in Samuel R. Levin, *The Semantics of Metaphor*, Baltimore: Johns Hopkins University Press, 1978.

11 All quotations are from David Erdman and Harold Bloom, eds., *The Poetry and Prose of William Blake*, New York: Doubleday, 1965.

12 Friedrich Schelling, *Philosophie der Mythologie*, Munich: C. H. Beck, 1968 (1842). See especially pp. 133, 138, 290, 291. As Schelling says in this last citation, "In der Mythologie ist nichts aus der Natur genommen, sondern der Naturprocess selbst wiederholte sich als theogonischer Process im Bewusstsein. Es gibt Voraussetzungen, unter denen man von jedem Naturding sagen kann, es sey ein modificirter Gott." ("In Mythology nothing is taken from nature, but the natural process itself repeats [lit. "repeated"] itself as a theogonic process in the consciousness. There are hypotheses under which it can be said of every object in nature that it is a modified God.") This assertion would be easy to reconcile with the assumptions of Blake.

13 As Jacob Bronowski says (*William Blake, 1757–1827: A Man Without a Mask*, London: Secker & Warburg, 1943, 93), "Blake made for himself, twenty years

before, the dialectic of Hegel's formal thought"; quoted and discussed in Peter F. Fisher, *The Valley of Vision*, Toronto: Toronto University Press, 1961, 7.

14 S. Foster Damon, *A Blake Dictionary*, Providence: Brown University Press, 1965, 368.

15 Depending on the interactions in *Jerusalem*, Vala's functions can bend towards enslavement or towards liberation, assimilating always to some prominent aspect of the momentary complex:

> The Starry Wheels revolv'd heavily over the Furnaces;
> Drawing Jerusalem in anguish of maternal love,
> Eastward a pillar of a cloud with Vala upon the mountains
> Howling in pain, redounding from the arms of Beulahs Daughters.
> (5.46–49; p. 147)

and again:

> Vala would never have sought & loved Albion
> If she had not sought to destroy Jerusalem; such is that false
> And Generating Love: a pretence of love to destroy love.
> (17.24–26; p. 160)

Yet before long Vala will embrace rather than destroy Jerusalem:

> He found Jerusalem upon the River of his City soft repos'd
> In the arms of Vala, assimilating in one with Vala and
> The Lilly of Havilah: . . .
> Error & fault that is soon forgiven; but mercy is not a Sin
> Nor pity nor love nor kind forgiveness!
> (19.40–42; 20.24–26; pp. 163–64)

Much later we have a whole series of identifications with Vala:

> Vala replied in cloud of tears Albions garments embracing
>
> I was a City & a Temple built by Albions Children.
> I was a Garden planted with beauty I allured on hill & valley
> The River of Life to flow against my walls & among my trees
> Vala was Albions Bride & Wife in great Eternity . . .
> Art thou Vala? replied Albion, image of my repose
> O how I tremble! how my members pour down milky fear! . . .
> Is not that Sun thy husband and that Moon thy glimmering Veil?
> Are not the Stars of heaven thy Children! art thou not Babylon?
> Art thou Nature Mother of all! is Jerusalem thy Daughter
> Why have thou elevate inward: O dweller of outward chambers
> (29.33–35, 30.2–3, 7–10; p. 174)

and again:

> Man is adjoind to Man by his Emanative portion:
> Who is Jerusalem in every individual Man: and her
> Shadow is Vala, builded by the Reasoning power in Man
> (39.38–40; p. 185)

but this simultaneously shades into a destructiveness:

> Then Vala the Wife of Albion, who is the Daughter of Luvah
> Took vengeance Twelve-fold among the Chaotic Rocks of the Druids
> Where the Human Victims howl to the Moon & Thor & Friga
> Dance the dance of death contending with Jehovah among the
> Cherubim.   (63.7–10; pp. 211–12)

This links Vala to her origin in Scandinavian mythology. But another verse asserts all these functions: "Then All the Daughters of Albion became One before Los: even Vala!" (64.6; p. 213).

16 Harley Parker and Marshall McLuhan, eds., *Through the Vanishing Point*, New York: Harper, 1968.

17 Anne K. Mellor (*Blake's Human Form Divine*, Berkeley: University of California Press, 1974) disengages the sources of Blake's representations of the human figure. Of his subject matter, she says, "In his episodes from early British history, Shakespeare, and the Bible (all subjects recommended by Burke as suitable for the sublime style), Blake followed contemporary history painters in their predilection for large idealized figures, rhetorically grouped configurations, static attitudes, and 'morally elevating' events" (105). As W. J. T. Mitchell says ("Blake's Composite Art," in John E. Grant and David Erdman, eds., *Blake's Visionary Forms Dramatic*, Princeton: Princeton University Press, 1970, 61), "Blake's critique of the implication of *ut pictura poesis* can be understood most clearly in terms of his reception of the idea of Nature assumed by this doctrine. For Blake, the dualistic world of mind and body, time and space, is an illusion which must not be imitated, but which must be dispelled by the processes of his art: 'But first the notion that a man has a body distinct from his work is to be expunged; that I do by printing in the infernal method, by corrosives, melting apparent surfaces away, and displaying the infinite which was hidden.'" And further (p. 63), "No scene in the poem corresponds to this picture, and yet it is a perfect representation of the poem's theme, the marriage of contraries." (Cf. Plate 3 of *The Marriage of Heaven and Hell*.) In his subsequent book (*Blake's Composite Art*, Princeton: Princeton University Press, 1978), Mitchell develops in detail his typology of relations between the picture and the verbal text in the illuminated books, stressing the at times independent and supplementary signification of the pictorial images. All the given terms of eighteenth-century practice in this mode are subject to redefinition by Blake, with his predilection for such dynamic forms as the vortex (69–77) and for the complexity of "living form" in *Jerusalem* (166–218).

18 Since Blake sometimes shifted plates around, this is alternatively Plate 46.

19 In one of Blake's first tries at a Prophetic Book, *Tiriel*, three generations of faintly allegorical persons are all overwhelmed by weariness and old age in an overburdened listlessness akin to that of *Hyperion*. It is as though Blake had to conjure up so dim and dominant a past in order, thereafter, to set it aside and center his new kind of poem on events always open to the energies of the future.

20 Northrop Frye, *Fearful Symmetry*, Princeton: Princeton University Press, 1947, 50. As evidence of some perception of instability, Frye immediately qualifies Blake's couplets: "The twofold vision here, however, is not that of Generation, but the ability to see an unfallen world as well as a fallen one."

21 "Wenn er nun ganz in die Beschauung dieser Urerscheinung versinkt, so entfaltet sich vor ihm in neu entstehenden Zeiten und Räumen, wie ein unermessliches Schauspiel, die Erzeugungsgeschichte der Natur, und jeder feste Punkt, der sich in der unendlichen Flüssigkeit ansetzt, wird ihm eine neue Offenbarung des Genius der Liebe, ein neues Band des Du und des Ich. Die sorgfältige Beschreibung dieser innern Weltgeschichte ist die wahre Theorie der Natur; durch den Zusammenhang seiner Gedankenwelt in sich und ihre Harmonie mit dem Universum bildet sich von selbst ein Gedankensystem zur getreuen Abbildung und Formel des Universums." Novalis, "die Lehrlinge zu Sais," in Carl Seilig, ed., *Gesammelte Werke*, Zurich: Bühl, 1945, I, 390.

22 As Aaron Fogel says ("Pictures of Speech: On Blake's Poetic," *Studies in Romanticism*, 21, 1982, 217–42), "Blake's names are primarily dialogical, directing us to types of natural speech rather than to simple categories like 'guilt'" (217). The indefiniteness of Blake's names is well argued here, though speech is really only an aspect of the function of Leutha or Orc's chains. Fogel also correlates the features of sound in Blake's poems to the process of action in them (226–32).

23 Thomas J. J. Altizer, *The New Apocalypse*, East Lansing: Michigan State University Press, 1974, 78.

24 I have provisionally counted them but will not impose a list of them on the reader.

25 Albert Cook, "Milton's Abstract Music," in *University of Toronto Quarterly*, 29, 1960, 370–85. For a clear, complex account of Blake's own metrics, see William Kumbier, "Blake's Epic Meter," *Studies in Romanticism*, 17, 1978, 163–92.

26 One may find these changing emphases in the earliest of the major Prophetic Books, *The Four Zoas*. For example, Night the Seventh offers a considerable "terrific" run (91.1–20; p. 395). "Mild and gentle" or "prosaic" passages occur throughout, as 119.12–28 or 126.18–37. One can sometimes catch the transition, as across the flattened accents of "humanizing" in this passage (132.36–40; p. 386):

> Joy thrilled thro all the Furious form of Tharmas humanizing
> Mild he Embracd her whom he sought he raisd her thro the heavens
> Sounding his trumpet to awake the dead on high he soard
> Over the ruind worlds the smoking tomb of the Eternal Prophet . . .

This quickly returns to "terrific" numbers after "Sounding," sustaining them through the amplification caught up in the elision of "the Eternal."

27 Jacques Lacan, *Écrits*, Paris: Seuil, 1966, 765–92.

28 Altizer, *The New Apocalypse*, 6–8.

Sin, *Verstand*, and the Love of All Things: The Vacillation of Coleridge

1 Thomas McFarland (*Romanticism and the Forms of Ruin*, Princeton: Princeton University Press, 1982, 346) quotes Novalis: "Die Trennung von Poet und Denker ist nur scheinbar — und zum *Nachteil* beyder" ("The separation of poet and thinker is only apparent — and to the disadvantage of both," N, 111, 406). And see n. 3 below.

2 *Archaeologiae Philosophicae sive Doctrina Antiqua de Rerum Originibus* Libri Duo, London, 1692, 68. The translation is by Mead and Foxton, 1736, as cited by Kathleen Coburn, ed., *The Notebooks of Samuel Taylor Coleridge*, New York: Bollingen, 1957, I: Notes, 1000 H n. (Hereafter cited as *Notebooks*.)

3 In his magisterial and expansive demonstration of Coleridge's intricate relationship to the current of the *Pantheismusstreit* in prior speculation, Thomas McFarland defines Spinoza's doctrines as the main challenge to refutation. As he summarizes them (*Coleridge and the Pantheist Tradition*, Oxford: Clarendon Press, 1969), "'individual things are nothing but modifications of the attributes of God'; Whatsoever is, is in God, and without God nothing can be, or be conceived. Again, Spinoza says that 'substances' and 'modes' form 'the sum total of existence,' but since 'modes' are merely 'the modification of substance,' and since 'besides God no substance can be conceived,' then 'modes' become 'merely modifications of the attributes of God' and we are left with only two basic entities, substance and God. The equation therefore, reduces itself to 'the sum total of existence' equals 'God or substance.' *Deus, sive substantia,* . . . 'individual things are nothing but modifications of the attributes of God.' Hence Spinoza is inextricably bound up to the category of 'thing' for his ultimate projection of God, and God becomes in this projection *res extensa* — an extended thing. . . . Since, on the one hand, the essence of a thing, what 'it is,' must, by the grammar of the question, imply an affirmation, and since all modification or relation is, by the *determinatio negatio est*, a form of negation, the form of ultimate abstraction from a thing must eschew modification or relation, and thereby all limit whatever, thus bringing us to the '*fulcrum atheismi*,' the identity of all substance. . . . Now in this development of a 'particular thing' into the 'sum total' of all things, into the 'extended thing' that Spinoza calls 'God, or Nature' (*Deus, sive Natura*), the unemphasized original element — the I, the self, the wonderer — is, . . . ontologically demolished" (63–67). And further, in his account of Coleridge's relation to Spinoza and the questions he raises, McFarland says (170, n.), "At the time of the poem's composition ["The Rime of the Ancient Mariner"], moreover, there are indications of Coleridge's mental upheaval with regard to theological problems."

4 "Atheism or Spinosism," in Earl Leslie Griggs, ed., *The Letters of Samuel Taylor Coleridge*, Oxford: Clarendon Press, 1957, II, 1196 (hereafter cited as *Letters*), as cited and discussed in McFarland, *Coleridge and the Pantheist Tradition*, 182.

5 Robert Graves, *The White Goddess*, New York: Farrar, Straus and Giroux,

1966 (1948), 433: "his description in the *Ancient Mariner* of the woman dic-
ing with Death in the phantom ship is as faithful a record of the White Goddess as exists."

6 Perhaps this works in some sort of congruence with the psychoanalytic implications of Coleridge's father's early death; thus the father is dead, and
the mother becomes by that fact a dominant presence, threatening as well
as nurturing, a Life-in-Death. The numerous sailors perhaps also parallel
Coleridge's large family.

7 "Madness may perhaps be defined as the circling in a stream which should
be progressive and adaptive" ("Lecture VIII" of "A Course of Lectures [1818],"
as reprinted in Samuel Taylor Coleridge, *Essays*, London: Everyman, 1907,
251), a definition that parallels the poem in its water metaphor.

8 John Livingston Lowes (*The Road to Xanadu*, Boston: Houghton-Mifflin, 1955
[1927], 69–72, and passim) identifies "The Rime of the Ancient Mariner" as
incorporating the project entitled "Hymns to the Sun, the Moon, and the
Elements," part of no. 16 in a list (*Notebooks*, I, 61): "Burnet's *theoria tel-
luris* translated into blank verse, the original at the bottom of the page." Both
Lowes and Meyer H. Abrams (*Natural Supernaturalism*, New York: Norton,
1971, 99–101) stress the complicated doctrinal and rhetorical interaction of
Burnet's ideas with Coleridge's. Since both these notebook entries connect
Burnet with a blank verse project, the strikingly successful ballad meter of
the poem to which he finally appended this quotation from Burnet may help
him to keep the tension of a necessary distance from Burnet. The argument,
amplified in the 1800 version and omitted in subsequent ones until the addition of Burnet in 1817, and the marginal glosses added just beforehand in
1815–16, may all be taken as attempts to spell out less delphically the poem's
conjunction of natural and supernatural.

9 McFarland, *Romanticism and the Ruins of Time*, passim.

10 Eleanor S. Shaffer, *"Kubla Khan" and "The Fall of Jerusalem": The Mythological School in Biblical Criticism and Secular Literature, 1770–1880*, Cambridge: Cambridge University Press, 1975.

11 Stith Thompson (*Motif Index of Folk Literature*, Bloomington: Indiana University Press, 1958) lists actually not one but a number of motifs on which
the events surrounding the Albatross may be seen to touch: a bird as a helper
on a quest (H 1233.6.2), as a messenger (B 291.1), as a messenger of the
gods (A 155.3), as a scout from an ark (A 1021.2), and as the shadow of god
(A 195.3); a bird rescues a man from the sea (B 541.3); a man shoots a bird
(F 661.5.2; J 641.1). It was Wordsworth, as it happened, who suggested the
Albatross to Coleridge.

12 Roberta F. Brinkley, *Coleridge on the Seventeenth Century*, Durham, N.C.:
University of North Carolina Press, 1955, 694, as cited by Thomas Mc-
Farland, "The Origin and Significance of Coleridge's Theory of Secondary
Imagination," in Geoffrey Hartman, ed., *New Papers on Coleridge and
Wordsworth: Selected Papers from the English Institute*, New York: Colum-
bia University Press, 1972, 201. To this in a supernatural context may be
added Eichhorn's praise of imagination, *Einbildungskraft* (Johann Gottfried

Eichhorn, *Einleitung in das Alte Testament*, Leipzig, 1780–83, 382, as cited and translated by Eleanor Shaffer, *"Kubla Khan,"* 125): "The imagination does not remain within the narrow bounds of the oral transmission, it ranges yet further in the realm of possibilities and raises much of what it glimpses in the mists of time to gigantic proportions and transforms sagas into truly magical ideas."

13 J. Robert Barth, S.J., *Coleridge and Christian Doctrine*, Cambridge: Harvard University Press, 1969, 111–17, 150, and passim.

14 What Barth (ibid., 67) says of Coleridge's theological doctrines is applicable here: "He seems to have fallen at one point into the fallacy of confusing his distinction between inspiration and revelation—both of which are supernatural gifts—with the traditional distinction between the providential and the miraculous, which is meant precisely to distinguish the natural and the supernatural"—and we are led back again to Burnet's categories as singled out by Coleridge for application to "The Rime of the Ancient Mariner."

15 The Mariner, as George Whalley points out ("The Mariner and the Albatross," *University of Toronto Quarterly*, 16, 1946–47, as reprinted in Kathleen Coburn, ed., *Coleridge*, Englewood Cliffs: Prentice-Hall, 1967), has many points of congruence with Coleridge himself. So that the personal sense the Mariner carries and the Wedding-Guest carries away would offer the only mode of unifying the supernatural and the natural worlds, just as "conscience" or "love" or "belief" serve to get beyond Spinoza's implied atheism in Coleridge's theology. Taken psychoanalytically and read as a dream, "The Rime of the Ancient Mariner" splits Coleridge into two figures: the man who will shortly sail to Germany and then later to Malta, who has drifted around England and has already begun to feel the pall of dejection creeping over him, does indeed resemble the Mariner. But he also resembles the Wedding-Guest: he dreams, so to speak, that his anguished self has detained his festive self before he attends the ceremony that he has already been coming to regret, himself-as-bridegroom displaced into himself-as-kin.

The question of identity, indeed, haunts the last transaction in the Mariner's tale, the one that has brought him before the kirk to repeat the tale:

> 'O shrieve me, shrieve me, holy man!'
> The Hermit crossed his brow.
> 'Say quick,' quoth he, 'I bid thee say—
> What manner of man art thou?'
>
> Forthwith this frame of mine was wrenched
> With a woeful agony,
> Which forced me to begin my tale;
> And then it left me free.   (574–81)

The question "what manner of man art thou" throws the Mariner into something not unlike an epileptic fit, from which the only release is to tell the tale. But does the tale answer the Hermit's question? And does telling it, in a sort of protopsychoanalysis or expanded confession, satisfy the condition for shriving? Coleridge passes by both these questions.

16 Thomas McFarland, "The Origin and Significance of Coleridge's Theory of Secondary Imagination."
17 *Letters,* IV, 600–601; III, 2560.
18 Eleanor Shaffer, *"Kubla Khan,"* 94.
19 A convenient survey of themes and traits is given by Albert B. Friedman, *The Viking Book of Folk Ballads,* New York: Viking, 1956.
20 Herbert Read, *English Prose Style,* London: G. Bell, 1949 (1928), 83.
21 *Letters,* IV, 578.
22 For further theoretical implications of such short utterances, see my "The Speech and Silence of the Proverb" in Albert Cook, *Myth and Language,* Bloomington: Indiana University Press, 1980, 211–24.
23 In Adorno's words, "Discontinuity is essential to the essay, its matter always an immobilized conflict" (T. W. Adorno, *Noten zur Literatur,* Frankfurt: Suhrkamp, 1958, I, 35).
24 "A lukewarm admirer"; S. T. Coleridge, *The Friend,* ed. Barbara E. Rooke, London: Routledge and Kegan Paul, 1969 (1818), I, 137.
25 Ms. Egerton 2800, ff. 43–45, as printed in Kathleen Coburn, *Inquiring Spirit,* New York: Funk and Wagnalls, 1968 (1951), 63–68.
26 W. K. Wimsatt, Jr., "The Structure of Romantic Nature Imagery," in Harold Bloom, ed., *Romanticism and Consciousness,* New York: Norton, 1970, 82–83.
27 Clint Goodson, "Kubla's Construct," *Studies in Romanticism,* 18, 1979, 405–25.
28 "The Stateman's Manual."
29 *Essays,* 231.
30 Ms. Notebook 23, ff. 43–44, as quoted by Eleanor Shaffer, *"Kubla Khan,"* 136. In *Letters* V, 91, again he distinguishes metaphor from symbol: "For such men it is either literal or metaphorical. There is no third. For as to the *symbolical* they have not arrived."
31 The circle closes the other way, so to speak, by elevating the process of association or language in the mind to the handling of "symbols" under the pressure of desire (he is writing about Sara Hutchinson): "All minds must think by some *symbols* — the strongest minds possess the most vivid Symbols in the Imagination — yet this ingenerates a want, pothon, desiderium, for vividness of Symbol: which something that is *without,* that has the property of *Outness* (a word which Berkeley preferred to 'Externality') can alone fully gratify even that indeed not fully — for the utmost is only an approximation to that absolute Union, which the soul sensible of its imperfection in itself, of its Halfness, yearns after" (*Notebooks,* III, 3325).
   Still another association, this time of Fancy, under the influence of the wine of Dionysus or Bacchus (but not of opium), as it emerges into "images," the last word being cast in a German Coleridge has further ciphered into Greek letters under a sort of linguistic excitation — a "fear and feeling in feeling": "An hour of productive Fancy required, to invent the Birth or Origin of these [intoxicants]. The former *hedone methuskios* from Thoughts, and Action . . . as communication — the latter introversive from fear, feeling in feeling, till the intensity manufactures the *schemata* into *bilder!* " (*Notebooks,* III, 3263).

32 Walter Jackson Bate characterizes the achievement of the Conversation Poems in terms of stylistic fusions (*Coleridge*, New York: Macmillan, 1968, 47): "he was able . . . to lift almost effortlessly the late Augustan reflective mode into something that could fulfill many of the poetic needs and interests of the next century and a half."

33 Owen Barfield, *What Coleridge Thought*, Middletown: Wesleyan University Press, 1971.

"Dejection: an Ode," however, was originally written in the form of a letter to Sara Hutchinson; its context was first seen as momentary and occasional, since her name, which he elsewhere puts into cipher in his journal, is written out there (*Letters*, II, 790). This suggests still another series of connections in his theory between "feeling" and "image"— for which there would in turn be much evidence, as: "Pleasure and Pain comparatively with general ideas in general — not so much generic *terms — something* in themselves into Images; but (perfect). Individuality is gained by Image — therefore the more *Feeling* and less Image, the more substance yet the less Individuality — and a certain middle state where there is a particular, and yet not quite a definite, sharply outlined Individual, makes an abstract Idea which is more than a generic term or Image acting, according to Descartes, as a generic Term" (*Notebooks*, III, 4068, April 1811). This may be seen to anticipate a great deal of the theory Mallarmé offers.

Or: "I feel strongly, and I think strongly; but I seldom feel without thinking, or think without feeling. Hence tho' my poetry has in general a *hue* of tenderness, or Passion o'er it, yet it seldom exhibits unmixed and simple tenderness or Passion. My philosophical opinions are blended with, or deduced from, my feelings: and this, I think, peculiarizes my style of Writing" (*Letters*, I, 279).

Or: "The more I think the more I am convinced that the greatest of differences is produced when in the one case the feelings are worked upon thro' the imagination and the Imagination thro' definite Forms (i.e. the Religion of Greece and Rome); in the other case where the feelings are worked upon by Hopes and Fears purely individual, and the Imagination is kept barren in definite Forms and only in cooperation with the Understanding labours after an obscure and indefinite Vastness — this is Christianity." (*Letters*, I, 466).

Or: ". . . my heart within me *burns* . . . to *concenter* my free mind to the affinities of the Feelings with Words and Ideas under the title of 'Concerning Poetry and the nature of the Pleasures derived from it'" (*Letters*, II, 671).

Hölderlin's Brink

1 Martin Heidegger, *Hölderlins Hymnen "Germanien" und "Der Rhein,"* in *Gesamtausgabe*, vol. 38, Frankfurt: Klostermann, 1980 (1934–35); *Erläuterungen zu Hölderlins Dichtung*, Frankfurt: Klostermann, 1951.

2 As Marshall Brown says ("'Errours Endlesse Traine': On Turning Points and the Dialectical Imagination," *PMLA*, 99, 1984, 11), "Literary art is constantly

literalizing that turning point when actions outstrip comprehension." While Brown makes a strong case for this turn in much if not all literature and philosophy, most of his examples, and perhaps his most telling ones, come from works written since the advent of Romanticism.

3 Heidegger, *Hölderlins Hymnen*, 34–35.

4 As John Baker says ("The Gods Weighed in the Balance: Demythologization as Transition to Hölderlin's Late Poetry," unpublished manuscript), "Hölderlin's Gedächtnis is rather the memory of an immemorial past, of a past which, in any positive sense, never was and which history therefore cannot narrate. . . . The temporal structures of 'Brod and Wein' are at least as fundamentally simultaneities as they are chronological progressions, or periodicities. . . . The structural tensions of the poem reticulate, as it were, the special shape of the poem's memory and the correspondingly special sense in which 'Brod und Wein' is an elegy — a lament for a past which has not yet come to be."

5 Most citations are from Friedrich Beissner, ed., *Stuttgarter Hölderlin-Ausgabe*, Stuttgart: Kohlhammer, 1946–74. Those marked "F" are from D. E. Sattler, ed., *Friedrich Hölderlin's Sämtliche Werke, Frankfurter Ausgabe*, Frankfurt: Roter Stern, 1976–79.

6 By stressing the ontological difference between words and flowers, and by looking at the dead metaphor in *entstehen* as though it were live, Paul de Man first isolates the negative element in the dialectic of Hölderlin's struggle with language and then reads "Worte, wie Blumen, entstehen" in "Brod und Wein" (2.93) against the current of the poem and against the force of such statements in his poetry generally ("Intentional Structure of the Romantic Image," in *The Rhetoric of Romanticism*, New York: Columbia University Press, 1984, 1–17). "The image is essentially a kinetic process," as de Man well says (3) — and yet we should insist that part of its kinetic movement is intended to surpass the momentary differences in favor of the simply asserted similarities. "'Entstehen' with its distancing prefix equates origin with negation and difference" only if the metaphor is put on a par with the lexical entry "originate" for the word. To do so is to perform a sleight of substitution against which Paul Ricoeur is particularly eloquent (*La Métaphore vive*, Paris: Seuil, 1975, esp. 365ff.). As it happens, the whole passage is dropped in the "Konstituierter Text" of F, I, 260. Heidegger (*Erläuterungen zu Hölderlins Dichtung*, 7) stresses in this poetry a quality of bells ringing through snow. De Man gets at something of this quality, but to put this in terms of an exclusion is to put it too simply: "in poetic language words are not used as signs, not even as names, but in order to name" (3). But all three functions are present in poetry, interactively. Heidegger's own formulation (34) better preserves the striving towards expression that is the fundamental communicative thrust of Hölderlin's intentionality. "In it [speech] can the purest and the most hidden, just as can the confused and the common, come into expression [*zu Wort*]" (34). Hölderlin himself emphasizes the "Verbindungsmittel zwischen Geist und Zeichen" ("the binder between mind and signifier," (4.1.248). In this essay, "Über die Verfahrungsweise des poetischen Geistes" ("How the poetic mind [*Geist*] proceeds"), a persistent goal for Hölderlin is a union variously named as *das*

Reine, das Harmonische, und *die unendliche Einheit* (italicized by Hölderlin, 251). "Die Erkenntnis die Sprache ahndet, so erinnert sich die Sprache der Erkenntnis" ("Knowing surmises speech; thus speech recalls knowing," 261). Moreover, flowers themselves in Hölderlin function as signs of plenitude. As Anke Bennholdt-Thomsen well says (*Stern und Blume: Untersuchungen zur Sprachauffassung Hölderlins,* Bonn: H. Bouvier, 1967, 9), "The flower is to that point a sign for the whole of nature. In this signification the flower plays an exceptional role all through Hölderlin's poetry." Flowers speak for Empedokles (cited p. 13):

> Es sprechen, wenn ich ferne bin, statt meiner
> Des Himmels Blumen, blühendes Gestirn
> Und die der Erde tausendfach entkeimen,
> Die göttlichgegenwärtige Natur
> Bedarf der Rede nicht.

> There speak, if I am afar, instead of me
> Flowers of heaven, a blossoming constellation
> And they teem from the earth a thousandfold,
> Nature in the presence of the godly
> Needs no talking.

The last statement — as a kind of demonstration of the casualness of the comparison — reverses the equation "flowers are like words." *Entkeimen* is a hyperbolic near-synonym for *entstehen,* and if the prefix "ent-" here remains live at all, it is to emphasize not separation but rather an exalted and abundant teeming forth. Hölderlin also compares word to flower in a letter (28.11.98 in 6, 293, no. 169, 13–17, cited by Bennholdt-Thomsen, 22).

Hans-Heinrich Schottman (*Metapher und Vergleich in der Sprache Friedrich Hölderlins,* Bonn: Bouvier, 1960, 109) characterizes the flower image as a comprehensive one, and says that it implies an inspiration underlying speech when it is applied to words: "and thus, too, the word spoken in a blest moment, one not based on personal caprice but awaked by the God, is his witness and celebrates him."

As de Man well says himself in another connection, "A metaphoric style like that of Hölderlin may not be described in conceptions of the antinomy of allegory and symbol" ("Allegorie und Symbol in der europäischen Frühromantik," in *Typologia Litterarum: Festschrift Max Wehrli,* Zurich: Atlantis, 1969, 406). And see also n. 10 below. There is no doubt that de Man wishes to assert "negation," "difference," and "forgetting" (4–5) in much if not all discourse. He can only attribute such notions, or even such effects, to Hölderlin's poetry by straining and falsifying it in ways that no deconstructivist argument can legitimize.

7 Heidegger (*Erläuterungen,* 25) offers another proportion for the fusion of joy and sorrow: "Darum ist die Freude des Dichters in Wahrheit die Sorge des Sängers" ("Therefore the poet's joy in truth is the singer's sorrow"). Walter Höllerer (*Zwischen Klassik und Modern: Lachen und Weinen in der Dichtung einer Übergangszeit,* Stuttgart: Ernst Klett, 1958) presents a com-

prehensive elaboration of interactions between joy and sorrow in the representations of such later figures as Grabbe, Heine, Büchner, and others, followed by Droste-Hülshoff, Stifter, and Mörike.

8 The elaborate derivations of such notions from ancient philosophy and their assimilation from contemporary thought into literature are discussed by Meyer H. Abrams, *Natural Supernaturalism*, New York: Norton, 1971.

9 Heidegger (*Erläuterungen*, 142) stresses the function of *aber* in Hölderlin's usage to suggest, and by not going beyond suggestion to resolve, a nascent contradiction.

10 Lawrence J. Ryan, *Hölderlins Lehre vom Wechsel der Töne*, Stuttgart: Kohlhammer, 1960. As Ryan says (44), "The division into three — and exactly these three — modes of poetry is therefore a necessary consequence of Hölderlin's interpretation of 'metaphor' and its relation to the phases of movement in the whole as it divides itself and arrives at itself."

11 As Wolfgang de Boer says (*Hölderlins Deutung des Daseins*, Frankfurt: Athenäum, 1961, 27), "He recognizes his bondage to the senses, not here or there, before or after. Even this limit must a man take upon himself while he becomes finite, releases himself from one being, and as a special form turns into existence [*Da-sein*]. In that way he loses the absolute oneness with all that is. . . . This loss becomes manifest to him as a lack . . . and because this can happen does the secret of finite mind subsist. The loss is not to be understood in such a way that what is lost falls into forgetfulness, but so that it remains powerful in existence from then on — thus a counterstriving ideal or primal image."

12 Heidegger (*Hölderlin's Hymnen*, 225–33) stresses Hölderlin's use of the demigod as a figure to express this double possibility.

13 The new, profound historicism of the time was leading people to raise this question, and Hölderlin manages to poeticize the questioning in what might be called a first phase.

In a second phase, as the elaboration of historical philology is under way, we get such more detailed imaginings as Clemens Brentano's on Adam's learning to speak:

> Des Vokals Belebend Wunder,
> Eh' geheimnis der Diphtonge,
> Und der Konsonanten Hunger
> Lernt' er draus zu Worten kochen.
> In dem A den Schall zu suchen,
> In dem E der Rede Wonne,
> In dem I der Stimme Wurzel,
> In dem O des Tones Odem.

> The vowel's lively wonder
> Before the diphthongs' secret,
> And the consonants' hunger
> He learned to boil out into words.
> In the A to seek the ring,
> In the E the charm of talking,

> In the I the root of voice,
> In the O the breath of tone.

Gesammelte Schriften, Frankfurt, 1852–55, IV, 183, as cited in Emil Staiger, *Die Zeit als Einbildingskraft des Dichters*, Zurich: Atlantis, 1953, 30.

In a third phase come such re-poeticizations of detailed phenomena as Rimbaud's sonnet on the vowels.

14 Michael Hamburger, *Hölderlin*, London: Routledge and Kegan Paul, 1966, 2.

15 These developments are too powerful to allow for the simple darkening of mood in Hölderlin's later poetry that Peter Szondi traces (*Hölderlinstudien*, Frankfurt: Insel, 1967) and takes to erupt when the draft of what is later called "Hälfte des Lebens" is superimposed on the worksheets of "Wie wenn am Feiertage" (46).

The "modern-Orphic" note comes through here and there elsewhere, as in "Andenken":

> An Feiertagen gehn
> Die braunen Frauen daselbst
> Auf seidnen Boden,
> Zur Märchenzeit,
> Wenn gleich ist Nacht und Tag,
> Und über langsamen Stegen,
> Vom goldnen Träumen schwer,
> Einwiegende Lüfte ziehen.   (2.188)

> On holidays they walk,
> The brown women, right there,
> On a silken floor,
> In the time of March
> When equal are night and day,
> And over slow paths,
> Heavy with golden dreams,
> Blow cradle-rocking breezes.

Heidegger (*Erläuterungen*, 102f.) makes *einwiegende* heavy with the poet's sense of human destiny. *Seidnen*, paired by rhythmical position and syntax with *braunen*, makes the brownness of the women something other then a Cereslike festive appearance, a Mediterranean trait, or just the natural beauty of the "nut-brown maid" of the medieval English lyric. As Heidegger says suggestively about *seidnen*, "tender and still it glistens in the preciousness of the hidden kingdom of the earth that has been scarcely touched."

Leopardi: The Mastery of Diffusing Sorrow

1 All quotations are from Giacomo Leopardi, *Tutte le Opere*, ed. Walter Binni and Enrico Ghidetti, Florence: Sansoni, 1969.

2 Sebastiano Timpanaro (*La filologia di Giacomo Leopardi*, Florence: Le Monnier, 1955) assesses his professional philological career in detail. As a translator Leopardi was a scrupulous literalist, like Hölderlin but unlike Shelley.

As Gilberto Lonardi says (*Classicismo e utopia nella lirica leopardiana*, Florence: Olschki, 1969, 4), "For the twenty-year-old Leopardi Greek still has a functional aspect: that of language, or rather a jealous and ingenious code for a cryptography of the sentiments."

3 The distinction is stressed by Domenico Consoli (*Cultura Coscienza Letteraria e Poesia in Giacomo Leopardi*, Florence: Le Monnier, 1967, 21–24): "La concezione leopardina dello stile poetico è essentialmente antiretorica."

4 In this light, it would take some dialectical twist to justify Lonardi's remark, quoted in n. 2 above.

5 "Discorso di un italiano interno alla poesia romantica," ll. 914–48.

6 Iris Origo remarks on this practice (*Leopardi*, London: Hamish Hamilton, 1953, 89–92), citing a lecture series by Attilio Momigliano, *La Poesía di Leopardi*.

7 Karl Kroeber (*Artifice of Reality*, Madison: University of Wisconsin Press, 1964) develops at length the analogy between Wordsworth and Leopardi.

8 Peter Baker has demonstrated how intensely, and with what complexity of theoretical implication, a number of post-Romantic poets have addressed the questions of memory and absence, especially the absence of a loved person who has died. The terms of his manuscript study, "Poetic Practice," help define the power Leopardi has enlisted by combining, as it were, memory and absence.

9 Cesare Galimberti makes much of Leopardi's use of negation as a rhetorical device (*Linguaggio del Vero in Leopardi*, Florence: Olschki, 1959, 68–130).

10 "The sentiment felt on the view of a countryside or anything else inspires in you thoughts that are vague and indefinite, however delightful, and just like a delight that cannot be grasped, it can be compared to somebody who runs after a beautiful colored butterfly without being able to catch it; and yet it always leaves in the soul a great desire: just this is the sum of our delights, and everything that is determined and certain is very much further from satisfying us than that which for its uncertainty can never be satisfied" (*Zibaldone*, 75; 2.47).

Stendhal and the Discovery of Ironic Interplay

1 Notably Friedrich Schlegel, "Über die Unverständlichkeit," in Ernst Behler, Jean-Jacques Anstett, and Hans Eichner, eds., *Kritische Friedrich Schlegel Ausgabe*, II, Paderborn, 1967. Schlegel's many statements about irony are classified and commented on in Ingrid Strohschneider-Kohrs, *Die romantische Ironie in Theorie und Gestaltung*, Tübingen: Niemeyer, 1977. See Gary Handwerk, *Irony and the Ethics of Intersubjectivity*, New Haven: Yale University Press, 1985.

2 The implications of this identification by philosophers in the early nineteenth century and later are discussed by Thomas McFarland, *Romanticism and the Ruins of Time*, Princeton: Princeton University Press, 1981.

3 In a lecture at SUNY-Buffalo, 26 October 1976. His discussion of Schlegel

is in "The Rhetoric of Temporality," in *Blindness and Insight* (Expanded ed.) Minneapolis: University of Minnesota Press, 1982.

4 De Man, to be sure, lists Stendhal at one point as a kind of exception. I am asserting that he is something more central: a supreme exemplum that subsumes many others — as de Man does go on to suggest, though at the cost of reading the fine interactions of *La Chartreuse de Parme* in too exclusively allegorical a light, almost as if Stendhal's novel were a sort of later *La Nouvelle Héloise*. Actually Marshall Brown (*The Shape of German Romanticism*, Ithaca: Cornell University Press, 1977, 99–102) heavily qualifies de Man's reading even of Schlegel, in whom Brown finds that "utopian expectation underlies even the apparently most destructive forms of Schlegel's irony."

5 René Bourgeois also touches on Stendhal's mechanism, while restricting it to notions of "théâtre" (*L'Ironie romantique*, Grenoble: Presses Universitaires, 1974, 107): "Romantic irony . . . is a philosophical disposition according to which the world is looked at as a theater where one must hold one's role with full consciousness, referring oneself to another universe, born of the imagination, which is at once in opposition to the first and in correspondence with it." This sounds, in fact, very much like what I have been characterizing as a threshold consciousness. The problem, as always, is to characterize where one goes from such a preliminary and what verbal techniques bring it about.

6 De Man suggestively aligns this phrase of Baudelaire's with an ironic view.

7 Beda Allemann, *Ironie und Dichtung*, Stuttgart: Neske, 1969, 17.

8 See Albert Cook, "Dialectic, Irony, and Myth in Plato's *Phaedrus*," *American Journal of Philology* (forthcoming).

9 *The Meaning of Fiction*, Detroit: Wayne State University Press, 1960, 53: "If we set Stendhal's quotation from Ronsard about astrology in *La Chartreuse de Parme* against the eager, sometimes possibly prescient, astrology of the Abbé Blanès on the one hand and an informed skepticism on the other, we may schematize the following contradictions. Each bracket stands for an irony:

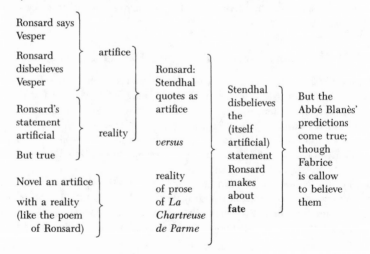

Since any bracket (the artifice-reality of Ronsard) may be identified with any other (Stendhal's belief-disbelief in astrology), and any pair of brackets in turn, the brackets, that is, the ironies, can be multiplied *ad infinitum*."

10 Stendhal, *Romans et nouvelles* (Pléiade), I, ed. Henri Martineau, Paris: Pléiade, 1952, 677 (hereafter cited as *Romans*); *Oeuvres intimes* (Pléiade), ed. Henri Martineau, Paris: Gallimard, 1955, 7 (hereafter cited as *Oeuvres intimes*").

11 Mais si je trouve le Dieu de Fénelon! il me dira peut-être: Il te sera beaucoup pardonné, parce que tu as beaucoup aimé. . . .

Ai-je beaucoup aimé? Ah! j'ai aimé Mme de Rênal, mais ma conduite a été atroce. Là, comme ailleurs, le mérite simple et modeste a été abandonné, pour ce qui est brillant. . . .

Mais, aussi, quelle perspective! . . . Colonel de hussards, si nous avions la guerre; secrétaire de légation pendant la paix; ensuite ambassadeur . . . car bientôt j'aurais su les affaires . . . , et quand je n'aurais été qu'un sot, le gendre du marquis de La Mole, a-t-il quelque rivalité à craindre? Toutes mes sottises eussent été pardonnées ou plutôt comptées pour des mérites. Homme de mérite, et jouissant de la plus grande existence à Vienne ou à Londres. . . .

— Pas précisément, monsieur, guillotiné dans trois jours.

Julien rit de bon coeur de cette saillie de son esprit. En vérité, l'homme a deux êtres en lui, pensa-t-il. Qui diable songeait à cette réflexion maligne? (*Romans*, I, 677.)

12 "Zwei Seelen wohnen, ach, in meiner Brust" (*Faust*, 1112) is perhaps echoed. Stendhal gives Goethe's title "Les affinités électives" to a chapter (I, vii). Goethe himself admired *Le Rouge et le noir*; he says of its women, "They all show great observation and deep psychological understanding (*Tiefblick*)." *Gespräche mit Eckermann*, 17 January 1831, Berlin: Aufbau, 1955, 706.

13 Belle réponse! pensa-t-il, et il s'endormit. Quelqu'un le réveilla le matin en le serrant fortement.

— Quoi déjà! dit Julien en ouvrant un oeil hagard. Il se croyait entre les mains du bourreau.

C'était Mathilde. *Heureusement, elle ne m'a pas compris. Cette réflexion lui rendit tout son sang-froid.* Il trouva Mathilde changée comme par six mois de maladie: réellement elle n'était pas reconnaissable.

Cet infâme Frilair m'a trahie, lui disait-elle en se tordant les mains; *la fureur l'empêchait de pleurer.*

— N'étais-je pas beau, hier, quand j'ai pris la parole? répondit Julien. J'improvisais, et pour la première fois de ma vie! il est vrai qu'il est à craindre que ce ne soit aussi la dernière.

Dans ce moment, Julien jouait sur le caractère de Mathilde avec tout le sang-froid d'un pianiste habile qui touche un piano. . . . L'avantage d'une naissance illustre me manque, il est vrai, ajouta-t-il, mais la grande âme de Mathilde a élevé son amant jusqu'à elle. Croyez-vous que Boniface de La Mole ait été mieux devant ses juges?

Mathilde, ce jour-là, était tendre sans affectation comme une pauvre fille habitant un cinquième étage; mais elle ne put obtenir de lui paroles plus simples. *Il lui rendait sans le savoir, le tourment qu'elle lui avait souvent infligé.*

On ne connait point les sources du Nil, se disait Julien; il n'a point été donné à l'oeil de l'homme de voir le roi des fleuves dans l'état de simple ruisseau: ainsi, aucun oeil humain ne verra Julien faible, d'abord parce qu'il ne l'est pas. Mais j'ai le coeur facile à toucher; *la parole la plus commune, si elle est dite avec un accent vrai, peut attendrir ma voix et même faire couler mes larmes.* Que de fois les coeurs secs ne m'ont-ils pas méprisé pour ce défaut! Ils croyaient que je demandais grâce: voilà ce qu'il ne faut pas souffrir! . . . On peut devenir savant, adroit, mais le coeur! Le coeur ne s'apprend pas. (*Romans*, I, 678–79.)

14 *Oeuvres intimes*, 1478.

15 Balzac, *Oeuvres diverses*, III, Paris, 1940, 277.

16 Albert Cook, *The Meaning of Fiction*, 55.

17 "Il faut s'amuser. . . . Il n'y a que cela de réel dans la vie." (*Romans*, I, 477.)

18 It is striking that Rousseau's novel has recourse to the same evasions and silences I have discussed above in the Introduction with respect to *Wuthering Heights*. In *La Nouvelle Héloïse* too, the woman, all the while protesting the absolute sublimity of her love, and all the while perfectly free to marry, rejects the lover out of a deference to family wishes, a deference so feebly expressed in the text that this nearly inarticulate and capital act of refusal takes on the air of unresolved contradiction before the large and easy flow of the amorous assertions in it.

19 *Romans*, I, 1393.

20 "Pour Julien, comme pour la postérité, il n'y avait rien entre Arcole, Saint-Hélène, et la Malmaison." (*Romans*, I, 440.)

21 *Romans*, I, 285.

22 *Oeuvres intimes*, 1302.

23 Cependant cette victime, ce Poloski si envié, était presque aussi malheureux que la duchesse. Il n'avait été qu'un instant près de la jeune Bianca. Il était toujours devant elle dans un état violent: plongé dans le silence; et alors il lui semblait que tous les yeux lisaient son amour dans les siens: — ou, s'il voulait parler, le feu qui le dévorait passait dans ses discours et leur donnait presque les caractères de la folie. C'était, de tous les caractères, celui qui était fait pour choquer le plus la comtesse. (*Le Roman de Métilde*, in *De l'amour*, ed. E. Abravanel, Lausanne: Rencontre, 1961, 520–21.)

24 Je fais tous les efforts possibles pour être *sec*. [Italics Stendhal's.] Je veux imposer silence à mon coeur qui croit avoir beaucoup à dire. Je tremble toujours de n'avoir écrit qu'un soupir quand je crois avoir noté une vérité. (*De l'amour*, chap. 9 entire, 66.)

25 Stendhal, *Correspondance* (Pléiade), I, ed. Henri Martineau and V. Del Litto, Paris: Gallimard, 1962, 1040.

26 Miss Cornel, célèbre actrice de Londres, voit un jour entrer chez elle à l'improviste le riche colonel qui lui était utile. Elle se trouvait avec un petit amant qui ne lui était qu'agréable. "M. un tel, dit-elle tout émue au colonel, est venu pour voir le poney que je veux vendre." "— Je suis ici pour toute autre

chose," reprit fièrement ce petit amant qui commençait à l'ennuyer, et que depuis cette réponse elle se mit à réaimer avec fureur. (*De l'amour,* 132.)

27 Il y vint trente-trois jours de suite sans y voir Ernestine; elle ne paraissait plus à l'église; on disait la messe au château; il s'en approcha sous un dé- guisement, et deux fois il eut le bonheur de voir Ernestine. Rien ne lui parut pouvoir égaler l'expression noble et naive à la fois de ses traits. Il se disait: "Jamais auprès d'une telle femme je ne connâitrais la satiété." Ce qui tou- chait le plus Astézan, c'était l'extrême pâleur d'Ernestine et son air souffrant. J'écrirais dix volumes comme Richardson, si j'entreprenais de noter toutes les manières dont un homme, qui d'ailleurs ne manquait pas de sens et d'usage, expliquait l'évanouissement et la tristesse d'Ernestine. (*De l'amour,* 496.)

28 "My judgments are only flashes." (*Oeuvres intimes,* 1393.)

29 *Oeuvres intimes,* 1428.

30 *Oeuvres intimes,* 1475.

31 "It spoils sentiments so tender to tell them in detail." (*Oeuvres intimes,* 395.)

32 En faisant ces tristes réflexions, Octave se trouvait placé sur un divan, vis-à- vis une petite chaise qu'occupait Armance de Zohiloff, sa cousine, et par hasard ses yeux s'arretèrent sur elle. Il remarqua qu'elle ne lui avait pas adressé la parole de toute la soirée. Armance etait une nièce assez pauvre de mes- dames de Bonnivet et de Malivert, à peu pres de l'âge d'Octave, et comme ces deux êtres n'avaient que de l'indifférence l'un pour l'autre, ils se parlaient avec toute franchise. Depuis trois quarts d'heure le coeur d'Octave etait abreuvé d'amertume, il fut saisi de cette idée: Armance ne me fait pas de compli- ment, elle seule ici est étrangère à ce redoublement d'intérêt que je dois à de l'argent, elle seule ici a quelque noblesse d'âme. Et ce fut pour lui une consolation que de regarder Armance. Voilà donc un être estimable, se dit-il, et comme la soirée s'avançait, il vit avec un plaisir égal au chagrin qui d'abord avait inondé son coeur qu'elle continuait à point lui parler. (Pléiade, *Romans,* I, 39–40.)

33 "Un homme qui, s'il avait su s'abstenir d'un malheureuse pédanterie, êut été le Mozart de la langue française et aurait produit un bien plus grand effet que Mozart sur les coeurs des hommes. Mais il voulait en être le législateur et non pas les ravir." (*Oeuvres intimes,* 940, 7 June 1810.)

34 *Oeuvres intimes,* 695, 30 April 1805.

35 "Je suis le contraire de J.-J. Rousseau en beaucoup de choses sans doute." *Oeuvres intimes,* 1241, 15 September 1813.

36 Beda Allemann, *Ironie und Dichtung,* 23.

37 "L'égotisme, *mais sincère,* est une façon de peindre ce coeur humain dans la connaissance duquel nous avons fait des pas de géant depuis 1721, époque des *Lettres Persanes* de ce grand homme que j'ai tant étudié, Montesquieu." *Oeuvres intimes,* 1448.)

38 Friedrich Nietzsche, *Unzeigemässe Betrachtungen,* in *Werke,* ed. Karl Schlechta, Munich: Hanser, 1966, I, 258.

39 Paul de Man, "The Rhetoric of Temporality."

40 Merleau-Ponty repeated this phrase in a lecture course at the Collège de France, winter 1952–53.
41 Beda Allemann, *Ironie und Dichtung*, 83.

Pushkin: The Balance of Irony

1 "Ironie ist klares Bewusstsein der ewigen Agilität, des unendlich vollen Chaos." Friedrich Schlegel, *Ideen*, 69, in Ernst Behler, Jean-Jacques Anstett, and Hans Eichner, eds., *Kritische Friedrich Schlegel Ausgabe*, II, Paderborn, 1967, 263.
2 Gérard Genette, *Figures II*, Paris: Seuil, 1969.
3 In my text I give proper names in their usual English spelling. Elsewhere I follow a slightly modified form of the Library of Congress transcription system.
4 Pushkin's simplicity was already noted by Gogol during Pushkin's lifetime, in "Some Words About Pushkin," written in 1832 and published in 1834 (V. Dorofeev and G. Cheremina, eds., *A. S. Pushkin v russkoi kritike*, Moscow: Gosudarstvennoe Izdatelstvo Chudozhestvennoi Literatur'i, 1950, 41–46): "There is all: both enjoyment and simplicity . . . all is simple" (46). And Belinsky says in "Russkaia literatura v 1841 godu" (ibid., 79), "The simplest sensation sounds in him with all its strings and so a monotone." The *monotonnost* may be related to, and derived from, Pushkin's conflation and re-distribution of the five stylistic elements of diction in the Russian literary language listed by Lomonosov, as noted by V. V. Vinogradov (*Ocherki po istorii russkogo literaturnogo yazyka*, Leiden: Brill, 1949 [Moscow, 1938], 96–98). In this conflation he resembles his Romantic contemporaries in other literatures. B. Tomashevsky (*Poeticheskoe nasledie Pushkina*, Moscow-Leningrad, 1941, I, 312–20) asserts that Pushkin did not follow Lomonosov's distinction between high and low styles but fused them together, though I would add that to do so in itself constitutes "damping" either style by an ironic play gainst the other. But Pushkin only gradually developed this "realism" out of the "romanticism" of his early work (T. A. Tukovsky, *Pushkin i problema romanticheskogo stila*, Moscow, 1957, 5ff.).
5 Pushkin's collection (adapted from Mérimée) of the songs of the Western Slavs, his frequent adversion to folklore materials in the *skazki* and elsewhere, and his many remarks on *narodnost* (assembled under that heading in *Russkie pisateli o literaturnom trude*, Leningrad: Sovietskii Pisatel, 1954, I, 304–10) are all typical for his period and easily associable with "high" literary interests. For example, the minor poet A. I. Turgenev (1781–1803), in a short life that ended while Pushkin was still an infant — though his brothers entered into association with Pushkin — is said by Lotman to have taken Schiller's lead toward an interest in both folklore and Shakespeare. (Yury M. Lotman, *Poety 1790–1810 Godov*, Leningrad: Sovietskii Pisatel, 1971, 231–32.)
6 *Prostoi*, along with its forms and compounds, covers most of six pages in the *Slovar yazyka Pushkina* (Moscow: Gosudarstvennoe Izdatelstvo Inostrannikh i Natsionalnikh Slovarei, 1959, III, 844–50). "Simplicity" may be seen as a way to combine accuracy and brevity in poetry as well as prose, which Push-

kin states by 1822 to be the goal of prose ("O proze," *Polnoe sobranie sochinenii*, Moscow: Nauka, 1957, VII, 15; hereafter cited as *Pss*).

7 Vladimir Nabokov, trans., *Eugene Onegin*, New York: Bollingen, 1964.

8 *Slovar yazyka Pushkina*, s.v. Before the poem begins, the letter of the epigraph charges Onegin with vanity, pride, indifference, and a sense of superiority — all of which are ironically tested by his last encounter with Tatyana, his own sense of irony further ironized by the narrator.

9 Of course, Pushkin did not see Byron's attitudes as easy; he admired him, exaltedly, as his contemporaries generally did. Still his remarks on tragedy (*Pss*. X, 774–76) qualify Byron's postures. Pushkin's brother, as quoted by Tomashevsky (*Poeticheskoe nasledie*, I, 104), stated that Pushkin heard only French from his tutor and that their father's library contained only French books. Nabokov (*Eugene Onegin*, passim) demonstrates abundantly the dependence of Pushkin on French models, even to the extent of using French translations of Byron and others. Byron's own view of his poem could be fairly simple and undialectical, as revealed in his tentative agreement to abandon it: "At the particular request of the Contessa G. I have promised *not* to continue *Don Juan*. You will therefore look upon these three cantos as the last of that poem. . . . The reason of this . . . arises from the wish of all women to exalt the *sentiment* of the passions and to keep up the illusion which is their empire. Now *Don Juan* strips off this illusion, and laughs at that and most other things. I never knew a woman who did not protect *Rousseau*, nor one who did not dislike de Grammont, Gil Blas, and all the *comedy* of passions, when brought out naturally." *Letters and Journals*, V, 6 July 1821, as quoted in Peter Quennell, *Byronic Thoughts*, London: John Murray, 1960, 52–53.

10 V. M. Eikhenbaum, *Stati o Lermontove*, Moscow: Sovietskii Pisatel, 1961, 47.

11 Pushkin was taken almost immediately with Stendhal's novel. As he wrote to E. M. Khitrovo in the second half of May 1831, "Je vous supplie de m'envoyer le second volume de Rouge et noir. J'en suis enchanté" (*Pss*., X, 31). There is a Stendhal-like tone in the opening of *Metel*, published in 1830, and the increased frequency of epigraphs in *Pikovaia Dama* could possibly have been suggested by Stendhal's growing fondness for this common practice.

12 Vladimir Nabokov, *Eugene Onegin*, II, 370. He was tempted to intermingle these too fully here in a stanza about them that he later canceled from this passage, as he canceled two further stanzas enjoining sympathy in the reader for Tatyana. The three stanzas left from the six originally drafted at this point serve to keep the focus neutral for at once framing and sharpening the postures contrasted.

13 Of course, under each of these plain terms a rich mixture of feelings is at work within its range. Of the metaphoric use of fire in Pushkin, here evidenced in "flaming heart," A. D. Grigoriev writes (*Poetichesky frazeologia Pushkina*, Moscow: Nauka, 1969, 211), "The image of fire is attractive to poets for the following characteristic feelings and states: rapture, heroism, vexation, regret, friendship, greed, envy, rage, hope, indignation, despair, zeal,

jealousy, remorse, humility, diligence, generosity, fury, etc." While all of these could not be concurrently present, more than one would be evoked in a given use of the image.

14 Pushkin's neutralizing control appears not only in his straightforward, largely unmetaphorical diction. His control, I would assert, may be traced also, and notably, to his masterly handling of syllables — an ordonnance of words whose syllable lengths are equal complements to the development of accentual patterns within the line of his syllabotonic meter, as discussed by Tomashevsky and others (a). Though there was some discussion in Pushkin's time of the number of syllables in a word — as, for example, whether the "u" in *Taushev* counted as a syllable (b) — and though syllabic meters had been firmly supplanted, the metrical pattern itself, iambic or another, is too simple to account for Pushkin's practice, and the deployment of the syllables in a line provided an opportunity for delicate stresses of balancing sound (c).

Pushkin himself on at least one occasion equated the number of syllables with the metric numbers of his line in asserting the joy and mastery of poetic composition:

> How pleasant to conduct your verses
> By numbers, in order, line by line,
> Not letting them stroll to the side
> Like troops scattering in battle rout!
> So each syllable is marked and in honor,
> So each verse sees itself a hero.
> And the verse-maker, with whom is he equal?
> He is Tamerlane or Napoleon.
>
> (*Domik v Kolomne*, v)

And he has just made the same point a little more explicitly:

> The syllable is a soldier! —
> All fit and formed for service: but we have no parade.   (III, 7–8)

And he continues:

> Lo, feminine and masculine syllables,
> Bless them, let's try them out, listen!
> Even it out, stretch out the feet
> Or by three in a row go on for an octave!
>
> (IV, 1–4)

In the control of Pushkin's verse, we are already far from the lightly versified chatter of Byron. The octosyllables of *Eugene Onegin* offer a pattern as simple as possible without the restriction of the trimetric *skazki*, where the short line immediately demands a corresponding restriction of other linguistic resources. While he joked about tiring of the "four-stopped iamb" (d), this measure in Pushkin's hands afforded him a play of language unparalleled in any narrative poet who had used it since Chaucer. The measure is simple enough for disposition to offer a constant tonic sense, neutralized in its tight handling away from any possibility that it would echo with some

primitive base, though in fact it is the oldest known Indo-European meter
(e). The iambic tetrameter is a simple pattern in which the elaboration of
conversation, seemingly associative and rambling and full, is suspended as
in the sort of optic glass to which Gogol compared Pushkin's verse (f).
Eugene Onegin offers a large repertoire of variations, taken line by line.
Consider the passage justifying Tatyana's letter (III, xxiii–xxv). In this stretch
of forty-two lines, there happens to occur no notable run of repeated syllable
pattern except the 3-3-2 of "Pugaia robkuiu liubov," repeated five lines later
in "Kazalsia inogda nezhnei'," and again after skipping a stanza, in XXV,
ii, "Revnivim ozhivim ognëm," and two lines later, at the end of the whole
run, "vsechasno virvatsia gotov." There are other approximations of the pattern in this stanza: 3-/2-1/-2 instead of 3-(3)-2) in the second line, a pattern
repeated in lines 9 and 13. So that the stanza moves, at the end, towards
the closure of syllabic approximation: 3-2-1-2 / 3-3-2 / (1-1-3-4)- 3-2-1-2 /
3-3-2. Of these five lines, four have a duplicate syllable pattern, except for
the variation between 2-1 and 3 for slots four through six in the line form.
So the gloom-sadness, emptiness-yearning, the toska, unfolds differently
in its different syllabic disposition within each of these lines:

> Chevo mne zhdat'? Toska, toska!   (Journey, 5.9)
> Opiat toska, opiat liubov!   (I, xxxiv, 8)
> Toska liubvi Tatianu gonit   (III, xvi, 1)
> eë revnivaia toska   (VI, iii, 7)

Here the line does more than activate the little plot from beginning to
end, as Donald Davie has pointed out for controlled poetry generally (g).
The disposition of syllables and the positioning of toska in a sound-pattern
with other words changes its effect. In the first line it is not only the repeti-
tious outcome of the question "What awaits me?" Its bisyllables open out
against the two immediately preceding monosyllables. The second line quoted
firmly controls it in the exact symmetry of 2-2-2-2, "again yearning, again
love." The trisyllabic Tatianu dominates the next line, and we will see her
only momentarily nonplussed by the fact that love's yearning drives her. In
the last illustration the four syllables of revnivaia fill out the whole center
of the line and interfuse the toska, so that jealousy comes to seem to dominate the sadness.

Unfolding the checkerwork of his syllabic repetitions and variations, Pushkin makes the ponderation of the syllable tightly exemplify what Lotman
(h) calls the relation between detail and the boundaries of the frame.

(a) B. V. Tomashevsky, O Stikhe, Munich: Fink, 1970 (1929). Complicated
rules and statistical proportions govern the occurrences of ictuses in a line
with binary rhythm, as pointed out by Kiril Taranovsky, "O ritmicheskoi
strukture russkikh dvuslozhnikh razmerov," in A. S. Bushmin, ed., Poetika
i stilistika russkoi literatury (Vinogradov Festschrift), Leningrad: Nauka, 1971,
420–29. These may be reckoned as having the effect of throwing syllable
count into further relief. I would argue that syllable count is definite, however proclitics are counted.

(b) Tomashevsky, *O Stikhe*, 39.

(c) Tomashevsky, citing Biely (50 and passim), discusses Pushkin's skillful handling of pyrrhics, the interaction in his verse of the accents (by rule only one to a word) and caesural pause (99–100), as well as the proportions he used of individual words that scanned as chorees (trochees), iambs, amphibrachs, and single beats (101–21). All these features at once qualify and underscore the syllable counts of the individual words.

(d) *Domik v Kolomne*, 1.

(e) The dimeter or eight-syllable line is a constituent of the *anastubh*, the simplest Vedic stanza (E. V. Arnold, *Vedic Metre in Its Historical Development*, Cambridge: Cambridge University Press, 1905). The centuries-long establishment of an octosyllabic meter with iambic emphasis in Slavic usage generally is demonstrated by Roman Jakobson in "Slavic Epic Verse: Comparative Studies in Comparative Metrics," *Selected Writings*, IV, The Hague: Mouton, 1966, 448–51. See also Antoine Meillet, *Les origines indo-européennes des mètres grecs*, Paris: Presse Universitaire, 1923.

(f) N. V. Gogol, "Some Words about Pushkin," 41.

(g) Donald Davie, *Articulate Energy*, London: Routledge & Kegan Paul, 1955.

(h) Yury M. Lotman, *Analiz poeticheskogo teksta*, Leningrad: Prosveshchenie, 1972, 12.

15 In *Die Wahlverwandtschaften* the irony is too faint and the narrator's sincerity too self-indulgent for the schematism to generate profundities other than those occasioned by such a subject, once it had been chosen by Goethe's astute instinct for significant plots. Walter Benjamin convincingly examines its charged locus of feeling, and yet there is something disproportionate between his grand categories and this blundering group. Eduard and Charlotte seem almost wholly unable, at the outset, in spite of their vague discussion, to cope with the possibility that a nubile, orphaned girl introduced as house guest into a childless, somewhat incompatible household may alter the erotic balance. Except insofar as the sentiment is true of all literature, it is impossible to assent fully to "The Mythic is the content of this book . . . a mythical shadow-play in the costumes of Goethe's century" (*Illuminationen*, Frankfurt: Suhrkamp, 1969 [1955]). In Pushkin's "novel in verses" there is not a jot more mythical shadow-play than the schematism would allow, nor is "Eros thanatos" (133) other than a truisitic category for him, or other than a backdrop of pathos for Goethe. Staiger's words of seeming tribute also conceal comparable uncertainties (*Goethe*, Zurich: Atlantis, 1956, 501): "The laws of nature and morality, elementary forces and conventions in their annihilations, counterplay, insinuations, magnetic fields, oracles, and dreams shake up the classic plasticity that charmed us in 'Hermann und Dorothea.'" But the simpler hexameter poem is more clearly realized than the finally pretentious novel. Nor does Tony Tanner's discussion, sophisticated and informed as it is, carry conviction (*Adultery and the Novel*, Baltimore: Johns Hopkins University Press, 1979). Tanner's demonstration of coherences in language and action could be applied with equal appositeness to ephemeral and trivial

novels, nor does he address either Goethe's smugness or his unquestioning recourse to stereotypes of emotion and class. For a discussion of the principles involved here, see Albert Cook, *The Meaning of Fiction*, Detroit: Wayne State University Press, 1960, chap. 5, "The Language of Fiction," 83–95, and chap. 13, "Platitude, Sentiment and Vision," 260–67. Tanner does cogently expound the force of Goethe's chosen plot, the instinctual "summary" of emotional problems that it encapsulates. And some of the afflatus of Goethe's language, its automatic quality, may be attributed to the "dream" element that I discuss in the Introduction. But Goethe in this novel is a far more soporific dreamer than the Melville of *Pierre*.

16 Elsewhere in Pushkin's work an ethnic difference highlights the terms of symmetry and also the possibility of breaking it. Age's love for youth and the politics of war extend the symmetry in *Poltava*, and then break it the more crushingly as the aging son-in-law avenges himself on his treacherous father-in-law, thereby losing his beloved forever. The Caucasian maid's submission to the asymmetrical fate of being left by her Russian lover because she frees him may explain Pushkin's preference for *The Prisoner of the Caucasus* over *The Fountain of Bakchisarai*, where the female Christian captive of Arabs merely dies before her rescue succeeds. (This relative assessment is discussed in D. D. Blagoi, *Tvorchesky put Pushkina*, Moscow: Sovietskii Pisatel, 1967, 96.)

It is with an asymmetrical description of moral contrasts that the father of the gypsy adulteress in *Gypsies* sends away the avenging Russian husband, who thought he was restoring a sort of order. "We are shy and good of soul / You are evil and bold — leave us." Shrunk to such essentials also are the last words of husband and wife, "Aleko: 'Then die!'" "Zemfira: 'I die in love.'"

"All passions are destined / And from fate there's no defense." The concluding words themselves draw the circle of reaction a little smaller than the poem, since "passions" (*strasti*) emphasizes the erotic over the vengeful. Pushkin, as the tale anyway makes clear, inclines towards the sentiment of the father, though the maxim can also be made to include Aleko: it is the only summary he is given, and so it covers his first connection with Zemfira but not his vengeance.

In short compass as in long, Pushkin reduces the components of a symmetry in dissolution or in formation to its bare essentials, as in this complete, late poem (1835):

> Bitterly sobbing, a jealous girl scolds a youth.
> Leaning on her shoulder the youth suddenly dozed off.
> The girl at once went still, cherishing his light sleep,
> And smiled at him, letting flow silent tears.

17 V. V. Vinogradov, *Ocherki*, 164–78.

18 In the poem *Osen* ("Autumn") a comparable effect is carried off in the poised presentation of the landscape itself. Throughout his career, as Vinogradov emphasizes, Pushkin has gradually freed himself from the habitual association-patterns of given words and their contrasting terms. He produces fresh con-

trasts, deepening the paradoxes, as in the tubercular girl who haunts "Autumn" (*Ocherki*, 268), a powerful impression underscored by syntactic condensations and sudden breaks, by ellipses or shifts of verb tense (344f.), or by a seemingly excessive involutedness (346).

Associated with Autumn in the poem is an opposition between boredom (*skuchna*) and yearning (*toska*) that much resembles the emotional base of Eugene Onegin's feeling for Tatyana, where boredom leads him at once to associate with her, undervalue her, and finally counteract his own feeling by a yearning come too late.

> Now it is my time; I do not love the springs;
> Boring to me is thaw; begone mud — of spring I'm sick,
> The blood rambles; feeling and thought are constrained while
> yearning —
> With stern winter I am much more content.   (II, 1–4)

A tone is set that makes a harmony of "sternness" (*surovoiu*) and "content" (*dovolen*). Autumn is bounded on either side, before by an opposite and ahead by an increase of delight. Autumn, spring, winter, summer, is a sequence that takes us through four of the nine completed stanzas, and Summer "ruined all the spiritual fruitfulness" (IV, 3). The "season of mists and mellow fruitfulness" in Keats's "Ode to Autumn" is not entered into for its plenitude, and the plaint of *Ubi sunt* is implicitly nullified. While Keats had "Where are the songs of Spring ay, where are they? Pushkin says, "Oh, beautiful summer! I would have loved you" (IV, 1). The elegiac convention has been put through the transformation of an objectivity whose ironizing is enriched by contrasting detail:

> How to explain it? It (*ona*) pleases me
> As, in truth, does a tubercular girl
> In season please you. Condemned to death
> The poor thing submits without murmur or vexation,
> A smile visible on withering lips;
> Of the tomb's precipice she (*ona*) hears no yawn.
> A crimson flower is still playing in her face,
> She is still alive today, tomorrow not.

> Despondent season. "Enchantment of the eyes."
> I love the splendid withering of nature,
> The woods clothed in crimson and in gold,
> In their canopies the wind's hum and fresh breathing,

> And the skies covered with a wavy haze,
> And the rare rays of the sun and the first frosts,
> And the rare prolonged threats of grey winter.   (VI, i–vii, 8)

19 As cited by V. V. Vinogradov, *Ocherki*, 247.
20 Lotman stresses that Pushkin's role (*Analyz*, 25) as a founder of Russian prose is only possible on the base of a poetic culture. He cites (29) Belinsky on the prosaic element in Pushkin's poetry and points out that the movement to-

wards simplicity, as it unites both prose and poetry, is a late development for Pushkin (26), as is Pushkin's adversion to prose in the first place.

21   Thus did he write, "Obscurely
and limply" (what we call romanticism —
though no romanticism at all
do I see here; but what is that to us?)   (VI, xxiii, 1–4)

22 *Slovar yazyka Pushkina*, s.v. Also *Pss.* VII, passim, especially "O poezii klassicheskoi i romanticheskoi," 32–35.
23 *Pss.*, X, 774–76, on tragedy, with strictures against Byron. "Both classics and romantics based their rules on *verisimilitude*" (italics Pushkin's). See also *Slovar yazyka Pushkina* s.v.
24 *Pss.* VII, 15.
25 Victor B. Shklovsky, *Zametki o proze Pushkina*, Moscow: Sovietskii Pisatel, 1937, 50. Though his title refers to prose, Shklovsky's examples at this point are drawn from *Domik v Kolomne* and *Eugene Onegin*.

Baudelaire: The Assessment of Incapacity

1 All page references are to Baudelaire, *Oeuvres Complètes*, Paris: Pléiade, 1961.
2 Baudelaire is notable, again, for centralizing and deepening, not for introducing, the scandalous subject of Lesbianism. It is a commonplace of eighteenth-century shock-writing, lingering on in the *Marseille* of André Chenier (1794; printed in *Oeuvres Complètes*, Paris: Pléiade, 1958, 535–43) and *La Fille aux yeux d'or* of Balzac.
3 Albert Feuillerat, *Baudelaire et sa mère*, Montreal: Variétés, 1944, as against Georges Blin, *Baudelaire*, Paris: Gallimard, 1939, and Michel Butor, *Une Histoire extraordinaire*, Paris: Gallimard, 1963 (1947). See also Leo Bersani, *Baudelaire and Freud*, Berkeley: University of California Press, 1977, which emphasizes a community of doctrine between the two.
4 John Sullivan, *Propertius: A Critical Introduction*, Cambridge: Cambridge University Press, 1976, 91–93.
5 Jacques Crépet, ed., Baudelaire, *Oeuvres Complètes*, Paris, 1935, vol. 7, IX.
6 Albert Béguin, *L'Âme romantique et le rêve*, Paris: José Corti, 1967 (1939). Béguin insists on the positive emphasis of revery in Baudelaire.
7 Jean-Pierre Richard, *Poésie et profondeur*, Paris: Seuil, 1955.
8 Georges Poulet, *Études sur le temps humain*, Paris: Plon, 1952.
9 Or she. Baudelaire sent this poem anonymously to Madame Sabatier.
10 Other Romantic poets undertook the bolder but weaker notion of showing the angel himself in a fallen state: Shelley's *Alastor*, Lermontov's *Demon*, Lamartine's *La Chute d'un ange*.
11 See Marshall Brown, "'Errours Endlesse Traine': On Turning Points and the Dialectical Imagination," *PMLA*, 99, 1984, 9–25.
12 Laurent Jenny, "Le Poétique et le narratif," *Poétique*, 18, 1976, 440–49.
13 The passage is the same one in which he registers the initial symptoms of

his mortal paresis: "aujourdhui 23 Janvier, 1862. J'ai subi un singulier aver-
tissement, j'ai senti passer sur moi *le vent de l'aile de l'imbécilité*."

14 Feuillerat, *Baudelaire et sa mère*, points up the positive, intellectual side of
Baudelaire's relation to his mother.

15 Walter Benjamin (*Illuminationen*, Frankfurt: Suhrkamp, 1969 [1955], 185–
246) has highlighted (rather faintly, after all) Baudelaire's dependence on
the modern city. He has also maintained that the "aura" around the art work
tends to disappear in the era of mechanical reproduction. But this alternative will not quite cover even Baudelaire's work as an art critic, where his
concentration on line and color usually renders such a distinction irrelevant,
wholly absorbed as he is in the perception of the artist. While Delacroix has
a sort of "aura," as Baudelaire's discussion of him implies, Daumier and Guys
really do not. Baudelaire's poem on the masters of painting declares them
to have something at once stronger and more direct than an aura, not a non-
aura but a super-aura. They are lighthouses, "Les Phares" (12).

16 *L'Éducation sentimentale*, too, offers a vision of incapacity. Fréderic misses
a career and his life drifts by under a well-nigh Baudelairean condition of
loss. The sentiments, as he gets educated to them, are somehow drained away.

17 For Baudelaire's generation *Le Lac* would have been a classic expression.
Geoffrey Hartman (*The Fate of Reading*, Chicago: University of Chicago
Press, 1975) finds a register in "Hesperian poetry" from Collins on. But, as
it happens, Baudelaire's twilights fall outside that register. Baudelaire takes
it from the earlier Romantics and transforms it, as he transforms everything.

18 Paul Valéry, *Oeuvres*, Paris: Pléiade, 1957, I, 598–613.

19 Chateaubriand was early a kind of mid-passage and mediator for Baudelaire:

> En moi qui des quinze ans vers le gouffre entrainé
> Déchiffrais courament les soupirs de René. (199)
>
> And I who from age fifteen, drawn to the gulf,
> Fluently deciphered the sighs of René.

Ovid is applied to Delacroix through Chateaubriand (1052).

20 It offers, as his poems do, an evocation of inevitable transience in a natural
landscape at twilight. And the final sense of fusion and whole retention is
not entirely alien to the element of nascent illusion in Baudelaire's perception of twilights and seas:

> Qu'il soit dans le zephyr qui frémit et qui passe,
> Dans les bruits de tes bords par les bords répétés,
> Dans l'astre au front d'argent qui blanchit ta surface
> De ses molles clartés.
>
> May it be in the zephyr that trembles and passes by,
> In the sounds of your shores repeated by those shores,
> In the star of silver brow that blanches your surface
> With its soft clarities.

Lamartine, *Oeuvres*, Paris: Pléiade, 1963, 40.

Here too, as in Baudelaire, we are given a concentration on the significance of visual impressions, sub-metaphoric and sub-symbolic.

21 De Vigny, *Oeuvres*, Paris: Pléiade, 1948, 601–2.

22 De Musset, *Poésies*, Paris: Pléiade, 1957, 331.

23 Leslie Marchand (*Byron: A Biography*, New York: Knopf, 1957, III, 1063), however, quotes Byron as it were against himself: "I suppose you expected me to explode into some enthusiastic exclamations on the sea . . . but the truth is, I hate cant of every kind and the cant of the love of nature as much as any other."

24 Lionel Trilling (*Sincerity and Authenticity*, Cambridge: Harvard University Press, 1971) emphasizes, quite properly, the less conservative side of the transformation in the newness of the terminology and the deep views implied by its use.

25 Béguin, *L'Âme romantique*.

26 Ernst Cassirer, *Rousseau, Kant, Goethe*, Princeton: Princeton University Press, 1945.

27 Richard is here suggestive on the way the aspiration tends to do itself in. *Poésie et profondeur*, 102–4 and passim.

28 "Le Cygne": "et bien d'autres encore"; "Le Voyage": "pour trouver du nouveau"; and inside that poem the whole of section VI, "Et puis, et puis encore?"

29 Valéry, *Oeuvres*, I, 611.

30 Gérard de Nerval, *Oeuvres*, Paris: Pléiade, 1960, 3.

31 Ibid., 4.

32 Albert Cook, *Prisms*, Bloomington: Indiana University Press, 1967.

33 Letter to Cazalis, October 1864, cited in Suzanne Bernard, *Le Poème en prose*, Paris: Nizet, 1959, 98, n. 6.

34 *Oeuvres*, II, 571, cited by Bernard, *Le Poème en prose*, 123, n. 124.

Mallarmé: The Deepening Occasion

1 "Je dis: une fleur! et, hors de l'oubli où ma voix relègue aucun contour, en tant que quelque chose d'autre vue les calices sus, musicalement se lève, idée même et suave, l'absente de tous bouquets" (368). (All page references are to Stéphane Mallarmé, *Oeuvres Complètes*, Paris: Pléiade, 1945.)

2 Jacques Derrida, "La Double Séance," in *La Dissémination*, Paris: Seuil, 1982, 199–318. This is perhaps the most intricate reading of Mallarmé in existence, and yet it tilts towards imbalance in its willingness to enlist the poet at a vanishing point he deeply resisted as well as deeply invoked. So the negative formulations tend to oversimplify him, as "Mallarmé maintient ainsi la structure différentielle de la mimique ou de la *mimesis*, mais sans l'interprétation platonicienne ou métaphysique, qui implique que quelque part l'être d'un étant soit imité." ("Thus Mallarmé maintains the differential structure of miming or mimesis, but without the interpretation, Platonic or metaphysical, that implies that somewhere the being of an existent is imitated," 234). This vacillates between a platitude about all imitation and a willingness to lock

Mallarmé too simply into a negative doctrine. As Jean-Joseph Goux more proportionately puts it (*Les Iconoclastes*, Paris: Seuil, 1978, 133), "la rupture mallarméenne . . . ne s'agit pas encore de supprimer tout renvoi à l'objet (au modèle, au référent), mais d'entretenir un autre rapport avec lui que le lien reproductif et réaliste" ("the Mallarméan break [*rupture*] does not yet involve suppressing all reference to the object (the model, the referent), but engages another relation with it than the reproductive or realist tie").

3 Paul Valéry, *Oeuvres*, Paris: Pléiade, 1957, I, 636.

4 As he said in his later autobiographical statement to Verlaine, "La Dernière Mode, dont les huit ou dix numéros parus servent encore . . . à me faire longtemps rêver" (664).

5 Leo Bersani, in the course of a discussion about Mallarmé angled somewhat differently from mine, has also remarked on the pervasively occasional nature of his work (*The Death of Stéphane Mallarmé*, Cambridge: Cambridge University Press, 1982). "We should, I think, find him close to the most familiar moves of ordinary consciousness" (ix). "Almost everything Mallarmé wrote during the last twenty-five years of his life was 'occasional,' in response to particular solicitations of all sorts" (48). "It could even be said that obscurity in Mallarmé's writing is frequently a mode of his sociability" (60). If Bersani's book had not come out well after the writing of mine, I might have worked still further points of convergence with it into my text.

6 In the detail of such poetry, too, there is surpassed the neoclassic penchant for typical utterance. The standard statement of the pre-Romantic notion that particularities are to be avoided in literature is, of course, Dr. Johnson's injunction against "number(ing) the streaks of the tulip" (Samuel Johnson, *Rasselas*, chap. 10), a notion that in Wimsatt's reading implies a priority given to the "concrete universal." (W. K. Wimsatt, *The Verbal Icon*, Louisville: University of Kentucky Press, 1954, 69–84.)

7 On the implications of such unspecified generality of reference in Mallarmé and other modern poets, see Albert Cook, *Prisms*, Bloomington: Indiana University Press, 1967, 25–73.

8 The account of the actual reading reveals the play of feeling in the performing poet himself. "A fine smile on his lips, his eye just a bit ecstatic, moved, trembling like a young virgin on whom the looks of a whole assembly weigh, the president of the seventh banquet, this pure poet, this delicious man, Stéphane Mallarmé, rises, takes his cup, and with a voice sonorous though ill-assured, speaks the exquisite poem" (1406–7). ("Un fin sourire sur les lèvres, l'oeil tant soit peu extatique, ému, tremblant ainsi qu'une jeune vierge sur qui pèsent les regards de toute une assemblée, le président du septième banquet, ce pur poète, cet homme délicieux, Stéphane Mallarmé, se lève et d'une voix sonore, quoique mal assurée, dit l'exquis poème.")

9 The lament for the dead, to begin with, is one of the oldest of literary occasions (H. M. and Nora Chadwick, *The Growth of Literature*, Cambridge: Cambridge University Press, I, 1932), and the *planh* of lament for a dead notable is one of the oldest forms in Romance poetry. Mallarmé's structure does not depart very far from that of the *planh* whose elements are sum-

marized by Martin de Riquer (*Los Trovadores*, Barcelona: Planeta, 1975, I, 60), following S. C. Aston and Caroline Cohen:

En el planh trovadoresco se suelen encontrar los siguientes motivos:

a) Invitación al lamento.
b) Linaje del difunto.
c) Enumeración de las tierras o personas entristecidas por su muerte.
d) Elogio de las virtudes del difunto (es el motivo principal).
e) La oracion para impetrar la salvación del alma del difunto.
f) El dolor producido por su muerte.

In the troubador *planh* the following motifs are usually encountered:

a) invitation to the lament;
b) the lineage of the deceased;
c) enumeration of the countries or persons saddened by his death;
d) praise for the virtues of the deceased (the principal motif);
e) a prayer to obtain salvation for the soul of the deceased;
f) the sorrow produced by his death.

10 Paul Valéry, *Oeuvres*, I, 660–62.

11 "A quoi bon la merveille de transposer un fait de nature en sa presque dispari- tion vibratoire selon le jeu de la parole, cependant; si ce n'est pour qu'en émane, sans la gène d'un proche ou concret rappel, la notion pure." "What good is it to transpose a fact of nature almost into its vibratory disappearance ac- cording to the play of the word, however, if it is not to have emanate there- from, without the embarrassment of a near or concrete recall, the pure no- tion" (368).

12 Paul Valéry, *Oeuvres*, I, 631.

13 Charles Baudelaire, *Oeuvres Complètes*, Paris, Pléiade, 1961, 76–77.

14 The term is one whose usage Robert G. Cohn (*Modes of Art*, Saratoga, Calif.: Anma Libri, 1975) has stressed in Mallarmé, applying it to the syntactic struc- ture of *Un Coup de dés* at first, and then to a range of other phenomena in a general aesthetics of symbolization.

15 For the theoretical extensibility of hyperbaton in poetry generally I am in- debted to a study in progress by Margaret Hausman.

16 Valéry, *Oeuvres*, I, 623.

17 Ibid., 646.

18 "Rag substituted bloody with the bear, who, his instincts recovered prior to a higher curiosity that the theatrical radiance gave him, fell on all fours and, as though carrying the Silence amid him, went with the padded walk of the species to sniff at, to put his teeth in, that prey."

19 So, too, in Mallarmé's verse, extensive and multiple revisions worked towards syntactic complication as much as towards the (related) tightening and deeping of attributions in individual words. So, for example, the first version of the sestet to "Ses purs ongles" in 1868:

> Et selon la croisée au nord vacante, un or
> Néfaste incite pour son beau cadre une rixe
> Faite d'un dieu qui croit emporter une nixe

> En l'obscurcissement de la glace, Décor
> de l'absence, sinon que sur la glace encor
> De scintillations le septuor se fixe.   (1488)

This, of course, lacks the powerful downturn of opposition at the transition from the first tercet to the second. While containing already most of the elements, and even the words, of the final 1887 version, it lacks the firm syntactic suspensions, and even the balancing, almost levitating touch of *sitôt* in the last line. *Selon* moves to a much more pivotal position, and *Encor/que* is made into the arch carrying almost all the last tercet:

> Mais proche la croisée au nord vacante, un or
> Agonise selon peut-être le décor
> Des licornes ruant du feu contre une nixe,
>
> Elle, défunte nue en le miroir, encor
> Que, dans l'oubli fermé par le cadre, se fixe
> De scintillations sitôt le septuor.   (68)

The sestet of "Ses purs ongles" raises the pitch of such suspensions, and especially in the last tercet. Working against each other here too, as in the prose sentence from "Un Spectacle Interrompu" quoted above, is a falling movement, derived from the status of the whole clause as an apposition to *nixe*, and a rising movement, also derived from the delay of the voice as each phrase piles up without sentence resolution. Strong emphasis is given the rising movement by the enjambment that breaks the parts of a conjunction, *encor/que*, and by the inversion of the last line built around the hanging adverb *sitôt*.

Mallarmé's handling of word order has a metaphysical dimension, as spelled out by Gaston Bachelard: "Time no longer flows. It bursts forth. . . . To retain, or rather to rediscover, this stabilized poetic instant, there are poets like Mallarmé who directly brutalize horizontal time, who tangle syntax, who arrest or deflect the consequences of the poetic instant." *L'Intuition de l'instant*, Paris: Gonthier, 1966 (1932), 106.

20 On the other hand, one could attribute figurative uses to the phrases. Mallarmé's "generality," as in "Ses purs ongles," lends itself especially to alternate and combined figurative attributions: as Suzanne Bernard says (*Le Poème en prose*, Paris: Nizet, 1959, 297) of another such phrase: "'vêtu encore du séjour informe des cavernes' is at once an abstraction, an ellipsis, and a hypallage."

21 As Valéry says of Mallarmé's verbal remanipulations, "Il a substitué au désir naif, à l'activité instinctive ou traditionelle de ses prédécesseurs, une conception artificielle, minutieusement raisonée, et obtenue par un certain genre d'analyse" (*Oeuvres*, I, 635). ("He substituted for the naive desire of predecessors, for their instinctive or traditional activity, an artificial conception minutely reasoned, and gained by a certain kind of analysis.")

22 A series of loci where Mallarmé employs the image of "la chevelure" is given in *Oeuvres*, 1467.

23 Mallarmé, less flagrant than such *épateurs*, resolutely excluded the one obscene poem he wrote — also occasionally — for the *Parnasse Satyrique* from the editions of his poems that he supervised during his lifetime.

24 Jean-Pierre Richard, *L'Univers imaginaire de Mallarmé*, Paris: Seuil, 1961, 135.

25 This complex image is more characteristically his own because it is his fantasy: there is no coin ancient enough to be contemporary with a Roman arena that would at the same time have a numerical figure, rather than another image, on its reverse. Large numbers on the reverse are characteristic of nineteenth-century coins, but not of ancient ones. A number of correlations between writers and money have been made in the recent writings of Jean-Joseph Goux and Marc Shell.

26 "Tandis que devant et derrière se prolonge le mensonge exploré de l'infini, ténèbres de toutes mes apparitions réunies, à présent que le temps a cessé et ne les divise plus, retombées en un lourd somme, massif . . . dans le vide duquel j'entends les pulsations de mon propre coeur." This links the state to a slumber (*somme*). ("While the tie of the infinite, explored, prolongs itself before and behind, shadows of all my apparitions reunited, now that time has ceased and divides them no more, fallen into a heavy slumber, a massive one . . . into the void where I hear the pulsations of my own head," 438).

And he extends the power of *rêves* into a realism of high generalizing power: "Seul interêt qui poigne à raison de rêves — Quand même survivrait, acceptation courante d'une entre les Chimères, la religion en cette épreuve liminaire, la Justice —." ("The only interest that gets reasonably at dreams — Even so there would survive, the current acceptation of one among the Chimerae, religion in this threshold test, Justice —," 392).

Emily Dickinson's White Exploits

1 All quotations are from *The Poems of Emily Dickinson*, ed. Thomas M. Johnson, Cambridge: Harvard University Press, 1955.

2 Of Emily Dickinson's emphasis on death, Richard Chase (*Emily Dickinson*, New York: Random House, 1951, 122) well says, "We cannot see her work very clearly until we perceive that her best and most characteristic poems proliferate from this one center of energy." Albert J. Gelpi (*Emily Dickinson: The Mind of the Poet*, New York: Athenaeum, 1967, 112) emphasizes the contemporary context of verse sentimentalizing death.

3 These points were made by Robert A. Gross in "Lonesome in Eden: Emily Dickinson and the Problem of Community in Nineteenth-Century New England," a paper given at the Emily Dickinson Symposium, Amherst, Massachusetts, October 4, 1980.

4 Clark Griffith (*The Long Shadow: Emily Dickinson's Tragic Poetry*, Princeton: Princeton University Press, 1964, III, 198) touches on Emily Dickinson's prophetic affinity for Heidegger.

5 Perry Miller (*Jonathan Edwards*, New York: Meridian, 1948) sees even Jonathan Edwards' theology as affected by the tendency persistently to modify this strict Calvinism into a more ecumenical, a more catholic, view.

> Exultation is the going
> Of an inland soul to sea,
> Past the houses — past the headlands —
> Into deep Eternity —   (76)

Anyone is the subject here, and anyone is the speaker of the earliest version of this metaphor in her work, "Land Ho! Eternity! / Ashore at last!" (4).

Again, it is implied that all share in the "Vitality" of death, in contradistinction to the inequalities of existence in this life:

> A Death blow is a Life blow to Some
> Who till they died, did not alive become —
> Who had they lived, had died but when
> They died, Vitality begun.   (816)

See also 964. The incomparably large crowd at the resurrection (515) implies such an all-inclusiveness.

6 This term "Compound Vision" is opposed to "Covered Vision" (715) by James Guthrie in an unpublished dissertation on Emily Dickinson ("'Compound Vision' and 'Covered Vision,'" SUNY–Buffalo, 1975). She herself says (*The Letters of Emily Dickinson*, ed. Thomas H. Johnson, Cambridge: Harvard University Press, 1958, II, 430), "There is no first, or last, in Forever — It is Centre, there all the time." And later she says, "Life is death we're lengthy at, death the hinge to life" (II, 424). The last statement could, indeed, be used as a summary of Heidegger's eschatology.

7 Emily Dickinson often dwelt on metaphors of size, as in 508, which speaks of "My second Rank — too small the first —." See also the discussion below of 451, 131, 350, 352.

8 For so complex a poem there are relatively few variants: "Played" alternates with "strove" in line 9, "leisure" thereby alternating for "labor" in the activities of those most likely to have the former. "Their lessons scarcely done," the variant for line 10, spells out the play alternative too explicitly and omits the image of the circle in space. "In the Ground" of line 20 emphasizes the rudimentary character of the house rather than the power of the apocalyptic earth over transient human habitation. "But each" (for "and yet") in line 21 underscores the centuries in separation, whereas "and yet" lumps them together by contrast with the day of realizing where the Horses' Heads were pointing.

9 Otto Bollnow makes Rilke a comparably intricate thinker, one who also adapted meditation on last things to a vision of this life. In this essay I am following Bollnow's practice of matching passage against passage to ascertain the complexities of a doctrine. Otto Bollnow, *Rilke*, Stuttgart: Kohlhammer, 1951. Death is dealt with especially in 88–97 and 289–301.

10 Gelpi (*Emily Dickinson*, 85) is precise in his attribution of hymn meters to the poems of Emily Dickinson: "Copies of Watts' *Christian Psalmody* or his collection of *The Psalms, Hymns, and Spiritual Songs* were fixtures in every New England household. Both were owned by Edward Dickinson, and are inscribed with his name. The latter is bound in brown sheepskin and bears

his name in gold on the cover." "The principal iambic meters are these: *Common Meter*, alternately eight and six syllables to the line; two lines of six syllables, followed by one of eight, then one of six. Each of these meters has properly four lines to the stanza. . . . Each may also be doubled in length to make eight-line stanzas. Each may also have six lines to the stanza. . . . The *Long Meter*, eight syllables to the line; and *Short Meter*, two lines of six syllables followed by one of eight, then one of six. Each of these meters has properly four lines to the stanza. . . . Each may also be doubled in length to make eight-line stanzas. Each may also have six lines to the stanza. . . . The principal trochaic meters are *Sevens*, *Eights and Sevens*, *Eights and Fives*, *Sevens and Fives*, *Sixes and Fives*, *Sixes*. . . . The dactyls . . . were arranged principally in *Elevens*, *Elevens and Tens*, and *Tens and Nines*. . . . It is significant that every poem she composed before 1861—during the years she was learning her craft—is fashioned in one or another of the hymn meters named above." For a discussion of Emily Dickinson's inventive modification, of received meters, see James Guthrie, "'Compound Vision.'"

11 See Dolores Dyer Lucas, *Emily Dickinson and Riddle*, DeKalb: Northern Illinois University Press, 1969.

12 Her letters, however, occasionally recount dreams, and one poem, 1670, gives an account of a dream. That she could not do much with dreams is indicated by 1376:

> Dreams are the subtle Dower—
> That make us rich an Hour—
> Then fling us poor
> Out of the Purple Door
> Into the Precinct raw
> Possessed before—

Poem 518 offers a possible dream that helps locate a "Fiction."

13 I owe the comparison to a lecture by Geoffrey Hartman at Buffalo, 1965.

14 The triple lenses are obscure and may correlate the Trinity with the stages of mental perception. There is a theological tradition for this, going back at least to St. Bonaventure's *Itinerarium Mentis ad Deum* (translated by George Boas as *The Mind's Road to God*, New York: Liberal Arts Press, 1953).

15 *Letters*, no. 105, I, 226.

16 James Guthrie, "'Compound Vision.'"

17 Jack Lee Capps (*Emily Dickinson's Reading*, Cambridge: Harvard University Press, 1966, as cited by Richard B. Sewall, *The Life of Emily Dickinson*, New York: Farrar, Straus and Giroux, 1974, II, 688–93) points out that the family owned nineteen Bibles. Emily Dickinson owned and used the *Imitatio Christi*.

Dostoevsky: The Apocalypse of Anguish

1 For a discussion of the interiority of fiction, see Albert Cook, *The Meaning of Fiction*, Detroit: Wayne State University Press, 1960. See also Arnold Wein-

stein's sensitive and encompassing studies, *Vision and Response in Modern Fiction*, Ithaca, Cornell University Press, 1974, and *Fictions of the Self, 1550–1800*, Princeton: Princeton University Press, 1981.

2 Mikhail Bakhtin, *La Poétique de Dostoevsky*, Paris: Seuil, 1970.

3 Ibid., 174, 221.

4 This is the term Victor Terras uses for implied contradictions or shifts in Dostoevsky ("Dissonances and False Notes in a Literary Text," in Andrew Kosjak, Michael J. Connolly, and Krystyna Pomorska, eds., *The Structural Analysis of Narrative Texts*, Columbus: Slavica, 1980, 82–95). See also Albert Cook, *The Meaning of Fiction*, 167–71.

5 Joseph Frank, *Dostoevsky*, Princeton: Princeton University Press, I, 230–38.

6 In a letter of 1867, quoted in Leonid Grossman, *Poetika Dostoevskogo*, Moscow: Akademii Nauk, 1925, as cited by Bakhtin, *La Poétique*, 63.

7 Valery Yakovlevich Kirpotin, *Razocharovanie i krushenie Rodiona Raskolnikova*, Moscow: Sovietskii Pisatel, 1970.

8 All references are to F. M. Dostoevsky, *Polnoe sobranie sochinenii*, Leningrad: Nauka, 1972. The following English versions are cited in the text: Jessie Coulson, trans., George Gibian, ed., *Crime and Punishment*, New York: Norton, 1964; Constance Garnett, trans. *The Possessed*, New York: Random House, 1936; Constance Garnett and Ralph Matlaw, trans. *The Brothers Karamazov*, New York: Norton, 1976.

9 P. M. Bitsilli links Dostoevsky's repetition of key words with his delineation of internal psychological processes, as in the anaphoric use of "suddenly" (*vdrug*) at a point where he is discussing the flow of Raskolnikov's feelings. P. M. Bitsilli, *K Voprosi o vnutrennei forme romana Dostoevskogo*, in Sofia Universitet, *Godishniki*, 42, 1945/1946, as reprinted in Donald Fanger, ed. *O Dostoevskom*, Providence: Brown University Press, 1966, 7–9.

10 Albert Cook, *The Meaning of Fiction*, chap. 11, "Plot as Discovery," 202–41.

11 V. Kozhinov ("*Prestuplenie i nakazanie*" *F. M. Dostoevskogo*, Moscow: Chudozhestvenaia Literatura, 1971, 144) comments on the unity for Dostoevsky between the social-psychological and the philosophical-moral.

12 The feeling of *toska* is as important for Dostoevsky as it is for the Romantic poets who are his predecessors and contemporaries. The underground man, too, renders his upheavals in terms of *toska*: "there smouldered above this a *toska*; there appeared a hysterical thirst for contradiction, for contrasts, and Lo! I also let myself grow depraved" (V, 127). Golyadkin expresses a comparable range of sentiments just before his double appears on the scene (I, 139–40).

13 R. P. Blackmur, *Eleven Essays on the European Novel*, New York: Harcourt Brace, 1964, 188.

14 Edward Wasiolek, ed., Victor Terras, trans., *Dostoevsky's Notebooks for "The Possessed,"* Chicago: University of Chicago Press, 1968, 58.

15 Bakhtin, *La Poétique*, 229.

16 Konstantin Mochulsky, *Dostoevsky*, Princeton: Princeton University Press, 197–208.

17 Cited in Bakhtin, *La Poétique*, 132.

18 Ibid., 62.

19 Albert Cook, *The Meaning of Fiction*, "Plot as Discovery."

20 Kirpotin analyzes these pairings in great detail in *Razocharovanie*, 158.

21 Yakov Emmanuelovich Golosovker, *Dostoevskii i Kant*, Moscow: Izdatelstvo Akademii Nauk, 1963.

22 Bakhtin, *La Poétique*, 114–17.

23 Lev Shestov, *Dostoevsky, Tolstoi and Nietzsche*, Columbus: Ohio State University Press, 1969.

24 Vladimir Soloviev, *Dukhovnie osnovy zhizni*, Brussels: Zhizn s Bogom, 1958 (1882–84).

25 Ibid., 53. Kirillov in *Devils* echoes Soloviev's notion of fear as a first religious step (pt. one, II, VIII).

26 Bakhtin, *La Poétique*, 303, speaks of Raskolnikov's "two voices."

27 Kirpotin, *Razocharovanie*, 86.

28 Dostoevsky comments on Poe in *Russkie pisateli o literaturnom trude*, Leningrad: Sovietskii Pisatel, 1954, III, 139–40.

29 Golosovker, *Dostoevskii i Kant*, 24ff.

30 Vasily Rozanov, *Dostoevsky and the Legend of the Grand Inquisitor*, Ithaca: Cornell University Press, 1972 (1891).

31 This aspect of the novels is discussed revealingly by Edward Wasiolek, *Dostoevsky: The Major Fiction*, Cambridge: M.I.T., 1964, 144–60, as reprinted in Ralph E. Matlaw, *The Brothers Karamazov: A Critical Edition*, New York: Norton, 1976.

The Moment of Nietzsche

1 One could say of Nietzsche what he says of Kant, "The moral tarantula Rousseau has bitten him too." *Morgenröte*, 1:3; in *Friedrich Nietzsche: Werke*, ed. Karl Schlechta, Munich: Hanser, 1966, I, 1013. I cite this edition except where otherwise specified.

Deep currents of Romantic thought run through the writings of both Rousseau and Nietzsche, a fact that complicates the question of Nietzsche's relation to Rousseau. One can emphasize Nietzsche's declared rejection of Rousseau, with Karl Joel (*Nietzsche und die Romantik*, Jena: Eugen Diederichs, 1925, 114): "so sieht die Romantik wie Nietzsche in Rousseau den verdorbenen Verderber; beide erheben ihn zum Epochentypus, zur Inkarnation der ihnen verhassten Zeittendenzen." ("Romanticism thus sees in Rousseau, as Nietzsche did, the corrupted corrupter. Both elevate him to an epochal type, to an incarnation of tendencies in the time that they hate.") Here "die Romantik" means the German Romantics, narrowly construed.

On the other hand, a careful construction of Rousseau's views may bring them into approximation with Nietzsche's. As W. D. Williams well says (*Nietzsche and France*, Oxford: Blackwell, 1952, 11): "Although Rousseau sometimes speaks as though the 'natural' man were simply to be understood as primitive man, he has in mind usually a conception of 'natural' man as the inner core of all men at all times. Indeed, he insists at times that 'natural' man, as he pictures him, is a logical construction rather than a portrait of any particular type of man who has existed in history. He wants, he says:

> bien connaître un état qui n'existe plus, qui n'a peut-être point existé, qui probablement n' existera jamais, et dont il est pourtant nécessaire d'avoir des notions justes, pour bien juger de notre état présent . . . ["to know well a state that no longer exists, that has perhaps never existed and probably will never exist, and of which it is nevertheless necessary to have exact notions to judge well of our present state"]. (*Discours de l'Inégalité, Oeuvres*, I, 79.)

Nietzsche, indeed, calls for a 'rebirth of tragedy' in the same way as Rousseau called for a 'return to nature,' and though these are not the same thing, they are both declarations of opposition to what Nietzsche calls 'theoretical' man, both thought of as permanent human possibilities, with more than a purely historical application."

See also Peter Heller, "Nietzsche in His Relation to Voltaire and Rousseau," in James C. O'Flaherty, Timothy F. Sellner, and Robert M. Helm, eds., *Studies in Nietzsche and the Classical Tradition*, Chapel Hill: University of North Carolina Press, 1976, 109–33.

2 *Die fröhliche Wissenschaft*, 100; II, 107: "Es bedarf ganzer Geschlechter, um auch nur eine höfliche Konvention des Dankes zu erfinden."

3 Gilles Deleuze (*Nietzsche et la philosophie*, Paris: Presses Universitaires, 1962, 80ff.) aptly discriminates between Nietzsche's idea's and Hegel's, though one could also point out their similarity with Karl Löwith, *Von Hegel zu Nietzsche*, Stuttgart: Kohlhammer, 1964 (1941), especially 37, 48. (English edition, New York: Holt, Rinehart and Winston, 1964.)

4 *Die fröhliche Wissenschaft*, 54; II, 73.

5 *Unzeitgemässe Betrachtungen*, 5; I, 241.

6 Ibid., I, 251.

7 Ibid., I, 263.

8 *Morgenröte*, 3:169; I, 1127–28. Tracy Strong develops the complex senses in which Nietzsche used history, Greek history in particular. Tracy Strong, "Nietzsche and Politics," in Robert Solomon, ed., *Nietzsche*, New York: Doubleday, 1973, 258–92.

9 Giorgio Colli and Mazzino Montinari, eds., *Nietzsche's Werke: Kritische Gesamtausgabe*, Berlin: de Gruyter, 1967– (hereafter cited as "Colli and Montinari"), VIII:2, 143.

10 *Morgenröte*, 1:18; I, 1027. This notion may be said further to energize and historicize the *Sittlichkeit* of Hegel in *die Phänomenologie des Geistes*, where Hegel had already given the lead.

11 Colli and Montinari, V:2, 393.

12 Ibid., V:2, 403.

13 *Die fröhliche Wissenschaft*, I:18ff; II, 50ff.

14 Ibid., 23; II, 57.

15 III, 485.

16 *Die fröhliche Wissenschaft*, 5:343; II, 205.

17 Colli and Montinari, V:2, 431.
18 *Unzeitgemässe Betrachtungen*, I, 214.
19 Ibid., I, 217.
20 Draft of a letter to Malwida von Meysenbug, November 1882, in Ernst Pfeiffer, *Friedrich Nietzsche, Paul Rée, Lou von Salome: Die Dokumente ihrer Begegnung*, Frankfurt: Insel, 1970, 259.
21 *Die fröhliche Wissenschaft*, 2:79; II, 88.
22 Ibid., 1:9, II, 423.
23 *Die fröhliche Wissenschaft*, 2:107; II, 114.
24 From Karl Jaspers, *Nietzsche*, as excerpted, translated, and reprinted in Robert Solomon, ed., *Nietzsche*, 131–55.
25 *Die Geburt der Tragödie*, I, 99, 114.
26 Colli and Montinari, V:2, 425; I Corinthians 12.28–31.
27 *Menschliches, Allzumenschliches*, I, 515.
28 *Die fröhliche Wissenschaft*, Vorrede, 3; II, 12.
29 Ibid., 5:370, II, 244.
30 *Morgenröte*, 1:10; I, 1021.
31 *Jenseits von Gut und Böse*, 1:19; II, 581.
32 Colli and Montinari, VIII:2, 156–57. In its full form, this draft has many qualifications, as shown in the German text.
33 Deleuze, *Nietzsche et la philosophie*, 54–56, 99ff.
34 Ibid., 88.
35 *Die Geburt der Tragödie*, 1, 9.
36 Colli and Montinari, VIII: 3, 268.
37 *Also sprach Zarathustra*, II, 359–72.
38 As Heidegger well says (Martin Heidegger, *Nietzsche*, Pfullingen: Neske, 1961, I, 119), "das Gefühl ist nichts, was nur im 'innern' sich abspielt, sondern das Gefühl ist jene Grundart unseres Daseins, kraft deren und gemäss der wir immer schon über uns weggehoben sind in das so und so uns angehende und nicht angehende Seiende im Ganzen" ("Feeling is nothing that only plays itself out 'on the inside,' but feeling is that basic means of our existence [*Dasein*] by virtue of which and in accord with which we are perpetually lifted beyond ourselves into certain things in being [Seinde] in the whole that concern us and things that do not concern us.") And of will (I, 64–65): "Dass Nietzsche den Willen bald als Affekt, bald als Leidenschaft, bald als Gefühl bezeichnet, soll sagen: Nietzsche sieht etwas Einheitlicheres, Ursprünglicheres und zugleich Reicheres hinter dem einen groben Wort 'Wille.' Wenn er diesen einen Affekt nennt, so ist das nicht eine blosse Gleichsetzung, sondern eine Kennzeichnung des Willens in Hinsicht auf jenes, was den Affekt auszeichnet. Dasselbe gilt für die Begriffe Leidenschaft und Gefühl. Wir müssen noch weitergehen und den Sachverhalt umkehren. Was man sonst als Affekt und Leidenschaft, und Gefühl kennt, ist für Nietzsche im Grunde seines Wesens Wille zur Macht." ("That Nietzsche designates the will now as affect, now as passion, now as feeling, means that Nietzsche sees something more unified, more original, and at the same time richer behind one crude word "will." . . . We must go still further and invert the content. What was other-

wise known as affect, passion, and feeling is for Nietzsche in the ground of his essence [*Wesen*] a will to power.")

39 The notion has a Renaissance history. Milton "dares find" Spenser a better moral teacher than Aquinas, and the abstract doctrine is to be found, somewhat surprisingly, in Descartes: "Atque ita non modo intelligere, velle, imaginari, sed etiam sentire, idem est sic quod cogitare" ("So not only to perceive, wish, and imagine, but also to feel, that is what thinking is"). *Principia Philosophiae*, I, 9, as quoted in Heidegger, *Nietzsche*, II, 156.

40 *Jenseits von Gut und Böse*, 36; II, 600; see also *Die fröhliche Wissenschaft*, 2:119; II, 193.

41 *Jenseits von Gut und Böse*, II, 601.

42 Arthur Danto, *Nietzsche the Philosopher*, New York: Macmillan, 1965, as excerpted in Robert Solomon, ed., *Nietzsche*, 33. But as Deleuze says (*Nietzsche et la philosophie*, 168), "On se gardera pourtant d'accorder aux concepts nietzschéens une signification exclusivement psychologique" ("One should guard against giving Nietzsche's concepts an exclusively psychological signification"). And Heidegger is still more explicit (Martin Heidegger, *Holzwege*, Frankfurt: Klostermann, 1963 [1950], 218): "Nietzsche begreift daher den Willen zur Macht nicht psychologisch, sondern er bestimmt umgekehrt die Psychologie neu als Morphologie und *Entwicklungslehre des Willens zur Macht*" (italics Heidegger's). ("Hence Nietzsche does not conceive of the will-to-power as psychological, but, the other way round, he determines psychology anew as the study of the morphology and *development of the will-to-power*.")

43 *Jenseits von Gut und Böse*, A:23; II, 587.

44 *Morgenröte*, 138; I, 1038.

45 As, for example, Sarah Kofman, "Le/les 'Concepts' de culture dans les 'Intempestives' ou la double dissimulation," in *Nietzsche aujourd'hui?* Colloques de Cerisy, Paris: Plon, 1973, II, 119–46. By selecting passages strategically from Nietzsche's work, including material he left in manuscript, Paul de Man (*Allegories of Reading*, New Haven: Yale University Press, 1979) has been able to make an astute but partial case for enlisting Nietzsche as a representative of his own version of deconstruction, a self-subverting complex shift between literal and figurative, grammatical and rhetorical uses of language. "The result [of binary models] is cumulative error, 'the consequence of all previous causal fictions' which as far as the 'objective' world is concerned are forever tied to 'the old error or original Cause.' This entire process of substitution and reversal is conceived by Nietzsche . . . as a linguistic event" (108) — but not, taking him globally, as exclusively a linguistic event. "And since, if one wants to conserve the term 'literature,' one should not hesitate to assimilate it with rhetoric, then it would follow that the deconstruction of metaphysics, or 'philosophy,' is an impossibility to the precise extent that it is 'literary'" (131) — an impossibility if one accepts without qualification de Man's "aporia between performative and constative language [that is,] merely a version of the aporia between trope and persuasion." Nietzsche's working between all these terms, in ways de Man helps to spell out, does

not add up to his assenting to such propositions. De Man would doubtless have been willing (while at the same time implying that his own demonstration escapes such a process by building in awareness of it) to subject his own terminology to the infinite regress its categories imply. But Nietzsche's whole posture implies that he expects a philosophical yield from the interfusion of philosophical and literary procedures. De Man also quotes Philippe Lacoue-Labarthe (96) on the centrality of Schopenhauer's "music is the unmediated image of the will" for *The Birth of Tragedy,* and yet the historical and psychological dialectics of that work are not "undermined" to issue in a "negative valorization of representational realism." Derrida (*Eperons*, Paris: Flammarion, 1978) goes still further in "deconstructing" the surface of Nietzsche's text, often adding gratuitous psychoanalytic inferences to his readings: "dazu gehört aber, zuerst and vor allem — Distanz! " ("thereto belongs, first and above all — distance! ").

> "Sous quel pas s'ouvre cette Dis-tanz? "
> L'écriture de Nietzsche déjà la mime, d'un effet de style écarté *entre* la citation latine (*actio in distans*) parodiant la langage des philosophes *et* le point d'exclamation, le tiret suspendant le mot *Distanz:* qui nous invite d'une pirouette ou d'un jeu de silhouette à nous tenir au loin de ces voiles multiples qui nous font rêver de mort . . . (36–37)

> "With what step does this Dis-tanz [*Tanz* is "dance" in German] open?"
> The writing of Nietzsche already mimes it in an effect of style distanced *between* the Latin citation (*actio in distans*) parodying the language of philosophers *and* the exclamation point, the dash suspending the word "distance," which invites us to a pirouette or a shadow play, to hold us far from the multiple veils that make us dream of death . . .

"Le renversement revient au même dans la déclaration bruante de l'antithèse. D'où l'hétérogénéité du texte" ("The reversal comes to the same thing in the noisy declaration of the antithesis, whence the heterogeneity of the text"), he declares. But Nietzsche's text is neither merely antithetical nor merely heterogeneous.

46 *Morgenröte,* 1:34; I, 1037.
47 In still another reversal, he speaks of "*Mood as argument* — with it all bases can be replaced and all counterbases overcome." ("Die Stimmung als Argument — damit kann man alle Gründe ersetzen und alle Gegengründe besiegen!") *Morgenröte,* 1:28; I, 1033.
48 *Menschliches, Allzumenschliches,* I, 729.
49 Ibid., I, 539.
50 *Der Fall Wagner,* II, 904ff.
51 *Die fröhliche Wissenschaft,* 2:99; II, 105: "das eigentlich Wagnerische an den Helden Wagners — ich meine, die Unschuld der höchsten Selbstsucht, der Glaube an die grosse Leidenschaft als an das Gute an sich, mit *einem* Worte, das Siegfriedhafte im Antlitze seiner Helden" ("what is really Wagnerian in Wagner's heroes — I mean, the innocence of the highest self-seeking, the belief in the grand passion as in something that is good in itself, in one single word the Siegfried-like in the countenance of his heroes").

52 *Jenseits von Gut und Böse*, 2:40; II, 603.

53 *Die Geburt der Tragödie*, I, 56: "die echt hellenische Freude an dieser dialektischen Lösung ist so gross, dass hierdurch ein Zug von überlegener Heiterkeit über das ganze Werk kommt, der den Schauderhaften Voraussetzungen jenes Prozesses überall die Spitze abbricht. Im 'Ödipus auf Kolonos' treffen wir diese selbe Heiterkeit, aber in eine unendliche Verklärung emporgehoben" ("the true Hellenic joy in this dialectical resolution is so great that through it comes a pull of powerful gaiety over the whole work, one that breaks all the peaks in the grisly expositions of that process. In 'Oedipus at Colonus' we meet the same gaiety, but elevated into an endless transfiguration").

54 *Götzendämmerung*, II, 941: "was wäre nötiger als Heiterkeit?" ("what is more needed than gaiety?").

55 Colli and Montinari, VIII:3, 14–15.

56 *Die Geburt der Tragödie*, I, 12.

57 *Morgenröte*, 134, 137; I, 1107–9.

58 Colli and Montinari, V:2, 470.

59 III, 785.

60 III, 504.

61 III, 422. "Der Mensch hat, im Gegensatz zum Tier, eine Fülle *gegensätzlicher* Triebe und Impulse in sich grossgezüchtet: . . . Der höchste Mensch würde die grösste Vielheit der Triebe haben, und auch in der relativ grössten Stärke, die sich noch ertragen lässt." ("Man has brought to full size, as opposed to a beast, a plenitude of *opposing* drives and impulses. . . . The highest man will have the greatest multiplicity of drives, and also in what is relatively the greatest strength that can be borne.") On Nietzsche's avoidance of the simplistic reconciliation of opposites, see Peter Heller, *Von den ersten und letzten Dingen*, Berlin: de Gruyter, 1972, 36.

62 *Menschliches, Allzumenschliches*, I, 485.

63 *Die fröhliche Wissenschaft*, 4:326; II, 188.

64 *Morgenröte*, 1:14; II, 1022–24.

65 *Unzeitgemässe Betrachtungen*, I, 314–15.

66 Colli and Montinari, V:1, 650–51.

67 "Nietzsches Denken gehorcht der verborgenen Einheit der Metaphysik, deren Grundstellung er ausmachen, beziehen, und durchbauen muss." ("Nietzsche's thought obeys the hidden unity of metaphysics, whose basic position he must arrange, set into relation, and thoroughly construct.") Heidegger, *Nietzsche*, II, 329. The persistent power of Nietzsche to enlist an attention aimed at systematic definition, in such commentators as Danto and Deleuze, testifies to his "professional" integrity as a philosopher.

68 Colli and Montinari, VIII: 2, 27.

69 *Die fröhliche Wissenschaft*, 1:21; II, 53.

70 Colli and Montinari, VIII:2, 171.

71 For Kant, however, the actual term *Vorstellung* is a shifting adjunct to a complex of other terms: *Begriff, Urteil, Anschauung, Gegenstand, Wahrnehmung, Erscheinung, Verstand,* and others.

72 Colli and Montinari, V:2, 465.
73 Albert Cook, "Heraclitus and the Conditions of Utterance," in *Myth and Language*, Bloomington: Indiana University Press, 1980, 69–107.
74 III, 678.
75 Löwith, *Von Hegel zu Nietzsche*, 126.
76 *Die fröhliche Wissenschaft*, 1:11; II, 44. "Diese lächerliche Überschätzung und Verkennung des Bewusstseins hat die grosse Nützlichkeit zur Folge, dass damit eine allzuschnelle Ausbildung desselben *verhindert* worden ist." ("This laughable overvaluation and misconstrual of consciousness has as a consequence the great advantage that thereby is prevented a rapid delineation of it.")
77 *Die Geburt der Tragödie*, I, 86. "Nun aber eilt die Wissenschaft, von ihrem kraftigen Wahne angespornt, unaufhaltsam bis zu ihren Grenzen, an denen ihr im Wesen der Logik verborgener Optimismus scheitert." ("Now learning hastens, spurred on by its forceful madness, without stopping, on to its limits, where its optimism, hidden in the nature of logic, runs aground.")
78 Ibid., I, 87.
79 *Unzeitgemässe Betrachtungen*, I, 148.
80 *Die fröhliche Wissenschaft*, 2:110; II, 117.
81 Colli and Montinari, V:2, 369.
82 *Götzendämmerung*, II, 1004.
83 *Die fröhliche Wissenschaft*, 1:39, II, 64: "Meinungen . . . sind nur Symptome des veränderten Geschmacks." "Opinions are only symptoms of a changed taste."
84 *Zur Genealogie der Moral*, 2:13; II, 820.
85 Heidegger, *Nietzsche*, I, 35. Robert Solomon, ed., *Nietzsche*, 204–8, lists nine senses for "Nihilism" in Nietzsche's work.
86 Heidegger, *Nietzsche*, I, 183. As he further says (*Holzwege*, 202), "Solange wir das Wort 'Gott ist tot' nur als die Formel des Unglaubens fassen, meinen wir es theologisch-apologetisch und verzichten auf das, worauf es Nietzsche ankommt, nämlich auf die Besinnung, die dem nachdenkt, was mit der Wahrheit der übersinnlichen Welt und mit ihrem Verhältnis zum Wesen des Menschen schon geschehen ist." ("So long as we take the expression 'God is dead' only as a formula for disbelief, we mean it as theologic-apologetic and renounce what Nietzsche arrives at, that is, the consideration that meditates on what indeed has happened with the truth of the suprasensual world and its relation to the essence of man.")
87 Gilles Deleuze, *Nietzsche et la philosophie*, 175.
88 Colli and Montinari, VIII:2, 305–7.
89 *Der Fall Wagner*, II, 903.
90 *Die fröhliche Wissenschaft*, 1:48; II, 70.
91 *Morgenröte*, 2:115; I, 1090.
92 *Ecce Homo*, II, 1104.
93 Colli and Montinari, V:1, 382.
94 Ibid., 620.
95 III, 705.
96 Colli and Montinari, VIII: 2, 144.

97 Ibid., V:2, 184.

98 For a discussion of this feature of Nietzsche's style, see Eric Blondel, "Les Guillemets de Nietzsche: philologie et généalogie," in Nietzsche aujourd'hui?, 153–78.

99 Colli and Montinari, VIII:2, 406.

100 "One example is the use of the idea that a man, after a struggle against himself, has still more devils than before." Menschliches, Allzumenschliches, I, 902–3.

101 Jenseits von Gut und Böse, 4:153, II, 637.

102 Die fröhliche Wissenschaft, 4:324; II, 187. Heidegger uses this passage as his epigraph for Nietzsche.

103 Heidegger, Nietzsche, I, 324.

104 Götzendämmerung, II, 995.

105 Die Geburt der Tragödie, I, 82–83.

106 Heidegger, Neitzsche, I, 166.

107 Die Geburt der Tragödie, I, 87 and passim. Frederick Love (Nietzsche and St. Peter, Berlin, New York: De Gruyter, 1981) demonstrates the progressive weakening of Nietzsche's canons for the music of others.

108 Letter to Paul Rée, August 1881, as cited in Ernst Pfeiffer, Neitzsche, Rée, Salome, 82. Generally Nietzsche tends to expand the Romantic doctrine of emotion-encoding-thought, "Die Musik als . . . unmittelbare Sprache des Gefühls" (Menschliches, Allzumenschliches, I, 573), into a sort of tonal equivalent for the achievement of all that his philosophy aims at. This is more than even music can comfortably bear, and it may help explain his disappointment over Wagner's failure to carry off a comparably Herculean task. Wagner's lapse in Parsifal into what Neitzsche calls a simple version of Christianity, and his toying with the Siegfried myth, are intellectual failures in his eyes, and he stresses these more than he does the musical inadequacies in Wagner about which Adorno is so eloquent. Myth only reinforces the cri de coeur at the heart of tragedy in ways that Pautrat (Bernard Pautrat, Versions du Soleil, Paris: Seuil, 1971) spells out. Opera, too, is scored for its "unnaturalness" (Die fröhliche Wissenschaft, 2:80; II, 89). Nietzsche is not content with Schopenhauer's idea that music is abstract; he revises it to a "lebhaft bewegte Geisterwelt" ("a world of spirit in lively motion," Die Geburt der Tragödie, I, 92), making it incorporate myth in a way that reverses Wagner's enterprise to make myth incorporate music. Again, Nietzsche invests music with all the recollecting power of Proust's mémoire involontaire: "Ein paar Töne Musik riefen mir heute einen Winter und ein Haus und ein höchst einsiedlerisches Leben ins Gedächtnis zurück und zugleich das Gefühl, in dem ich damals lebte: — ich meinte ewig so fortleben zu können." ("A pair of musical tones recalled to me in remembrance today a winter and a house and a highly hermitlike life, and at the same time the feeling in which I was living then — I intended to be able to live on that way eternally." Die fröhliche Wissenschaft, 4:317, II, 185.) He remarks, too, of Delacroix, Stendhal, and Flaubert, on the passion of the Romantics for music and their impulse to transform its perceptions into equivalent forms (III, 890–91).

109 *Die fröhliche Wissenschaft*, 4:333; II, 192.

110 *Menschliches, Allzumenschliches*, I, 903.

111 *Also sprach Zarathustra*, II, 306.

112 *Die fröhliche Wissenschaft*, 2:94–95, II, 100–101.

113 Ibid., 5:354, II, 221. "Der Zeichen-erfindende Mensch ist zugleich der immer schärfer seiner selbst bewusste Mensch" ("The sign-discovering man is at the same time the ever-keener self-conscious man").

114 *Menschliches, Allzumenschliches*, I, 923: "jeder Tragiker nimmt den Stoff in noch *kleineren* Stücken als sein Vorgänger, jeder aber erzielt eine *reichere* Blütenfülle innerhalb dieser abgegrenzten, umfriedeten Gartenhecken" ("every tragedian takes his material in still *smaller* pieces than his predecessor but aims at a *richer* blossoming inside this limited, pacified garden hedge").

115 *Die fröhliche Wissenschaft*, 2:92; II, 99.

116 Colli and Montinari, VIII:2, 436.

117 *Also sprach Zarathustra*, II, 443ff.

118 *Götzendämmerung*, II, 1027. Nietzsche here calls this element in his style Roman, deriving it from Horace and Sallust!

119 *Die fröhliche Wissenschaft*, 2:96; II, 101.

120 Colli and Montinari, VIII:2, 436.

121 In dealing with the madness of Nietzsche, any apocalyptic speculations must be qualified by the probability that he was responding to a syphilis contracted long before any of his major writings. So too for Hölderlin, some allowance must be made for sheer accident: the dismissed tutor reestablishing himself far away in Bordeaux happens one day to hear of the death of Diotima; at once impulsively makes his difficult way on foot all the way back to the German world; and arrives in a state of madness from which he never fully recovers. And he was also plagued by the very real fear of political arrest, according to Pierre Bertaux, *Hölderlin-Variationen*, Frankfurt: Suhrkamp, 1984, esp. 7–53 and 183–88.

122 III, 482.

123 Colli and Montinari, VIII:1, 105–7.

124 Nietzsche reverts to *The Birth of Tragedy* in *Ecce Homo* to describe that book, and again near the end of his work in 1888 (Colli and Montinari, VIII:3, 318–23). In *The Birth of Tragedy* itself, seeing Dionysus behind the mask of every tragic figure from Prometheus to Oedipus, Nietzsche derives what amounts to the whole Greek world from that single figure: "Aus dem Lächeln dieses Dionysus sind die olympischen Götter, aus seinen Tränen die Menschen entstanden" ("Out of the laughter of this Dionysus arise the Olympian gods, out of his tears, men," (I, 61–62).

125 *Ecce Homo*, 9; II, 1159.

126 *Ecce Homo*, II, 1073.

127 *Jenseits von Gut und Böse*, 295; II, 755.

128 Gilles Deleuze, *Nietzsche* (Philosophes), Paris: Presses Universitaires, 1968, 41.

129 All these points combine and spill over into Nietzsche's personal identifica-

tions, as so often, in one of the last "mad" letters, to Cosima Wagner, now more than five years a widow, whose whole text reads, "Ariadne, ich liebe Dich. Dionysus" (III, 1350).

130 *Die Geburt der Tragödie*, I, 25.

131 *Also sprach Zarathustra*, II, 281.

132 III, 497. "Die Täuschung *Apollos*: die *Ewigkeit* der schönen Form; die aristokratische Gesetzgebung 'so soll es immer sein!' *Dionysos*: Sinnlichkeit und Grausamkeit. Die Vergänglichkeit könnte ausgelegt werden als Genuss der zeugenden und zerstörenden Kraft, als *beständige Schöpfung*." ("The deception of Apollo: the *eternity* of beautiful form; the aristocratic law-giving, 'it shall ever be thus!' *Dionysos*: sensuality and horror. Transitoriness can be analyzed as a pleasure in a creating and destroying power, as a *constant creation*."

133 *Götzendämmerung*, II, 996. "Was bedeutet der von mir in die Ästhetik eingeführte Gegensatz-Begriff *apollonisch* und *dionysisch*, beide als Arten des Rausches begriffen?— Der apollonische Rausch hält vor allem das Auge erregt, so dass es die Kraft der Vision bekommt." ("What do the opposing concepts that I introduced into aesthetics mean, the *Apollonian* and the *Dionysiac*, both conceived as kinds of intoxication?—The Apollonian intoxication first of all keeps the eye aroused, so that it attains the power of vision.")

134 *Die Geburt der Tragödie*, I, 41.

135 *Also sprach Zarathustra*, II, 305.

136 Heidegger, *Nietzsche*, II, 133.

137 *Götzendämmerung*, II, 995.

138 *Morgenröte*, I, 1188–89.

139 Gilles Deleuze, *Nietzsche*, 40.

140 II, 1138–39.

141 Hegel, *Die Phänomenologie des Geistes*, Hamburg: Meiner, 1952 (1807–41): "das *Gefühl* des Wesens herstellen" (13); "das Wahre nicht als *Substanz*, sondern eben so sehr als *Subjekt* aufzufassen und auszudrücken" (19); "Dies Werden . . . ist es, was diese *Phänomenologie* des Geistes darstellt" (26). ("To construct the feeling of essence"; "To grasp and express the true not as *substance*, but very much as *subject*"; "This becoming . . . it is that which this *phenomenology* of spirit represents.")

Index

Abrams, Meyer H., 261n, 267n
Abravanel, E., 272n
Adorno, Theodor W., 9, 12, 248n, 263n, 298n
Ahearn, Edward, 252n
Alcman, 250n
Allemann, Beda, 111, 123, 270n, 273n, 274n
Altizer, Thomas J. J., 259n
Anstett, Jean-Jacques, 249n, 269n, 274n
Apollinaire, Guillaume, 96
Aquinas, Saint Thomas, 16, 294n
Arac, Jonathan, 246n
Aristotle, 88
Arnold, E. V., 278n
Arnold, Matthew, 14, 253n
Aston, S. C., 285n
Aupick, Madame, 149
Austen, Jane, 12, 116

Bachelard, Gaston, 286n
Bacon, Francis, 64
Baker, John, 247n, 255n, 256n, 265n
Baker, Peter, 269n
Bakhtin, Mikhail, 16, 203, 204, 214, 251n, 290n, 291n
Balzac, Honoré de, 13, 115, 142, 144, 154, 203, 250n, 272n
Barfield, Owen, 80, 264n
Barth, J. Robert, S.J., 69, 262n

Barthes, Roland, 247n
Bate, Walter Jackson, 247n, 264n
Bateson, F. W., 253n
Baudelaire, Charles, 3–4, 5, 9, 18, 19, 139–61, 162–79 passim, 204, 213, 220, 270n, 281–83n, 285n
Bayle, Pierre, 128
Beckett, Samuel, 255n
Becquer, Gustavo, 7
Beer, Samuel, 250n
Beethoven, Ludwig von, 149
Béguin, Albert, 14, 18, 156, 252n, 281n, 283n
Behler, Ernst, 249n, 269n, 274n
Beissner, Friedrich, 265n
Belin, A., 249n
Belinsky, Vissarion, 274n, 280n
Benjamin, Walter, 152, 278n, 282n
Bennholdt-Thomsen, Anke, 266n
Berkeley, George, 263n
Bernard, Suzanne, 283n, 286n
Bersani, Leo, 281n, 284n
Bertaut, Pierre, 299n
Bertrand, Aloysius, 4, 160
Biely, Andrei, 278n
Binni, Walter, 268n
Bitsilli, P. M., 290n
Black, Max, 252n
Blackmur, R. P., 203, 209, 290n
Blagoi, D. D., 279n
Blake, William, x, 3, 5, 7, 8, 13, 14,

Blake, William (continued)
19, 27, 28, 29–62, 63, 71, 78, 80,
83, 84, 88, 97, 111, 134, 155, 178,
179, 183, 188, 199, 221, 232, 234,
239, 245n, 249n, 252n, 256–57n,
258n, 259n
Blanc, Louis, 157
Blanchot, Maurice, 254n
Blin, Georges, 143, 281n
Blodgett, Harold W., 249n
Blondel, Eric, 298n
Bloom, Harold, 256n, 263n
Boas, George, 289n
Boehme, Jacob, 32
Boileau-Despréaux, Nicolas, 18, 178
Bollnow, Otto, 288n
Bonaventure, Saint, 289n
Bosch, Hieronymus, 45
Bostetter, Edward E., 255n
Bourgeois, René, 111, 270n
Bowles, Reverend Samuel, 200
Bradley, Sculley, 249n
Brentano, Clemens, 7, 267n
Brillat-Savarin, Anthelme, 148
Brinkley, Roberta F., 261n
Bronowski, Jacob, 35, 256n
Brontë, Branwell, 13
Brontë, Charlotte, 8, 13
Brontë, Emily, 11–12
Brontë family, 8, 13
Brown, Marshall, 252n, 264–65n,
270n, 281n
Büchner, Georg, 267n
Burke, Edmund, 134, 245n, 258n
Burnet, Thomas, 64, 65, 66, 69,
261n, 262n
Bushmin, A. S., 277n
Butor, Michel, 143, 281n
Butts, Thomas, 42, 47
Byron, George Gordon, 8, 9, 12,
101, 108, 117, 127–33 passim, 138,
149, 155, 157, 248n, 275n, 276n,
281n, 283n

Callimachus, 93
Calvin, John, 249n

Capps, Jack Lee, 289n
Carr, E. H., 248n
Carroll, Lewis, 18
Caserio, Robert, 251n
Cassirer, Ernst, 236, 283n
Cazalis, Henri, 283n
Cézanne, Paul, 51
Chadwick, H. M., 284n
Chadwick, Nora, 284n
Chamfort, Nicolas, 72, 237
Chase, Richard, 287n
Chateaubriand, François René, 61,
74, 113, 153, 154, 235, 251n, 282n
Chatman, Seymour, 252n, 256n
Chatterton, Thomas, 149
Chaucer, Geoffrey, 276n
Chénier, André, 281n
Cheremina, G., 274n
Clare, John, 7
Claudel, Paul, 163
Coburn, Kathleen, 248n, 250n,
260n, 262n, 263n
Cohen, Caroline, 285n
Cohn, Robert G., 285n
Coleridge, Hartley, 80
Coleridge, Samuel Taylor, 8, 19, 27,
63–82, 88, 91, 97, 98, 99, 103, 134,
188, 220, 236, 245n, 250n, 255n,
256n, 260–64n
Colli, Giorgio, 292n, 293n, 296–99n
Collins, William, 83, 164, 282n
Condillac, Étienne de, 76
Connolly, Michael J., 290n
Consoli, Domenico, 269n
Constable, John, 44, 51
Constant, Benjamin, 116
Cook, Albert, 255n, 256n, 259n,
263n, 270n, 272n, 279n, 283n,
284n, 289–91n, 297n
Corneille, Pierre, 91
Corot, Jean Baptiste Camille, 156
Coulson, Jessie, 209, 218, 290n
Crépet, Jacques, 281n

Damon, S. Foster, 257n
Dante, 30, 50, 98, 106, 108

Danto, Arthur, 229, 294n, 296n
Danton, Georges-Jacques, 112, 142
Darbyshire, Helen, 252n
Darwin, Charles, 155
Daumier, Honoré, 149, 282n
d'Aurevilly, Barbey, 176
Davie, Donald, 253n, 277n, 278n
de Boer, Wolfgang, 267n
Delacroix, Ferdinand Victor Eugène,
   157, 282n, 298n
Deleuze, Gilles, 227, 234, 239, 292n,
   293n, 294n, 296–97n, 299–300n
Del Litto, V., 272n
de Maistre, Joseph, 157
de Man, Paul, 5, 15, 28, 84, 110,
   124, 155, 246n, 250n, 252–53n,
   265–66n, 270n, 273n, 294–95n
Dembrowska, Métilde, 118
Democritus, 40
De Quincey, Thomas, 10, 153, 155
de Riquer, Martin, 285n
Derrida, Jacques, ix, 162, 245n,
   254n, 283n, 295n
de Sade, Marquis, see Sade.
Descartes, René, 70, 73, 156, 254n,
   264n, 294n
de Selincourt, Ernest, 252n
des Pres, Terence, 246n
de Tracy, Destutt, 115
de Vigny, Alfred, 149, 153, 154, 283n
Dickens, Charles, 16, 203, 209, 218
Dickinson, Edward, 288n
Dickinson, Emily, x, 3, 19, 179–202,
   213, 220, 287–89n
Diderot, Denis, 16, 123, 164
Diogenes Laertius, 222
Donne, John, 22
Dorofeev, V., 274n
Dostoevsky, Feodor, 3, 10, 13, 16,
   203–19, 289–91n
Droste-Hülshoff, 267n
Duval, Jeanne, 143

Edwards, Jonathan, 287n
Eichhorn, Johann Gottfried, 64, 69,
   261n

Eichner, Hans, 249n, 269n, 274n
Eikhenbaum, V. M., 128, 275n
Eliot, T. S., 58
Emerson, Ralph Waldo, 73, 160,
   187, 199, 229
Empedocles, 30, 90, 92, 93, 266n
Epicurus, 115, 166
Erasmus, Desiderius, 72
Erdman, David, 256n, 258n
Euripides, 250n

Faner, Robert D., 249n
Fanger, Donald, 290n
Fénelon, François de Salignac de la
   Mothe, 113, 271n
Feuillerat, Albert, 143, 281n, 282n
Fisher, Peter F., 257n
Flaubert, Gustave, 5, 9, 16, 137,
   152, 298n
Fletcher, Angus, 245n
Fogel, Aaron, 259n
Fontenelle, Bernard, 237
Foucault, Michel, 18, 252n
Frank, Joseph, 204, 290n
Frazer, Sir James George, 236
Freud, Sigmund, x, 10, 12, 18, 117,
   121, 143, 229, 247n
Friedman, Albert B., 263n
Friedrich, Kaspar David, 51, 152
Fry, Roger, 165
Frye, Northrop, 123, 259n
Fuseli, Henry, 44

Galimberti, Cesare, 269n
Garnett, Constance, 206, 290n
Gaskell, Edith, 13
Gautier, Théophile, 154, 157, 167
Gelpi, Albert, 287n, 288n
Genette, Gérard, 125, 274n
Ghidetti, Enrico, 268n
Gibbon, Edward, 128
Gibian, George, 290n
Gilbert, Susan, 200
Giorgione, 96
Giotto, 45
Glivenko, 217

Godwin, William, 8
Goethe, Johann Wolfgang, x, 4, 8,
  13, 14, 76, 102, 114, 133, 149, 154,
  227, 231, 238, 242, 246n, 249n,
  250n, 271n, 278–79n
Gogol, Nikolai, 9, 203, 274n, 277n,
  278n
Goldsmith, Oliver, 12
Golosovker, Yakov Emmanuelovich,
  215, 217, 291n
Gongora y Argote, 171
Goodson, Clint, 27, 75, 255n, 263n
Goux, Jean-Joseph, 284n, 287n
Grabbe, 267n
Grant, John E., 258n
Graves, Robert, 65, 260n
Gray, Thomas, 46
Greene, Thomas, 16
Griffith, Clark, 287n
Griggs, Earl Leslie, 260n
Grigoriev, A. D., 275n
Grillparzer, Franz, 248n
Gross, Robert A., 287n
Grossman, Leonid, 204, 290n
Guardini, Romano, 206, 214
Guthrie, James, 200, 288n, 289n
Guys, Constantin, 150, 282n

Hamburger, Michael, 91, 250n, 268n
Handwerk, Gary, 255n, 269n
Hartley, David, 76
Hartman, Geoffrey H., 7, 20, 22, 54,
  245n, 247n, 252n, 253n, 255n,
  261n, 282n, 289n
Hass, Robert, 248n
Hausman, Margaret, 285n
Haussmann, Baron, 152
Hawthorne, Nathaniel, 16
Hazlitt, William, 74
Hegel, Georg Friedrich Wilhelm, ix,
  x, 3, 13, 33, 35, 74, 88, 96, 123,
  154, 177, 217, 222, 223, 224, 229,
  233, 242, 246n, 257n, 292n
Heidegger, Martin, 32, 83, 84, 87,
  102, 180, 220, 232, 234, 236, 239,

  256n, 264–68n, 287–88n, 293–
  94n, 296–98n, 300n
Heine, Heinrich, 155, 267n
Heller, Peter, 292n, 296n
Helm, Robert M., 292n
Hemingway, Ernest, 19
Heraclitus, 33, 229, 231, 233
Herder, Johann Gottfried, x, 31, 91,
  156
Herzen, Alexander, 248n
Hesiod, 93
Higginson, Thomas Wentworth, 200,
  201
Hirsch, E. D., 282n
Hoffman, E. T. A., 16, 155, 157,
  250n
Hoffman, Werner, 15, 111
Hölderlin, Friedrich, 4, 9, 10, 15,
  19, 31, 33, 83–96, 97, 151, 179,
  187, 199, 233, 256n, 264–68n,
  299n
Höllerer, Walter, 266n
Homer, 40, 93
Horace, 93, 172, 299n
Hugo, Victor, 7, 10, 98, 153, 154,
  156–57, 163
Hume, David, 98
Hutchinson, Sara, 263n, 264n
Huysmans, Joris, 5, 176

Itard, Jean, Doctor, 8

Jakobson, Roman, 256n, 278n
James, Henry, 137
Jaspers, Karl, 225, 293n
Jenny, Laurent, 147, 281n
Job, 192
Joel, Karl, 291n
John, Saint, 107
Johnson, Samuel, 150, 284n
Johnson, Thomas M., 287n, 288n
Jones, John, 23, 253n
Jonson, Ben, 27–28
Josephus, 66

Joubert, Joseph, 72
Joyce, James, 222

Kafka, Franz, 76, 197
Kant, Immanuel, 3, 56, 60, 64, 69,
   74, 175, 215, 217, 220, 223, 224,
   232, 245n, 291n, 296n
Keats, John, 5–7, 27–28, 49, 57, 74,
   78, 85, 92, 141, 172, 187, 246n,
   247n, 251n, 255n, 256n, 280n
Khitrovo, E. M., 275n
Kierkegaard, Soren, ix, 10, 73, 111,
   183, 220, 221, 224, 233, 234, 250n
Kirpotin, Valery Yakovlevich, 204,
   217, 290n, 291n
Kofman, Sarah, 294n
Kosjak, Andrew, 290n
Kozhinov, V., 290n
Kroeber, Karl, 269n
Kumbier, William, 259n

Lacan, Jacques, 60, 255n, 259n
Laclos, Choderlos de, 115, 142
Lacoue-Labarthe, Philippe, 295n
Laforgue, Jules, 158
Lamartine, Alphonse Marie Louis de
   Prat de, 7, 152–55 *passim*, 157,
   163, 281n, 282n
Lamb, Charles, 8, 73
Landor, Walter Savage, 78
La Rochefoucauld, François de, 72
Laurent, Méry, 163, 164
Lautréamont, Comte de, 253n, 254n
Lawrence, D. H., 213
Le Cat, 255n
Lenau, Nikolaus, 246n
Lenz, 10
Leonardo da Vinci, 120
Leopardi, Giacomo, 7, 15, 19, 22,
   88, 97–109, 179, 188, 199, 220,
   235, 268–69
Lermontov, Mikhail Yurievich, 128,
   155, 281n
Lessing, Gotthold, 249n
Levin, Samuel R., 256n

Lewis, Gregory, 248n
Lindenberger, Herbert, 27, 255n
Locke, John, 76
Lomonosov, Michael, 274n
Lonardi, Gilberto, 269n
Lotman, Yury M., 274n, 277n, 278n,
   280n
Love, Frederick, 298n
Lovejoy, Arthur O., 246n
Lowell, Amy, 19
Lowes, John Livingston, 261n
Löwith, Karl, 292n
Lucas, Dolores Dyer, 289n
Lucian, 204
Lucretius, 30–31, 93
Luini, Bernardo, 120
Lukacs, Georg, 12
Luther, Martin, 235

Mai, Cardinal, 97
Malherbe, François, 18
Mallarmé, Stéphane, x, 4, 19, 160,
   162–78, 199, 264n, 283–87n
Malthus, Thomas Robert, 247n
Mandelshtam, Osip, 96
Manet, Edouard, 164
Marchand, Leslie, 283n
Martineau, Henri, 271n
Marx, Karl, 12, 247n
Massey, Irving, 16, 30, 251n, 256n
Matlaw, Ralph E., 206, 290n, 291n
McFarland, Thomas, 63, 66, 69,
   251n, 260n, 261n, 263n, 269n
McKenzie, Henry, 4
McLuhan, Marshall, 44, 258n
Meillet, Antoine, 278n
Mellor, Anne K., 258n
Melville, Herman, 9, 16–18, 76,
   251n, 252n, 279n
Mendelssohn, Felix, 14
Menippeus, 203, 204, 237
Mérimée, Prosper, 274n
Merleau-Ponty, Maurice, ix, 124,
   274n
Michelangelo, 44

Miller, Perry, 287*n*
Milton, John, 3, 56–60, 71, 245*n*,
254*n*, 294*n*
Mitchell, W. J. T., 258*n*
Mochulsky, Konstantin, 212, 290*n*
Momigliano, Attilio, 269*n*
Montagu, Basil, 8
Montaigne, Michel Eyquem de, 72,
73
Montesquieu, Charles Louis de
Secondat, 123, 273*n*
Montinari, Mazzino, 292*n*, 293*n*,
296–99*n*
Moorman, Mary, 248*n*
Mörike, Eduard, 267*n*
Moses, 113
Moynahan, Julian, 248*n*
Mozart, Wolfgang Amadeus, 10,
122, 273*n*
Musset, Alfred de, 101, 153, 154,
283*n*

Nabokov, Vladimir, 275*n*
Napoleon, 4, 112, 113, 114, 117, 118,
247*n*
Nekrasov, N. A., 7, 10
Nerval, Gérard de, 143, 151, 153,
154, 159, 252*n*, 283*n*
Newton, Sir Isaac, 40, 233
Nietzsche, Friedrich, ix, x, 3, 9, 14,
56, 72, 73, 97, 111, 123–24, 142,
160, 177, 200, 213, 218, 220–43,
248*n*, 273*n*, 291–300*n*
Novalis, 13, 27, 72, 188, 249*n*, 259*n*,
260*n*

O'Flaherty, James C., 292*n*
Ogarev, Nikolai, 10
Ogden, Terence, 255*n*
Ohmann, Richard, 252*n*
Olson, Charles, 96, 251*n*
Origen, 77
Origo, Iris, 269*n*
Ortega y Gasset, José, 206, 214
Ossian, 23
Ovid, 40, 93, 98, 282*n*

Parker, Harley, 44, 258*n*
Parmenides, 30
Pascal, Blaise, 72
Pater, Walter, 148
Paul, Saint, 64, 225
Pautrat, Bernard, 298*n*
Perse, St.-John, 163, 253*n*
Peter the Great, 135
Petrarch, 10, 32, 102, 105
Pfeiffer, Ernst, 293*n*, 298*n*
Pico della Mirandola, 32
Pindar, 91, 225
Plato, 86, 98, 111, 123, 175, 283*n*
Poe, Edgar Allen, ix, 61, 91, 143,
148, 149, 153, 157, 167, 188, 291*n*
Pogov, 135
Pomorska, Krystyna, 290*n*
Pope, Alexander, 30, 150, 164
Porterfield, William, 255*n*
Poulet, Georges, 143, 281*n*
Praz, Mario, 5, 7, 246*n*
Priestley, Joseph, 255*n*
Propertius, 143
Proust, Marcel, 14, 15, 134, 141, 144,
156, 170, 178, 195, 222, 298*n*
Puccini, Giacomo, 19
Pushkin, Alexander, 19, 125–38, 142,
274–81*n*
Puvis de Chavannes, 167

Quennell, Peter, 248*n*, 275*n*

Rabelais, François, 16
Racine, Jean, 159, 212
Randel, Fred V., 251*n*
Raphael, 44
Read, Herbert, 72, 254*n*, 263*n*
Rée, Paul, 224, 298*n*
Renan, Joseph Ernest, 235
Richard, Jean-Pierre, 148, 177, 281*n*,
283*n*, 287*n*
Richardson, Samuel, 16, 120, 128,
215
Ricks, Christopher, 246*n*
Ricoeur, Paul, 265*n*
Rilke, Rainer Maria, 93, 160, 288*n*

Rimbaud, Arthur, 18, 19, 148, 161, 164, 171, 194, 268n
Rohde, Erwin, 224
Roland, Madame, 142
Ronsard, Pierre de, 270–71n
Rooke, Barbara E., 263n
Rousseau, Jean-Jacques, x, 5, 13–14, 15, 31, 37–38, 40, 61, 72, 73, 74, 91, 122, 123, 128, 143, 147, 154, 155, 156, 157, 164, 204, 221, 223, 230, 231, 237, 246n, 249n, 250n, 272n, 273n, 275n, 291–92n
Rozanov, Vasily, 212, 218, 291n
Russell, Bertrand, 18
Ryan, Lawrence J., 88, 267n

Sabatier, Madame, 143, 281n
Sade, Donatien, Marquis de, 61, 142, 156, 247n
Sainte-Beuve, Charles Augustin, 154
Sale, William, 248n
Sallust, 299n
Salomé, Lou von, 224
Sand, George (Madame Aurore Dudevant), 156, 157
Sanger, Charles Percy, 248n
Sartre, Jean Paul, ix, 143, 248n
Sattler, D. E., 265n
Saussure, Ferdinand de, 173
Schelling, Friedrich, 31, 73, 74, 256n
Schiller, Johann Christoph Friedrich, 15, 83, 84, 101, 156, 248n, 249n, 274n
Schlechta, Karl, 248n, 273n, 291n
Schlegel, Friedrich, ix, x, 13, 31, 110, 111, 123, 124, 125, 188, 249n, 255n, 269n, 270n, 274n
Scholes, Robert, 256n
Schopenhauer, Arthur, 220, 222, 226, 230, 232, 295n, 298n
Schottman, Hans-Heinrich, 266n
Scott, Sir Walter, 70
Seelye, John, 251n
Seilig, Carl, 249n, 259n
Sellner, Timothy F., 292n
Sewall, Richard B., 289n

Shaffer, Eleanor S., 66, 70, 71, 261n, 262n, 263n
Shakespeare, William, 10, 27, 30, 73, 187, 247n, 258n
Shaw, George Bernard, 72
Shell, Marc, 287n
Shelley, Percy Bysshe, 5, 7, 8, 9, 10, 19, 29–30, 61, 78, 99, 109, 172, 188, 246n, 250n, 253n, 268n, 281n
Shestov, L., 216, 291n
Shklovsky, Victor B., 138, 281n
Sidney, Sir Philip, 156
Socrates, 123, 222, 236
Solomon, Robert, 292–94n, 297n
Soloviev, Vladimir, 216, 217, 291n
Sombart, Werner, 13, 249n
Sophocles, 85
Spenser, Edmund, 188, 245n, 294n
Spinoza, Baruch, 64–65, 69, 233, 237, 260n, 262n
Staiger, Emil, 15, 249n, 250n, 268n, 278n
Starobinski, Jean, 5, 110, 246n
Stendhal (Beyle, Marie Henri), 3, 110–24, 125, 126, 128, 136, 138, 154, 157, 269–74n, 275n, 298n
Stenzel, Gerhard, 249n, 250n
Sterne, Laurence, 138
Stifter, Adalbert, 267n
Strauss, David, 222, 235
Strohschneider-Kohrs, Ingrid, 269n
Strong, Tracy, 292n
Stryk, Lucien, 250n
Sullivan, John, 281n
Swedenborg, Emanuel, 32, 61
Swinburne, Algernon Charles, 5
Szondi, Peter, 110, 268n

Tanner, Tony, 278–79n
Taranovsky, Kiril, 277n
Tennyson, Alfred Lord, 155, 157, 251n
Terras, Victor, 290n
Thompson, E. P., 14, 249n
Thompson, Stith, 261n
Thomson, George, 3, 57, 58

Thorslev, Peter L., 248n
Tieck, Ludwig, 248n, 250n, 251n
Timpanaro, Sebastiano, 268n
Titian, 45
Tiutchev, Fyodor, 7, 19
Tomashevsky, B. V., 274–78n
Trakl, Georg, 248n
Trilling, Lionel, 14, 246n, 250n, 283n
Trollope, Anthony, 116
Tukovsky, T. A., 274n
Turgenev, A. I., 274n
Turgenev, Ivan, 14
Turner, William, 44–45, 51

Valéry, Paul, 19, 98, 153, 154, 159,
    160, 168, 171, 188, 253n, 282–86n
van Gennep, A., 245n
Vauvenargues, Comte de, 72
Vergil, 93, 172
Verlaine, Paul, 167, 284n
Vico, Giambattista, 13, 15, 37, 221,
    232
Villiers de l'Isle Adam, 176
Villon, François, 151
Vinogradov, V. V., 274n, 279n, 280n
Voltaire (François Marie Arouet),
    37–38, 40, 117, 123, 233
von Arnim, Bettina, 14
von Meysenbug, Malwida, 293n

Wagner, Cosima, 300n
Wagner, Richard, 9, 157, 167, 176,
    222, 230, 234–37, 239, 250n,
    295n, 298n
Walpole, Hugh, 248n
Wasiolek, Edward, 290n, 291n
Watteau, Jean Antoine, 144
Watts, Isaac, 288n
Weinstein, Arnold, 289–90n
Whalley, George, 262n
Wharton, Edith, 19
Whitman, Walt, 14, 178, 183
Wickert, Max, 248n
Wilamowitz, Otto, 221
Wilde, Oscar, 5, 174
Williams, W. D., 291n
Wimsatt, W. K., 75, 263n, 284n
Winckelmann, Johann Joachim, 44,
    84, 97
Wittgenstein, Ludwig, 232
Wolf, F. A., 97
Wordsworth, Dorothy, 8, 9, 66
Wordsworth, William, 3, 5, 8, 9, 12,
    15, 19–27, 29–30, 49, 58, 61, 66,
    71, 74, 75, 78, 80, 85, 87, 98, 99,
    100, 105, 134, 141, 144, 151, 155,
    156, 157, 166, 184, 188, 193, 195,
    252n, 253n, 254n, 255n, 261n,
    269n

Young, Edward, 44, 46, 57

Zola, Émile, 170, 176